Improving Student Learning Skills

A Comprehensive Guide to
Successful Practices and Programs
for Increasing the Performance
of Underprepared Students

Martha Maxwell

Improving Student Learning Skills

Jossey-Bass Publishers

San Francisco • Washington • London • 1979

IMPROVING STUDENT LEARNING SKILLS
A Comprehensive Guide to Successful Practices and Programs for Increasing the Performance of Underprepared Students
by Martha Maxwell

Copyright © 1979 by: Jossey-Bass, Inc., Publishers
433 California Street
San Francisco, California 94104
&
Jossey-Bass Limited
28 Banner Street
London EC1Y 8QE

Library of Congress Catalogue Card Number LC 79-83582

International Standard Book Number ISBN 0-87589-413-5

Manufactured in the United States of America

JACKET DESIGN BY WILLI BAUM

FIRST EDITION

Code 7912

The Jossey-Bass
Series in Higher Education

Preface

This book is about the problems students have in adapting to the academic demands of college courses and about the learning-support services colleges provide to help them. It is based on more than thirty years of my experience in working with college students and on a thorough review of the programs and research that have emerged from the past fifteen years of radical change in our institutions of higher learning.

In a sense, this book was written by seven persons named Martha Maxwell, for my career spans many roles—counselor, teacher, academic adviser, reading/learning-disabilities specialist, researcher, administrator, and perennial student. I have counseled college students and trained others to counsel, taught both graduate and undergraduate courses in psychology and education, advised potential psychology majors, and researched problems in

college learning and reading skills. I have also developed and administered a large student learning center at the University of
California at Berkeley and taught more special programs for low-
achieving college students and adults than I can count.

My biases are clear. First, I believe that college students
should be treated as the adults they are. Not only should their
interests and needs be considered in planning academic support
services, but the students themselves should play a part in decisions
about the types of services and the delivery systems to be provided.
I also believe that individual students who have learning difficulties
must have a voice in the diagnosis of their problems. Second, I feel
strongly, as I have for thirty years, that if student services are to be
effective, they must be closely coordinated with one another and
with academic departments. Third, I hold that good, explicit teaching and appropriate, college-related materials and methods are
needed if students with learning problems are to learn. The
strongly motivated, high-achieving student will succeed despite
poor teaching and inappropriate materials, but the underprepared
student will not. Fourth, I believe that instruction and programs
for the poorly prepared student need not be so costly and ineffective as they apparently have been in many colleges and universities
during the past fifteen years. Fifth, I believe that one cannot discuss the problems of special groups—such as educationally disadvantaged minority students, returning women, or the learning-
disabled—without considering the problems that typical college
students have always faced. Too often those who design programs
and develop policies lack this perspective.

Why this book? Open-admissions programs and other attempts to enroll a broader spectrum of the population in higher-
education have already generated many publications on the problems of underprepared students, but each has focused on some
aspect of the problem. Cross (1971, 1976) surveyed community
college programs and analyzed their remedial course offerings and
curriculums designed to meet the needs of "New Students"—that
is, those college students who score in the lowest third on traditional measures of academic achievement. Her excellent observations of the characteristics of these particular students and the curricular changes that must be made to accommodate them have

influenced the policies and goals of many programs and will continue to do so. Rossman and others (1975), in *Open Admissions at City University of New York: An Analysis of the First Year,* surveyed students to learn how they responded to their freshman-year open-admissions experience, described the major issues of the open-admissions concept, and examined the curriculums and other programs implemented by different City University of New York (CUNY) campuses. Rosen and others (1973) visited open-admissions concept, and examined the curriculums and other programs implemented by different City University of New York (CUNY) campuses. Rosen and others (1973) visited open-Pitman, 1972; Roueche and Kirk, 1973; and Roueche and Snow, 1977) have written several books on how community colleges have responded and should respond to the needs of open-admissions students, basing suggestions on survey data. Reed (1974) surveyed and visited peer-tutoring programs for the educationally disadvantaged and provides some excellent suggestions on how these programs should be evaluated and improved. In *The Learning Center* (1975), Peterson presents a model for the development of a comprehensive community college learning-resources center but mentions only briefly the characteristics and skills of the students for whom the program is designed. Karwin's *Flying a Learning Center* (1973) details the costs and design of facilities for a satellite learning center located in a community remote from the central campus, but it deals mainly with costs, equipment, space, and facilities; it does not discuss staff qualifications and training. And in *Errors and Expectations* (1977), Shaughnessy describes in exquisite detail the writing problems of underprepared college students and the knowledge needed by effective instructors. Many of her suggestions have been used for generations by remedial college instructors, but no one else has produced so comprehensive a treatise on how to teach nonwriters to write.

However, with the exceptions of Peterson and Shaughnessy these authors have all been "outsiders" to the programs they studied—researchers who have peered in our windows, read our reports, interviewed our students, visited our programs, and written books about us. Their books reflect useful insights and philosophies but sometimes fail to take into account the practical problems in implementing their golden goals. None of them provides specific information for faculty members or administrators who are developing or managing a comprehensive academic support service, such as today's learning-assistance centers, or a tutorial program.

Most "insiders," I suspect, are much too busy with daily commitments to write books about their experiences (and are not likely to be rewarded if they do). So as an "insider" who is very aware of the practical problems in providing student services, I designed this book to fill the gap between liberals who eulogize the egalitarian goals of college and conservatives who condemn all efforts to help students as "spoon-feeding" and as failures.

It is my hope that those faculty members who find themselves thrust into positions in which they must develop, teach, or administer academic support services will find in this book ideas, suggestions, information, and resources that will enable them to create stronger and better programs.

While I was writing this book my editors and I discussed whether it should be addressed to the college administrator, the learning-center director, or the learning-skills specialist/remedial instructor. I suspect that most college administrators have neither the time nor the interest to read books outside the sphere of their immediate concerns. They hurl books at the heads of their subordinates, who, in turn, pass them on down the line. So I have tried to write a book that will be useful to the person at whom the buck (or book) stops. I hope that it will enable readers to find specific information that can be applied to their teaching and administrative concerns, as well as ideas that can be passed back up the line to their administrators.

In the two chapters that form Part One of the book, I describe the learning needs of today's college students and the techniques for identifying students with learning difficulties, diagnosing their problems, and placing them in skills programs. In the four chapters of Part Two, I discuss ways of organizing learning-support services through tutorial programs and learning centers, plus ways to overcome the problems these administrative units face, and to evaluate their success. The six chapters in Part Three focus on methods for understanding the characteristics of underprepared students and programs for helping them improve their skills in reading, writing, studying, mathematics and science. Finally, the resources at the end of the book point to available tests, publications, and forms for possible use or adaptation by program directors and instructors.

I am indebted to over a thousand college reading- and learning-skills specialists who have been kind enough to share their ideas, failures, frustrations, and successes with me over many years. I am deeply appreciative of the many people who have read and commented on sections of this book, but especially to Candace Dawson, Nancy Ames, Bruce Bennett, Ronald P. Drucker, Gordon Cox, Karen Franklin, Friedel Gordon, Rondi Gilbert, Gloria Rapinchuk, Hadas Rin, Carl Mampaey, and Carolyn Walker.

Many of the ideas and programs described in the book have not been published before. If I do not cite a reference, it is because the information has been gathered informally through a telephone conversation, a scribbled note, or a hasty conversation while waiting for a restaurant table at a convention.

I dedicate the book to Michael Agron, who for nine years has been urging me to write it and get on with the rest of my life.

Berkeley, California Martha Maxwell
April 1979

Contents

Part Two: Organizing Successful Programs

Part Three: Solving Special Skills Problems

Part Four: Resources

The Author

MARTHA MAXWELL is academic coordinator and lecturer in education at the University of California, Berkeley. She was awarded the bachelor's degree in psychology (1946), the master's degree in psychology (1948), and the doctor's degree in education and psychology (1960)—all from the University of Maryland. She has founded learning centers and reading and study skills programs at the American University, the University of Maryland, and the University of California at Berkeley. Since 1976 she has coordinated Berkeley's summer institute for directors and staff of college learning centers.

Maxwell has published over seventy-five professional articles in educational and psychological journals and is the author of *Skimming and Scanning Improvement* (1968). She has had extensive experience in college positions, having served for many years as a teacher, scholar, researcher, counselor, administrator, diagnostician, and academic adviser. Her major professional interests are in college reading, program evaluation, the motivational problems of college students, and problem solving. Her major avocational interest is ethno-biology of tropical jungles.

Improving Student Learning Skills

A Comprehensive Guide to
Successful Practices and Programs
for Increasing the Performance
of Underprepared Students

1

Confronting the Growing Need for Skills Programs

This book focuses on the problems students have in adjusting to the *academic* demands of college, the nature of these problems, their causes, strategies for their prevention and treatment, and the programs that have been developed to ameliorate them. Certainly academic skills are not the only problems college students face for they must make personal and social adjustments to a new environment and they are just as susceptible to problems with their families, health, and finances as others in their age group. However, I believe that the central concern of college students is success in academic work; if faced with academic difficulties, they are overwhelmed. They feel inadequate and fear failure and these feel-

1

ings affect all spheres of their lives. Conversely, when students are able to overcome learning problems, they gain confidence in themselves, and this confidence enables them to cope more effectively with other conflicts.

Most, if not all, entering students experience problems in adjusting to college courses. In contrast to high school, where attendance is required, college gives students greater freedom, for professors assume that they have the self-direction and self-discipline to study and learn on their own. Furthermore, college students are expected to develop new and higher-level skills. As Townsend (1956, p. 112) says, "Many of the reading skills, habits, and attitudes which are effective in producing good high school achievement are inadequate tools for college reading, even though they are still necessary and still constantly in use."

The permissive environment of today's high schools, their lowered standards as reflected in high absentee rates and grade inflation, and their deemphasis of traditional college preparatory courses have produced a generation of students that is weaker in skills than students of the 1950s. Faculty members and administrators in colleges throughout the country are deeply concerned about the continuing decline in college entrance test scores and in measures of proficiency in basic skills. As increasing numbers of students from poverty backgrounds and with weak academic preparation enter college, supported by federal and state financial aid, the pool of highly qualified college applicants seems to grow smaller each year. The problem of underprepared students affects every institution—indeed, it is viewed as a national crisis. Newspapers regularly report on the crisis in the three R's, the illiteracy of today's college students, and the fact that providing the necessary remedial instruction is taxing college budgets and resources. Most colleges are requiring freshmen to take basic reading, writing, and mathematics review courses, while some are still struggling with the question whether credit should be awarded for preparatory work that faculty members (and state legislatures) insist should have been taught in high school. But the problems are growing and an end is not in sight.

Who are the underprepared students?

I define *underprepared students* as those whose skills, knowledge, and academic ability are significantly below those of the "typical" student in the college or curriculum in which they are enrolled. By this definition, whether a student is underprepared for higher education depends on the particular institution— its entrance standards, the expectations of its faculty, and the characteristics of its average student. The more than 2000 institutions of higher education in the United States vary tremendously in their goals, their programs, and the students they attract. Students who are underprepared for the University of California or the University of Wisconsin may be adequately prepared to enter a community college. Thus "underpreparedness" is relative. The further students fall below the college's norm, the more likely they are to have serious academic difficulties, and the harder it is to help them.

There are also wide differences in the preparation and skills required for success in different majors within the same institution. If students admitted to a college with high standards have very weak reading and writing skills, then I would consider them underprepared for the regular freshman literature course and would think it most unlikely that a one-term basic writing course would prepare many of them for it. Or if an engineering program in a university accepts minority and women students who have not taken the prerequisite mathematics courses in high school (or have done poorly in them), then I would consider these students underprepared for engineering. They might, however, be adequately prepared for other programs that do not require mathematics.

The terms *underprepared* and *underachieving*, as I use them, also encompass students who are labeled "misprepared," meaning that although they earned high grades in high school, either they did not take college preparatory courses needed for their college programs or their courses were academically weak.

What constitutes "basic skills" at the college level is also subject to different interpretations. Some administrators and faculty members insist that *basic skills* refers to the reading, writing, computational, speech, and listening skills that should have been mastered in elementary school. Others, in more selective institutions, use the term *basic skills* to describe skills and knowledge normally acquired in high school. Sometimes professors confuse immaturity and inadequate knowledge of new subjects with skill deficiencies. Students cannot understand textbooks if they have not grasped the concepts, are unfamiliar with the technical vocabulary, or lack the information necessary to interpret the examples and references. Similarly, students cannot write skillful essays on topics about which they know little. Sometimes professors overlook the gaps in students' preparation for college as well as their skills limitations. A professor who assumes that all students in the class have completed high school chemistry may attribute to poor skills the difficulties of the many who have not.

Faculty members espouse common, but erroneous, beliefs about "appropriate" college-level work, materials, and courses. Because of our grade levels in public schools, many assume that college students should be able to read books written at the Grade 13 level. However, to implement a universal standard such as requiring all students reading below the Grade 12 level on a standardized test to take a course in remedial reading ignores the great variability among college populations. For example, entering freshmen at Stanford average 615 on the verbal part of the Scholastic Aptitude Test (SAT), while those entering Coppin State College (Baltimore, Maryland) average 273. It stands to reason that the entry-level reading and composition courses at the two institutions will and should be markedly different. Each college must decide on the essential skills required for its curriculums, and each must take a cold, hard look at the characteristics of the students it enrolls. If most of the applicants lack the skills and preparation for the basic courses offered, then new programs and courses must be instituted unless the college is satisfied that it has a large enough pool of applicants that it need not be concerned about very high attrition rates.

Do *remedial* and *developmental* mean the same thing? The major approach used by colleges to cope with the vast numbers of underprepared students who entered in the 1960s and 1970s was to establish or greatly expand remedial programs. In this context, the terms *remedial* and *developmental* merged in meaning. Cross (1976, p. 31) explains that developmental education gives attention to the fullest possible development of talent and aims to develop strengths as well as correct weaknesses. Remediation, she says, aims to overcome academic deficiencies and is a part of developmental education. In the past, the term *developmental* was reserved for programs that helped the "average" student improve, but it often subsumed programs for students who needed intensive skill building. For many years we used the term *developmental* to avoid the stigma of calling a program "remedial." In addition, many public colleges are prohibited by their state legislatures from offering remedial courses, and so they term their skills programs "developmental." I will use the term *remedial* for programs that offer intensive help to students with the weakest preparation relative to their peers in a given college.

Is Underpreparedness New?

The current euphemisms applied to underprepared college students disturb me, for they imply that we are dealing with a new species of student. We have always had academically weak, poorly prepared college students. Perhaps we have them in greater numbers today, but then, more students are currently attending college than ever before. I recall the first university course I taught—an English course called "Reading Improvement." Of the twenty-six students who enrolled, four would be considered barely literate even by today's standards. Two were recent graduates of rural black high schools, one a student from Appalachia, and the other a first-generation college student of Lithuanian ancestry from a coal mining district in Pennsylvania. The other students in the class ranged from government clerks to a navy captain. Individualizing instruction was a necessity, and each student had his or her* own special assignments and goals.

Are today's underprepared students so different from those who had difficulties with college courses in the past? Indeed, although we call them culturally or educationally deprived or learning-disabled, they share the traits of poor achievers of previous eras as Pitcher and Blaushild, (1970, pp. 107–108) note:

> Cultural deprivation is now accepted as a fact by most people. . . . Still the feeling persists that deprivation belongs only to

*The English language lacks an accepted word to denote the third person singular pronoun and encompass both men and women. The author finds *she/he* awkward and chooses to use *he* throughout this book.

a special ghetto population and has nothing in common with the learning problems of the white, middle class and upper economic classes of America's children who go to college. Although it is generally accepted that emotional problems can interfere with learning and cut across every class, economic, and color line, the idea of cultural deprivation cutting across these lines is new. Yet the same symptoms found in ghetto populations are found in the wealthy. Both the underachieving wealthy and the deprived student can have the same inability to plan long-range goals and the same indifference to grades; both groups can remain in worlds that are cut off from the academic, the wealthy in his car-filled playground, the ghetto student in his street gang. Both groups can show reading, writing, or speaking problems in the academic sense, and have the same ups and downs in academic performance. Both can be exclusively involved and preoccupied with the activities of their own pocket-cultures and uninterested in the values and goals of the larger society.

Both wealth and poverty can create similar learning problems in students . . . explained in two key words: *motivation* and *gratification*. . . . The rich child can become as deprived as the ghetto child . . . and expect instant gratification—however, the poor receive sympathy and the guilt of the culture. The middle- or upper-class youngsters are not so lucky . . . they are the casualties.

The need for intensive basic skills services for college students is not a recent phenomenon but has deep historical roots. To put our present problem in perspective, we should remember that American higher education has historically had an egalitarian thrust. College has provided the principal way for children of immigrants and the poor to advance socially and economically, while it has also served to preserve the status of the children of the rich. Private colleges, from their beginnings, have admitted the talented children of the poor and given them scholarships, and working one's way through college is a time-honored American custom for students whose families could not afford to support their college aspirations. In addition, our most prestigious private colleges have always found places in their freshman classes for the untalented scions of their wealthiest alumni. So student diversity is certainly not a new experience for college faculties.

In large public institutions, failure has always been an inherent part of academic life. Even before the days of open admissions, state universities admitted large numbers of freshmen each fall, many of whom failed or dropped out before the end of their first year. Colleges, in those days, were not termed "revolving doors"; a better metaphor might be "stone walls" over which few passed. Pitcher and Blaushild (1970, p. 3) describe the traumatic effects of college failure on students and their parents: "Every year, more than 380,000 students fail out of college and are looked upon with pity, suspicion, and even anger. Their problems are loudly worried about, but ultimately swept under the academic carpet. No one seems to know what to do with this huge army of human beings . . . they are stranded in their confusion, guilt, and failure. . . . Colleges dump thousands on the failure pile annually . . . and the young person is often isolated on his island of rejection and left feeling there is no alternative to failure. The college takes little interest or responsibility for him . . . parents are frequently as overwhelmed with shame, defeat, and worry and fear as he is."

Today there is greater concern about retaining students in college, for our declining birthrate bodes ill for the institutions competing for young high school graduates to fill their classrooms. Although college grades are currently higher than they have ever been, many students continue to drop out of college, and others are taking longer to complete degrees.

For those who insist that college students in the old days were somehow superior to present students—and for those who are too young to remember—a glimpse at some of the milestones in the history of American higher education may be enlightening (source: Brubacher and Willis, 1976).

- 1852   Henry P. Tappan, in his inaugural address as president of the University of Michigan, stated that American colleges were too much involved in teaching rudimentary courses that belonged in intermediate or even primary schools and that universities were lowering their standards by admitting poorly prepared students. He asked, "Of what avail could the learned professors and preparations of a University be to juvenile students? . . . To turn raw, undisciplined youth into the University to study the Professions, to study the Learned Languages and the Higher Sciences is a palpable absurdity."

- 1862   President Lincoln signed the Morrill Act, establishing land-grant colleges to teach agricultural and mechanical courses. A few years later, Iowa State College required that entering freshmen be fourteen years old and able to read, write, and do arithmetic. If they lacked these skills, they were placed in the college's preparatory department.

- 1874
Harvard first offered freshman English at the request of faculty members who were dissatisfied with students' preparation in formal writing.

- 1890
The Second Morrill Act increased federal aid to colleges for implementing programs in applied science and mechanical arts. This act freed American colleges from their classical and formal tradition. The rationale of the bill was that every American citizen was entitled to receive some form of higher education.

- 1890
The College Entrance Examination Board was founded, representing an attempt to make college admission requirements uniform.

- 1907
Over half the students who matriculated at Harvard, Yale, Princeton, and Columbia failed to meet entrance requirements. (Since colleges were competing fiercely for students they were willing to admit students who did not meet their standards in order to fill their classes.)

- 1915
Three hundred fifty colleges in the United States reported to the U.S. commissioner of education that they had college preparatory departments, suggesting that a gap remained between high school preparation and the expectations of colleges. Historians attribute this gap to the fact that states, in that era, were spending most of their money for education on elementary schools and little on high schools.

- 1930 to 1939
Remedial reading programs were emphasized in the public schools, and by the end of the decade, colleges and universities were establishing remedial reading clinics. New York University's Reading Laboratory began in 1936; Harvard instituted a

remedial reading course for its students in 1938, and Francis Triggs founded a reading clinic at the University of Minnesota in the same year. (I suspect that one impetus for the development of college reading services came from the introduction of general survey courses in 1929. Courses that required lengthy reading assignments, like "Introduction to Contemporary Civilization," became popular.)

- 1934   The University of Minnesota established a separate General College in response to the state legislature's mandate that the university accept all state high school graduates. (During the 1930s, public school graduates who felt unprepared for state college took a postgraduate year in high school or, if their families were wealthier, enrolled in a private preparatory school for a year or more before entering college.)

- 1941 to 1945   During World War II, colleges reduced the amount of time required to complete college degrees by shortening courses and adding intensive summer sessions. Frank Robinson of Ohio State University developed his SQ3R method for reading textbooks to help servicemen learn more quickly and effectively in their condensed, eight-week college courses.

- 1944 to 1955   The G.I. Bill enabled millions of former servicemen to attend college. Government funding allowed colleges to establish veterans' guidance centers, reading and study skills programs, and tutoring services. As the number of veterans attending college declined, these services became institutionalized as counseling centers and were open to all students.

- 1950s   College programs continued to expand, and community colleges spread across the country, making it possible for state universities to set higher admission standards. Following the launching of Sputnik, education in general, and colleges in particular, received funding for improving mathematics and science courses. These programs emphasized the identification and training of the most intellectually able students. (Having tried repeatedly to get funding for training marginally qualified college students during that period, I can attest to the number of federal agencies that turned a deaf ear to programs that did not concern the upper 10 percent of the college population.)

• 1961

Shaw (1961, pp. 336–337) summarized the reading problems of college students in the late fifties as follows: "Estimates of the prevalence of reading and study deficiencies among college freshmen are quite alarming. Observations and criticism of the situation by educators and laymen are confirmed by studies which show that . . . 68 percent had never been taught to read a chapter effectively; 70 percent had not been taught to concentrate on a reading activity; 70 percent had not been taught to evaluate a writer's bias. Two thirds of the freshmen lack the reading skills required for college success; 95 percent lack study skills." College faculties blamed the high schools and denied that colleges shared the responsibility of teaching the reading skills, study skills, and attitudes necessary for college work—but, at the same time, many offered remedial and study skills programs for students who needed them.

• 1960 to
  1980

Colleges, aided by government funding and pressured by the politics of the day, opened their doors to low-income groups, especially women and minorities that were underrepresented in academic and other professional careers. Open-admissions policies were adopted by most two-year and many four-year colleges. Prestigious universities enlarged their special-admissions programs. In 1964 the federally funded Upward Bound program started, marking the beginning of efforts to identify large numbers of disadvantaged minority students in high school and encourage them to prepare for college. Other federal programs soon followed. By 1970, one half million students—one seventh of those enrolled in U.S. colleges—came from poverty backgrounds. Open-admissions policies were implemented in the large City University of New York (CUNY) system; this program lasted six years. Throughout the country, colleges instituted learning centers and tutorial programs—at first to aid the minority students, but later to serve others as well.

More recently, legislation aimed at increasing college access for the handicapped. As a result, many colleges are admitting students with learning disabilities and other special problems who have been denied higher education in the past. These students require special academic support services.

The seventies were also the era when adults, particularly women, returned to undergraduate institutions in larger numbers than ever before. In 1976 two thirds of the students enrolled in California's huge community college system were working adults. Harvard admitted a sixty-three-year-old freshman, and many colleges are now actively seeking senior citizens for their undergraduate programs. Women outnumber men in college classes for the first time since World War II. Although today's Betty Coed is not as likely to be a grandmother as an eighteen-year-old, the day is fast approaching when this may be true. Already in some large urban universities, the average age of entering students is thirty-two.

Will the Present Diversity Continue?

In the near future, at least, colleges will continue to enroll a diverse group—in age, race, sex, economic background, and other characteristics. Almost all institutions are still recruiting disadvantaged students. The quantum jump in financial aid packages to students over the past decade is and will continue to be vital to the financial survival of many colleges in this age of apparently endless inflation. Federal Basic Educational Opportunity grants and 88 percent of state scholarships are presently awarded on the basis of financial need, not academic merit. The Basic Educational Opportunity grants have become the WPA of the 1970s. Many students today, in contrast to past periods, are paid to attend college, and both they and their colleges need their tuition scholarships. Middle-class students, who were the major group served by small private colleges, find they no longer can afford the rising tuition and board costs, and many are choosing to live at home, attend local public colleges part-time, and hold jobs. So colleges, including private ones, compete for students to fill their financial aid quotas and become increasingly dependent on the monies low-income students bring in the form of government grants. It is important financially for colleges to retain these students as well as to admit them, and special services and programs are needed if they are to remain in college.

Of the many changes that have occurred in American higher education since 1960, four complex and interrelated events are probably the most important—open admissions, federal policies mandated to increase access to higher education for educationally disadvantaged students and women, declining basic skills of college students (as exemplified by the lower scores on college admissions tests), and grade inflation. Also, the percentage of entering freshmen who rank in the top quarter of their high school graduating classes who chose to attend four year colleges has been steadily declining (Peng, 1977). Perhaps this decline is caused by the rising costs of attending college or perhaps it reflects the growing disenchantment with the benefits of a college degree and increasing disinterest in academic education (see Bird, 1975, for a discussion of these arguments).

Open Admissions. Although other colleges embraced open-admissions policies in the 1960s, the rapid and traumatic experiences of the City University of New York (CUNY) were the most controversial, best publicized, and most heavily documented

(Castro, 1974; Donovan, 1976; Kaufman and Botwinick, 1975; Kramer and others, 1974; Piasco and others, 1974; Rosen and others, 1973; Rossman and others, 1975). In 1970, when open-admissions policies were implemented, the CUNY system comprised ten senior colleges and eight two-year colleges. Although some of the two-year colleges had historically accepted students from the lower ranks of high school graduating classes (that is, students whose grade-point averages were below 2.5 on a four-point scale), most of the four-year institutions required that students have GPAs of 3.0 or higher and a pattern of college preparatory courses, and some schools had even higher standards. In 1970 all CUNY colleges were required to accept students with poor high school records. Many of these students were deficient in English, mathematics, and other basic skills.

Open-admissions students traumatized both faculty members and other students. Faculty members in four-year colleges, where open-admissions students were fewer, were generally indifferent to their needs or uncooperative, although some tried very hard to teach them. Even in community colleges with a decade or more of experience with disadvantaged students, there were serious problems in that faculty members found the massive numbers of students enrolled in their classes unmanageable.

Each institution developed its own methods for dealing with the educational deficiencies of the low-achieving enrollees. For example, Hunter College faculty members offered additional remedial work and tutoring within the departmental structure and found that the new students did not use these services. Queens College assigned each open-admissions student to a faculty adviser/counselor, and neither students nor advisers followed through. Medgar Evers faculty members designed a special interdisciplinary course, "The City of Man and Man in the City," taught in modules by different instructors, and this failed in differing degrees because instructors did not understand their roles as language teachers, use the resource center, or change their style of teaching to accommodate the underprepared students. Furthermore, they did not see the need to do so.

Other colleges treated open-admissions students like any other students and assumed that they would seek help from faculty members when they needed it. This approach failed also, and during the second year of open admissions, each institution introduced required remedial classes (if it had not already done so) and centralized tutoring and counseling services. Whether these support services were used by open-admissions students varied from campus to campus and seemed to depend on whether the support services were accepted by both faculty and other students (Rossman and others, 1975).

In brief, the initial year of open admissions at CUNY showed clearly that all the programs that depended on large-scale faculty support and involvement failed.

Inadequate budgets for remedial programs plagued CUNY's open-admissions programs from the beginning. During the second year of the program, open-admissions students were allocated fewer dollars each than regular students were, and the result was very large enrollments in remedial classes. But even if faculties had had more funds, they still would have lacked the knowledge of what might work with these students. In the third year of the program, there was some respite when $3 million in funds was "found," enabling colleges to hire more remedial instructors, mostly elementary and high school teachers. Some colleges tried to teach professors and remedial teachers to work with the new students, but most of the faculty members rejected these efforts. So the remedial teachers and professors learned the hard way about what does not work with underprepared students. By 1976, when the city's budget crisis forced massive cutbacks, CUNY was spending over $40 million a year on remedial instruction.

CUNY colleges had tried virtually every technique they could dream up to teach open-admissions students. Programs ranged from requiring the whole freshman class to take remedial English (Medgar-Evers) to quickly developing and implementing a dozen noncredit remedial courses (Bronx Community College) to a kind of benign neglect in which open-admissions students were assumed to be like everyone else.

Follow-up studies of the CUNY freshmen who entered during the first year of open admissions (Kaufman and Botwinick, 1975) reported that there was no evidence that the large-scale admission of low-achieving and economically disadvantaged students had produced either significant changes in the instructional methodology used or higher retention and success rates of students than would have been predicted from high school records and socioeconomic backgrounds. No relation between the number of required noncredit remedial courses offered to low-achieving students and their persistence was found—in fact, a negative relation was suggested. Over the four-year period studied, retention of *all* students—from high, average, or low socioeconomic backgrounds—declined at a small but significant rate. In the twenty-six studies on remedial instruction at different CUNY colleges, no clear trends emerged. Colleges that had longer experience with underprepared students fared no better in retaining them; indeed, they did less well than selective colleges with no experience.

Every four-year college graduated or retained a higher proportion of its lower-achieving students than any community college did (Kaufman and Botwinick, 1975, pp. 34–35). To be sure, the selective colleges did not have to deal with the massive numbers of open-admissions students, but there may be other reasons for the difference in graduation/retention rates. Perhaps the underprepared students who entered senior colleges were more highly motivated than those who entered junior colleges, or perhaps the expectations of the faculty in four-year colleges that students will complete college made a difference.

In the great push to establish programs for the disadvantaged both in open-admissions colleges and in the special-admissions programs of selective universities, program directors focused on their own students' problems ignoring the experiences of the black colleges that had taught educationally disadvantaged students for generations. As Langston Hughes said, "Black colleges are all caught up in the 'sweet flypaper' of life—they really know how to be relevant in community affairs." Students in black colleges have long viewed a college education as the means to a secure future, and most choose the helping professions, such as teaching and social work, as majors (Willie, 1973).

Historically, black colleges have emphasized technical and vocational courses and the professions, and black students have generally considered liberal arts courses useless and unrealistic.

Different black colleges have concentrated on different specialties. For instance, Dillard University in New Orleans emphasized remedial education, especially reading and language enrichment. Morgan State College in Baltimore concentrated on developing test-taking sophistication. Howard University, Fisk, and Morehouse attracted the top black students and prepared them for professional schools.

Gordon (1973) accuses white colleges of repeating the same mistakes that black colleges learned to avoid, because they failed to consult black colleges when they began their programs. In particular, white colleges insisted on implementing traditional remedial courses, assuming that that was the way to provide an adequate compensatory program. Furthermore, Gordon claims that the open-admissions efforts, particularly those at CUNY, were tainted by expediency and underfunded. Although this may be true, CUNY's experiences illustrate the problems most colleges faced, though CUNY's efforts and failures were on a grander scale.

The greatest burden fell on our most selective institutions. They had always admitted underprepared students in small numbers, but not in the quantities that they accepted in the sixties. Black scholar Thomas Sowell (1974) points out that the special pressures that governmental affirmative action demands placed on prestige and other institutions created a demand for black students at precisely those institutions least fitted to the students' educational preparation—that is, at research-oriented universities more concerned with filling their quotas, or "doing their part," than with seeing that the students were appropriately prepared and interested in their programs. The mismatch between students and colleges, as Sowell describes it, worsened when prestige institutions were convinced that they should adapt to serve students who did not meet their highly specialized requirements, and the possibility of sending black students to institutions whose normal standards they could meet was almost totally ignored (Sowell, 1974). Even worse, by government edict prestige colleges established special programs to admit black students who could not meet the colleges' normal standards: "Those institutions which most rapidly increased their enrollments were those in which the great majority of white Americans could *not* qualify" (1974, p. 180). In fact, regulations for the Educational Opportunity Program (EOP) and other programs specified that the students selected should have substandard academic performance as well as lower socioeconomic status. Sowell reports that black students themselves have said they are afraid to perform at their best in high school for fear of reducing their chances of getting the financial aid they need to go to college.

The question of whether black and other minority students receive covertly given special treatment at selective white institutions is still controversial. Sowell (1974, p. 184) reports: "As for the prevalence of dishonest and clandestine double standards, its nature is such that it can only be estimated impressionistically. My interviews with academics from coast to coast convince me that double standards are a fact of life on virtually every campus, but not necessarily in a majority of courses. This situation may in fact present the maximum academic danger to the black student: enough double standards to give him a false sense of security and enough rigid-standards courses to produce academic disasters."

Stanley (1971) questions an assumption underlying the programs for disadvantaged students: that they need less of the verbal ability measured by the SAT than the more advantaged students do. The proponents of accepting high-risk students into selective institutions seemed to imply that students from the ghettos would study harder and more effectively than advantaged students or perhaps would have developed more effective coping skills that would serve them well in college, despite their difficulties with traditional elementary and secondary schoolwork. Stanley further argues that there seemed to be more emphasis on the high-risk students' persisting in college than in their earning high grades and points out that "there is no magic in a degree from a usually selective college if it is not in one's preferred field, if it represents little real educational achievement, or if the recipient has falsely convinced himself that he is stupid" (p. 644).

Decline in SAT Scores. One symptom of the great change that has occurred in higher education is the decline in average scores of entering students on college admissions tests, especially the SAT. SAT scores began to drop in 1960 and have declined steadily since. Although the causes for the drop are complex, the basic reason is that more students are finishing high school and more are going on to college. As educational opportunities for educationally disadvantaged and minority students have expanded, more have sought college and therefore taken the SAT. For example, one half of U.S. high school graduates in 1970 went on to college, compared with one quarter in 1960. Blacks and students from low-income families have traditionally averaged 100 points lower on the SAT than whites and students from high-income families—and the greatest increase in college attendance in the 1970s occurred among low-income black students. Moreover, the percentage of women in college showed steady increases, and white women's SAT scores in mathematics average 50 points lower than the scores of white males.

The Advisory Panel on the Scholastic Aptitude Score Decline established by the College Entrance Examination Board (Wirtz and others, 1977) analyzed the reasons for the drop in scores during two periods—the 1960s, when they found that three fourths of the decline could be explained by the changing population who took the test, and the 1970s, when they concluded that the causes were more complex. The large increases in enrollment of disadvantaged students occurred in the 1960s, and, although colleges also enrolled large numbers of disadvantaged students in the 1970s, other factors appear to account for the continued score decline. The Wirtz Report cites such factors as the increase in absenteeism accompanying the higher retention rate that resulted from efforts to prevent high school students from dropping out. Absenteeism, the report explains, slows classroom progress and makes for repeated lessons and student boredom. Other suspected causes are these:

- The reading level for high school textbooks has dropped. Most eleventh-grade books currently used in high schools have reading levels at the ninth or tenth grade, but SAT questions are aimed at the eleventh- to fourteenth-grade levels.
- Enrollment in high school English courses dropped significantly between 1971 and 1973. English courses in grades ten through twelve enrolled 50 percent fewer students in 1973 than in 1971. Although there were more students in high school during the

later period, they were permitted to substitute other courses for English.

- Automatic promotion, grade inflation, and declines in the amount of homework assigned may have affected students' test scores.
- Student motivation toward college and especially toward taking standardized tests has changed. Students, knowing that colleges will accept them, are less motivated to do well on the SAT.
- The breakdown of the family and greater distance between its members, the hours students spend watching television, a general decline in academic motivation, and the social confusion surrounding such issues as the civil-rights movement, the Vietnam War, and Watergate were also mentioned as factors suspected of adversely affecting students' test performance.

Grade Inflation. Grade inflation began in high schools as they adopted automatic promotion and made other efforts to prevent students from dropping out of school. Students were given more choices of courses, and many colleges changed their entrance requirements; for example, students were no longer required to take four years of high school English or three years of laboratory science to qualify for college entrance.

Similarly, when the large group of disadvantaged students entered colleges under open admissions, these institutions made many concessions to accommodate these students. As a result of open-admissions policies and the student protest movement, colleges dropped some requirements, such as foreign-language courses, and allowed students to substitute a wide range of electives for lower-division general-education courses. Some faculty members who were forced to teach large numbers of underprepared students were either unable or unwilling to modify their courses, and they instead lowered their grading standards. Faculty members who maintained their standards ran the risk of being attacked by students as "racist" and "elitist" and considered not supportive of the efforts to help disadvantaged students get college degrees. Students from the ghetto brought with them survival skills that academics had never experienced—intimidation, threats, and emotional confrontations. In addition, to fail a student meant that the faculty member must justify his grading practices through a series of grievance hearings or conferences with administrators. Many felt that it was just not worth the time or effort. Finally, student groups were publishing course evaluations in efforts to change professors, and if one had the reputation of a tough grader, one's courses would attract fewer students.

College courses have not been equally affected by grade inflation. Social science courses have been the most susceptible to grade inflation while science grades have shown smaller increases. Social science courses, however, have been more popular with disadvantaged students than have science subjects. In addition, the students in the 1960s and early 1970s demanded that courses be relevant, and this led to new courses in current social issues and ethnic studies. Not only were the new courses different in content but also in method and assignments, often requiring that students discuss issues rather than write essays or take examinations. Grades in these new courses tended to be higher than those in traditional courses—after all, how can one fail "The Chicano Experience" course if one is a Chicano? In the minds of many students, relevant was equated with easy. As a result of these and other influences, more college students today are receiving A's than C's.

Faculty members faced pressures from both administrators and students to change their grading practices as well as student pressures. Teaching-accountability procedures were implemented that affected teaching and grading practices. A brief case history of one college's attempt to mandate faculty accountability illustrates this problem. In 1972 Passaic Community College's employment and promotion policy was hailed as a necessary means of getting the faculty to implement mastery learning techniques and as a reflection of the dynamic leadership of the college president (Roueche and Pitman, 1972). Following a simple rationale that faculty promotions should be based on ability to produce measurable learning in increasing numbers of students, the college required faculty members to sign contracts specifying their responsibilities. For instance, the contract for full professors stated that they would "design, implement, manage, and evaluate learning experiences for a minimum of 960 credit hours per semester and see that 90 percent of the students enrolled in the classes will achieve stated objectives at a level satisfactory for transfer to a senior institution if in a transfer course or at a level satisfactory for employment if in an occupational course." Faculty members at lower academic ranks were expected to teach fewer students and "succeed" with a smaller percentage of the class. An instructor was responsible for teaching 240 student credit hours each semester and was expected to prepare 60 percent of the students for transfer or employment (Roueche and Pitman, 1972).

In September 1976 Passaic College made news again by suspending or putting on probation 468 students—roughly one third of the student body—for unsatisfactory performance. Prior to the "midnight massacre," there were no entrance requirements. The implementation of a requirement that students must read at the tenth-grade level was an attempt to set minimum standards. Compelled by budget cuts, the college sought to restrict its enrollment equitably and maintain open admissions while requiring reading competency. While the faculty had been under contracts to improve students' skills and knowledge or else, grade-point averages had risen steadily. The faculty members set their own objectives for their courses, and many must have tried to attain the goals necessary to qualify them for promotions—at least, they gave higher grades.

So open admissions and other efforts to bring disadvantaged students into higher education led to major changes in U.S. higher education, including declines in traditional measures of college aptitude and grade inflation, which at the time seemed peripheral to the major social changes and student protests that brought violence into the halls of ivy. A generation before, the G.I. Bill had changed U.S. higher education by enabling massive numbers of young men from all walks of life to participate in higher education. But the veterans had returned to classes peacefully, whereas the masses of disadvantaged and minority students entered at a time when campuses were erupting and emotions were high. In the long run, the events of the 1960s and early 1970s may be viewed as having a greater impact on higher education in this country than any other event. And although the furor and demands for college entrance for all have died down, today many colleges are actively seeking students—any students—to fill their classrooms.

Are College Remedial Courses Failures?

Critics maintain that traditional college remedial courses are failures and are not the best way to help underprepared students gain the skills and knowledge they need (Davis and others, 1975; Gordon, 1973; Jason and others, 1977; Roueche and Kirk, 1973; Roueche and Pitman, 1972). In fact, some experts believe that such courses are the worst possible way to deal with the problems of academically weak freshmen because they kill student motivation (Klingelhofer and Hollander, 1973; Jason and others, 1977).

It is generally conceded that remedial college courses do little to increase the retention of underprepared college students over what might be expected from their high school records and their test scores. The large-scale federally funded programs to help disadvantaged students attend and remain in college, such as Upward Bound and the Special Services Programs, have fared poorly in follow-up evaluation studies. (Comptroller General of the United States, n.d.; Davis and others, 1975).

Many reasons have been given for these failures. Remedial programs are invariably classified as "special" or "supportive" and are often founded in a climate of hostility with very little consideration given to making them a part of the academic mainstream (Jason and others, 1977). Students in remedial programs are always considered different from other students. They are labeled "slow learners" or "poor achievers," and their motivation and strengths are overlooked, while the work they are assigned is obviously at the high school level, usually of the skills-drill format, which does not inspire them to learn. Often colleges place unnecessary bureaucratic obstacles in their way, such as time constraints on completing courses, so that they become discouraged, confused, or unable to cope with the system.

College faculty members, perhaps in a mood of eternal optimism, believe that remedial courses—even those that have existed for almost a century—are temporary and that the need they fill will soon disappear. Since remedial programs are considered unrelated to the main functions of a college, they are usually allocated minimal staffing and resources. Without an academic power base like other programs, they are vulnerable to budget cuts and reduced staffing when money is tight.

College administrators, in general, do not consider remedial instruction an effective way to use faculty resources, and faculty members do not perceive their role to include teaching basic skills. Faculty members are rarely experienced, skilled, or interested in teaching remedial students. Teaching remedial courses offers little prestige; indeed, it may be viewed as punitive when it takes instructors away from colleagues in their academic departments and from their research—the keys to promotion and tenure.

The stigma attached to both taking and teaching remedial courses is important in discouraging students. If the program is viewed as a salvage operation, both instructors and students suffer low morale. The situation is worsened when unwilling instructors are drafted to teach remedial courses. They may lack both interest and skills and be unable to relate to the students.

Another factor that has prevented remedial courses from succeeding is the impossible expectations for them. For example, under special-admissions programs in selective universities, where the weakest students were enrolled with the best, disadvantaged students were exposed to one course in writing skills while carrying regular courses concurrently. It was hoped that their problems would be eradicated in one term. If students are recruited whose skills are far below their classmates', no program can make them fare as well in their courses as the regular admits. Nor can any reading program raise students' reading ability four grade levels in ten weeks, yet this expectation is often implied in curriculum schedules. If students enter college with below-eighth-grade reading skills, they also lack information and knowledge that come from reading in high school. College remedial reading courses are not designed to fill information gaps or to help students gain quickly the cognitive skills that must develop slowly with extensive practice.

Within the remedial courses themselves, the three R's are fractured. Remedial writing is taught by an English instructor, mathematics by a mathematics instructor, and reading by yet another instructor in another department—perhaps the department of education or the counseling service. Speech and listening, although important skills for college survival, are not generally included—in fact, speech is not regarded as a remedial subject. And within each course, instructors further fractionate the skills into small, discrete subskills like reading for details or mastering word endings, and they may not help the students integrate these subskills into the real activities they must perform in other courses, such as reading college textbooks.

Remedial courses have also been criticized as being easy, watered-down versions of the content of college courses aimed at improving students' self-concepts or attitudes rather than their learning. Some instructors, in their zeal to remedy the students' deficiencies, may limit the course to skills drills on basic phonics or grammar without relating this information to the broader skills needed in future composition or social science courses. As a result, students may pass the remedial course and fail their other courses.

Certainly the goal of remedial courses should be to help students develop the skills and knowledge they will need for advanced work in college, but sometimes this is difficult. In mathematics the route is clear—algebra precedes trigonometry, for example. Students may not view a course in reading improvement as relevant to their particular goals.

If, for the reasons just cited, remedial college courses have failed to help underprepared students succeed academically, one might wonder why they are proliferating. The answer is that they may serve other functions. If they exist to protect faculty members from having to teach weak students or if they are designed to discourage poorly prepared students from pursuing college goals, then they might be viewed as quite successful. Many colleges today that are faced with declining enrollments and the threat of financial failure are reexamining their programs and are deeply concerned about student retention (Astin, 1975, 1977). Under these exigencies, institutions may have incentives to develop better ways of instructing students whom they formerly preferred to reject or to condemn to ineffective remedial programs.

Certainly student diversity will remain a characteristic of higher education for some time. Community college instructors are struggling to find ways of motivating and retaining the wide range of students in their classes, yet dropout rates remain as high as 75 percent. And highly selective colleges and universities are concerned with resurrecting academic standards that have eroded for twenty years. Some are developing competency-based examinations that students must take at different points in their college years. For example, Brigham Young University has introduced examinations for its breadth requirements. To qualify for junior standing students must pass a proficiency test in each breadth-requirement area, whether or not they have taken and passed the respective course. Other universities are following the new Harvard model and reintroducing required lower-division courses, including foreign languages, philosophy, and other courses that were made electives in the 1960s.

In short, the attempts we made in the past to extend college educational experiences to greater numbers of students have led to grade inflation and a weakening of academic standards. Many of the efforts were token attempts at best, ignoring the experiences of black colleges and other institutions that have historically provided college experiences for educationally disadvantaged or otherwise underprepared students. The chaos surrounding the open-admissions programs of the 1960s and early 1970s, particularly those in formerly selective colleges, has abated. Despite protestations that institutions want to help underprepared students succeed, the dropout rates remain high, suggesting that colleges may be effective only in reinforcing the negative attitudes toward education that students may have developed in their earlier school experiences

However, underprepared students will not disappear from college classrooms, nor can most colleges expect to restrict admissions to the best prepared—there are too few of them, and average students' skills have deteriorated also. Under these circumstances it is clear that colleges must continue to offer comprehensive and intensive academic support services to their students.

Out of the failures of the 1960s and 1970s some programs have emerged that show promise and others suggest caveats to be observed in planning instructional services. I hope that this book will indicate some directions and present some ideas that will help us avoid past mistakes and plan more realistically for the future.

2

Diagnosing the Basic Skill Difficulties of Students

Colleges and universities differ widely in the procedures they use to determine which students will take basic skills programs. Programs may be for credit or noncredit; enrollment, required or voluntary. Specific policies reflect the philosophy and standards of the college and the number of students accepted who are considered underprepared.

Some colleges do not accept obviously underprepared students, carefully monitoring the qualifications of the students they admit. At the same time, they offer special reading and study skills programs, tutoring, and other academic support services for their students who turn out to have difficulties.

Some selective institutions limit admission of underprepared students to a fixed number or percentage within each entering class while holding higher admissions standards for the majority of their freshmen. These "special admits" may be (1) required to take remedial courses with or without credit, (2) accepted into regular courses and given intensive tutoring and other help, and then, if they fail to make progress, required to take remedial courses, (3) permitted, required, or encouraged to take reduced course loads, or (4) required or encouraged to attend special summer bridge programs; or some combination of these policies may be applied.

Most open-admissions colleges require weak students to take basic skills courses, but some put students in regular courses.

Skills Courses—Required or Voluntary?

The question whether basic skills courses should be required or voluntary has been debated by college educators for many years. Experts disagree. Jones (1959, p. 25) expresses the view held by many skills specialists: "The selection of students for college and university reading programs should be *entirely* on a voluntary basis. At this level, students will be successful only if they want to be and not because they are forced." Others insist that if colleges admit students who have deficient skills, they should require skills-improvement courses for the weakest students. Blake (1956) argues that freshmen admitted on probation in a selective college benefit from a required course in reading and study skills. Shaw (1961), after teaching both kinds of courses, takes a middle position. He believes it is a mistake to assume that all beginning freshmen have the insight to determine whether they should enroll in a skills course and, once enrolled, whether they should continue to attend regularly. But, Shaw cautions, if students resist taking the course, they should be allowed to drop it as they would any other course.

In practice today, some colleges require skills courses, some counsel certain students to take them, and others open them to all students as electives. Each policy has advantages and disadvantages.

Required Skills Courses. At one extreme, all students judged academically weak are required to enroll in basic skills courses. Students with low skills are identified in one of three ways: (1) Scores on the college's admissions test are used. For example, a basic skills program might be required for students scoring in the lowest quartile on the institution's norms—or those scoring below a cutoff score on national norms—on the SAT, the ACT (the test of the American College Testing Program), or some other standardized test. Or students scoring below the twelfth-grade level on the Cooperative English Test might be required to take a reading course. (2) Some combination of test scores and high school grades or rank in high school graduating class is used. (3) Students scoring low on the admissions test are held for special qualifying tests in reading, writing, and mathematics, and those who fail the qualifying tests are required to take basic skills courses. (This third method is commonly used to determine students' ability to take freshman English, the qualifying test being a departmentally administered writing-sample examination.)

Mandatory skills courses have a number of advantages. First, identifying and placing students with skills deficiencies is automatic. A formula of grades and test scores or a cutoff score is programmed into a computer, and all students scoring in the designated category are given enrollment cards for the skills courses. Compulsory enrollment in skills courses is cheap, simple for administrators and advisers, and efficient.

If skills classes are filled by the registrar under a college requirement, skills instructors need not worry about attracting students to their classes, for this is done automatically. Besides, their task is easier in that they teach groups of students relatively homogeneous in ability. Many instructors prefer teaching this type of class.

Many faculty members and administrators view requiring basic skills courses as fairer and more objective than other methods of selecting students into these courses because the placement criteria (test scores and prior grades) are specific and measurable. In addition, administrators can be certain that those students who need help the most will get it, for underprepared students may not volunteer to take basic skills courses.

Another advantage is that compulsory basic skills courses protect the faculty members who teach regular freshman courses from having to teach underprepared students and deal with their problems in the same classes as better-prepared students.

Mandating enrollment in basic skills courses has an equal number of disadvantages. Since requiring remedial courses has been the most common placement policy and since many have been viewed as failures, one should carefully consider the problems and plan strategies to avoid them if one decides to require these courses.

First, the psychological effects of being required to take a remedial course and being stigmatized as dumb are shared by both students and instructors. As Felton and Biggs (1977, p. 7) point out, "Remediation, as it is sometimes practiced, may help the student to label herself as stupid, and this may in turn affect the teacher's attitudinal responses to that individual. This means that under-achievement often is caused directly in the classroom and in the 'helping' provided there. This is a painful irony." Requiring students to take special unchallenging courses is equivalent to creating an intellectual ghetto for a subgroup of students and instructors.

Second, the task of instruction is made more difficult in that instructors must bear the responsibility for motivating unmotivated and often quite resistant students. As a result, instructors must fight against developing a self-fulfilling, pessimistic prognosis for their students.

Third, without realistic role models to show what the regular college students are like, remedial students may not make the progress they should. Their instructors too may lose perspective of the skills and intellectual knowledge that the institution requires of its students, because they are teaching only the lowest. As a result, they may dilute their course material to make it easier and more palatable to their resisting students, thus effectively pushing the students further from their goals.

Fourth, segregating students into basic skills courses, particularly when those courses do not fit into a clear sequence of advanced courses, may lead to a proliferation of remedial courses. Skills instructors identify their weakest students and request that those students be assigned to a separate, simpler, more intensive class. As Malvina Reynolds' song goes, "Hit bottom? Oh, no! There's a bottom below." So the skills instructor focuses on the bottom group and finds more and more layers of deficiency. Soon the writing instructors are offering a series of courses from essay writing down to paragraph writing down to sentence writing. The reading instructors begin to specialize, too. Starting with a course in improving speed and comprehension, they add courses in basic comprehension skills, vocabulary building, word-attack skills, and finally basic phonics and decoding skills. The inevitable result— and it has occurred in some community colleges—is that students are required to take as many as fifteen noncredit remedial courses before being permitted to register for any regular college classes. They are, in effect, majoring in being remediated. Invariably, this results in high student attrition.

Proliferation of remedial courses usually occurs when the faculty rigidly adheres to traditional curriculums and standards while the institution admits large numbers of unqualified students. The basic skills instructors, who cannot hope to advance to teaching higher-level courses, respond by specializing. They plan new, pre-liminary courses in order to build a power base and compete with other departments for student full-time equivalent (FTE) and funding. Thrust into a role in which they must teach students who cannot expect to qualify for the institution's normal programs, they too play the traditional academic game—that is, identify a topic, label it, and expand it into a full-term course. Then they demand that students get credit for taking it. (If this trend continues, I expect that there will come a time when college students will get credit for three separate courses—one in prefixes, another in suf-fixes, and a third in roots.) By fragmenting and oversimplifying skills courses, instructors are actually pushing students further from their college goals intellectually as well as setting up imposing time hurdles. For the weakest students—those who, even if they persist through the remedial series, will never be able to compete in traditional programs—the effect is tragic. Unfortunately, those who offer such courses do not see it that way. They are convinced that they are meeting their students' needs.

In summary, compulsory programs, by definition, permit

students no options. Some students may not be motivated to improve their basic skills. In teaching mandatory basic skills courses, instructors play a dual role, that of motivating students as well as teaching them. Counselors can provide some assistance to resistant students but are usually placed in a reactive position—that is, they must explain and justify the rationale for the courses—and students may feel that their individual needs are not being considered. Required remedial courses protect the faculty from the need to modify its courses and curriculums, but if a college has large numbers of underprepared students, the remedial programs will proliferate. The remedial/developmental skills department grows in size, but few students are able to make the transition from remedial work to regular majors. What makes the difference is whether the students admitted have skills close to those demanded by the professors for their specialties and whether the remedial courses are closely articulated with advanced courses.

Placement Through Counselor Recommendation. Another approach to identifying students for placement in basic skills courses involves counseling. This technique might be viewed as midway between compulsory and voluntary enrollment. A voluntary program assumes that students are motivated to improve their skills and will choose to do so. To choose wisely, however, students need solid information about their skills and how they compare with the demands and expectations of the faculty. The counseling approaches address this problem.

One method is to have advisers identify students with weak high school backgrounds and low entrance-test scores and encourage them to enroll in basic skills courses. Encouragement may range in intensity from a gentle nudge to a strong shove. I recall how advisers in a small, selective, liberal arts college used to do it. Entering freshmen were required to take a standardized reading test, and their percentile ranks were recorded on their permanent grade records. It took little urging from advisers to persuade students with low scores to volunteer for the reading-improvement course, for they were told that if they completed the reading-improvement program, they could retake the test and raise their scores. Since these students aspired to attend graduate and professional schools, they were highly motivated to get those low scores off their transcripts so as not to jeopardize their chances for getting into advanced programs.

In some colleges, advisers refer students with low entrance-test scores or weak high school grades to the testing service for diagnostic testing. A learning-skills counselor interprets the results of this testing and encourages those who need skills help to enroll in the program, but the student has the option of refusing. Most counseling and learning-support programs that offer diagnostic testing encourage students to come in on their own for skills testing as well as accepting referrals from faculty members. The self-referred student who needs skills courses will be encouraged to enroll in the program.

Skills Courses as Electives. In some colleges, the skills courses are open to any student who wishes to take them. Underprepared and even learning-disabled students are channeled into these pro-grams. For example, in the comprehensive program at West Valley College, (Saratoga, California) a reading course is offered as an elective to any student (Peterson and others, 1978). West Valley College, an open-admissions community college, does not require students to take entrance tests for admission. Students learn about the reading course through friends, advertising, counselors, advis-ers, faculty members, and other means. During the first two class meetings, students enrolled in the reading course are given reading tests and, on the basis of their scores, divided into two sections. This is easily accomplished, as two sections of the course are scheduled each hour of the school day in adjoining classrooms. Instructors use different criteria to assess the progress of the high- and low-scoring sections.

Advantages of mainstreaming are that it ensures that students enrolling in the class are motivated and it minimizes the remedial stigma. Instructor morale is higher too, reflecting the level of motivation of the students. A disadvantage is that the pro-gram may not reach all students who need it. Without entrance tests, there is no systematic way to determine how many students avoid the class, but as classes fill regularly, one can conclude that the program is popular with students.

Since instructors offering elective skills courses must compete with those offering other kinds of courses, their success in attracting students depends on having a strong public relations program to convince both students and faculty of the value of their courses. In addition, a successful course must provide ancillary services for the weakest students—diagnostic services, counseling, and individualized intensive practice in a learning laboratory. The qualities of the staff, of course, are important in attracting students and in developing and maintaining the support of other faculty members. If markedly deviant students, such as those with severe learning disabilities, are enrolled in the course, then flexible procedures that permit students to repeat the course are needed. To summarize, a successful elective basic skills course must be part of a comprehensive, well-coordinated program of student services.

In the West Valley College model (Peterson and others, 1978, p. 16), students with limited functioning are identified and assessed through a network of services and the development and expansion of regular college programs. The discrepancy between an individual's functioning and the required functioning (that is, meeting the demands of the curriculum, the classroom environment, and so on) is determined by input from fifteen different services, including community agencies, and diagnostic testing. On the basis of this information, the student is helped to find practical solutions, which may be of four kinds: remediation (cure), amelioration devices (tutoring, adaptive physical education, speech, and so on), modifying requirements, or changing his or her goal (through counseling, community agencies, and other services).

Other Ways to Organize and Present Basic Skills Services

Basic skills may be presented to students as part of their regular courses, as by incorporating reading and study skills units into freshman English or requiring students in a course to complete learning modules on particular skills in a learning center as part of their assigned work. Adjunct skills courses—programs, generally noncredit, that parallel the work in a given subject and focus on the skills needed throughout the term—are another way of ensuring that students learn needed skills. (See Chapter Eleven for descriptions of adjunct skills courses.) These techniques may require special skills of the faculty or at least a willingness to refer students to support services, but they have the advantage of relating basic skills to what students consider real learning—that is, to the content of regular college courses.

Summer Bridge Programs. Special summer bridge programs are a way of organizing basic skills and other support services for underprepared students and are widely used by both undergraduate and graduate institutions. Entering students with weak academic backgrounds are identified before enrolling in college and encouraged to attend a special summer school session. Most summer bridge programs include tutoring, counseling, advising, skills programs, and regular academic courses. If students are required to attend a summer session in order to qualify for fall admission, the number of applications for admission and enrollments of underprepared students will drop sharply. (In programs I have observed and worked in where summer attendance was mandatory, only about half of those who applied for admission attended the summer session.) Special programs for disadvantaged students attending graduate and professional schools usually do not show reduced enrollments in a summer bridge program, but these students tend to be very highly motivated. In undergraduate programs, a higher percentage of students will attend the summer session if scholarships and financial aid are included.

One advantage of summer bridge programs is that they give students an opportunity to test out college courses and receive intensive skills help at the same time. Further, they offer students an opportunity to adjust to college at a time when the pace is less hectic. Some argue that summer programs are advantageous to underprepared students because they enable them to start at a slower pace; I disagree, because most summer courses are condensed into intensive six- or eight-week sessions, in which students must cover a full semester's worth of work in a shorter time. At any rate, summer-session enrollment is much lighter at most colleges and universities than during the academic year, and so bridge students can be taught in smaller classes, where they find the atmosphere less competitive than in the fall and spring terms.

Another advantage of summer bridge programs is that they employ the skills staff in the summer, when there is otherwise very little demand for its services.

On the negative side, summer bridge programs can be expensive, particularly when they offer scholarships, personal counseling, tutoring, skills assistance, and instruction in regular academic subjects. Whether this expense is an important consideration to a college depends on the reasons for the program and the functions it fulfills. If a large number of freshmen fail or drop out of the institution at the end of every fall term, then a summer bridge program designed to prevent attrition may be viewed by the administration as cost-effective. Even if the program only screens out those students who would leave college anyway, this can cut many costs—for instance, the cost of dormitory rooms that fill in the fall and are half-filled in the spring or the cost of hiring instructors for freshman courses by the year who have few courses to teach in the spring. If a college is mandated by the federal government to accept larger numbers of minority students, summer bridge programs are used to attract them and improve their skills.

However, there is little evidence that summer bridge programs are any more effective than programs offered during the academic year. Indeed, they may generate special problems for the students who attend them. As an example, one selective private university, which recruited minority students from Harlem ghettos, abandoned its special summer programs for EOP students when it discovered the culture shock these students experienced when they returned to college in the fall. Although the summer bridge program offered a full range of services, only disadvantaged students (EOP and Upward Bound) enrolled in campus courses during the summer session. When the regular student body returned in the fall, the small group of minority students found themselves like a few peas in a bushel of apples. Outnumbered and outdistanced in background by their peers, many of the disadvantaged students became discouraged and dropped out of college.

Attending summer school drains students' energies and financial resources, even when scholarships are given. Conscientious, underprepared students invest a tremendous amount of energy and time in succeeding in the summer program. When, after a few weeks' vacation, they enroll again in more rigorous, competitive fall classes, they may be tempted to relax and enjoy the social and other extracurricular activities the college offers, with the result that they do not study, and they make low grades or fail.

Reduced-Course-Load Programs. An alternative—or an adjunct—to summer bridge programs is to permit underprepared students to take a lighter course load than regular students. Study units—ungraded credits that do not count toward graduation— are given for participation in basic skills programs so that the student may qualify for financial aid or veterans' benefits. Reduced-course-load programs may be required or voluntary. If students are tested and counseled and work out contracts with their counselors or advisers that specify the skills courses and/or other activities they will complete, this type of program can be beneficial. Since students with poor preparation for college generally take longer to complete degrees, if they graduate at all, building a longer time span into their college plans seems realistic. Some colleges call these programs "extended degree programs" or "ninth semesters."

All-Freshmen Skills Courses. Some highly selective as well as many open-admissions colleges require that *all* freshmen take basic skills courses, such as composition, reading and study skills, and general mathematics and do not differentiate sections as remedial. A small number of outstanding students may be exempted from this requirement, but the rest of the freshmen are held for the course. High-risk freshmen are enrolled in the same classes as better-prepared students. Special services such as study skills specialists, tutors, and learning laboratories are available for students who need or want to use them.

One advantage of the all-freshmen skills course is that it lacks the stigma associated with separate remedial courses. As a result, underprepared students are not so hesitant and resistant about taking it. (Of course, some students resent taking any required course, and they will object to this one too, but they are usually few.) Instructors are less likely to water down or simplify the course, since a wide range of students are enrolled in it. It is therefore easier to keep the course requirements consistent with the level of the college's other freshman courses. A further advantage is that faculty and student morale can generally be maintained at a higher level, and students are less subject to instructors' negative expectations.

A disadvantage is that there are limits to the number of students and the range of abilities that some teachers can handle effectively in a single classroom, so that this method requires better and more sophisticated instructors than when students are segregated by ability. Another disadvantage is that some students who need extra help will not use the services provided and may fail the course or receive grades of incomplete and need to repeat it.

Of course, many other factors are involved, and some colleges have found that retention of underprepared students is higher when they are placed in regular courses than when they are segregated into separate remedial programs.

It should be obvious that an all-freshmen skills course in which a handful of nonreaders are registered amidst a group of students who read at the thirteenth-grade level or higher will not help the nonreaders and may drive the instructor up the wall. If a selective institution must admit students with very low skills, then special programs and curriculums for them are needed, not mainstreaming. Since the present accuracy of our best predictors of college grades are far from perfect, enrolling students who may not need the course or who can quickly improve their skills in a full-term course may be a waste of students' time, the institution's time, and the resources of the college.

Skills Courses—Credit or Noncredit?

Another often-debated issue about basic skills courses is whether credit should be given. The issue is unresolved, although there is a strong trend to award at least partial credit for such courses if students are required to take them. In a survey of public two-year colleges in the Midwest, Ferrin (1971) found that most gave some credit for both remedial and developmental courses. Cross (1976) reported that the percentage of two-year colleges offering credit for remedial courses increased from 32 to 53 between 1970 and 1974. Other authors have indicated that colleges are increasingly offering credit for basic skills courses (Roueche and Snow, 1977; Sullivan, 1978). Cross (1976) argues that disadvantaged students need the immediate and tangible reward of credit, and skills specialists insist that without credit, academically weak students will not attend classes. Faculty members and administrators, however, maintain that educationally disadvantaged students are being shortchanged when they are awarded credit toward graduation for skills training they should have had in high school or earlier. Grobman (1972) takes the position that if academically weak students are given credit for a series of skills courses, they are not able to fulfill the breadth requirements or to take as many courses in their majors as other students. A number of reading experts are currently arguing that general reading-improvement courses ought to be awarded credit and be open to all freshmen, as freshman English is (Hertz and others, 1977; Shepherd, 1977).

The reason most often cited for an institution's not awarding credit for skills courses is that the faculty feels that giving credit for remedial courses would lower standards. Although this attitude among the faculty may indeed play a part, the major determinants of whether a college awards credit for basic skills courses are more pragmatic: where the program gets its funding and who teaches the courses. If the basic skills instructors are paid by academic departments or developmental skills departments funded by monies earmarked for instruction, the college is apt to give credit. But if the skills courses are offered by nonacademic units, such as counseling centers, learning centers without departmental affiliations, and library services, the program generally does not carry credit. (There are exceptions, of course.)

Who teaches the course makes a difference. If a senior faculty member in a prestigious university becomes discouraged with the math preparation of his students and develops a course to reeducate students from the beginning up to college, he usually can get credit approved by his department. A lowly teaching associate who develops a precalculus course may find it much harder to secure departmental approval to offer the course for credit. However, if the topic is pursued long enough and students support credit for the course, the department may be persuaded to grant at least partial credit for the course.

The point is that credit courses in most institutions are taught by faculty members in academic departments, and if offering skills courses for credit will increase departmental student FTE (or, in private colleges, their tuition income), then it is to the department's advantage to offer courses for credit developed and taught within their own departments. Programs staffed by counselors or learning-skills specialists are often budgeted from a different fund than academic departments and are less likely to secure approval to award credit for their courses.

A closer look at the way colleges grant credit for skills courses reveals some interesting facts. The credit awarded may be temporary, as for a precalculus course in a university. The student earns up to two credits for completing precalculus, but if he or she completes calculus, the credits for precalculus are removed. Similarly, in community colleges a reading course may carry credit that counts for an Associate of Arts degree but not for transfer to a senior college.

The student consumer movement in the early 1970s and pressures to admit and retain disadvantaged students led many institutions to award credit for skills courses that had traditionally been noncredit. Currently, faculty members in many institutions seem more willing to grant credit for skills work as graduate enrollments shrink and as administrators scrutinize their workload measures and set arbitrary faculty/student ratios. Offering basic skills courses to freshmen is one way an education department, for instance, can attract enough students to offset the declining enrollments in graduate courses.

In summary, the number of colleges and universities offering academic credit for basic skills courses has increased greatly since the mid sixties. However, such courses may carry partial credit—for instance, two credits may be awarded for a course requiring the same amount of time as a three-credit regular course —or disappearing credit, which is good for financial aid and veterans' benefits but not for graduation or transfer to a senior college or which is removed if the student completes a more advanced course.

Noncredit basic skills courses are often offered in large universities. They may or may not be required. If voluntary, they are usually given as short minicourses; students who are—or think they are—weak in a subject or skill may enroll. Requiring noncredit remedial courses is an effective way to reduce the number of unqualified students who enroll in an institution and will increase freshman attrition. One university requires students who fail a qualifying mathematics test to take three sequential noncredit math courses in order to be eligible for general calculus. They must take algebra, solid geometry, and trigonometry, and the courses are not flexible, so that the student who has a few gaps in one of the subjects must still complete all three. Only the most highly motivated do.

Identifying Students with Weak Skills

Whether basic skills courses are required or voluntary, credit or noncredit, the key to a successful program is early identification of students with weak skills, preferably before they are accepted by the college. Precollege screening and counseling are essential. Prospective students must be evaluated in light of the college's existing programs and the characteristics of current students on the following points:

- Reading—Are prospective students able to read well enough to understand freshman textbooks and hold their own with other students?
- Writing—Can they expect to succeed in the lowest-level writing course the college offers?
- Mathematics—Have they the skills to handle the basic math course? For example, if the college's mathematics course assumes that students have had algebra, then those who are deficient in basic arithmetic and have had no algebra should not be admitted until they have completed courses elsewhere and can qualify.
- Science—If students aspire to science majors, have they adequate mathematics skills, prior courses in chemistry, and the analytic thinking skills needed to succeed in beginning courses?
- Expectations and Motivation—Are students interested in and knowledgeable about the courses and majors offered by the institution? For example, if a student expects that a university business administration major prepares students to be clerk-typists, she is likely to be disappointed in the freshman courses she takes.

Are students aware of the time and effort it takes to learn in college, and are they willing and able to make this investment?

If a college admits students whose skills and background are far below the level of the average student in that college or the level expected by the faculty, there will be high attrition among the underprepared group, dissatisfied faculty members, and/or lowered standards.

Colleges use different ways to determine the skills and motivation of their prospective students. Private schools will send out teams of interviewers and also use their local alumni to contact prospective students and evaluate them. Most institutions require admissions tests and have special summer orientation programs, which often include parents. Currently, community colleges are trying the same approaches—that is, loading new students into a bus for a weekend retreat to orient them to the demands and expectations of the faculty, to get to know them, and to give them a head start on skills they will need. (I know of few colleges that invite spouses to orientation, but I feel that it would be an excellent idea, because so many of today's college students are married and the spouses' attitude can make a great difference in the students' success.)

In addition to information about programs offered by and skills needed for a particular college, students need information about themselves. Testing assesses students skills and provides information for them. Colleges and universities use standardized tests, locally built tests, and informal instruments to place or guide freshmen into appropriate skills courses in mathematics, reading, and writing. (See Appendix A for a list of frequently used tests.)

Reading Tests. Ninety-five percent of college reading programs in this country use standardized reading tests to select, place, and/or evaluate the progress of students (Geerlofs and Kling, 1968; Fairbanks and Snozek, 1973). The Nelson-Denny Reading Test is most often used for pre- and posttesting, probably because it takes less time to administer than most reading tests (30 minutes) and its subscores —speed, comprehension, and vocabulary—reflect students' gains in rate of reading. Other popular college reading tests are the Cooperative English Test, the McGraw-Hill Basic Skills

Test—Reading, and the Diagnostic Reading Test—Survey Section. The Cooperative English Test yields two scores—rate of comprehension (the number of items answered correctly with a correction for guessing) and level of comprehension (based on number of correct responses to items in the first section, which nearly everyone completes). In contrast to tests using words-per-minute as the index of rate, this scoring system uses rate of comprehension. It is harder for students to raise their rate of comprehension scores as a result of a short course than to increase their reading speed.

The McGraw-Hill Basic Skills Test—Reading uses longer passages to measure leisure reading and reading of the kind done when studying and arrives at a flexibility ratio (speed versus difficulty of material). It also includes a section on skimming and scanning and a paragraph-comprehension test that can be scored for specific comprehension skills, such as understanding scientific principles, so that students who are weak can be directed to the appropriate workbook in the McGraw-Hill Basic Skills System. Although there are only five items per comprehension category, I have found this paragraph-comprehension section very useful in writing "blind" diagnoses on students from high school through graduate level. It is also a useful screening test to determine whether students can hold their own in a speed-reading course.

The Diagnostic Reading Test was once considered too easy for college students by many reading experts, but times have changed. It contains timed reading exercises and multiple-choice questions. The vocabulary test yields scores on English, mathematics, science, and social science vocabulary, and there are silent and oral word-attack tests.

Open-admissions community colleges that enroll a wide diversity of students generally use a quick screening test such as the Wide Range Achievement Test, which takes one minute to give individually and requires the student to pronounce words ranging from *milk* to *synecdoche*. The score yields a rough grade placement. Another screening test is the Reading Progress Scale, which can be administered quickly, involves silent reading, and indicates whether students read below fourth grade, below eighth grade, or higher. A quick screening test can help the instructor or reading specialist decide whether to administer further diagnostic testing, which takes much longer.

It is unfortunate that there are no standardized tests that measure students' ability to read material of textbook-chapter length on different subjects. Maintaining Reading Efficiency Tests come closest in format to this goal. The five tests each contain 5,000-word passages on the history, geography, government, and culture of different countries—Brazil, Japan, India, New Zealand, and Switzerland. Although these tests are somewhat limited in that their content is restricted to social science, and some of the passages are poorly written (but, one might argue, so are some textbooks), they do approximate the college student's reading task.

For instructors who are concerned about whether students can read critically, there is the Watson-Glaser Test of Critical Thinking. Herlin (1976) is building a critical-reading test to be used as a qualifying examination for a part of the breadth requirements at Brigham Young University. His test has three sections—analyzing the structure of writing, logic, and interpretation. The structure-of-writing section measures the level at which students can generalize about paragraphs and essays and gives students a method of diagraming their generalizations.

College reading specialists who work with students with very limited reading skills (below eighth grade) often use the Stanford Diagnostic Reading Test to determine students' skills gaps and to plan appropriate programs. The California Phonics Test is another interesting diagnostic test for students with minimal reading skills and is administered by tape recorder. Students enjoy taking this test—a rare situation with standardized tests.

A new battery, Descriptive Tests of Language Skills, has been published by the College Entrance Examination Board (CEEB). These tests have not yet been normed. They are designed to identify students with language and reading problems, particularly in open-admissions schools, so as to promote individualized instruction and aid in placement in remedial courses. The topics of the reading selections appear to have more interest for today's college students than those in many traditional standardized tests.

Writing. There are a number of standardized tests on language usage, sentence structure, grammar, and spelling which may be used to place students in writing courses. However, most English departments determine who must take remedial writing not just on the basis of standardized tests but on the basis of a writing sample, usually an essay, which is graded by the instructors. The standardized tests are useful for diagnostic purposes and to assess improvement in an individualized program, but the student's ability to write a theme is considered more important.

See descriptions of the Descriptive Tests of Language Skills, the Westinghouse Patterns of Language (measuring dialect interference), and others in Appendix A.

Mathematics. As in other basic skills, there are many standardized tests in mathematics. (See Appendix A for descriptions of the McGraw-Hill Basic Systems—Mathematics, Wide Range Achievement Test—Arithmetic, Stanford Diagnostic Mathematics Test, and others.) Many institutions use their own mathematics screening tests to place students, and some use self-administered tests so that students can select the appropriate mathematics course for themselves.

A test that is gaining popularity in community colleges is the Comparative Guidance and Placement Test, a self-scoring test that can be given to late enrollees as they are waiting to see a counselor or academic adviser. It saves both the student and the adviser time, because the results are immediately available to use in planning a program and scheduling the student in appropriate skills courses.

Study-Habits Inventories. A number of published inventories purport to measure students' attitudes toward study, reading, and college, such as the Brown-Holtzman Study Skills, Habits, and Attitudes Inventory (SSHA), The Reader's Inventory, and Christ's SR/SE Inventory. (See Appendix A for details.) The value of these inventories depends on the student's willingness to answer honestly. Their main use is for counseling purposes, but they are also often used in studies of reading and study skills programs. Some instructors find that a simple checklist of problem areas works as well as a published attitude questionnaire, and as a result many learning centers have developed their own study-problem checklists.

Other Self-Assessment Instruments. Rather than submitting a large group of new students to a mass testing program and waiting for the results to come from the computer-processing service, some educators are using self-rating and self-analysis instruments so that students are involved in making their own decisions about courses and placement. For example, Gwen H. Rippey developed a Self-

Assessment and Course Selection Inventory for students at El Centro College. As part of their orientation program, students rate their likes and dislikes, abilities, and high school grades in reading, mathematics, and writing. Their responses are weighted, and they can determine from a chart whether they can probably do the reading for such courses as psychology and history or whether they should take developmental reading, and also their needs in mathematics and writing. Although students also take standardized tests as part of orientation, the self-assessment gives them an understanding of how their backgrounds and skills fit with the demands of freshman courses and whether they should enroll in remedial/developmental courses. They are guided through the process by a counselor. Having access to information, the students make better choices and are less likely to drop out, and the system is reported to improve faculty morale as well. (For another example of a self-assessment test, see "Are You Prepared for Chem. 1A?" in Appendix F.)

Whether a college uses standardized tests or self-assessment instruments or both to guide students to appropriate basic skills courses or sections, it is important that the instruments have local norms and validity for the purposes for which they are used. Too often, instructors use standardized tests and national norms to place students without knowing the distribution of scores within the college. When the test is not appropriate for the student population, this practice can lead to assignment of too many students to remedial courses or, more rarely, too few.

Diagnosing the Learning Problems of Students Who Voluntarily Seek Help

With so many colleges expending so much effort to identify underprepared students for placement in remedial/developmental courses, the average student is often overlooked. Other students, who are neither underprepared nor disadvantaged, often need skills help too. So let us look briefly at the problems of students who volunteer for special help in basic skills and some of the ways their problems can be diagnosed and these students supported.

To diagnose students' learning problems, the learning-skills specialist (counselor) must recognize and understand their expectations, symptoms, and self-diagnosis and the conditions that lead students to seek help. Diagnosing a learning problem does not take place in a vacuum, nor can it be done solely by administering a battery of tests. The counselor must have a thorough understanding of the academic context in which the student's problems occur and the dynamics of the interaction between the student's needs, skills, attitudes, knowledge, and abilities and the instructors' expectations, teaching strategies, and characteristics. Such factors as peer competition and the institution's policies and standards must also be considered and weighed. To achieve the insights which must precede and accompany successful treatment, students must be helped to identify the most important causes of their problems and differentiate between those factors that are intrinsic and those that stem from extrinsic conditions. Intrinsic causes refer to personal limitations, such as attitudes, visual defects, or lack of background. Some intrinsic limitations can be improved; others cannot and the student must find ways to compensate for these if he is to remain in college. Extrinsic factors refer to conditions imposed by the academic environment over which the student has little control and with which he must learn to cope if he is to succeed. Another integral part of the diagnostic process is to help the student examine alternative programs and choices.

So the question that must be addressed is how to differentiate between the environmental factors that create problems for students and the subjective causes (such as lack of preparation, fear, or limited skills). The solution may involve three alternatives: (1) modifying the external conditions; (2) changing the student's behavior; and (3) changing the student's goals or plans.

It takes a certain kind of courage and a touch of desperation for students to seek help voluntarily from an academic support service, because doing so means that they admit they have a problem. It also implies that they realize that they are not up to the level of their peers. Superstrivers, who are very anxious about their ability to compete in college, are usually the first to volunteer for help—a fortunate circumstance for the image of the service. At the beginning of the fall term, anxious new freshmen, transfer students, and even beginning graduate students come for assistance in large numbers. Academically weak students, particularly those who have negative attitudes toward their previous teachers, may avoid learning-assistance services at the beginning of the term—unless they have been personally counseled concerning their needs and have met the staff. If weak students do not seek help early in the school term, their problems may be intensified, and, when they realize they are failing, they are angry and difficult to help.

External Reasons for Students' Problems. The academic situations that cause problems for average and above-average students are not different in kind from those that cause problems for underprepared students. However, well-prepared students are often more sensitive to the institution's standards and requirements, and have stronger fears that they will fail, than their less well-prepared peers. (When learning skills services are available, average and above-average students often seek help in greater numbers than do academically weak students.) Getting into college may have been such a struggle for the underprepared students that they may not be aware of or concerned about what is expected from them now that they are admitted.

Most students who seek learning assistance recognize that they are facing new demands on their abilities. This recognition may take the form of a feeling that college courses generally are going to be harder than high school courses were or that a particular professor's standards are so high that the skills that earned high grades in the past are not sufficient to succeed in this course. Coming for assistance may reflect a student's concern about succeeding in a new subject—such as philosophy or economics—in which the ideas are strange and the textbook hard to read. Or it may reflect the student's reactions to the amount of work expected—for instance, longer reading lists than he or she has ever been assigned before—or confusion about how to approach a particular assignment. New vocabulary, complex syntax, erudite lecturers who assume their students are familiar with the terms and ideas in their subjects are other factors that exacerbate the student's insecurity. (See Figure 1 for a model of some of the factors that lead students to seek help.)

A second, very common problem occurs when students find they do not understand the professor's criteria for grading and

Figure 1. Precipitating Factors That Lead a Student to Seek Help for a Learning Problem.

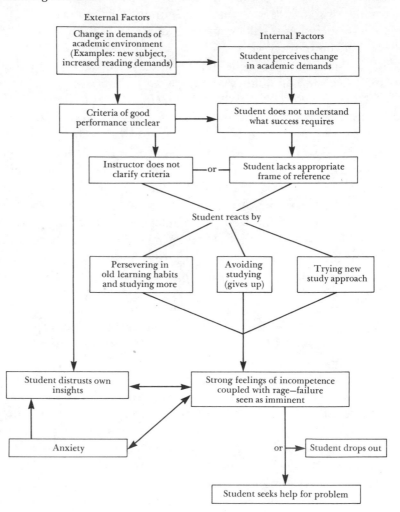

standards for judging good performance. Instructors may not clarify their expectations, or they may make vague statements that grades will be based on a paper and class participation or say only, "There will be three midterms and a final in this course." Such statements may be sufficient for the experienced student, who can find out about the course from friends or who is willing to meet with the professor. But new students hesitate to ask for clarification for fear of being judged dumb. Professors too may become frustrated when students ask basic questions about how to tackle an assignment. For example, Jonathan, a freshman, came into the learning center to improve his reading speed after asking his geography professor how to approach the ten books assigned in the course. The professor had replied impatiently, "Read every word, of course. You will be responsible for all the material." I asked Jonathan what he had to do with the information he would collect from reading all the books, and he responded that he had an hour exam the following week covering four of the books. Then I could discuss with him how much he could write about four books on an hour exam, what questions the instructor was likely to ask, and which concepts, theories, and information he must know to answer the questions.

Some instructors espouse the philosophy that what college students need is to find their own way through life's maze. These instructors appear to revel in the role of maze builders who deliberately obfuscate the path with unstructured lectures and vague assignments. Others are so deeply committed to their own intellectual interests that they fail to recognize that students lack the background to understand them. Textbooks, too, are sometimes written as if the author considered it a disservice to the reader to present ideas in clear, explicit prose.

Another strategy that provokes anxiety in students is faculty members' frequent failure to provide constructive information to students about their progress. Uncertain of the professor's expectations, students find themselves unable to judge the quality of their own work, particularly when only one paper is assigned and it is due at the end of the term. In such situations even very well-prepared students may seek help, while less-prepared students procrastinate and, if they seek help, are likely to do so at the last minute. Similarly, if the instructor assigns only letter grades to papers, without comments, students have no basis for assessing their work and no guidelines for future papers. A grade of B, the most common grade given currently, is particularly devastating, if given without comments. It gives students no hint of what they need to do to improve.

Instructors may not recognize that students do not share their frame of reference or do not have the conceptual framework necessary to learn and retain the course content. For example, engineering students taking their first economics course may not understand that the formulas in economics are mere metaphors and cannot be solved like the formulas in engineering courses. Or an English teacher tells her class, "Write a theme on a controversial topic." The physical education major does not understand that the controversial issues that concern his swimming coach are not considered controversies by his English teacher, and so she fails him.

Absorbing the instructional traditions and learning the foibles of individual professors are situations that create problems for college students. Perhaps these problems could be termed communication difficulties, for the student must be indoctrinated into another language and different customs in order to communicate with his instructors. Faculty members, who are usually knowledgeable about the differences and schisms in their own fields, may be naive about the viewpoints of students, who make errors because they are using a different reference base than their instructors.

Unless the instructor presents a conceptual framework for his subject or helps students build their own, the information he presents in lectures may become an indigestible mass of facts that the student cannot organize, learn, or retain. As a result, students revert to memorization and, when asked to discuss issues, implications, or assumptions of the course, cannot. Asking and answering "why" questions is not a widely practiced skill in high school courses. So students who lack this experience become frustrated at their inability to perform well on tests that require them to generalize, compare different viewpoints, and draw inferences. Indeed, they become enraged.

Few faculty members realize how their instructional strategies and general teaching approaches adversely affect student attitudes and performance. Nor do they recognize how their teaching styles increase the anxiety that lowers performance, although they may be aware that their students are anxious.

But faculty members have been trained in the content of

their disciplines, not in teaching techniques. Most are convinced that they are good teachers, but even those judged most competent by students have some class members who seek assistance because they cannot learn and who complain about the teacher's strategies. The student's problem may reflect poor or inappropriate teaching strategies, or it may represent the student's perception of poor teaching. Either way, the result is the same—the student becomes discouraged and angry, compounding his other difficulties.

In addition to the problems that result from faculty expectations and teaching methods, students may be burdened further by rigid institutional rules and policies, such as the requirement to carry a full schedule of classes to maintain financial aid or to remain in a major. Scheduling difficulties and poor academic advising may add extra burdens on the student, who enrolls in inappropriate courses.

Internal Reasons for Students' Problems. There are many kinds of personal limitations that may cause learning problems for college students—such physical disabilities as poor vision, speech impediments, hearing losses, or poor health; weak learning skills, inadequate high school preparation; social adjustment difficulties, limited intellectual ability; or emotional and attitudinal problems. Sometimes physical limitations are overlooked by the learning counselor in his zeal to search for psychological explanations or to place the student in remedial courses.* For instance, concentration problems, spelling problems, and slow reading may result from poor visual acuity. If the student's vision can be corrected, glasses may be more effective in treating the problem than counseling or remedial courses.

Other conditions that are unique to the student—that is, those not a function of the academic environment—may distract the student from learning or impair his efficiency. Such activities as holding down a full-time job (or working several part-time jobs), family pressures, and difficulties with roommates or friends are among the many situations that may prevent the student from achieving in college.

Frequently, however, the student's learning problem stems from his own attitudes, expectations and emotional outlook. If a student has an unrealistically high estimate of the level of performance that professors expect or if his expectations of himself are unrealistically high, then each two-page paper becomes an impossible struggle as he strives to write one of Nobel Prize–winning caliber.

By setting impossibly high standards for themselves, students ensure that they will never meet their goals. Whether their problem arises from not understanding what the instructor expects, from having an inappropriate frame of reference, or from misperceiving what they should be able to accomplish, students who are motivated to succeed in college will react. Some react by studying harder but using the same ineffective methods. Others try a new study approach, but even if it seems to be working well, they are still insecure if they have no way of verifying their intuitive feelings without feedback from their instructor in the form of comments or grades. Still others become discouraged and give up, stop studying, and stop attending the class. Each of these responses reflects the student's strong feelings of incompetence. Increased frustration, anxiety, and rage ensue. Students—at least freshmen—seldom direct their rage at their instructors. More often they are angry and disillusioned with themselves. When they seek help from the learning center, however, their frustrations may spill over on the receptionist or other staff member.

The Student's Self-Diagnosis. Students seek learning-assistance services anxiously with more or less well-defined symptoms that they label as rather specific ones, such as not being able to read fast enough, poor comprehension, inability to concentrate or remember, and often problems in writing, spelling, or vocabulary. (See Figure 2.) In general, clients tend to blame themselves for their difficulties, and the more symptoms they list, the greater their anxiety. However, one should realize that students who seek help do not differ in their symptoms from those who do not seek help. I have given study-problem checklists to my graduate classes and found that they check the same problems with about the same frequency as learning-center clients do. (I have tried the checklist on only a few faculty members, but I suspect that they too would indicate that they too had problems in concentration, remembering, reading rate, and comprehension.)

Figure 2. The Diagnostic Paradigm

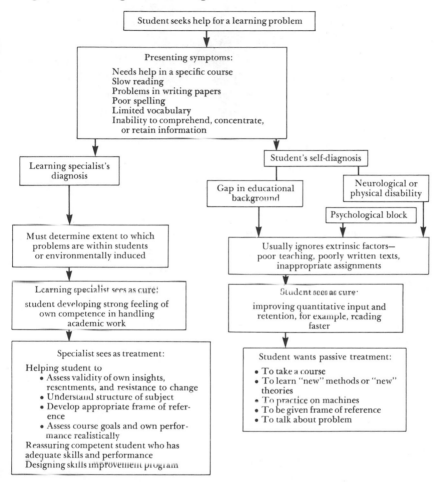

The reasons students give for their problems are revealing. Many attribute their present difficulties to gaps in their educational background. They say things like "I've always had trouble with reading because I was never taught phonics." "No one ever showed me how to diagram sentences." "I was ill in third grade and missed most of the year. Since then I have always felt behind in school." Another common self-diagnosis—or rationalization, if you prefer—occurs when a student feels that his intellectual functioning is impaired by some neurological or physical disability. "My eyes

won't move fast enough." "I think I'm developing a brain tumor
like my mother (or other relative) had." "Perhaps I have narcolepsy
(or hypoglycemia or some other condition), which would explain
why I'm so tired." To make sure there is no medical cause, it is
extremely important that students be referred for medical screening. Occasionally students do have medical problems whose treatment can improve academic performance. The slowest reader I
ever worked with was an overweight freshman with a very low
energy level. I referred her to a physician, who discovered a
hypothyroid condition. When she began taking medication, her
reading rate increased dramatically. Some students, however, prefer a medical label for their difficulties because it helps them save
face. It is more socially acceptable to give a medical reason for one's
problem than to admit that one cannot stand up under the competition or that one lacks ability. Students faced with the threat of
failure may diagnose in themselves rare disorders like dyslexia.

Clients are usually quite willing to discuss their psychological
blocks to learning. (Today, people prefer to call these same
symptoms "anxieties." Consequently, we have math anxiety, writing
anxiety, test anxiety, and so on.) Generally students who block on a
subject or are anxious about it have avoided taking courses that
require the skill. They expend great effort in finding ways to es-
cape the subject, and so I think it more appropriate, in most cases,
to call their problem math avoidance or writing avoidance. If the
student blocks and avoids the subject, he does not have an opportunity to engage in the practice necessary to develop skills and
acquire understanding. People who claim to have math anxiety
have usually excluded mathematics from their personal universe.

Inevitably, students can recall some embarrassing or traumatic incident in elementary school which they feel triggered their
emotional block. For example, Jake recalled being forced to take a
remedial reading course in summer school when he was in the
fourth grade. He said that he could remember little about it, except
that he had to cross town to get to the class. On further questioning,
he recalled that once when he had been asked to read orally in
front of the class, he fainted. He awoke to find himself lying on the
floor, looking up at the faces of the other children who were staring
down at him—a most humiliating experience. At age twenty-five,

he still saw himself as a retarded reader although he was making excellent grades in science courses. His reading block prevented him, he felt, from doing well in nonscience courses.

If a student is helped to recall the emotional event that precipitated the learning block, he has taken the first step toward overcoming it. However, this will not cure the problem. Students with this kind of problem must practice and, in most cases, learn or relearn the fundamentals. One does not expect to become a professional musician in three or four hours of practice (or even as a result of a few hours of psychotherapy). One should not expect to remedy five or ten years of deficiencies in the basic skills in a few hours, but sometimes students expect miracles.

Many students are unable to differentiate those problems that stem from their own limitations (or avoidance) from those that result from poor teaching, poorly written textbooks, or other factors in their academic environment.

What Does the Student See as the Cure? Clients usually seek simple cures and are convinced that the cure is a formula, short course, or technique that will alleviate their symptoms and one that will require minimal effort and time. Some seem to have an almost mystical faith in a magic cure. "If only," they say, "I could read a thousand words per minute. I could absorb more information and get A's on all my exams." Or "Isn't there a new law of learning (or new drug) that will help me increase my memory so I can retain all the facts in my biology book?" Many students see the cure for their problems as finding a way to increase the quantity of information they can absorb, retain, and regurgitate, they fail to see that remembering requires them to organize and understand the major concepts, not just cram in the facts. Others, who are convinced they have a psychological block, are sure their problems will be cured if they can just talk about them with a counselor, even though practice and intensive effort may be needed if these students are to develop skills commensurate with their peers'. The treatments students suggest usually reflect their desire to remain in a passive, receptive role and to let the skills counselor provide the effort and the cure. (See Figure 2.)

The Role of the Skills Counselor. Faced with a student who suppresses his anger, presents a variety of symptoms, has an over-simplified diagnosis of his difficulty, and expects a quick cure, what does the learning-skills counselor do? The skills counselor must explore the basic question "To what extent are this student's problems due to his own educational deficiencies and attitudinal or motivational confusion and to what extent to the constraints and stress created by the academic environment in which he struggles?" Some students willingly assume the blame for their problems and feel helpless, stupid, and discouraged. Others blame the instructor, the textbook, or the academic policies of the college. The learning skills counselor must help the student with a problem determine realistically how much of his difficulty stems from his own limitations and how much is a function of the academic situation. Although usually little can be done to change instructors' teaching strategies or assignments (or to improve textbooks), it is therapeutic for the student to be reassured that he is not to blame. Often when this happens, he finds ways to cope. However, when students' problems stem from their own limitations, the counselor must hold out hope that they can catch up on the skills or knowledge needed to achieve and show how this can be accomplished. If the student can develop better insight into the real causes of his problem and the steps that must be taken to solve it, he is on his way to a solution.

Inevitably, the college student who seeks help for a learning problem also has an emotional problem, which may be a low self-image, resentment of authority, resistance to change, or simply an active hatred of the college environment. But even if the student understands and changes his emotional outlook, he still must learn to cope with academic realities. For some well-prepared students, this may mean that the skills counselor must provide reassurance that their new study approaches will work. For the less prepared and for those whose anxieties mask a weakness, it means that the skills counselor must help them recognize the need for, and embark on, a skills program that will take time and effort. Convincing the student that he can improve and that improving will make it easier for him to attain his goal is crucial. The skills counselor must provide support and encouragement as the student works and must help him learn to recognize his own progress and the ways he can apply the skills in his other course work.

Michelle's case serves as an example. An archeology major, Michelle was having difficulty in the history of archeology and complained that she was unable to comprehend and retain the information in the textbook. She felt very depressed, as she had done well in previous courses in her major. As I quickly skimmed the book, I commented that it was poorly organized. In fact, it looked as if the author had handed his secretary an outline and dumped a stack of note cards down the stairs, gathered them up, and given them to his secretary with instructions to type ten cards under each heading. After noting other limitations, I watched Michelle breathe a sigh of relief and exclaim, "Yes, I wondered how the author managed to pass freshman English." Since her professor presented well-organized lectures, I asked her whether she felt it essential to read the textbook. She felt she must read it, because her study ritual dictated that one always read the textbook before going to lectures. We were able to work out a compromise of sorts in that she agreed to take lecture notes first and then skim the textbook for further ideas that might fit into her notes. Common sense? Perhaps, but even the brightest students are often quite rigid and superstitious about their study methods. Would Michelle's problem have been revealed by a standardized reading test? I doubt it, as she was an excellent reader.

In diagnosing specific difficulties in college courses, the skills counselor must play a detectivelike role, examining both the materials students read and study and the methods they use.

The key to effective treatment of learning problems is a thorough assessment of the task the student must perform and helping him understand not only what is being asked of him but the steps he should follow to complete the task. This assessment includes determining what skills and information the student needs and aiding him in assessing the validity of his own insights, resentments, and resistances within the class context. Once the student is realistically aware of the tasks required to succeed, he is in a position to determine how much effort and time he must invest to learn what he wants to know and to attain the grade he wants. (For further information on task analysis see Gladstein, 1967; Johnson, 1977.)

3

================================

Creating
Tutoring Services

================================

Tutoring *is* individualized instruction. Group instruction, even under ideal conditions, must be supplemented by individualized instruction if all students are to learn well. In college classrooms where group instruction through lectures is the norm, some students will need intensive help, and most students, even the brightest and most highly motivated, will need individual instruction at various times as a supplement to group instruction. If the instructor is unable (owing to the large size of the class) or unwilling to provide individual help, then tutoring can fill the gap.

Historically, the wealthy and elite have always hired tutors for their children, and in some historical eras, tutoring was the main avenue to learning. Since the Middle Ages, going to a European university has usually meant traveling to a city, renting a room, hiring a tutor, studying for years, attending lectures, and taking the examinations for a degree when one felt prepared.

Oxford and Cambridge, after which Harvard and other early colleges in the United States were modeled, have had a somewhat different arrangement. At Oxford and Cambridge, students lived in residential units with tutors and dons, a setting in which study and social life were merged. The English dons did not have the responsibility of examining, grading, and disciplining students, so that they were able to provide a supportive, collegial atmosphere and develop close, personal relationships with students. The early United States colleges, however, never quite achieved the same collegial atmosphere. Even in colonial days, American professors assumed disciplinary and examining roles and did not live with their students. In the nineteenth century, when Harvard attempted a residential system with tutors, the program was modeled after the British system but was not a replica. American tutors and professors preferred not to live with their students, and providing individual tutors for each student soon proved too expensive. During a later period, President Lowell of Harvard, determined to excite superior students to their maximum attainment and avoid mediocrity, implemented rigorous examination to challenge the students. This policy created a need for tutors, and so professors, graduate assistants, and undergraduates helped younger students prepare for the tests. When Woodrow Wilson was president of Princeton, he introduced preceptors (typically graduate students) whose function was to establish informal associations with students and stimulate and guide their intellectual endeavors. Whereas most of the earlier Harvard tutors had been members of the faculty, the Princeton preceptors were predominantly students.

Tutors have long been available in public colleges and universities, if a student could afford to hire them. Academic departments keep lists of qualified tutors, and some departments— particularly in the sciences and mathematics—pay tutors to tutor lower-division students. Tutoring has also been a way for poor students to work their way through college, while student members of honor societies, motivated by a sense of noblesse oblige, have a long history of offering free tutoring to their less academically successful peers. Student-athletes, too, receive intensive tutoring along with their athletic scholarships, and since World War II the G.I. Bill package of services for veterans has included funds for tutoring. To summarize, tutoring has been an accepted part of academic life, but it has been considered a low-paying, low-prestige, entry-level position for teachers despite the needs it fills.

Tutoring continues to be a service contracted for by students with money. A recent example is the college education of Princess Rima of Saudi Arabia, whose father arranged to enroll her in the University of Houston's Open University Program. The university agreed to send two women professors and books, films, tapes, and other learning materials to the princess' quarters in the palace in Riyadh, Saudi Arabia. This may go down in history as the most expensive college education ever arranged and the ultimate in individualized instruction, but it does signal a breakthrough in the education of women in Arabia, where very few females enter high school and even fewer attend college.

In the 1960s, when U.S. colleges and universities began to admit large numbers of low-income, educationally disadvantaged students, tutorial services were among the first programs organized on a large scale to help these students. Although figures from national surveys vary because of differences in the colleges sampled, there is clear evidence that formal, cross-disciplinary tutorial programs have increased. Sixty-three percent of the 2,381 institutions of higher education surveyed in an Educational Testing Service study in 1971–72 reported having special tutoring by faculty members or students for educationally disadvantaged students (Burkheimer and others, 1973). Cross (1976) found that more two-year colleges were offering peer-tutoring services in 1974 (65 percent) than in 1970 (36 percent). In a national survey of learning centers, Devirian and others (1975) reported that 80 percent of the four-year institutions responding and 68 percent of the two-year colleges answered questions about their peer-tutoring programs. Woolley (1976) found that 94 percent of California community colleges provided tutorial services in 1974–75 and all the others but one planned to establish tutorial services. Seventy-five percent of the California community colleges started tutoring programs between 1969 and 1975.

Although at the start of open-admissions programs, tutors hired to work with underprepared students were faculty members, by 1970 most tutoring services were using peer tutors (other undergraduate students) rather than graduate students, faculty members, or paid paraprofessionals (Reed, 1974).

One of the insights that researchers and others gained from the open-admissions and special disadvantaged-student programs of the 1960s was that regularly admitted students need help too. Davis and others (1975) stressed that disadvantaged students will benefit more from a tutorial program that is not stigmatized as a remedial service or a "salvage operation." Reed (1974, p. 68) took an even stronger position: "Peer-tutoring programs have embellished traditional college teaching in a highly significant manner. The growth of these programs throughout academe attests to their success. Originally implemented to meet the academic needs of the educationally deficient students, these programs are becoming the *sine qua non* for all students."

The development of learning centers in the seventies, resulting from mergers of tutoring programs for minority students with traditional reading and study skills services, made it possible for existing student personnel services to offer tutoring to a larger segment of the student body. The general philosophy that seems to pervade present programs is that tutoring should be free, voluntary, and available to any student, not restricted to economically disadvantaged or wealthy students (Davis and others, 1975; Gourdine, 1976a; Hubin, 1976; Reed, 1974). Although today more college programs offer tutoring to a greater range of students, inflationary costs and limited budgets have forced many university programs to restrict tutoring to entry-level courses or to special groups for whom extramural funding is available. In private colleges, tutoring may be offered to clients who can pay or for whom departments can be charged. Community colleges continue to offer tutoring to a wide spectrum of their students—when there is state or federal funding. At the City University of New York in 1976 when budgets were slashed, many tutorial programs were abandoned or offered on a free, voluntary basis—that is, both tutors and tutees volunteered.

Who Seeks Tutoring?

As a director of a large voluntary tutoring and skills program, I found that many underprepared, nontraditional students as well as insecure, traditionally prepared students seek tutoring when the curriculum includes required courses taught in large lecture sections and students perceive the professors and teaching assistants as indifferent, punitive, and unavailable. In this setting, the tutoring program, if open to all students, acts as a barometer of the institution's undergraduate teaching. If a course goes awry and the professor sets unreasonable standards, assigns an excessive amount of work, or teaches poorly, many students seek tutoring services. There are courses in which students rarely, if ever, seek help. These tend to be well-planned and well-organized courses, self-paced or Keller-plan courses (in which student tutors or monitors are available in the classroom), courses involving team projects or individual contracts in which students play a major role in deciding on the work they will accomplish. The key to whether there will be a large demand for tutoring seems to be whether the professor and/or the teaching assistant is available and supportive and can convey this to students, not the nature or content of the course itself.

In some courses, almost every student may need individual assistance, and if help is not available from the instructor or teaching assistant, the more assertive students seek help from their friends, other students, or even their parents. Freshmen (particularly underprepared students) may feel too intimidated to ask the instructor, teaching assistants, or even other students for help and prefer to seek tutoring from a program in which they know the assistance they will get is nonjudgmental and will not have a negative effect on their course grades. They feel that if they ask a question in class, they will be judged stupid. The goal for tutors working with these students is to improve their confidence and knowledge to a level at which they are comfortable enough to ask the professor or teaching assistant a question and informed enough to understand the answer.

As one minority student in our program said, "When I got into my classes at Berkeley, I found that in some subjects things were fuzzy and unclear. The classes and sections were too large to deal with individual questions adequately; there is just very little personal attention. Also, I was reluctant to ask questions in large classes. After coming to the center two or three times, I began to notice that those fuzzy areas were clearing up."

To summarize, tutoring demands on a learning center are heavy when—

1. The material is difficult for the average student to learn or highly abstract in content, students lack the appropriate precollege preparation, the competition is strong, or classes are taught in large lectures. (Examples are chemistry, calculus, statistics, and economics.)
2. The professor stresses theory and expects students to be intellectually mature and have excellent reading and writing skills—skills that are higher than the average student possesses (for example, political-theory courses, anthropology). Student difficulties are manifested as problems in reading and comprehending the material or as problems in determining which topics to address in a term paper and how to organize the paper.
3. There is a group of students whose skills and background are lower than those of the institution's typical students.
4. There is little opportunity for individual conferences between instructor and students, or students perceive the instructor as distant, uninterested in them, and unapproachable.

There is a very light demand, if any at all, for tutoring when

1. Instruction is given through the Keller plan or is self-paced.
2. The academic department maintains a well-staffed and well-equipped course center with audiovisual aids, teaching assistants, or paraprofessionals.
3. The department provides its own peer tutors.
4. The department has made special efforts to recruit minority TAs and train its TAs, and the TAs meet with students regularly.
5. The classes are small enough so that each student can meet regularly with his instructor or TA.

Should Tutoring Be Required or Voluntary?

The surveys just cited suggest that between 25 and 30 percent of the college tutoring programs in the United States today require that some students receive tutoring. Typically, tutoring is required for students who enter college with low high school grades or low test scores and/or show poor academic performance in college. Whether tutoring should be required or voluntary is a philosophical question and depends on whether one ultimately trusts students as adults to make responsible decisions about the help they need in order to succeed because they have chosen to attend college or whether one assumes that the goal of the institution is to motivate low-achieving, unmotivated potential dropouts to remain in college. Since students who lack strong motivation toward school and make poor grades often become depressed and discouraged, they may not seek help voluntarily. Required tutoring does provide a structure, although some students may resist accepting tutoring on these terms. However, the question whether required tutoring results in long-term improvement in grades and ultimate academic success is unanswered—and perhaps unanswerable, since once an institution adopts the policy of requiring tutoring for underprepared or low-achieving students, there is no opportunity to study those who might have succeeded without tutoring or with voluntary tutoring. In addition, unless extraordinary measures are taken to reduce the resistance of students who are required to receive tutoring, tutors will face difficulties, for it is virtually impossible to force the unwilling student to keep tutoring appointments.

The rationale for required tutoring programs is based on correlational studies that show that underprepared students who regularly attend tutoring sessions make higher grades than those having the same background and ability who do not use tutoring (for example, Donovan, 1976; Hedges and Majer, 1976; Watanabe and Maxwell, 1975). For example, the College Assistance Migrant Program (CAMP) at St. Edward's University in Austin, Texas, discovered that students who averaged four hours in tutoring a week earned a grade-point average of at least 2.3 their first semester, while those who received less tutoring earned less than 2.0 (Donovan, 1975, p. 32). As a result of these findings, a policy requiring all CAMP freshmen to spend at least three hours a week in tutoring was instituted. Students earning low grades were required to meet six hours a week with a tutor. Under the new policy, it will be difficult to demonstrate that required tutoring is more effective in improving student achievement than the old, voluntary program because the students who volunteered for tutoring may have been more highly motivated toward academic work. Their motivation, rather than the tutoring, may have enabled them to make higher grades. It may be impossible to determine whether tutoring raises grades independently of motivation. It will take both time and a sophisticated evaluation study controlling for student characteristics to determine whether requiring tutoring of all CAMP freshmen will ultimately result in significant grade improvement and reduced attrition.

A contract arranged between the student, his counselor, and his tutors is a way of ameliorating the motivational problems that may reduce the effectiveness of required tutoring programs. A tutoring contract can be tailored to the individual needs of the student.

The model programs funded by the "Alternatives to the Revolving Door" federal evaluation project typically provided "intensive care packages" for underprepared freshmen, and these packages included student contracts for tutoring. The directors maintain that contracting has the following advantages: (1) it places the responsibility for learning on the student; (2) it places the teaching responsibility on instructors and requires that they make their criteria for success explicit; (3) it provides a humane way of providing structure which allows for individual differences; (4) it is a way of teaching problem-solving skills; and, (5) it is a means of bridging the cultural differences between students and faculty ("Alternatives to the Revolving Door," 1976).

More specifically, the proponents of contracting argue that contracting places the responsibility for learning on the student who, as a victim of our educational system, has learned to be dependent on teachers, even though this dependency may conflict with his perception of himself as an adult in other ways. He often puts pressure on instructors to treat him as a dependent student, has a low estimate of his ability to perform academically, and attributes his success or failure to factors beyond his control, such as luck or the will of God. Even when successful, he tends not to repeat the activities that lead to success, because he does not attribute the successful outcome to his actions. Contracting with the student forces him to acknowledge the kind of action that will lead to rewards and thus helps him assume the responsibility for his own learning. Second, it is argued that care must be taken in introducing the low-achieving student to a learning environment in which he has mutual input with the instructor, since his first reaction will be disorganized and he will usually put pressure on the teacher to behave toward him in the traditional way or abuse the privilege. Experts stress that such students should begin in a structured environment, and once they learn, through contracting, to take responsibility for their own learning, then they can become involved in a learning experience that is exciting and rewarding both to the student and to the instructor.

While contracting puts responsibility on the student for learning, it simultaneously places the responsibility for teaching on the instructor. The instructor's role becomes a facilitating one, and through contracting, the instructor makes explicit what he can do and is willing to do to help the student.

Third, contracting is viewed as a humanistic way of imposing structure on the learning process, yet, at the same time, allowing for flexibility and individualization. Since the student's knowledge, skills, interests, and goals are considered in drawing up the contract, and the level of performance and time to complete the goal are specified, as is regular feedback on progress, the contract gives the student a fair and clear structure.

Fourth, contracting can be used to teach problem solving by encouraging the student to examine his environment and suggest ways he can reach the instructional goals of the course, a contrast to situations in which the instructor determines all work. As the student practices on short, simple contracts, he builds both his skills and a positive self-image that enables him to tackle larger problems both in educational and in noneducational settings.

Another advantage cited for contracts is that they can help bridge cultures, since contracting requires the student and the instructor to communicate their needs and expectations to each other. Both must understand that if one is to succeed, both must succeed ("Alternatives to the Revolving Door," 1976).

The tutor should take part in the development of the contract package, along with the instructor, counselor, and student, and the contract should specify not only the length and frequency of tutoring sessions but the specific objectives and skills relative to the course that the student will attain.

(An additional source of information on teaching by contract is Berte, 1975.)

Another way to reduce negative feelings about required tutoring—assuming that tutoring is not required for all students—is to see that tutoring is also offered to students who volunteer for it. Those required to receive it are not as likely to feel they are being stigmatized.

In conclusion, mandatory tutoring has advantages and disadvantages, and the choice depends on the institution's philosophy about accepting underprepared students. If faculty members see their goal as providing the opportunity for students who want higher education, they are likely to assume that students are mature or sophisticated enough to avail themselves of tutoring and other academic support services. If, however, the institution feels an obligation to see that underprepared students succeed, it is likely to provide "intensive care packages" including required tutoring. An intermediate measure is to arrange a three-way contract with the student, tutor, and instructor. If the contract contains clearly specified objectives and activities, the student will be less resistive and more likely to participate in tutoring.

Flexible Systems for Delivering Tutoring

Given a choice between individual and group tutoring, most students will choose individual work, since it is hard to get any individual help on large college campuses unless one is persistent and assertive. However, some students prefer group tutoring because they feel less threatened in a group, where others freely ask questions, than in one-to-one tutoring, where they feel they are on the line to perform.

Reed's survey (1974) found that 67 percent of peer-tutoring programs offered both group and individual tutoring. Group tutoring is most appropriate for large, introductory lecture courses—for instance, science and mathematics courses in which students need to review basic concepts and understand how to do homework problems. As business and economics courses increase in popularity and size, there is a greater demand for tutoring in these subjects, and group tutoring can be an effective strategy. It is most difficult to arrange group tutoring in courses where there are many sections and each instructor gives different assignments.

Different skills are required to tutor small groups than to tutor individuals. We have found that graduate students who have taught large classes by the lecture method often have problems in making the transition to conducting small discussion groups.

Recruiting and Selecting Tutors

A tutor is defined as a person having a minimum of special training who helps one or more students learn a particular skill or body of information in a course under the guidance of an instructor or supervisor. For tutoring to be both effective in enhancing student learning and cost-efficient, tutors should be carefully selected so that those who have a good background in the subject,* a natural predisposition for working with students, good communication skills, and appropriate personality traits can be hired. The goal should be to minimize the amount of training and supervision necessary to prepare tutors to work independently and effectively with students.

College tutoring programs use many kinds of people as tutors—faculty members, undergraduate and graduate students, students on work-study or taking courses in tutoring for credit as field study experiences, high school teachers and principals, paraprofessionals from the community, and volunteers. Volunteers may include students or ex-students, housewives (including faculty wives), local businessmen who are released by their employers for

*When tutors are enrolled in the same courses as the students they are tutoring (a true peer-tutoring situation), tutors will need intensive supervision and monitoring.

social service work, and the elderly (retired professors, former schoolteachers, or retired persons from other professional fields). Increasingly, librarians are serving as skills specialists and tutors (Douglas, 1971), as libraries come to house learning centers and tutorial programs. Most tutors work part time, whether paid or volunteers. Tutoring college students is not a field that is conducive to full-time work unless other duties are included, such as administration and supervision, teaching, materials development, or research.

Most tutoring programs have a mixture of paid tutors and volunteers. For example, in a recent survey of tutoring programs in ninety-eight California community colleges, 85 percent of the institutions with tutoring programs reported that they paid tutors, 100 percent selected students from the institution itself, 26 percent used graduate students, 27 percent selected undergraduates from four-year colleges and universities, and 47 percent had volunteer tutors (Woolley, 1976).

Programs use special incentives to entice volunteer tutors. For example, the Learning Assistance Center at California State University at Long Beach offers volunteer tutors, who are not students, the title of "Adjunct Professor," pays them a token $1 a term, gives them parking and library privileges, requires them to participate in staff-development activities, and considers them regular staff members.

Recruitment practices vary, but most programs solicit recommendations from academic departments or faculty members for prospective tutors. Other methods include listing positions in student employment offices, advertising in local college and/or community newspapers, soliciting recommendations from student organizations (especially ethnic organizations), and recruiting tutors from among former tutees of the program who are succeeding academically. To recruit volunteers from the community, program directors advertise in newspapers and through public service announcements on radio and television, obtain lists of community organizations and businesses that offer volunteer services and contact them, or enlist the support of the alumni association and campus faculty and staff organizations.

At the Student Learning Center at Berkeley, we rely heavily

on advertisements in the student newspaper, on referrals from a network of minority faculty and staff members, from academic departments, and from student organizations—such as ethnic student associations and the work-study and student employment services. Posters and notices are put up around campus in places where student traffic is heavy and on department bulletin boards. The tutor-for-credit program is also extensively advertised. Now that the program is well established, student tutors are referring their friends, and students who have been tutored are volunteering to tutor others.

When prospective tutors apply, they are given a brief description of the center's programs and objectives and written information on qualifications, personal characteristics, and duties. They fill out an application form, which contains questions about their class, their major, courses taken, and grades they received in the courses they wish to tutor, their ethnic background, any previous tutoring or teaching experiences, the reasons they want to tutor, and their attitudes toward and understanding of underprepared or low-achieving students.

We require that students seeking paid tutoring positions have a letter of recommendation from a faculty member in the subject they want to tutor. This letter serves two functions: it protects us from complaints by faculty members that we are hiring tutors who are not sufficiently knowledgeable in the course, and it helps publicize the tutoring service to the faculty. We have found faculty letters generally honest and helpful. Faculty members are given the option of calling the tutor supervisor instead of writing a recommendation.

The applicants for paid tutoring positions whose applications and recommendations look more promising are then screened by a team of three persons: a learning specialist in the appropriate subject, a senior tutor or learning specialist (who may be in another field), and a member of the clerical staff. We try to include at least one woman and one minority-group member on each screening team. During the screening interview, the applicant is presented with a role-playing situation planned in advance, involving a typical student problem. One of the team members, who need not be an expert in the subject, role-plays the tutee. Using the applicant's performance in the screening situation, the team rates the applicant on three major factors: knowledge of the subject, ability to explain and communicate this knowledge to the tutee, and sensitivity to students' problems.

Knowledge of the subject is the first prerequisite most tutorial directors look for in selecting tutors. Many directors (for example, Osguthorpe, 1976) insist that only outstanding, straight-A graduate students should be selected. However, we have found that many of our freshman clients relate well to undergraduate peer tutors who have average to good grades in the course and can explain the subject well. Often tutees categorize graduate students or A students as "experts", and find them intimidating. Some minority students prefer to work with tutors who come from their own ethnic background and reject tutors from other ethnic groups. Intensive recruitment is needed to find bilingual or minority tutors in the sciences and mathematics. In general, we look for tutors who are supportive and flexible enough to work with the wide range of students who use our services. We try to staff enough tutors in each subject so that students have a choice, but it is impossible to find tutors from each ethnic group for each subject. It is vital that tutors be sensitive, empathetic (not sympathetic), nonjudgmental people who can accept students as they are and who do not have unrealistically high expectations of what the tutee should have had in high school or should be able to do in college. Effective tutors must also have a clear understanding of the academic realities of the courses and instructional practices of the college.

Other traits we consider in screening tutors are willingness to undergo training, reliability, acceptance of continual evaluation by students and supervisors, commitment to making the learning success of their tutees the central concern of the relationship, interest in understanding students' problems and backgrounds, and ability to establish a supportive relationship. Obviously, some of these traits are hard to assess in a screening interview or from an application blank; however, if tutors are closely supervised during their initial training, supervisors usually can pinpoint those who are having problems relating to students.

We use similar, though less rigorous, procedures in selecting students admitted to our tutoring-for-credit courses and volunteer tutors. They too need faculty recommendations, and they are interviewed by a supervisor, who considers their background and motivation. Students who take the course just to earn a credit often make poor tutors.

Tutors-for-credit—who must have junior standing—sign up each quarter for the course. Although we encourage them to continue in the course for a full year (three quarters), often they are unable to because they must take required courses in their major. Supervisors of the tutors-for-credit select tutees and attempt to match them with tutors during their first quarter term, meet with the tutors regularly, and require them to keep logs or journals describing each session with their tutees and records of the time spent in each tutoring session.

Students who have had a quarter or two in our tutoring-for-credit program have been carefully followed and evaluated and make good candidates for our paid tutoring positions.

Tutor Training

Two current indicators of the gradual professionalization of college tutoring programs are the increasing number of tutor-training programs and the appearance of manuals and materials for tutor training. Surveys suggest that more than half the college tutoring programs today offer some form of training for their tutors (Roueche and Snow, 1977; Woolley, 1976).

Woolley (1976) states that 71 percent of the California community college tutor directors he surveyed reported they offered tutor-training programs. Roueche and Snow (1977) found that 56 percent of the programs at two-year colleges and 62 percent of those at four-year colleges report that they train peer tutors in teaching techniques; 44 percent at two-year colleges and 47 percent at four-year colleges train tutors in self-concept development; and 54 percent and 74 percent of the respective programs train tutors in study skills.

Currently, reports on college tutor-training programs are appearing more frequently in professional journals and on the programs of professional conferences (Ahrendt, 1971; Beitler and Martin, 1973; Brown, 1976; Hall, 1975; Hawkins, 1977; Hedges, 1975; Hubin, 1976; Osguthorpe, 1976—to cite just a few).

Many tutoring programs are developing training manuals and using videotapes, role playing, modeling, brainstorming, and handouts to train tutors through orientation programs and regular weekly or biweekly group or individual conferences with supervisors.

The most typical format is a short (half-day or one-day) orientation session for tutors followed by weekly or biweekly staff development meetings. In some programs, new tutors serve internships or are paired with senior tutors for training and supervision. If tutors are selected who are knowledgeable about their subjects, sensitive to students, and relatively mature and reliable, they do not need intensive training. However, they do need ongoing supportive supervision. Tutors for some groups need quite specialized training. For example, tutors for the deaf must master sign language and understand the special needs of deaf students. Osguthorpe (1976) describes an intensive two-week training program for tutor/notetakers who were selected to help deaf students enrolled in integrated (regular) classes at Rochester Institute of Technology. The hearing tutors were given six weeks of training in sign language and two weeks of intensive training in notetaking skills and tutoring techniques, using explanation, modeling, role playing or simulation, and applied practice. Tutors were trained to take careful notes and to define difficult vocabulary items, illustrate with examples, and draw diagrams or other visual aids to clarify concepts. In this program tutors were also required to work closely with faculty members.

A Model Tutor-Training Program

I have compiled the following guidelines for an effective tutor-training program on the basis of a survey of current literature and my own experiences. Tutors need—

1. Knowledge of the goals and objectives of the program and the appropriate behavior for a tutor and the opportunity to demonstrate these in practice (for example, in a role-playing or modeling situation).

2. Training in using appropriate materials and structured activities.
3. Training in conducting sessions: opening the session; establishing rapport; diagnosing or clarifying the student's problem; creating a supportive learning situation in which the tutee can demonstrate his learning; closing the session; determining when the student is progressing and helping the student focus on the task.
4. Training in how to develop a working relationship with faculty members.
5. Ways of explaining, presenting, and clarifying the basic concepts in the subject.
6. Strategies for helping students master concepts and basic skills.
7. An awareness of some of the typical tutoring problems they will encounter and ways of working with them.
8. An understanding of the recordkeeping and other procedures of the program and its organizational structure.

In our program, we have tutors sign a training contract specifying the various staff-development activities in which they will participate. These include small-group meetings with a member of the senior staff or the counseling psychologist, case conferences, videotaping sessions, talks by outside speakers, and courses that are related to improving their skills. New tutors are expected to attend weekly seminars conducted by their supervisors.

One model for tutor training is described below. (Not all the topics suggested are taught in formal training sessions; however, most that are not arise informally during the course.)

The overall goal of the program is to assist tutors in developing their own flexible, comfortable tutoring style that will result in improved learning for the diverse students who use the learning center. Toward this end, the program has the following objectives: (1) Increasing the tutor's knowledge and understanding of teaching, tutoring techniques, and his subject. (2) Increasing the tutor's knowledge of and sensitivity to students' different learning/cognitive styles and the effects of different tutoring strategies on learning. (3) Increasing the tutor's ability to become a facilitator of learning, not an answer machine. (4) Improving the tutor's knowledge of the basic learning and study skills required for mastering the subject and methods of teaching study skills. (5) Informing the tutor about the materials available to assist the student in learning the subject matter. (6) Increasing the tutor's knowledge of how to diagnose the student's difficulty and clarify the student's problem.

The program's activities fall into five categories: orientation, improving interpersonal effectiveness, improving intrapersonal skills, ethics and confidentiality, and evaluation as an ongoing process.

Orientation. The first step is to orient tutors to the mission and objectives of the center, its staff, organization, functions, and services, and how it fits into the administrative structure and the mission of the institution. (At Berkeley this is done through printed material and in a general orientation session for new tutors. The mission of our center is to assist students to become more efficient, self-confident, and independent learners—a goal that is reinforced in all formal and informal training sessions.)

1. *Description of center procedures and tutors' responsibilities.* Procedures and responsibilities described include keeping records on student contacts; scheduling appointments; groups entitled to priority appointments; keeping a regular work schedule and other business policies; contacting faculty members during the first week of class to get course syllabuses and discuss course objectives; attending lectures and maintaining contacts with faculty members and teaching assistants. These points are briefly presented in the general orientation program, and a checklist of procedures is given each new tutor. The checklist contains such items as getting employment forms signed, getting a mailbox, turning in schedules, getting one's picture taken, and turning in weekly student contact sheets. It also lists the names and functions of our clerical and program staff members.

2. *Information on tutor backup materials.* New tutors are taken on a tour of the Library-Laboratory, shown instructional materials and the computer-assisted-instruction programs in their specialties, and given a list of resource materials. The Library-Laboratory contains textbooks, self-paced instructional materials, how-to-study

books in different subjects, cassette recorders and tapes, reading
machines, reference books, old exams, and tutor-training
materials.

3. *Study skills training.* Learning specialists from science,
mathematics, writing, and reading present demonstration/
discussion sessions on the application of study skills techniques to
particular courses and describe techniques for analyzing a student's
skills level and needs. The Library-Laboratory offers a diagnostic
testing service to which tutors can refer students who need special
help. There are a number of minicourses for students who want to
improve exam skills, reading, general study skills, or math and
science skills. Tutors are encouraged to take the diagnostic tests
themselves and to sit in on minicourses to learn techniques. (For
additional information on skills training, see the chapters on study
skills, test taking, reading, and writing.)

4. *Referrals.* Tutors are advised how and when to make referrals to faculty members, counseling and other student services,
academic advisers, the ombudsperson, and others. Each tutor is
given a copy of the student services handbook, which briefly describes all the services on campus and gives their locations and
phone numbers. The counseling-center liaison person participates
in the general orientation, discusses how to make referrals to the
counseling and psychiatric services, and indicates his willingness to
work with individual tutors on general or special problems they
may have with students. Speakers from other student service units
and academic departments are also invited to speak at regular
staff-development meetings.

5. *Diagnosis and strategy development.* Tutors learn how to
diagnose the student's learning difficulty, recognize different
cognitive/learning styles, and develop appropriate strategies for
tutoring. Through observing a videotape of an actual tutoring
session by senior learning specialists (or, in some cases, a mock
session), attending seminars, or reviewing videotapes of his own
tutoring sessions with the supervisor, the novice tutor learns how to
determine the appropriate level and material for the tutee.

6. *Insight into typical problems students bring to the center.* Typical problems are discussed at the general orientation session and
modeled on videotaped modules, and tutors are given short jour-

nal summaries written by previous tutors and other reading materials, including "Difficult Tutoring Situations" (Rose, 1976), which is reproduced in Appendix C. The videotape modules illustrating tutee problems are discussed in the weekly training seminars where new tutors share their experiences with one another and the supervisor. Susan Kerwin of Champlain College, Quebec, uses several short (two- to five-minute) videotaped illustrations as a basis for discussion in her tutor-training program: (1) A smoothly running encounter between student and tutor. The tutor establishes rapport, reinforces the tutee's ideas, and develops common objectives, and together they work out a study contract. (Discussion centers on how the tutor achieves this.) (2) An apathetic student who gives very brief answers to anything the tutor asks. (Discussion centers on how to mobilize the student's energies and reinforce commitment.) (3) A client who is extremely negativistic and claims he cannot handle college work, is too dumb, does not belong in college, and so on. (Discussion centers on how to respond to this kind of student.) (4) A situation in which the tutor/student relationship becomes a peer friendship and the tutor gets sidetracked from the major issues of tutoring. (Discussion centers on how to get the tutoring session back on base.) (5) A situation in which the tutor plays a very dominating role and lectures the student, asks "yes" and "no" questions, and generally controls the session. (Discussion centers on how this situation might be improved.)

Improving Interpersonal Effectiveness. Several techniques are used to improve tutors' interpersonal skills: modeling and imitating the supervisor's role playing, critiques of their own videotaped tutoring sessions, seminars and role playing, handouts, and lecture/discussion presentations by a counseling psychologist. The following skills are stressed:

1. *Establishing rapport* and a positive relationship with the student without encouraging dependency.

2. *Jointly participating with the student* in setting objectives for each session, starting and ending the session, and handling interruptions. Tutors are given ways of ensuring that the student accepts control of his own learning.

3. *Improving listening skills and patience.* We use parts of Ivey and Gluckstern's video-microcounseling program on basic attend-

ing skills (1974). Others have found the video program by Kagan useful (Kagan, 1973, n.d.) (See also Ivey and Gluckstern, 1974, and Ivey and Authier, 1978, for information on microcounseling.) One difficulty in using many of the commercially available videotaped programs is that they are oriented toward training peer counselors and are less relevant for tutor training. In discussions with other tutoring directors, I have found that they have had the same experience and after using the commercially prepared tapes for a year or less, they either develop their own or use role playing instead.

4. *Developing effective questioning skills.* Through modeling and videotaping, tutors are trained to establish a dialogue with the student and develop ways of helping the student ask relevant, important questions.

5. *Avoiding lecturing and other nonfacilitative behaviors.* Videotaping actual tutoring sessions and critiquing these with the tutor helps reduce the tutor's tendency toward such nonfacilitating behaviors as lecturing. A paper by Napell (n.d.) for training graduate teaching assistants is also helpful for training tutors. Napell describes six nonfacilitating teaching behaviors, which adversely affect the quality and quantity of students' learning: insufficient wait time after asking a question; the rapid reward, in which the instructor effectively terminates thinking by saying "Right" to the first answer given, thus favoring the quick thinker and penalizing others in the class; the programmed answer, in which the teacher shoots a stream of questions that reveal the expected answer; nonspecific feedback questions, such as "Do you all understand?"; teacher's-ego-stroking and classroom-climate effects, such as stating, "Since I've explained this several times already, you all should know . . ."; and fixation at a low level of questions such as questions that yield one-word or yes/no answers. One goal of our training program is to help the tutor learn to recognize and avoid these behaviors.

6. *Ways of assessing the student's progress* using positive reinforcement. Tutors can find the appropriate cues in the material to convey what the student is to do to solve the problem or learn the material. Students who are too slow in responding in group situations can be rewarded for progress in individual tutoring sessions.

The tutoring situation also lowers the tutee's anxiety, since it is private. Tutors need to learn what kinds of reinforcement different students need and how to continuously monitor students' responses so that they are accurate and appropriate. They can explore the reasoning behind the student's wrong answers, something which is useful diagnostically and which classroom instructors rarely have the time or interest to do. Tutors can repeat material in different ways and alter cues to fit individual learners' needs, cultural backgrounds, and experiences. They can help students actively participate. Tutors provide encouragement and support as the student struggles with a concept, and they honestly praise him when he has mastered it.

7. *Techniques for dealing with special problems* —for example, the apathetic, passive student, the overly demanding student, the test-anxious student. Our counseling psychologist presents seminars on these topics and has developed handouts with suggestions for new tutors. We also use Rose's short case studies (see Appendix C).

8. *Avoiding student manipulation* —that is, not letting oneself be played off against the instructor and not "putting down" the instructor to gain rapport with students.

9. *Special role of the drop-in tutor* —learning to serve as facilitator to maximize informal (student-to-student) learning.

10. *Techniques in working with group seminars.* Sessions on group processes are provided by the counseling psychologist, and new tutors observe and critique group sessions run by senior tutors. (Hill's book, *Learning Through Discussion: Guide for Leaders and Members of Discussion Groups,* 1975, is helpful for training.)

Improving Intrapersonal Skills. Intrapersonal skills are presented in the videotaped model sessions and through role playing and are discussed in seminars as problems arise. The counseling psychologist presents talks and handouts on the following topics:

1. *Recognizing one's own fears and limitations.*

2. *Relaxing and concentrating,* tolerating ambiguity, not taking hostility directed toward the tutor personally, and so forth. The counseling psychologist conducts a series of two relaxation/concentration workshops for the staff; relaxation tapes are also available in the Library-Laboratory. Helping the tutor resolve his

own authority conflicts is often necessary, as the tutoring role requires that prospective tutors revise their perceptions of themselves as passive students or "good buddies."

3. *Understanding one's own learning style*. Self-analysis of the tutor's own learning style and study techniques is an important part of the seminar training.

4. *Learning to deal honestly with situations, feelings, and clients*. How to respond honestly to students is a topic that comes up often in the informal training sessions and in critiquing videotaped tutoring sessions.

5. *Figuring out what one does not know and articulating questions*. This skill is related to the one just mentioned. Tutors need to know what to do when they do not know the answer. They need ways of saying, "I don't know; let's try to work the problem together," or referring the student to an instructor.

Ethics and Confidentiality. The National Association of Tutorial Services' eighteen-point code of ethics ("Code of Ethics," 1977), which specifies the roles of tutors and their responsibilities toward their tutees, is discussed with new tutors. The code contains such propositions as "Subject proficiency and knowledgeability have top priority in my task as tutor" and pledges to build motivation and self-confidence, not impose one's own value system on clients, and so on. Since the code does not specify conditions under which information received from clients should be considered confidential, examples in this area are presented and discussed to augment the code.

Evaluation as an Ongoing Process.

1. Supervisors continually evaluate tutors and provide feedback.

2. New tutors evaluate the center's program and the training program through checklists and open discussions.

3. The supervisor writes up an evaluation of each new tutor's progress at the end of the quarter and discusses the evaluation with the tutor. Tutors are also evaluated by their tutees through phone calls and questionnaires. Finally, the center has a complaint box where students may drop suggestions, complaints, or kudos.

Resource Materials for Tutor Training

A resource library, well stocked with materials for student use and aids for tutors, is a necessity for an effective tutorial program. Materials for student use should include self-paced-instruction programs and audiovisual aids, including autotutorial systems, projectors with filmstrip programs, and audiotape cassettes with workbooks. Some tutorial services have computer-assisted-instruction facilities. Videotaped lectures and reading programs are also often included. (Other specific tutor backup materials are discussed in the chapters on reading, writing, mathematics, and science.)

There are a number of articles on how to train tutors and set up tutoring programs. Newman (1971) and Yuthas (1971) describe training student tutors and paraprofessionals to help students with reading problems. The Office of Academic Support and Instructional Services (OASIS) at the University of California at San Diego produces regular reports on its EOP tutor-training program (Hedges, 1975; Hedges and Majer, 1976; Shreve and others, 1976). Martin and others (1977) have outlined their tutor-training program, and Johnson (1977) and Lazar and others (1977) describe different approaches to training PSI proctors. Hawkins (1977) and Smith (1975) describe training students to tutor writing, and Houston (1976) discusses peer tutoring in English as a second language (ESL). New publications are appearing monthly in professional journals. (See Appendix D for a list of publications by professional associations.)

Handbooks for student tutors with suggestions, instructions, and plans are also available. In reading, Rauch's *Handbook for the Volunteer Tutor* (1969) and Fry's *Emergency Reading Teacher's Manual* (1969) have practical suggestions on how to help poor readers. Hawkins' *Benjamin: Reading and Beyond* (1972) describes a tutor's struggle to help an adult learn to read. ESL tutors will find Black's *Dear Arby* (1975) a practical cookbook for working with non-English-speaking students. Jolly and Jolly (1974) also have written a handbook for ESL tutors. Martin and others (1977) include scenarios for tutors to follow in teaching vocabulary, reading, and other skills in different subjects, and Shaughnessy's *Errors and Expectations* (1977) is eye-opening for the beginning writing tutor or the novice instructor.

Some excellent books on general tutoring are Kozma and others' *Guide for PSI Proctors* (1976), Osguthorpe and others' *Tutor Notebook* (n.d.), and Driskell's *Guide to Tutoring* (1977).

Many tutoring programs are developing their own videotaped training modules for orienting new tutors. Others are using tape and slide presentations, audiotaped training sessions, and materials on other audiovisual equipment.

Most tutoring programs have written guidelines with specific instructions, policies, and tips for new tutors, and these are becoming longer and much more explicit.

Incorporating Counseling Skills into Tutor Training

As tutoring components have become integrated with counseling and learning-skills services, there is greater recognition of the need to train tutors in interviewing and counseling techniques. The counseling philosophy most frequently adopted by tutor trainers might best be described as eclectic with a heavy emphasis on cognitive counseling approaches, such as Glasser's Reality Therapy (1965) or Ellis' Rational-Emotive Therapy (1973, 1977), usually coupled with behavior modification. For example, Susan Kerwin at Champlain College has tutors ask students to keep a log of their feelings as they study and to bring it in for discussion. The tutors are familiar with Albert Ellis' "common irrational beliefs" (listed below), and when, for example, a student expresses negative self-perceptions or anxiety, the tutor may choose to refute the irrational belief that "I must be perfectly competent in everything I do."

Albert Ellis' Common Irrational Beliefs

1. The idea that it is a dire necessity for an adult human being to be loved or approved by virtually every significant person in his community.

2. The idea that one should be thoroughly competent, adequate, and achieving in all possible respects if one is to consider oneself worthwhile.
3. The idea that certain people are bad, wicked, or villainous and that they should be severely blamed and punished for their villainy.
4. The idea that it is awful and catastrophic when things are not the way one would very much like them to be.
5. The idea that human unhappiness is externally caused and that people have little or no ability to control their sorrows and disturbances.
6. The idea that if something is or may be dangerous or fearsome, one should be terribly concerned about it and should keep dwelling on the possibility of its occurring.
7. The idea that it is easier to avoid than to face certain life difficulties and self-responsibilities.
8. The idea that one should be dependent on others and that one needs someone stronger than oneself on whom to rely.
9. The idea that one's past history is an all-important determinant of one's present behavior and that because something once strongly affected one's life, it should forever have a similar effect.
10. The idea that one should become quite upset over other people's problems and disturbances.
11. The idea that there is invariably a right, precise, and perfect solution to human problems and that it is catastrophic if this correct solution is not found [Goldfried and Goldfried, 1975].

Illustrative of the trend toward incorporating counseling techniques into tutor training are the short case studies developed at UCLA to help tutors deal with difficult tutoring situations. (See Appendix C.)

Special Considerations in Managing Tutors

On Matching Tutors and Tutees. Although it is inevitable that tutors will work better with some students, it is often impractical to try to match tutors and tutees. Logistically, it can be an impossibility, since tutors' and tutees' schedules may not mesh. Rather than try to match tutors and tutees, we staff several tutors in each key subject, with flexible hours, so that students have a choice of tutors. We post tutors' schedules and pictures (taken with a Polaroid camera in color) in the reception area to help students learn tutors' names and recognize tutors readily.

One disadvantage in allowing students free choice of tutors is that inevitably some tutors will be more popular than others and their schedules will fill rapidly. By offering different types of tutoring—small-group work as well as individual help—the more popular tutors can work with more students.

In addition to providing students with a choice of tutors, it is important that procedures permit students to change tutors if the relationship is not productive. The supervisor should be alert to problems that arise between tutors and tutees, so that students who need intensive tutoring do not become discouraged and give up. Students should understand that if they are dissatisfied with a tutor, they can talk to the tutor's supervisor to make other arrangements. In an open-choice tutoring arrangement, there will inevitably be students who are tutor-hoppers, shifting from one tutor to another until they have worked with all the tutors in the program. The supervisor should be aware of these students and help tutors coordinate their efforts so they can minimize the effects of students who play one tutor against another.

Sometimes it is surprising what tutor/tutee combinations work well. For instance, we once hired a paraplegic tutor who was very popular with student athletes, especially football players. However, some students are very concerned that the tutor be from their own ethnic background or of the same sex. We have found that many Chicano/Latino male students, as well as many male students from foreign countries, have difficulty working with female tutors. They can make the woman tutor feel very uncomfortable by denying that she knows her subject. These considerations may seem important to the student, but often students who insist on working only with tutors from a particular ethnic background or sex are rationalizing and using these demands as excuses for rejecting the tutoring program.

One cannot eliminate all complaints or fill all demands, particularly when the supply of tutors in some subjects is small. However, it is important that tutors represent, as far as possible, the ethnic and sex distribution of the students who seek help. If you are unable to locate a Native American female qualified to tutor physics (we did find one once, despite the small number of Native American students on our campus), the next-best strategy is to recruit and select tutors who are sensitive and flexible enough to work with a wide range of student problems.

For new, inexperienced tutors, I believe that supervisors, at least in the beginning stages of the training, should screen tutees and assign them to tutors, for the benefit of both the tutors and the students. As new tutors gain experience, they can work with a wider range of student problems, but if their first tutee relationship is poor, it can be a devastating blow to their self-confidence, and it will require much effort and time for the supervisor to undo the damage.

Flexible Scheduling. For a tutorial program to be most effective in reaching the students who need its service, the hours it is open must be compatible with students' schedules. In any institution, there are hours when most students will be in classes—for example, early morning hours—and this time can better be used by senior staff members in staff conferences or planning than in tutoring. Appointments at 8:00 A.M., like classes at 8:00 A.M., are not popular with students, and we have found that students are likely not to keep early morning appointments, a discouraging situation for motivated tutors. In our program, noon and late afternoon are popular tutoring times.

Woolley (1976) reports that 68 percent of the California community colleges surveyed offer tutoring in the evening and 25 percent on weekends. Some evening hours are a must if tutoring services are to assist employed students, those with heavy class schedules, and athletes for whom classes, coaching, and practice leave little free time during the day.

In scheduling night tutoring, building security and the safety of staff members and students must be considered. Other constraints are the budget and the willingness of staff members to work nights. Tutors who are also students frequently prefer night hours. If the service is located in a library, there are fewer problems with safety and security, as there are other staff members and students in the building, parking lots are well lit, and transportation service is usually available. Rather than attempt to keep our building open at night, we obtained rooms for evening tutoring in the undergraduate library, which was open until midnight. However, the program outgrew the space, and there were enough clients to open our building evenings. Another alternative is to use dormitory meeting rooms for evening tutoring.

In beginning an evening program, it is important that the service be well advertised through announcements in classes, in the campus newspaper, and on bulletin boards and that sufficient time elapse for students to learn about the service.

In the evening, drop-in and small-group tutoring services seem to work better than scheduled individual appointments, which students tend not to keep.

A major difficulty I have observed in visiting other tutoring programs is the problem of staffing a separate night shift of tutors, particularly in schools with large programs of night classes. Since instructors in night classes tend to be hired on a part-time or per-course basis and since many are moonlighting from other teaching jobs, they tend to be minimally involved with the institution's support services and administrative programs. This makes it difficult for tutors to contact and work with instructors. Besides, the night-shift tutors are not likely to have much contact with day-shift tutors and learning specialists, and unless special arrangements are made, they get little support or supervision. One way to eliminate the morale and other difficulties generated by separate staffs is to systematically schedule regular meetings with both day and night staffs and faculty members (at the beginning and end of each term, at least), pay staff members to attend, and allow time for them to interact socially on an informal basis as well as to discuss the program, its goals, and its effectiveness.

Staffing tutors on weekends can be expensive unless there is a regular and sustained demand for their services. The same problems of building security and safety that characterize evening tutoring sessions are encountered. However, adult part-time students who work full time and attend evening classes often need special help and are free only on weekends. A survey of students' needs for weekend tutoring, their willingness to use it, and their preferred hours can provide information on the feasibility of staffing a program on weekends and the most popular hours. For example, in our program we found that the most popular hours were from ten to three on Saturdays and that some Sunday hours are desirable in the week preceding examinations.

In summary, tutoring hours should be flexible so that students who need the service can schedule it. Holding to a rigid eight-to-five or nine-to-five schedule and closing at the noon hour for lunch will restrict the number of students who can be tutored and will penalize those who work part time or have heavy class schedules and may need tutoring the most.

Drop-In Centers. Many tutoring programs have drop-in services, most commonly for math and science. The success of this arrangement depends on the tutor's ability to work with more than one student at a time—with small groups or from student to student, spending just a few minutes with each. Our Drop-In Center has cafeteria tables each labeled with a course name and number, larger tables for small groups, and carrels where tutors can work privately with one or two students at a time. The carrels, built by students, consist of hexagonal Formica tables large enough to seat three persons and surrounded by three movable partitions, sound-resistant and covered with flameproofed burlap. The tables and carrels are movable and can be rearranged for large groups or to provide more privacy. There is also a graphics computer terminal, which students can use for computer-assisted instruction.

At the tables, the tutor's role is that of a learning facilitator, not an answer machine. The tutor helps students work together in groups of two to six and can assist them when they have difficulty. The objective is to create an informal, unpressured learning environment—a place where students can study with friends. (Libraries are too formal for many students, and librarians tend to frown on conversations. Besides, librarians usually cannot help students with their calculus problems.) One backup tutor at peak times can work individually with students who need more intensive help. (A warning: Some professors scoff at the study groups and comment that "the blind are leading the blind.")

The Drop-In area was constructed by knocking down several walls in our old World War II barracks building to create an open space 35 by 70 feet, carpeting the floor, and spraying acoustical material on the ceiling. The room will hold 110 people and is often filled to capacity. It is not quiet. There is a constant murmur of voices; however, this is not distracting, since it serves as white noise and masks individual conversations. In fact, it provides a more private atmosphere than our library, where we try to maintain quiet, but where conversations can be heard throughout the room.

We have observed that this arrangement attracts minority students as well as others. Students do not have to schedule formal appointments, and they like the idea of working with others with a tutor present.

Another aspect of the Drop-In Center is that it provides a comfortable place for commuter students to study. Many of the EOP students at Berkeley commute and lack a place to study at home. We are open evenings and Saturdays to serve commuters. At peak times—for example, before exams—we open longer hours on weekends and hold sessions on Sundays to aid commuters who cannot study at home.

The Drop-In receptionist has often reported that students come into the Drop-In area alone and ask whether they can just sit and study. They are welcome. In observing them, we find that within an hour or two they begin working with another student or a tutor. There is something that appeals to students about feeling that they are not studying alone—they are with a group and feel okay because there are a lot of other students there. And they can usually find someone who is in the same class as they are and work together. It is hard for the freshman student who feels alone and alienated to make friends in a large lecture class. Some solve this problem by taking the same courses as their friends. Others spontaneously form their own study groups in the Drop-In area and meet regularly. Others show up even when no tutor in their subject is scheduled. This environment seems to help the field-dependent student feel comfortable. However, some of the more capable students complain, "I came here to get tutoring and ended up being the tutor."

The Drop-In Center gets crowded at times. On some days we have 250 students in Drop-In, and the number of hours EOP students use the Drop-In area has increased each quarter. (Although EOP students have priority for individual appointments with tutors, many of them prefer the informal atmosphere of the Drop-In Center.)

The logistics of staffing tutors in the Drop-In to handle students at peak times are complex, but we have found this system generally more satisfactory for both tutors and tutees than limiting service to individual appointments held in rooms all over the building or in fixed-schedule groups. Students can make individual appointments in the Drop-In Center with a regular tutor if they prefer or can sign up for regularly scheduled groups. The problem of students who failed to keep appointments plagued us, as it has most centers that serve underprepared students. With the Drop-In Center, this problem is greatly reduced. If a student does not show for an individual appointment, the tutor can go to the Drop-In and work with another student or group of students. This improves the morale of the paid tutor or volunteer, since "no shows" are discouraging, especially if the tutor's pay or credit is determined by the hours he works with students.

Drop-in services present special problems in evaluation because they lack clear criteria for student entrance and exit. Since students typically use drop-in services only occasionally, often just once or twice, it is not feasible to try to measure the effects of this kind of tutoring on grades. Student satisfaction with the service is the criterion most often used. But, in a sense, evaluating a drop-in tutoring service is like evaluating a supermarket. If students (or customers) find what they are seeking, they are satisfied. If not, they are dissatisfied.

Problems Tutoring Programs Face

Tutoring services often face problems that are similar to those of other student services, and some are unique to tutoring. These include political problems, staff morale, logistical problems caused by a heavy student demand, and sometimes overt faculty hostility. Since tutoring programs typically serve special groups of students, especially underprepared and minority students, they can get caught in battles between student groups. They may have less autonomy than other services when administrators are concerned about the institution's image with special groups. For example, Reed (1974, p. 35) describes one tutorial program, which is not atypical in my experience, where both the program administrators and the faculty felt that friction between student ethnic groups about personnel and the basic philosophy of the program doomed it to failure. "At that school black and Chicano students felt that the program director and other key program personnel should be representative of their respective ethnic groups and that the program should manifest an orientation toward their cultures. Obviously, these concerns are legitimate, and the administration should provide resources strong enough to satisfy them. Apparently, the administration of that particular institution intentionally permitted the conflict between minority students to undermine the program. Unfortunately, the students involved did not appear to understand that the administration and perhaps others were not committed to the program." It is sad, but true, that students may turn against the services that offer them the most personal and important help and in a sense bite the hands that feed them.

Staff Morale. In addition to pressure from minority student groups, staff members can suffer from morale problems and "burnout" (Maslach, 1976) just as others in the helping professions do. When the workload is heavy, the pace is frantic, future funding and positions are insecure, and tutors are continually being evaluated by anxious students, staff morale may fall. Faculty cynicism and criticism can have a devastating effect on a conscientious tutor. Moreover, a tutor loses enthusiasm when there is little or no improvement in his tutee's learning as the end of the term is approaching, when both tutor and tutee have worked hard. A tutor becomes depressed when he fears the student will fail. Unrealistic expectations of what a student should be able to learn and a commitment to help the tutee sometimes conflict, and under pressure the tutor tends to do the work for the tutee or becomes impatient or overstrict. Tutors who expect gratitude from their tutees may be disappointed when the tutee brags, "I got a B+ and I did it all myself." (But, then, isn't that the ultimate goal?)

Tutors need support in setting realistic objectives for tutees, and they need clear ways to evaluate learning gains. Peer tutors sometimes have difficulty defining and maintaining a tutor role with their tutees because their closeness in age and desire to be liked may interfere with effective tutoring. Usually peer tutors compensate for lack of knowledge through their enthusiasm and willingness to help; however, some have problems with the tutoring role and need help clarifying ways to become effective.

Other staff problems are those that affect a tutor's comfort and sanity: sheer physical exhaustion, lack of time, losing patience, handling the desperate tutee who comes in at the end of the tutor's scheduled work period and wants "just five minutes," having too many students to work with at once, having another tutor grab one's tutee, and not being able to help a student work a difficult problem. All these problems can be worked through if there is a regularly scheduled time for the tutor to sit down to talk with a supervisor and/or other tutors.

We have found that team-building and relaxation/ concentration workshops given by the psychological consultant are most productive when they are given to the staff, not the students. (Our experience has been consistent with the study by Abramowitz and others (1974), who found that training counselors in deep-relaxation/concentration techniques was superior to encounter-group training in increasing their empathy, increasing their acceptance of aggressive clients, and enabling them to develop a deeper relationship, give more unconditional expressions of regard, and generally perform in a more facilitative way.) That faculty members seek this kind of program too was discovered when the Learning Assistance Center at Stanford recently offered a summer course for credit titled "How to Cope with Academe" in which relaxation/ concentration techniques were taught. Interestingly, more faculty and staff members signed up for the course than undergraduate students, for whom it was planned.

Another problem that plagues many programs is boredom and anxiety. Some directors propose the following solutions for improving staff morale: (1) Members of the program staff must be given autonomy over the program. (2) Job descriptions should change within the program structure as often as possible. No person should work in one area more than three years. (3) Staff members should be trained to be people-oriented, not subject- or cash-oriented. (4) In-service training for all staff members should include consciousness raising, discussions of self-survival, and discussions of how to design effective strategies for low achievers.

Logistical Difficulties. Most college tutoring programs attract more students than they can serve, and even with tightly controlled caseloads, there are periods before exams when students want and need extra help. The logistics of bringing students and tutors together, finding enough space, and providing materials become formidable. Tutoring programs using student tutors may collapse at the end of the term when students seek extra help and tutors themselves have to study. One can plan for these exigencies by limiting service and scheduling senior staff members for more time in group sessions. In one program, senior staff members were scheduled to cover all drop-in hours during the last two weeks of the term; we called them our "Band-Aid brigade," realizing that helping students reduce their anxiety before exams was a useful service. I have not tried the "study table and panic clinic," in which facilities are open twenty-four hours a day during exam week, but some feel that it is worthwhile (Enright, 1976).

There are also differences in opinion concerning whether group review sessions and mock-exam practice sessions are beneficial to students. Certainly, many students will attend these programs.

Even aside from end-of-term crowding, many tutoring programs soon find that they attract more students than they can effectively serve—even though they provide drop-in services, evening hours, and group and individual help. Unless the program has an unlimited budget and an endless supply of tutors, decisions have to be made about which students can be served.

Some program directors restrict tutoring service to special groups—for example, EOP students, athletes, or students on probation. Others restrict their services to certain courses—for example, freshman courses or entry-level lower-division courses—and to students bearing a letter from a faculty member attesting to their need for help. Restricting services to special groups is sometimes a requirement for federal funding, but this practice always entails the risk of the program's being labeled a "salvage operation."

If a program restricts tutoring to freshman courses, then it assumes that upper-level students do not need help. Advanced students who are well on their way to success but may need an occasional boost to help them pass a difficult upper-division course get no tutoring services. This may seem like educational "triage," but when a tutoring program has limited funds and resources, the director must decide whether to restrict services to those students who are most likely to profit from them or to those who are most in need of them (yet are so far behind that they cannot expect to pass). Or should he compromise and offer some help to both groups? Should a student who is impossibly behind the rest of the class continue to receive tutoring help to the exclusion of other students who are closer to passing? Should there be a limit on the amount of help a student may receive or the length of time he may be tutored? Most colleges set stringent limits on the length of time to allow a student to demonstrate that he can perform college-level work before dismissing him. Individual and even group tutoring tends to be expensive and popular; should ground rules for excluding students from tutoring be set, or should cases be decided individually? Each of these alternatives is used by some tutoring programs. Some require that all prospective tutees be screened by a learning specialist before they can be seen by a tutor. Others restrict their services to students who sign up before a certain date (except for emergency referrals from administrators or faculty members).

Faculty Negativism. Some faculty members have negative attitudes about tutoring. They have either had direct experience with abuses of tutoring or heard horror stories about tutors who did students' homework, read their books for them, wrote their papers, and even took exams for them. It takes patience and effort to help professors overcome these prejudices and educate them to the quality and kind of tutoring that your programs presently offer. Complaining about students' lack of skills seems to be an ingrained faculty position and one that new staff members may find most discouraging. A strong faculty advisory board can help strengthen the image of the tutoring service with other faculty members, as will the improved performance of students who are tutored, but it takes time and continual effort to build strong bridges of mutual trust between tutorial staff and faculty.

Research on Tutoring

Until quite recently, few studies on the effectiveness of college tutoring programs had been done. Tutoring did not capture the interest of researchers, because historically tutoring arrangements had generally been private and informal. If professors tutored, it was assumed that their students would learn. Similarly, if honor-society members tutored, they were considered qualified and their effectiveness was not questioned. The large tutoring programs developed in the 1960s to help minority and other disadvantaged students were not designed as educational experiments and tended to be informal and unstructured. Their effectiveness, when judged by post-hoc investigators, could not be validated (Davis and others, 1975; Reed, 1974). As tutoring programs become more formal, structured, and costly, their effectiveness is being questioned, and tutoring is beginning to attract greater interest from researchers.

However, a large body of research with implications for college tutoring programs exists: the program descriptions and studies generated by the tutoring explosion in the public schools. The curricular problems of the 1960s and the realization that education is vitally important in modern society resulted in desperation about the need for helping each child get a good education. Because of desegregation and the greater mobility of the population, teachers were faced for the first time with large numbers of children who did not learn with the customary materials and methods. Classrooms became diversified as tracking was abolished and achievement levels fell. Bloom (n.d., p. 4) states, "New materials, computer-assisted instruction, and other special programs were developed and tried with great fervor and high expectations. Only rarely have they proved to be successful in raising the learning level of pupils. Tutoring, on the other hand, has worked well enough to be embraced by many as the panacea."

At first, tutoring-program directors at both the elementary and college levels assumed that all that was necessary was to bring tutor and tutee together, thus releasing the creativity of the tutor, who, calling upon years of work as a student, would intuitively know how to tutor and would develop a successful, positive, and helping relationship with the tutee. As a result, Bloom found, some programs failed miserably. Other directors, who did not make this assumption, developed effective programs through trial and error.

Extensive reviews of studies on tutoring public school students have been produced by Allen (1976), Bloom (n.d.), and Gartner and others (1971). The most consistent finding that emerges from these reviews is that *structured* tutoring, when appropriately used, results in learning gains for tutees. (Structured tutoring means that tutors work on particular, prediagnosed skills and content.) For example, Bloom found that 80 percent of the studies involving structured tutoring yielded significant results. Structured tutoring is held to have the following advantages: (1) it makes it possible to divide material into sections, or modules, to provide limited and attainable goals with visible evidence when a student has mastered each unit or skill; (2) it may be used with regular classroom materials, and as Harrison (1972a, 1972b) has emphasized, structured tutoring is not just a set of materials, but a teaching technique that can be adapted to any subject; (3) it provides flexibility and allows continuity of tutoring even when there is a change of tutors. Bloom points out that in helping a student learn essential skills, the risk of failing is too great to allow dependence on tutor-selected materials, which may not be keyed to the appropriate starting point for the tutee. She adds that creating useful and appropriate materials is so complex and time-consuming that it is hard to maintain tutors' enthusiasm. Furthermore, tutor-prepared materials are more likely to reflect the tutor's preference than the needs of the tutee, and although students may progress with tutor-prepared materials, the opportunity to maximize the learning of essential skills is often lost.

One study on structured tutoring in reading may serve to illustrate some of the points discussed above. Ellson and others (1968) studied the effects of two types of paraprofessional tutoring given to inner-city first-graders by women trained and supervised by the experimenters. Scores on three reading tests administered in January and June were the dependent variables. The experimenters found that tutoring in reading without regard to kind or amount of tutoring yielded equivocal results. Structured, programmed tutoring was significantly more effective in raising children's reading scores than "directed" tutoring, which resembled the regular classroom activities with games and other techniques designed to motivate students. Although both students and staff members preferred the directed tutoring, it failed to show significant improvement in reading. Poorer readers gained significantly more from the structured tutoring program, compared with control subjects, than students at higher reading levels did. The experimenters concluded that structured, programmed tutoring has a "workmanlike atmosphere with clearly defined goals and tasks imposed at first by the tutor, but accepted by the child, and demands a close personal interaction" (1968, p. 345).

Many recent studies have been made on the effectiveness of peer tutoring for students in college classes using personalized self-instructional (PSI) programs or the Keller plan. Such classes provide a highly structured tutoring environment. Goldschmid and Goldschmid (1976a, 1976b) reviewed the studies on PSI tutoring and concluded that peer tutors, even those chosen from among students currently enrolled in the course, were effective in enhancing student learning.

Other investigators who have examined the effects of structured tutoring on college students' performance include Carman, 1975 (mathematics), Osguthorpe, 1976 (tutoring the deaf), Ott, 1976 (second-language learning), and Santa Barbara City College, 1970 (English). A variation of structured tutoring is tutored videotaped instruction, in which tutors lead group discussion sessions, stopping a videotaped lecture as needed by the students (Gibbons and others, 1977).

Carman's two-year follow-up study (1975) on community college students in a developmental mathematics course compared students from three classes. One group had programmed mathematical materials but no tutoring; the second group had programmed mathematical materials and "total tutoring"—that is, intensive individual and small-group tutoring for five hours a week; and the third had programmed materials and occasional tutoring. Carman found that 76 percent of the nontutored group withdrew from college their first semester, compared with 57 percent of the group receiving some tutoring and 49 percent of the intensively tutored group. Only 3 percent of the intensively tutored group withdrew from all math courses they enrolled in over the two years of the study. He concluded that the intense personal relationship formed with a tutor may be a significant factor in the positive changes observed in the "total tutoring" group, and he suggested that experiments on tutoring should look at improvement in attitudes toward learning and at persistence, not at GPA alone. The Santa Barbara City College study (1970) also included supportive data suggesting that low-achieving students who used the tutoring service persisted longer in English courses.

Hedges and Majer (1976) studied EOP students at the University of California at San Diego who were tutored by "outstanding math or science majors" taking a tutoring-for-credit course. Each tutor was assigned three students for the ten-week quarter and required to attend meetings of the class in which he tutored. Eighty-five tutored students in three freshman classes (1971, 1972, and 1973) were compared with eighty-five EOP students in the same classes who did not request tutoring. In two out of the three years, Hedges and Majer found statistically significant differences between tutored and nontutored students in cumulative GPA improvement between the freshman and sophomore years and in persistence at the end of the sophomore year when high school GPA and SAT mathematics and verbal scores were controlled. For the third year, they did not find significant differences between freshman and sophomore grades, but they reported that both groups earned unusually high grades their first year and had higher test scores. The investigators expressed concern that the close personal relationship between tutor and tutee should have improved grades more for the tutored group.

It is interesting that so many researchers who evaluate college tutoring tend to attribute achievement gains to the enhancement of the student's self-concept resulting from the close personal relationship developed with the tutor, while the researchers study-

ing elementary students stress the structured aspects of the tutoring session as having the greatest impact on improving achievement (though not negating the improvement of self-confidence
that comes from mastery of the material and from personal identification with a tutor). Although it is self-evident that tutors should
relate to underprepared students in an empathetic and nonjudgmental manner, I question whether confidence in one's ability
to achieve can improve unless one can see improvement in one's
learning skills and understanding of the subject matter. A structured program enables students to measure their progress in these
areas.

Another way to assess the effects of tutoring is to ask students whether they feel their achievement level has improved and
whether they would have dropped the course if they had not received tutoring. For instance, Woolley (1976) studied a random
sample of 424 community college students who had received more
than ten hours of tutorial assistance and found that 85 percent
reported that their achievement level had improved after the assistance and 57 percent stated that without it they would have
dropped the course. The responses of the tutoring services' directors on these two questions did not significantly differ from those
of the tutees.

A basic problem in studying the effects of tutoring is that
most students who receive tutoring are weaker in the subject than
those who do not, so that studies often reveal that the posttest
grades of students who were tutored are lower than those of students not receiving help. Hubin (1976) agrees that what many of us
have observed in voluntary tutoring services is true: Below average
students volunteer for tutoring and slightly above average students
volunteer for skills services. In addition, professors usually refer
the academically weakest students for tutoring.

Another factor that affects the results of research on tutoring is motivation to succeed in college. Wright (n.d.) reports that
those students whose grades are expected to be in the average
range (based on high school background and entrance tests) participate in tutoring the most and profit the most from it. The predicted lowest achievers profit the least from tutoring or do not use
it. (To clarify the apparent discrepancy between Hubin's and

Wright's statements about those who seek and use tutoring, one must understand that weaker students are more likely to seek tutoring than to enroll voluntarily in reading and study skills programs, but the weakest students may not seek tutoring or, if they are referred, are likely to not follow through or not profit from it.)

There is evidence, however, that underprepared college students receiving enough tutoring with enough regularity will get higher grades in the course, at least when tutoring is voluntary. Watanabe and Maxwell (1975) found that EOP students at the University of California at Berkeley who used the chemistry tutoring program on a regular basis (coming in at least three times and attending regularly at least once a week) earned significantly higher grades in chemistry than EOP students who used tutoring sporadically. Earlier studies on Berkeley EOP students had shown that tutored students made significantly lower grades, even after they had been tutored, than their nontutored peers.

Motivated and better-prepared students use tutoring more regularly than the less well prepared, who may either get discouraged or deny their lack of background. If there is a large discrepancy between the tutee's background knowledge and skills and those of the typical student in the institution, one cannot expect tutoring alone, no matter how intensive, to improve the tutee's grades. Furthermore, the weakest students may not come in for regular tutoring. Rose (1976) describes a pilot study on EOP students at UCLA which indicates that students with GPAs below 2.3 often deny their need for tutorial support with the same reasons offered by those with GPAs of 3.5 or higher: They give excuses like "It doesn't seem necessary" or "I can't fit it into my schedule."

To summarize, different studies have made contradictory findings: some have found that weaker students seek tutoring in preference to volunteering for counseling or skills programs while others have found that weaker students are not likely to refer themselves for tutoring or for skills help, although they need both. Additionally, they are not likely to profit much from tutoring when they do receive it. To improve this situation, the director must address the problem of how to identify those students who need tutoring early, to find ways to encourage them to accept help, and to make sure that the tutoring program is designed to meet their needs. Professors refer weak students for tutoring, and academically weak students generally prefer tutoring to other kinds of academic services (skills or counseling, for instance). For tutoring to be most effective with underprepared and academically weak students, tutors should be trained in teaching basic skills and using structured materials. Without this kind of preparation, tutors tend to emulate their professors, with the result that students who are motivated and closer to average in ability and background receive the most tutoring and profit the most from it. Tutors who have been selected for high achievement in a subject are not likely to use methods that differ from those used in their classes, and they are more likely to reward students who are motivated and can learn rapidly. Those tutees who do not fit this profile may soon become discouraged with the tutors' approach and stop attending tutoring sessions.

Underprepared students who are achieving poorly and deny the need for help pose a problem. Counseling and contracting may help if the student "doesn't know that he doesn't know," but if the student lacks motivation to study, it is hard indeed to help. It is important to understand that being tutored may have some negative psychological implications for the tutee, which may account for the reluctance of some to seek help. If tutoring is to reach more students who need it, ways must be found to avoid hurting their pride or making them feel inferior. Rosen and others (1977) hypothesize that people who are below par are reluctant to seek help when receiving help would lead to unresolved feelings of indebtedness. A person in need of help will avoid entering into an inequitable relationship with a potential donor. They add that some persons may refrain from seeking help to avoid validating the donor's implicit claim to superior status and the right to impose future demands.

Studying students in an educational psychology class who were assigned to tutor others in the class and then became tutees of the other students, Rosen and others found that participant satisfaction, perception of good performance, and actual performance were directly dependent on becoming the tutor and entering an equitable tutoring relationship. (An equitable tutoring relationship was defined as one in which the tutor's grades were equal to—not

higher nor lower than—the tutee's.) The investigators conclude
that it is better to tutor than to be tutored.

That tutoring improves the achievement and attitudes
toward school of the tutors as well as the tutees is amply documented in the studies of cross-age tutoring and peer tutoring in
public schools (Bloom, n.d.; Cloward, 1966; Gartner and others,
1971; Schell, 1976; Shaver and Nuhn, 1971). There is increasing
evidence that the same effects hold the college-student tutors.
McWhorter and Levy (1971) found that college students tutoring
elementary school children in phonics improved their own skills.
Jackson and Van Zoost (1974) found similar results for tutors in
study skills, and Hoover (1972) for tutors in English. Hedges and
others (1976) report that upper-division science students who tutored EOP freshmen earned higher scores on the Medical College
Admissions Test than classmates matched for courses and grades.
(These findings provide an additional incentive to prospective
tutors.)

Starting from the premise that one learns more by teaching
or tutoring others than by being tutored, Drucker and I designed a
program in which women and minority freshmen are apprenticed
to senior tutors in an effort to motivate them to major in the physical sciences and mathematics. Peer tutors are carefully selected,
paid for ten to fifteen hours a week, and enrolled in beginning
college mathematics and science courses. They tutor in these same
courses as they themselves are learning the concepts. This kind of
tutoring program requires intensive training and close individual
supervision. The peer tutors attend group tutoring sessions where
they observe the senior tutors' tutoring style, meet in weekly seminars on how to tutor, and receive intensive tutoring themselves.
Both tutors and tutees earned higher grades and remained
enrolled in the chemistry sequence longer than controls (Drucker,
1976). Three of the original group of ten freshmen are still working as tutors. Although this program is more expensive than
merely hiring tutors, it does seem to have a higher payoff in maintaining underprepared students' motivation to stay in college, in
the grades they receive, and in increasing the number of women
and minority students who remain in science and mathematics
majors.

To summarize, research on college tutoring, its programs, and, to a limited extent, its process is slowly increasing. The many studies of tutoring in public schools offer a framework for exploring more-sophisticated questions about college tutoring, including whether structured tutoring is more conducive to learning gains in students than looser, more humanistic approaches and how materials and interpersonal relationships interact to produce gains. Some studies suggest that the amount and regularity of tutoring are correlated with college course grades and retention of disadvantaged students. Other studies show that tutors benefit from the experience, perhaps even more than their tutees. More-complex studies that include the many individual and intervention variables involved in tutoring should be designed and an adequate data base developed so that programs can be compared. At present, tutorial-program directors are more frequently assessing student reactions to their services; this is a beginning, but additional studies are needed.

4

<hr>

Establishing
Learning Centers

<hr>

"Why do you call your service a learning center? Isn't that the mission of the whole college?" This is the question faculty members and administrators most frequently ask learning-center directors. The usual answer is that learning centers assist students in basic skills and learning beyond the assistance that faculty members have time for during their class sessions and office hours. Were it possible for colleges to offer small, homogeneous classes taught by professors deeply dedicated to and rewarded for teaching, perhaps learning centers would not be needed, and a skilled ombudsperson might suffice to negotiate and resolve problems. However, most public postsecondary institutions in the United States have become knowledge-dispensing factories. Mass production is as ingrained in American higher education as it is in automobile manufacturing, despite the lip service paid to the importance of working with individuals. Although students are permitted to choose individual colleges and their curriculums, they are subject to pervasive similarities in admission rituals, courses, credits, requirements, and teaching styles. In college one must adapt to the rituals and requirements in order to succeed, sometimes compromising one's own interests and needs with the demands and constraints set by faculty members and administrators. Learning centers exist to help our increasingly diverse students make this adjustment.

The majority of U.S. colleges and universities now have some kind of academic support service, apart from regular academic courses, to help students improve their learning skills. The most recent, and by far the most comprehensive, survey reveals that there are at least 1,848 learning-center components in 1,433 independent colleges and universities in English-speaking North America (Sullivan, 1978). From Vassar to the Virgin Islands, from Georgia to Guam, colleges are offering special professional help to underprepared students. Learning-center services are proliferating as colleges attempt to aid and retain underprepared students. The number of learning centers doubled between 1974 and 1977, with four-year institutions showing the greatest increase (Sullivan, 1978).

Learning Centers Defined

Learning centers are as varied as the institutions and the students they serve, yet, like other facets of academe, they share common functions, goals, and strategies. Sullivan (1978) defines learning-center components as containing some or all of the following elements: instructional resources, instructional media, learning-skill development, tutoring, and instructional development. He reports that a number of institutions have more than one department or unit offering these components.

Enright (1975, p. 81) defines a learning-assistance center as a "place concerned with learning environments functioning to enable students to learn more in less time and with greater ease, offering tutorial help, study aids in content fields, serving as a testing ground for innovative machines, materials and programs, and acting as a campus ombudsman." Peterson (1975, p. 9) offers a somewhat different description: "A learning center is an amalgamation of four services: library, audiovisual service, nontraditional learning activities (including tutoring), and instructional development service" (that is, the center assists faculty members in developing new teaching strategies, materials, and courses.) The Committee on Learning Skills Centers (1976) explains that a learning center is a special location where students can come—or be sent—for special instruction not usually included in "regular" college classes. The committee notes that centers offer various services, from individualized instruction or special classes to tutoring, and work on self-help materials. The New England Association of Academic Support Personnel (1977, p. 1) describes learning centers as "places of various sizes, where students can find personnel (professionals or trained peers) and materials (of varying degrees of sophistication) to help them with specific problems. Classes are run from the center, drop-ins are encouraged, and much individual counseling takes place." Many learning centers offer students such multiple services as individual and group skills programs, tutoring, preparation for graduate and professional exams, and media and materials for self-paced instruction. Some concentrate their programs on special groups such as student athletes, the disadvantaged, the physically handicapped, or international students; others serve all students. Some offer credit for reading and other skills courses; others do not. Whatever the local title, learning centers are found in public and private colleges, two- and four-year institutions, universities, and graduate and professional schools.

Historical Background

Campuswide learning centers that offer skills and tutorial services to all students are a relatively recent development. Enright (1975) notes that 57 percent of the learning centers in U.S. colleges have become operational since 1970 and that directors are considered mature practitioners after only four years in the field.

From a historical viewpoint, learning centers are merely the latest development in a long series of attempts to help students adjust to the academic demands of college. Study skills handbooks have been published since 1916, if not before, and "how to study" courses were required of underachieving applicants to the University of Buffalo as early as 1926.

During the 1930s remedial reading was popularized, and it swept through the public schools. Similarly, reading-improvement courses became a part of college "how to study" courses. The tachistoscope and other devices developed and used in psychological research on vision and perception were adopted by college reading specialists, who attempted to apply research findings—Javel's on eye movements, Buswell's on mature reading, and those of Huey, Tinker, and many others.

During World War II groups of young men attended college for brief periods as part of their armed-services training, and courses were truncated. Medical school training was reduced to three years, and numerous other efforts were made to speed the training of potential officers and skilled technicians. It was during this period that Frank Robinson of Ohio State University developed his SQ3R study method to help these young male students get the most from their brief exposure to college.

After the war, veterans flooded our colleges. Men from both rural and urban areas, who would not have considered going to college had it not been for the G.I. Bill, returned from service and tried their luck at getting a college degree. In many colleges the federal government funded vocational guidance centers, which later became campuswide counseling centers. Many of the veterans needed help with basic reading, writing, math, and study skills; programs, usually in counseling centers, were developed to help them.

By the late 1940s, college remedial and developmental reading and study skills courses were expanding rapidly. Many relied on the use of machines like bulky pacers (which required ripping books apart, since they held only one page at a time), tachistoscopes for increasing eye span (the number of words seen per fixation), films, and other devices. Reading specialists debated whether it was more effective to teach rapid reading with an instructor and a stopwatch or with a battery of machines. Spache (1955) says that college reading programs emerged from the laboratories of psychologists, traveled into the classrooms of education and English departments, and then moved into counseling services. Required college orientation courses proliferated in the 1950s, and reading and study skills were taught in these courses. Orientation courses were usually offered for full or partial credit. As separate college reading-improvement courses became more common, they too were given for credit. Causey's nationwide survey in 1950 found that about half the colleges offering reading courses gave credit for them (Causey, 1955).

Although American public universities have historically been based on an egalitarian philosophy, by the 1930s most state universities required that entering students present at least a B average in college preparatory courses. Even with these standards, a large number of students were expected to drop out before the sophomore year. In the mid forties, a number of state universities were faced with a threat from state legislators who were proposing laws requiring them to admit all state high school graduates, as the University of Minnesota had been forced to do in the 1930s. Minnesota founded a General College, which accepted any state high school graduate who failed to meet normal admissions standards. The General College offered its students courses and the opportunity to transfer to regular university courses if they earned high enough grades or the option of remaining in the General College and getting a degree there. (The General College is still viewed with some opprobrium by Minnesota students, who call it Nicholson High School because its classes are held in Nicholson Hall.)

As a result of similar legislative pressure, Pennsylvania State University established a special Counseling College where students admitted on probation received counseling, reading and study skills help, and other services while they took regular courses. The University of Maryland was faced with similar laws and, in 1947, developed a "holding college" for students entering with below C averages from high school. Originally a part of the extension division, it later became a separate department. Students were required to take a study skills and college orientation program their first semester called "College Aims," for which credit was given. They received special academic advising, tutoring, and counseling and were permitted to take a light load of basic courses required for their intended majors. During their second semester, they were required to take a reading-improvement course, also for credit.

They could transfer into a regular college if they earned an average of 2.5 (C+) their first semester or an overall 2.0 (C) for the year. Transfer students with poor academic records from community colleges were also required to participate in this program (originally called "Special and Continuation Studies"). By 1960 there were several thousand applicants for the program annually, and it was affecting dormitory spaces and departmental teaching schedules. To alleviate these pressures, all low-achieving applicants were required to take an intensive eight-week summer program consisting of counseling, reading, study skills, advisement, and two regular courses. (This program was named the Pre-college Summer Session.) Students who attained a C average were eligible for regular enrollment in the fall. The required summer session greatly reduced the number of students applying and overloading facilities in the fall.

Although the Maryland program included individual counseling, during most of the 1950s group or class work was the major approach to teaching study skills and reading. Weigand and Blake's *College Orientation* (1955) typifies the techniques used, many of which were based on Robinson's earlier work, *Effective Study* (1946/1970), a rather pedantic, psychologically sophisticated work. By the mid fifties, the major emphasis in colleges and universities was on finding ways of identifying and training the brightest students, and extramural funding for programs to help marginal students was practically nonexistent. With the launching of Sputnik, the pressure to develop the intellectually gifted increased.

By the late 1950s programmed learning materials based on B. F. Skinner's ideas were being developed at a rapid rate. The new technology and philosophy made possible the development of individualized reading programs at the University of Florida (Spache and others, 1959), the University of Maryland (Maxwell and Magoon, 1962, 1963), and the University of Minnesota (Raygor, 1965). Other colleges soon adopted self-instructional programs.

The spread of open-admissions policies in the 1960s offered opportunities for disadvantaged minorities and underprepared students to attend college in large numbers. Even the most selective institutions accepted small groups of "special admit" students who did not meet the school's admission standards. Government funding enabled colleges to establish special minority tutoring, counseling, recruiting, and advising centers independent of other services. Traditional reading and study skills programs also served these students, though in smaller numbers. The growth of educational technology plus the admission of large numbers of underprepared students led to the development of learning centers, often a product of the merger between minority tutorial programs and existing reading and study skills services. In 1966 I described plans for a campuswide multidisciplinary learning center (Maxwell, 1966a), and others expanded on this self-help, multiskills model. Christ (1971) describes a "cybernetic, student-oriented" learning-assistance center with diagnostic testing, specific objectives, and self-paced materials and machine programs geared to each student's needs. Christ's model operates with a small staff and does not offer credit programs. Many learning centers, particularly in the West, have patterned their programs after Christ's model.

As a rule, learning centers in public universities provide diagnostic testing, individualized laboratory work, tutoring, and skills groups (usually noncredit minicourses). Two-year public colleges are more likely to offer credit for their programs.

Centralized learning centers, like their prececessors, reading and study skills programs, are usually founded by administrative fiat, by pressure from academic departments, or, more rarely, by pressure from students (Committee on Learning Skills Centers, 1976). Some evolved from programs in counseling centers where trained counselors found working with underprepared students' learning problems difficult and less satisfying than counseling clients with personal and/or vocational problems (Kirk, 1969).

Improvements in educational technology and the resistance of many college librarians toward integrating media and self-paced instructional materials into their regular collections were other factors precipitating the development of learning centers. Some centers combine many functions, serving underprepared students and regular students as well as providing media resources for faculty members. For example, DeAnza College (Cupertino, California) has a large learning-resources center that helps faculty members develop courses utilizing media as well as offering tutoring and skills help to students. Peterson (1975) postulates that through merging current learning theory with technology, classroom instruction can be improved.

Learning centers in large public universities continue to grow rapidly and offer a broad range of services. However, some centers remain large reading and study skills programs and restrict their services to these general skills, while others have expanded their services and hired specialists in writing, sciences, mathematics, and other subjects.

Organizing a Learning Center

The first step in organizing a learning center is that one or more faculty or staff members become interested and see the need for the service. They then must convince the administration of the value of implementing such a program. Many learning centers evolved casually—serendipity rather than careful planning characterizes their founding—usually "sponsored" by a single, dedicated faculty member. Today's emerging center is more likely to evolve as a result of the deliberations and recommendations of a task force set up by the administration and comprising faculty members, students, counselors, and administrators.

Administrative Location of a Center. Where should the learning center fit in the institution's organizational hierarchy? Existing centers vary in their location. Some are independent units, others are under academic departments or counseling centers.

Ideally, the learning center belongs under the administrator who can provide maximum support and nurturance for its roles and who will permit the director autonomy. The precise administrative structure in which these conditions are optimal varies from institution to institution, and historical precedence, power politics, and departmental feuds are important factors in choosing a structure. In large public universities, the present trend seems to be for learning centers to become separate units under the dean or vice-president of student personnel. This arrangement has advantages and disadvantages. The center director must compete with long-established units, such as the counseling center, career planning and placement, and student activities, for diminishing dollars and other resources. However, the learning center may have more autonomy than if it were located in a counseling center or within an academic department, where the learning center's needs would be lowest in the hierarchy.

University programs nested in counseling centers often perform a function for counseling psychologists analogous to the services rendered by teaching assistants who instruct freshman classes for graduate professors. That is, by teaching the large undergraduate courses, TAs enable professors to teach small graduate seminars in their specialties. Similarly, the learning center, with its typically large number of student contacts and its lower-paid staff, often enables the highly paid counselors to continue their traditional role of one-to-one counseling. The student contacts of the learning-center staff inflate the total use figures of the counseling center and are most helpful in justifying budgets. Some counseling-center directors provide a very comfortable, supportive environment for their learning centers, enabling them to develop large, strong programs and insulating them from bureaucratic problems and campus politics.

People in power, programs, and priorities change, and the present administrative organizations of learning centers as well as their functions will change, too. With declining enrollments in upper-division English, education, and humanities courses, there is increasing pressure for academic control of remedial programs in four-year colleges and for learning centers to be staffed by tenured faculty members.

Setting Objectives. The next step in organizing and developing a learning center is to determine its mission and specific objectives. Functions will depend on institutional needs and funding. Specific objectives should be based on needs-assessment surveys of students and faculty members. The program's objectives should be clear enough to evaluate and to change when students' needs or curricular revisions dictate. Information describing the specific objectives of the learning center should be widely disseminated to students, faculty members, and administrators. The objectives should be developed with input from the center's staff and accepted by all staff members.

What are typical goals for learning centers? Reed's (1974) survey of seventy-eight college peer-tutoring programs for the disadvantaged lists the following student service goals of the institutions responding in his sample. I believe that these goals are also applicable to learning centers.

1. To provide academic support for students who lack the educational background for college work. (This means underprepared students.)
2. To ensure student retention in college and subsequent graduation.
3. To help students develop their self-concepts as learners.
4. To help students develop self-confidence and reduce fear of failure.
5. To improve human relations and the sense of campus community among students.
6. To provide individualized help.
7. To provide help in developing study skills.
8. To improve academic performance. (This goal is "concerned with improving the academic performance of students who are performing at academically successful levels but who may be capable of doing better work"—Reed, 1974, p. 10.)

Some other examples of learning centers' goals are these:

1. "To assist students in becoming more independent, self-confident, and efficient learners so that they will be better able to meet the university's academic standards and attain their own educational goals" (Student Learning Center, University of California at Berkeley).
2. To provide a place where faculty members can refer students in academic difficulty who need help in reading, writing, and study skills improvement or diagnosis of their learning problems.
3. To "support each educational method of each instructor, meet the separate and individual learning and study needs of each student, and . . . provide cultural and educational opportunities to the community" (Learning Center Unlimited, Cuesta College, San Luis Obispo, California).

This last goal illustrates the wide scope of a center that combines tutoring, skills help, and a learning-resources center/library serving students, faculty members, and the community.

The objectives listed above are mainly addressed to the *student service* functions of the learning center, and some have the merit that they are quite easily measurable. However, one should be cautious in establishing objectives that are either too broad or too specific to be realistic. If the skills and knowledge of the population to be served are two or more years below those of the average student in the college, it is unrealistic to expect that the center's program will "save" most of these students. If, for example, 20 percent of the high-risk students survive to graduation (a typical rate), the program may be considered a failure by administrators and professors who expect more. The national rate of persistence to graduation among regularly admitted college students is around 50 percent, and in some institutions the rate is much lower. It is important to know the completion rate in your institution and have background data on the success of high-risk students so that you can put the results of your program in proper perspective. Hinging the success of a learning-center program on unrealistic student retention goals or improvement in grade-point averages places the responsibility for underprepared students' success on the support service, not on the academic departments, so that the center risks being used to preserve the instructional status quo. Faculty members will resist making needed changes in their courses and curriculums if the center is solely responsible for survival of academically weak students.

Another caution in using client retention in college as the criterion for judging the effectiveness of a learning center is that dropping out of college may reflect a realistic and positive decision. For example, if students decide that they are better suited for a trade or technical career and leave college to enter on-the-job training, their decisions may indicate personal growth and maturity. Some way of accounting for such changes in student occupational goals should be a part of the center's evaluation plan. (For instance, learning-skills counselors could rate the degree to which a student's educational goal is appropriate or realistic.) In addition, the objectives described so far are limited mainly to the *student* service functions of the center. Another important goal might be to improve the academic performance of tutors or student aides as well as that of the clients. Improving tutors' skills requires a more intensive training program and closer supervision if students selected as tutors are not highly skilled and well versed in their subjects.

To summarize, learning centers need to clearly specify what their student services are and how those services are related to academic programs and the faculty. These goals should not be so broad in scope that they are unattainable and unmeasurable; however, they should describe the center's responsibility in improving instruction. If a center is to effectively help underprepared and low-achieving students, it must avoid assuming complete responsibility for redeeming failing students.

The Center as a Catalyst for Change. I prefer to think of the academic support service as a catalyst for the improvement of undergraduate instruction in the institution as a whole. This means that the learning center assumes a preventive role and attempts to make the campus academic environment more conducive to student success, rather than limiting its functions to serving the victims of poor teaching, unrealistically difficult examinations, and unreasonable faculty expectations. It does not mean promoting lower academic standards or helping students find in curriculums the loopholes that will help them avoid learning. Serving a catalytic role requires that the center develop ways of working closely with instructors, *not* only to alert them to student difficulties and special needs but also to encourage different ways of teaching. This is a difficult and sensitive area, but a great many instructors are concerned about how well students master their courses and welcome feedback about those who are having difficulty, especially since these students rarely complain.

The tutorial/skills program is a barometer of the undergraduate climate, for when courses go awry, many students seek help. If data on student demand are systematically collected, they can be used to examine the causes of student problems and to explore ways to ameliorate them. In this way, students can be helped who do not volunteer for services. The center might be viewed as a large ameba, reaching out to serve students in a particular subject, identifying needs and strategies for helping them, turning over the information to instructors, and then pulling back (or being pulled) into another area.

Heard (1976, p. 6) states that if we carefully define and intelligently limit the learning center's roles, "there should come a time when we don't measure our effectiveness by the numbers who walk in our doors. Rather we should observe the numbers whose needs are served *comprehensively* in a concerted effort throughout all departments on campus."

Selecting the Director. To succeed, any academic support service needs the commitment of both administration and faculty to its goals. After defining the general goals of the program and the responsibilities of the director, the next crucial step in organizing a learning center is to select a strong director. The director should be knowledgeable about the social and political realities of academic communities, recognize the sources of power, be respected by faculty and students, and be sensitive to student needs. The director must also sell the program to the college community and have good business-management skills.

Directors of learning centers and tutorial programs come from many backgrounds (Committee on Learning Skills Centers, 1976; Heard, 1976; Smith and others, 1975). Reed (1974) offers a profile of tutoring-program directors that illustrates their diversity from his study of centers at eighteen colleges. Directors ranged in age from forty-one to fifty; eight were women and ten men; seven were white, seven black, and two Asian. Male directors were more likely than females to hold regular faculty appointments and were likely to have been employed by the college for fewer years. Thirty-nine percent of the directors had backgrounds in English; the others were trained in a wide range of academic disciplines, including sociology, psychology, business, music, physics, and mathematics. Reed (p. 33) characterizes the directors of "outstanding" programs as having directed the program for two years or longer and holding a joint administrative/faculty appointment.

I recommend *A Guide to Higher Education Learning Centers in the United States and Canada* (Sullivan, 1978), which lists the names and addresses of directors of 1,848 learning-center components, to anyone who wants to undertake a demographic analysis of current learning-center directors.

What attributes are essential in a director? The director plays many roles—teacher, counselor, researcher, writer, public relations specialist, consultant, trainer of staff members and para-professionals, professional educator. In centers in small colleges, the director may be expected to perform all these functions. In centers where there is a large staff, the director may hire specialists to assume some of these duties. Successful directors must also function as catalysts for change within their institutions, as critical consumers of the emerging research and development literature in the field of college learning, and as administrators. They are expected to be excellent teachers, to be competent lecturers to groups of faculty members and students, and to be able to relate to both small groups and individual students. As administrators, they need the knowledge and skills necessary to plan, develop, and implement programs, supervise the staff, establish procedures, and make decisions. In this era of accountability, they must be able to evaluate and justify programs and justify their expenditures. (Accounting skills are useful.) The ability to develop good public relations is necessary, for the director must keep an ever-changing study body and peripatetic faculty informed of the center's services.

In our publish-or-perish academic society, directors— particularly those in larger four-year colleges and universities— are expected to do research and publish within their specialties. They must also prepare annual reports and descriptions of their programs for budget committees and the college administration, design and develop new programs to meet student and faculty needs, and obtain grants from outside funding sources.

Training staff members and paraprofessionals is a vital function, because few applicants for learning-specialist positions have either experience or formal training—and as budgets tighten, staffing must depend on paraprofessionals. Directors also serve as consultants and on campus committees, advising other faculty members within the institution as well as community and public school groups and other professional educators' associations.

Learning-center directors also need to be able to hold their own with other faculty members. Some directors maintain their identification with their own academic discipline—psychology, English, or whatever—as well as with reading, study skills, and educational professional associations.

Directors can function as catalysts for change within their institutions through serving on committees and working directly with faculty members in academic departments. In a sense, directors function as student advocates, and if they can contribute knowledge about student problems that are generated by rigid academic procedures, inappropriate instructional strategies, and unrealistic grading practices, they can help make the academic environment more responsive to student needs and prevent their own programs from being overloaded with students.

As a critical consumer of research and development in the fields relevant to learning and basic skills, the learning-center director must keep abreast of current publications and other sources of information. He should be wary of the misleading advertising claims of some publishers and commercial companies that promise quick and easy solutions to student problems. For example, there are a number of high-priced rapid-reading programs designed for business and professional people that are inappropriate in content and method for college students, yet the salespeople insist these programs are suitable for the college market.

Directors need a broad background in reading and study skills at all grade levels—the theories, philosophies, controversies, methods, materials, and research. They also need to understand the principles of individual diagnosis and treatment, testing, methods, and evaluation techniques. Knowledge of counseling theories and techniques is also important, as are the ability to, and interest in, continuing to learn and improve.

Directors must develop a thorough understanding of the academic procedures, customs, and rituals of their institutions in order to help students and train staff members. They need to understand faculty demands and expectations in different academic departments and be aware of instructional goals, teaching strategies, grading practices, and academic requirements. Directors must also know about the requirements and demands of professional and graduate schools, if they are working in four-year colleges where many students seek help in preparing for advanced work and in preparing for the admissions tests. In other words, directors must know how the system works and be alert to changes, particularly those that will affect the center. Ideally, directors of learning centers should participate in committees planning major changes in policies that affect undergraduates—changes in admission policies, degree requirements, departmental prerequisites for majors, and so on. But in reality, these decisions are usually made without input from the learning-center director, who is faced with revising his programs after the decisions are made. Directors also must know the other resources on campus for students so that they can refer students to appropriate units for help and develop cooperative rather than competitive programs.

In addition to being intelligent, creative, and nice, what other attributes are necessary for the successful learning-center director? Directors, particularly those running small programs, who work directly with students' problems should be able to relate well with students with diverse backgrounds—slow learners as well as fast learners, students with different learning styles and those from different socioeconomic backgrounds, members of ethnic minorities, foreign students, physically handicapped students, athletes, and many others. Directors must also be able to relate well to other administrators.

Directors should have broad intellectual interests. To develop strong programs in different disciplines, they need an understanding of the assumptions underlying different fields of knowledge and how knowledge is organized in different fields. Obviously one cannot be an expert in every field, but one should know how reading and study techniques can be applied to different subjects.

Perhaps the most important attribute the director of a small program needs is the ability to provide emotional support and encouragement to a student who has not learned how to learn but is now motivated to try. Directors of large programs must help their staff develop sensitivity and rapport with students, and it is the director who must provide the support for staff members and a favorable climate in which they can grow.

Flexibility and responsiveness to change, personal integrity, a high regard for intellectual goals and the individual, and a strong feeling of personal worth are other personal attributes that should be considered in selecting a director.

In summary, the center director serves many roles and needs much in the way of skills, knowledge, and personal attributes. Some of these skills can be learned, and knowledge can be acquired, but the personal attributes discussed may not be teachable. Those who select the director must, therefore, screen candidates for these characteristics. Since few of us can walk on water, it is highly unlikely that one individual will possess all the characteristics described, but they do represent areas that should be considered. Ideally, the director can then select specialists and other staff members to complement his abilities and fill in the gaps of his weaker areas.

Even if one were to possess all the abilities and skills described, it would help to have tenure in an academic department. With the vicissitudes of the current collegial *Zeitgeist*, one should not expect to grow old and retire as a learning-center director.

Staffing. Most learning centers have few full-time professional staff members. On the average, they employ a director and one or two learning specialists and rely on student help. In community college programs where remedial courses are given for credit, the usual pattern is to have several paid instructors and a learning laboratory staffed by paraprofessionals or work-study students. Often the courses are taught by part-time paraprofessionals as well.

College learning specialists, unlike college counselors and other college personnel workers, rarely have formal training or graduate study directly related to their positions. Coming from many backgrounds, including counseling, education, English, and psychology, they develop their skills in working with college students on the job. Few graduate programs in the country offer master's degrees in college reading and study skills. Until recently there has been only one, that offered by Dr. Alton Raygor at the

University of Minnesota (Raygor and Vavoulis, 1973; Vavoulis and Raygor, 1973). Since 1971, however, a number of universities have begun offering master's-level programs for community college reading and writing specialists, including Appalachian State University and the University of Florida, Gainesville. To be sure, there are many opportunities for direct experience with college students. Graduate students are usually offered teaching assistantships or internships in learning centers as part of their experience, and other schools offer credit practicum courses (Maxwell, 1966a) that train graduate students to work with students with difficulties. Generally, applicants with a degree in reading curriculum, counseling, or English seek jobs that offer experience in establishing and managing reading and study skills programs or other support services. They learn by doing. Professional associations provide institutes, special programs, and other in-service training, and local consortia of learning-center programs are forming all over the country to exchange information—for example, the New England Association of Academic Support Personnel, the Western North Carolina Consortium for Developmental Education, and the Regional Association of East Bay Colleges and Universities Basic Skills Committee, (northern California) to name just a few.

Universities have often been criticized for neglecting training in remedial teaching for their students who are planning to be college instructors (Bossone and Weiner, 1975; Schnell, 1974); yet the teachers themselves report that on-the-job experiences are more beneficial than their previous university courses. Learning specialists in mathematics and science tend to have degrees in these subjects but little training in remedial techniques or diagnosis; they are motivated to work with student problems and develop skills on the job. I have found that it is easier and faster to train a chemistry major to be a learning specialist in chemistry than to train a counselor to work with students with problems in chemistry.

Because of the wide range of duties and responsibilities of learning specialists and the newness of the field, few institutions have adopted guidelines for these positions. In June 1975, however, directors of learning centers and coordinators of tutoring programs from the nine campuses of the University of California met at Santa Barbara to address the problem of personnel classifications. The purpose of the conference was to develop guidelines and specifications for a job series that would clarify the roles and functions of learning specialists. Since many of the learning centers had emerged from or were still part of counseling centers, job titles and salaries varied widely from campus to campus. Most positions were classified as beginning counselors with a low and very restricted salary range. On other campuses, writing and mathematics specialists were classified as counseling psychologists, while others were titled program representatives or assistant or associate deans of students or bore other titles unrelated to their duties.

The conference generated job descriptions making up a new classification system, which was approved by the University of California statewide personnel office a year later as the set of job descriptions reproduced in Appendix B. These descriptions may be useful as a model for other state college systems or for individual institutions that wish to develop a professional job series for learning-center staffs.

A clerical staff is needed, too. Surveys suggest that learning centers have very few clerical positions unless they are federally funded. Large programs usually have an administrative assistant, a secretary-receptionist, and several clerical student aides. Some smaller programs have just one clerical worker, who functions as typist, receptionist, monitor of the self-help program, and recordkeeper. Others have only work-study student clerks and rely on other departments for typing reports or special work. The role of the secretary/receptionist is vital. In a personal communication, Sam Silas of William Paterson College (Wayne, New Jersey) says: "Whether the secretary/receptionist is a regular eight-hour-a-day staff member or a work-study worker, careful attention should go to this person's selection. It is normally the nature of the secretary/receptionist's job description that makes her/him the most visible person in the program. Hence, through the secretary/receptionist, the question of the program's public image becomes a critical issue. With the right person in this position, many glaring weaknesses can be skillfully covered up. With a slightly inept person in the secretary's chair, the possibility of negative misrepresentation forever hovers over the program. In brief, the secretaries of learning centers need to be sharp of mind and knowledgeable of office procedure and philosophy. Also, the secretary needs to be inordinately committed to the program's success and have a great deal of empathy for students."

Staffing costs vary according to the services provided and funds allocated. Some models follow:

Table 1. Personnel for a Satellite Learning Center

Title	Full-Time Equivalent	Total Salaries
Manager/Librarian	1	$ 12,000
Assistant Manager	1	10,000
Clerk-Typist	2	14,400
Senior Electronics Technician	1	11,000
Custodian/Groundskeeper	0.50	4,500
Counselor	4	48,000
Tutor/Facilitator	8	72,000
	Total	$171,900

Note: These are 1972 salaries and do not include fringe benefits.
Source: Karwin, 1973.

This staffing would enable 500 students to use the center between four and twelve hours weekly for use of learning stations and additional hours for counseling and tutoring.

Reed (1974) proposed the following budget for a peer-tutoring program to serve 200 students:

Table 2. Personnel for a Peer-Tutoring Program

Title	Full-Time Equivalent	Total Costs
Program Director	1	$15,000
Peer Tutors: 16 at $3/hour 8 hours/week for 36 weeks		13,824
Clerical Staff (secretary/receptionist)	1	8,000
Program Evaluation		1,600
Equipment and Supplies		4,000
Miscellaneous		942
	Total	$43,366

Source: Reed, 1974.

Computing projected costs for tutoring is the most difficult aspect of budget planning. Since tutors are often dependent on student demand for help in their particular specialties, it is hard to predict the number of hours needed. Surveys suggest that peer tutors were paid an average of $2.50 and hour in 1975. Most programs pay graduate tutors and tutors who conduct groups more ($4–$5 an hour) than they pay those who tutor individuals. Some strategies to reduce tutoring costs, are to give tutors credit instead of pay and to recruit volunteer tutors from the campus or local community.

Certainly the number of staff members budgeted affects the number of individual student conferences the center can provide and the nature of the program. Some learning centers serve all students on a first-come, first-served basis, and when hours are filled, students must wait untit the next term. Others provide free tutoring to special groups—athletes, EOP students, or students on financial aid, for example—but require other students to pay. Most study skills programs, particularly noncredit group programs, are open to any student without charge. Many private colleges charge extra tuition to students taking reading and study skills or remedial courses. Some centers charge a nominal fee to motivate students; for example, the Writing Clinic at the University of Southern California charges one dollar per visit. However, whether charging students additional fees is desirable is still a debatable question.

Learning centers often earn extra funds by providing services to faculty members and nonstudents for a fee.

Attracting Students and Developing a Positive Image. A learning center's success depends on its image to students. A program can be carefully developed, staffed with excellent people, yet remain unknown and unused by students. One good indicator that a program is succeeding is when students refer their friends; however, in starting a new program or in informing an ever-changing pool of students, the services must be publicized. Academic advisers in small private colleges (for example, McCallister, Wellesley, Simmons) write personal letters to new students describing the special academic services offered and counsel students into programs. Similarly, the counselors in most special programs for disadvantaged students or other target groups in larger institutions contact students individually by form letters and arrange conferences. In

large public universities with many student services and complicated registration procedures, however, new students receive so
many pieces of mail from the school that they ignore them. Many
student services departments now produce student handbooks listing and describing all the services on campus (a way of reducing
printing and mailing costs as well as coordinating services).

There are many ways to inform students about the program—movies, tape-and-slide presentations, or talks at freshman
orientation, brochures, bookmarks, articles and ads in the student
newspaper, television "commercials" (between closed-circuit-
television classes), speeches to classes and student groups. To ensure that students will use a program voluntarily, it seems that they
must learn about it from several sources. They may hear about the
learning center in freshman orientation, but often they are too
busy reacting to other students and the strangeness of the new
experience they are in to recall services discussed in orientation. Of
course, some students who fear that they are unprepared for college courses will sign up for programs immediately, but most need
more than one exposure to the fact that the program exists to recall
it. I find that many students hear about the center in orientation,
see newspaper ads about minicourses, hear about it from their
friends, and then see a small notice on a bulletin board that triggers
their coming in for assistance. Others have heard about the program many times but do not come unless referred by a faculty
member. In other words, students need to be reminded a number
of times, and when they feel the need for the service, they will
come. There may be a long incubation period between sending out
publicity and seeing students arrive at the doorstep. I recall Henry,
who carried an ad about our program in his wallet for two years
before coming in; and more recently, a group of students came in
with a brochure that was six years old asking about the old reading
laboratory.

Our center has brochures and bookmarks placed in the library and the checkout stands at the student bookstore and, of
course, announcements in the campus catalogue and student
handbooks advertising group programs, tutoring for credit, and
special services. We find that purchasing ads in the student news-

paper is the quickest and best way to attract students. We also send announcements to academic departments and other student services to post on their bulletin boards.

The effectiveness of our ads varies with the topic of the minicourse and the time of year. For example, an ad starting "Wanted: Slow Readers . . . to help us test and evaluate a new self-help program in speed reading . . ." drew 150 students in the winter quarter but only 5 in the spring quarter. "Can you tune out the trivial and zero in on the important ideas in listening to lectures . . ." (an ad for the Xerox Listening Program), attracted fewer than 5 students each time it was placed. Speed-reading courses inevitably fill if they are scheduled at convenient hours, although during the first few years of our program, the groups tended to be fairly small. Currently, with a dynamic instructor, this program attracts more than 1,000 students a year. Study skills programs offered on a voluntary basis tend to attract fewer students than speed-reading programs. We offered a minicourse titled "Academic Survival Skills: Coping with Berkeley's Course Demands" scheduled early in the fall, but few students signed up. Students apparently do not want to "survive"; they want to succeed. We changed the title to "The Academic Game: How to Play and Win" (from Hanau's 1972 book of a similar title), and about 20 showed up, but most dropped out by the third session. Undaunted, we scheduled informal one-hour sessions on particular skills; depending on the topics and when they were scheduled, they worked well. But watch the timing; do not schedule sessions on reducing test anxiety at the *beginning* of the fall term.

Usually it takes a few terms for a minicourse to "catch on." Two that I wish had been continued were "Improving Your Reading Skills—For Honor Students and Those Who Aspire to Be" and "How to Like Reading, an open-ended group dedicated to the proposition that reading can be fun, interesting, worthwhile, meaningful and that it need not be a bore or just a task." Only three students signed up for the latter course, and although they were enthusiastic about it, we did not offer it again.

In a recent talk, Patricia Heard suggests that the *least* popular programs (though they may be the most needed by students) be listed *first* in the center's publicity—such as groups in improving communication skills or improving reading comprehension. Students are usually highly motivated to take speed reading or attend review sessions for the Medical College Admissions Test and will spot these offerings even if they have to turn the page or search a long list.

Some publicity strategies that learning-center staff members have developed to attract students are very creative. For example, Brenda Wright at the University of Missouri Pharmacy School printed up colorful bookmarks in the form of prescriptions—Rx for academic success, listing the skills needed for textbook reading, test taking, notetaking, studying, and so on—and checked the box labeled "refill," typed each entering pharmacy student's name on top of a bookmark, and laminated them in plastic. Library displays also can be planned to illustrate services dramatically. I recall one we did years ago that featured an open book with a spider's web and a large rubber spider to illustrate the need for speed reading. Announcements on the campus radio station, recorded or call-in programs, such as dial-a-study-tip, center hotlines, and just about everything else, with the possible exception of sky writing, have been used to inform students of services.

Occasionally, new center directors find that they have been hired to manage a program that has a negative image among students, administrators, and the faculty. Perhaps the previous director alienated a group of faculty members, or perhaps students found the programs rigid, boring, or simplistic. The first things I would do in this case would be to change the name of the center, develop and advertise new programs, and set about building bridges with the faculty and student clientele.

What's in a Name? Choosing a name for your learning center is an important step in establishing an image. Students inevitably use acronyms, so be alert. *Academic Support Service* may sound like a reasonable title, but do you really want your center to be known as ASS and your staff members called "asses"? Even the popular term *Learning Assistance Center* has its drawbacks. McHargue (1975) reports that the Stanford program became known as "lack" and the staff members were dubbed "lackeys." The University of Texas

Reading Improvement Program (RIP), called by some "rest in peace," was changed to RASSL (pronounced "wrassle"). Although the service is no longer limited to reading and study skills laboratory, Patricia Heard, the director, refuses to change the name, because 90 percent of the 40,000 students at the University of Texas at Austin known about RASSL.

Titles for learning centers vary from *Academic Advancement Center* to simply *The Bridge*. If you feel the need for a new name for your program, I suggest that you sponsor a contest for naming the center and give a prize to the student who creates the best title. Not only will you get some clever entries, but this is an excellent way to publicize a new program.

Budget. Learning-center funds come from many sources—departmental instructional budgets, student registration or activity fees, chancellor's discretionary funds, affirmative action monies, profits from vending machines on campus, direct charges to student users. Many centers are funded from several of these sources, and often federal, state, or foundation grants make possible special services to underprepared or other target groups of students. Extramural funding, such as athletic funds or grants for veterans or the handicapped, may determine which students receive help. Some centers have no budget at all, and their staff and resource monies are contributed by different departments. For instance, one staff member may be paid by the counseling center and another from Department of English funds.

Budget size limits the number of staff members who can be hired, although in many colleges FTE (full-time equivalent) positions are harder to get than funds. Directors then must hire part-time or temporary staff members and live with high staff turnover. The best arrangement is to invest in a small permanent career staff (including both learning specialists and tutor supervisors) and hire part-time experienced tutors and/or paraprofessionals and train them to train others. Since so few experienced, trained professionals are available for recruitment, most centers train their own staff. Undergraduate tutors for credit and volunteers, if trained and supervised, can enable the service to reach more students at minimum cost. We have found that a half-time tutor or study skills supervisor can train and supervise ten new, inexperienced student tutors. Currently, programs are forced by budget cuts and inflation to reduce their full-time staffs and place career employees, including clerical workers, on nine- or ten-month contracts, making it harder to develop programs and to retain qualified staff members. Others are funded on "soft money," so that staff contracts are negotiated on a year-by-year basis, with continued employment contingent on the renewal of the grant. Surveys show that both learning-center directors (Committee on Learning Skills Centers, 1976) and directors of tutorial services (Reed, 1974) report they need more money for their programs, but in interviewing directors, Reed found that none had requested additional funds or was planning to do so. This same combination of complaint about lack of funding and reluctance to request additional funds for staffing characterizes remedial mathematics programs in academic departments (Moskowitz, 1976) and, perhaps, academic programs in general.

In an era of tightening budgets, directors must often fight to hold onto existing funds and positions, which are constantly jeopardized by inflation and steady-state budgets. Learning centers, particularly in private schools, are among the most vulnerable units for budget cuts, layoffs, and elimination. Even in large public institutions, where the need for learning centers is great, center directors are currently being pressured to obtain grants in order to keep their programs viable.

Besides salaries, discussed above under "Staffing," what must the budget include? Supplies and office expenses (including equipment maintenance) are essential items. Generally, these expenses make up 5 to 10 percent of the center's total budget, depending on the size and type of programs offered. In addition to supplies such as paper and office expenses such as telephone and mailing, the learning-center director should budget for replacement of instructional materials, tapes, and films. In centers with a large number of electronic aids, pieces of audiovisual equipment, or computer terminals, maintenance and rental costs may dictate that a larger percentage of the budget be spent on this item. Programs that serve large numbers of students find that advertising and handouts to students and other expendable materials—can be costly but important.

I have observed that when new centers are formed from existing departments, the hardest funds to transfer are the supplies and equipment expenses, for they are often buried within the larger budget. For instance, while positions and the salaries attached are usually clearly spelled out on budgets, phone expenses, duplicating costs, equipment, and furniture are averaged per employee. In the case of a learning center that is formed from some of the staff of a counseling center, the learning center staff needs may be greater than those of the average counselor for duplicating, materials, and phones.

Equipment is usually the costliest item in starting a new center. Tape recorders, audiovisual aids, reading machines, tachistoscopes, autotutorial machines, and computer terminals not only are very expensive but must be selected with care so flexible programs can be developed and maximal use obtained. Different filmstrip machines use different kinds of film, and even different tape-recording devices may require different tapes. Machines wear out and educational equipment becomes obsolete quickly. For example, at a recent institute I coordinated, one of the speakers wanted to show a videotape on tutor training. He had a three-quarter-inch color tape cassette, and I was unable to locate anywhere on campus a monitor that would play it. Our media system is geared to half-inch and one-inch black-and-white equipment.

It is well to select equipment which has the software you need for your student clientele and which can also be used for other purposes, such as developing your own materials (if you have the staff time and talent). In other words, unless you have a department that can print materials on Mylar film, it is better to buy reading machines that use standard 35-mm camera film, which you can use to make your own materials.

Karwin (1973) estimates that $53,000 will equip a center with forty-five study carrels wired for electronic equipment, twenty videocassette players, twenty color television receivers, five computer terminals, fifteen calculators, twelve electric typewriters, twenty microfiche viewers, fifty audiocassettes with headsets, and one cassette duplicator. Costs have risen on many of these items since 1973. The operational cost of an interactive computer system may be more than $500,000 per year. However, if your college has such a system, it is fairly easy to get a few terminals in the learning center. After the equipment is purchased, costs can be amortized over a five-year period, but with the rapid obsolescence of modern electronic equipment, it would be wise to compute rental costs on an annual basis and compare them with purchase costs before making a decision. I have visited many elaborately equipped learning laboratories where the costly machines are *never* used by students. Once the novelty wears off, the machines wait unused and quietly rusting.

Budgets should also include money for miscellaneous expenses, including travel costs (both for bringing in prospective employees for interviews and for sending staff members to professional conferences) and staff-training costs. Some educators recommend that 20 percent of the total budget should be allocated for evaluating the services, but learning centers rarely attain that goal unless funded by special grants under which evaluation costs have been allocated in advance.

In preparing the center's asking budget, it is important to remember that asking budgets are created to be cut. Each administrator who reviews the budget may, depending on his conception of his role, slice items before it reaches final approval. (For many years I headed a service where my supervisor inevitably red-penciled budget items. I requested a Reading Eye Camera, an expensive piece of equipment, each year for eight years, and since it was always at the bottom of the list of items arranged in order of priority and was expensive, he always red-penciled it. Thus, I was able to preserve staff positions and necessary materials and equipment.)

I like the model of the asking-budget process that some business executives advocate. They suggest thinking of the asking budget as a wheel with spokes and a hub. The hub represents the basic money you need to keep essential services operating. The spokes represent additional personnel or items that you would like and can prepare adequate justifications for. Ask for the wheel. You usually will not get the whole wheel, but you may get some of the spokes. If you request only the hub (the barebones budget), you are likely to have essential funds cut, with the result that you must either reduce your programs or overwork your staff.

When a center's budget for equipment and supplies is too small, the director usually writes a grant proposal for money to equip the center or modernize its materials and media. It inevitably takes months to receive the funds, if the grant is approved at all. In the meantime, if you are offering services to students and need materials, there are local sources—faculty, student associations, research projects, community groups, alumni associations. Frank Christ at California State University at Long Beach sent letters to faculty members requesting donations of textbooks, self-paced programs, audiovisual equipment and other learning aids and collected a great deal of equipment and materials. You may get some useful items, and you can realize a few dollars from the junk by selling it at the flea market or a garage sale.

Many years ago it was possible to buy sets of used texts (older editions of those currently required) for five cents a copy. This was an inexpensive way to acquire realistic material for class instruction in study skills. Prices of books, even used books, have risen tremendously since then, but it is still possible to find bargains. For example, our center was given a library of some 300 calculus textbooks by the mathematics department because the department lacked storage space. The books were reviewed by our mathematics staff and catalogued. A math specialist wrote brief comments on the textbooks he rated as most valuable such as:

"*Calculus* by X___: Covers concepts taught in our courses 1AB and 16AB. Nonrigorous, generally good reading. The author's explanations are often poor, but the book is full of comments inserted by the author's students, and these are quite illuminating. There is also a lot of excellent historical material. The examples and problems are very good and each chapter ends with six sample exams, four of which are one-hour length and two of which are longer.

Calculus by K___: Covers concepts in our 16AB. Nonrigorous and very good reading. This book comes closest to reading like a novel of any calculus text I know, but long-windedness is its major fault. It has little historical material, but the author tries to make sure that the real-world need for each technique is apparent before it is introduced. This is the antithesis of the approach used in the current required texts where theoretical sections are followed by applications sections. There are two good summaries in the appendix which would be useful as reviews, not as introductions, to analytic geometry and trigonometry."

These reviews were useful for students who cannot understand their present text or just want to learn math from a different perspective.

We also rented a $4,000 cathode-ray-tube computer terminal from the local stock exchange for $1 a month during a lull in the stock market and obtained several teletype computer terminals free from professors who had completed their research projects or had bought newer models. An incentive for professors to donate dollars, books, or equipment is the tax write-off benefit. If you estimate the fair market value of a donation of materials or equipment and write a "thank you" letter specifying the dollar value of the gift, the donor may use the letter to document the contribution for tax purposes. (Check with local Internal Revenue Service office for details). Occasionally, professors have turned over the royalties from their books to our program. These modest amounts help pay tutoring costs. Some centers have established programs for regular faculty donations through payroll deductions. The alumni branch of the women's honor society often donates funds for the purchase of special pieces of equipment, and a number of smaller foundations have been generous in providing funds to start innovative programs. And we have been able to purchase larger equipment, such as a computer multiplexer board and a videotape machine, through our regular budget channels by sharing the equipment and costs with other departments.

Space. Space and staff positions are the two territories over which academic power battles rage. It is the rare learning center that does not soon outgrow its allotted space—even when new buildings are designed especially for it. As staff and programs— especially tutoring—expand, the center is forced to schedule study skills groups in some far corner of the campus or to turn tutors loose to find empty classrooms, a corner of the library, or unused areas of the campus dining hall to meet their student clients. Part-time staff members are difficult to monitor when they are physically removed from the center's main facilities. As group programs draw more students, it requires the expertise of an experienced diplomat to find classrooms for minicourses or graduate-exam review sessions.

Learning-center directors sometimes find themselves involved in a continuous struggle to expand or hold onto their territory. They need some knowledge of architecture and facilities planning. Ideally the learning center should be located in an attractive building in the center of the campus. Occasionally this materializes, but on older campuses, centers tend to be housed in available space—for example, in "temporary" buildings on the wrong side of the tracks or in a corner basement office. When George Spache was director of the University of Florida's Reading and Study Skills Laboratory, he complained that students had to walk through his office to get to the reading laboratory. Winifred Cooke at Southeastern Community College (Whiteville, North Carolina) describes the offices of her staff as located on a balcony high above and overlooking the basketball court in the college gym. The RASSL program at the University of Texas, Austin, has no enclosed space for tutors, and so they sit with their tutees at tables in the corridor, under the skylight and next to the railing lining the atrium on the fourth floor of Jester Hall.

The facilities in which a program is located ostensibly reflect the institution's commitment to the program. However, since older campuses have had few funds for capital improvements for a number of years, newly emerging centers compete with expanding academic departments for space, and they are low on the priority list. Given the choice, I would select the facilities that are most conveniently located for students over a fancy suite of offices on the fifth floor of an office building on the periphery of the campus. In fact, we fought to retain our old World War II temporary building, rather than being moved to an upper floor of the student union building, by taking a traffic check of the number of students using our programs at noon and arguing that the move not only would restrict the number of students using our programs but would irritate other workers by tying up the two elevators during lunch hour, one of our peak demand times.

While fighting for additional space, one should also develop alternative plans for maximizing the utilization of existing space. I suspect that learning-center directors are already famous for the number of walls they have knocked down—I know I have ordered many walls removed to make room for learning labs, drop-in centers, and group programs. I learned long ago that it is better not to partition off space into small offices or carrels, for needs change. Movable furniture and dividers or screens are more practical and enable multipurpose use of space. If carpeting, drapes, and other sound-reducing materials are installed, the room can hold a number of staff members and students working individually or in small groups without the noise that seeps through plywood partitions. Although noise can never be totally eliminated, it is possible to reduce distracting noise by drop-in arrangements; the many conversations serve as white noise, masking individual voices.

There are few activities that cannot be handled well in an open room, properly furnished and arranged. Even individual counseling on personal problems can be offered this way if student and counselor are in a movable cubicle so visual distractions are minimized. Foreign-language tutors can tutor in a drop-in center as well as math and science tutors. If you offer tutoring in speech, drama, or voice, however, a soundproofed room is necessary, not only for the speech clients but also for the protection of the eardrums of the rest of the staff. Similarly, typing rooms need to be soundproofed and shut off from other activities.

Some students find any noise distracting. The best solution I have found is to buy headsets like those worn by workers in jet airports for students to wear while working. Giving tests and exercises by tape recorder with a headset focuses the student's attention on the material and minimizes distraction from external sounds.

The building plans of new colleges usually include learning-center facilities, either as separate units or, more typically, as part of the library or academic departments. For example, the National Training Institute for the Deaf at Rochester Institute of Technology has a learning-resource center in each department, and Los Medanos College in Pittsburg, California, a one-building school, has learning centers on each floor.

Karwin (1973) describes an idealized building for a community satellite learning center, with estimated building costs and space needed for different functions. For example, he recommends twenty-five square feet per person for individual study areas, twenty per person for seminar rooms, forty per room for tutorial rooms (with space for five persons), and sixty per room for counseling offices. (It is interesting that we allow more space for a student talking about himself to a counselor in a one-to-one situation than for students working closely together on a math problem. Perhaps the need for personal space is related to the perceived intimacy of the subject discussed.) In Karwin's blueprint, a space of 2,500 square feet accommodates 100 students who are studying independently.

One way of using existing space more efficiently is to extend hours to evenings and weekends and adjust staff schedules accordingly. One space that often appears underused in voluntary learning centers is the individualized learning laboratory, where students work on self-help materials. Community college programs seem to have little trouble filling their laboratory stations to capacity when credit is given for modules completed or assignments require students to complete modules as part of their regular course work. However, the laboratories in university programs are seldom filled to capacity when students use them voluntarily and without course credit. Use of laboratory facilities varies with time of year. Depending on the materials and programs available, the laboratory may be crowded when students are preparing for graduate or professional exams or for competency-based tests required for some course—or just before exams, when they use the laboratory as a place of study. Use of laboratory facilities also seems to depend on the people who staff the laboratory. If it is staffed with friendly, supportive people who can help students see the relation between the modules and their course work, more students will use it.

Since remodeling and redecorating costs at most institutions are exorbitant and steadily rising, it is important that directors plan ahead for future needs. Even routine repainting costs are high. Some centers brighten their walls with graphics or murals painted by students, rent or borrow paintings from the art department, and get leftover furniture from other units or the campus storehouse.

Furnishing a center is both costly and difficult unless special funds are available—that is, funds in addition to those allocated in your regular budget. The rule-of-thumb figure for furnishing a new center is 6 percent of the total cost of the building (Karwin, 1973, p. 17).

Operating Procedures and Recordkeeping. Once funds and space are allocated, the director's next step is to establish procedures for the operation of the program and for compiling and maintaining student use records. One of the most complex aspects of a tutorial program is the logistics of getting students and part-time tutors together so that scheduling procedures are clear and consistent. One might have a message center where the receptionist places student schedules in the tutors' boxes; each tutor is then responsible for calling the tutee and arranging a session. (If you use this system, be sure to ask the prospective tutee what hours are best to phone him. Otherwise, it may take a long time for the two to get together.) Another arrangement is for the tutee to call the tutor; or tutor and tutee may exchange phone numbers.

Tutors should be scheduled for some regular hours each week so tutees may sign up for appointments on the tutor's schedule. If you have a drop-in service, the tutor can work with other students if the scheduled client fails to keep the appointment. However, missed appointments are very discouraging to tutors, and most tutoring programs strictly limit the number of times a tutee can miss an appointment and still continue to get help. We encourage tutors to call the student who missed as soon as possible and find out the reason for the absence. Tutors determine whether students who miss appointments should be dropped from the program. When there is a large student demand for a service, it may be too costly to try to punish tutees who do not keep their appointments. If the service is small and students negotiate tutoring contracts, then careful checks can be made. Generally, there are fewer "no shows" in appointments with learning-skills specialists than with tutors, but even this varies with the season of the year and type of service.

Accurate records of student users' characteristics and student contacts are essential for budgetary justification and evaluation studies. Records should be as simple and short as possible and should be monitored regularly. The day has passed when tutoring programs saw their recordkeeping function as generating mountains of paper, lengthy written reports weekly on each tutee, which were unread and unnecessary. Complex data-collection systems and lengthy forms create resistance from both staff and students.

Minimal records should include a way of registering each student who uses the service and should include relevant demographic data and the subject and skill for which the student is seeking help. For example, we use a three-by-five card (reproduced in Figure 3) on which the student records his name, address, phone, campus registration number, sex, class, college, major, and ethnic background (optional) and the subject in which help is sought. The student also checks spaces for intercollegiate athletes or EOP status, if appropriate; these are our priority groups. The receptionist assigns the student a special learning-center identification number and gives him a small card that entitles him to use any of the center services for a year. For each course or skill in which the student is seeking help, he also fills out a short questionnaire on a half sheet of paper (Figure 4), which is given to the tutor or skills specialist. Information from the three-by-five card is entered into our computer system. By matching the student's identification

Figure 3. General Record Card Kept by Receptionist

SLC ID No. _____

Reg. No. _____   Date _____

NAME _____
            Last   First   Middle

ADDRESS _____
            Street   City   Zip

PHONE _____ _____ EOP _____ NON-EOP _____
        Area Code   Number

Athlete _____ Ethnic Background _____

Male _____ Female _____ Department _____ Major _____

CLASS: Fr. Soph. Jr. Sr. Grad. Other _____

Assigned to   Subject   Date

Figure 4. SLC Student Information Card

SLC ID# _____ Date _____

NAME _____
       (Last)   (First)   (Middle)

ADDRESS _____ PHONE _____
       (No./Street)   (City)   (Zip)

CIRCLE IF APPLICABLE: EOP Athlete Black Latino/Chicano Native American Filipino

CLASS (Circle): Freshman Sophomore Junior Senior Other MALE FEMALE

HOW DID YOU HEAR ABOUT THE CENTER? Faculty Referral ___ TA ___ Counselor ___ Adviser ___

Friends ___ Daily Cal ___ Bulletin Board ___ Other ___

COURSE _____ INSTRUCTOR _____ # UNITS CARRIED THIS QTR. _____

CHECK SERVICES YOU ARE INTERESTED IN USING:

___ Writing Reports/Papers
  ___ grammar
  ___ organization
  ___ spelling

* ___ Reading
  ___ speed
  ___ vocabulary
  ___ comprehension

___ Science
  ___ problem solving in science & math
  ___ Drop-in tutoring in _____
  ___ Chem Resource Center
  ___ Chem Cluster groups

* ___ Study Efficiency
  ___ time management/procrastination
  ___ exam skills
  ___ test anxiety
  ___ lecture note-taking

___ Math/Statistics/Computer Science
  ___ Drop-in tutoring in _____
  ___ study group programs
  ___ workshops & minicourses
  ___ other

___ Preparation for the GRE/LSAT/MCAT/Other _____

*Groups, individual appointments, handouts, and self-help materials are available through the Library/Lab. See Lab receptionist.

number with this information each time he sees a tutor or skills specialist or attends a group, the computer is able to generate a printout of the number and type of contacts a student has had during the year.

Keeping accurate records of student visits is also essential for payroll, budget, and accountability studies. We require staff members to fill out a weekly contact sheet (Figure 5) on which they record the student's name and identification number for each individual appointment and the time they spend in other activities (drop-in, outreach, preparation, training, and so forth). They also attach student sign-in sheets from group sessions. In the drop-in program, students keep their own attendance records on sign-in sheets. These sign-in sheets and the tutor contact sheets are computerized so that the demand for help in different subjects and the tutor and staff workload can be readily retrieved. (See also Christ, 1977, and Devirian, 1973, for suggestions on recordkeeping.)

Some programs adopt stricter procedures and require that tutees request tutoring help two weeks in advance. Others require tests before tutees are tutored. Others require that tutees be interviewed. About 75 percent of tutoring programs have no entrance requirements for tutees except their willingness to sign up (Reed, 1974). Similarly, students seeking help in study skills, reading, and so forth may be required to fill in lengthy questionnaires and complete test batteries or may use drop-in services with less paperwork.

Periodically supervisors prepare evaluations of staff members, including tutors (Figure 6). Supervisors base their evaluations on observations of the staff members' work with students, their reliability in recordkeeping and in keeping appointments, and their evaluations by students (Figures 7 and 8). The supervisor prepares a written report on each person, rates him or her as "more than satisfactory," "satisfactory," or "needs improvement" on each job function, and writes comments, including specific suggestions for improvement. These regular evaluations should come as no surprise to the staff member, since the supervisor has been working directly and conferring regularly with him or her.

Modern business practices based on a "systems approach" to management are being widely adopted by academic administrators,

Figure 5. Staff Contact Sheet

NAME _____ WEEK BEGINNING Monday _____ to Sunday _____
(tutor/specialist)

1. Individual Hours with EOP students |
2. Individual Hours with Non-EOP students |
3. Hours Spent in Groups |
4. Hours Spent in Drop-In |
5. Program Development Hours |
6. Training, Others |
7. Outreach |
8. Staff Development |
9. Component Administration |
10. Leave Holiday _____ |
      Other _____ |
11. TOTAL HOURS |

GROUPS AND MINICOURSES

Date	Hours	Course	EOP	Number of Students

Student's Name	Course	SLC ID#	Date	EOP	Hours	Name	Course	SLC ID#	Date	EOP	Hours
A											
B											
C											
D											
E											
F											
G											
H											
I											
J											
K											
L											
M											
N											
O											
P											
Q											
R											
S											
T											
U											
V											
W											
X											
Y											
Z											

Figure 6. Tutor Evaluation Form

Tutor Evaluation Form/Ed. 197, Sec. 19: _____ Quarter, 19 _____. Subject: _____

Tutor's Name _____ Grade in the course: PASS NOT PASS

Instructor's Name _____ SLC Staff Supervisor _____

Tutor's Status in the program: New _____ Returning: 2nd quarter _____ 3rd quarter _____

Rate the overall quality of the tutor's performance with students:

Excellent   Good   Average   Fair   Poor

How would you characterize the general response of tutees to this tutor?

Very satisfied   Satisfied   Mixed   Unresponsive   Dissatisfied

Did the tutor participate actively in and make significant contributions to the weekly seminar?

Nearly always   Most of the time   Sometimes   Rarely   Almost never

_____ This tutor was not able to attend regular seminars because of time conflicts, but agreed to meet frequently with the program supervisor instead.

To what extent did the tutor take advantage of the opportunities for private conferences with the supervisor?

Frequently   Whenever serious problems arose   Rarely   Almost never

Rate the quality of this tutor's journal or other written project:

Excellent   Good   Average   Fair   Poor

Did the tutor appear to grow during the quarter in terms of:

1. Improving mastery of subject matter and study skill: yes   no   questionable
2. Exploring facilitative techniques for working with students: yes   no   questionable
3. Developing and maintaining a personal, successful style of tutoring: yes   no   questionable

To the best of your knowledge, what resources did the tutor take advantage of?

_____ Books or articles on teaching _____ Videotape _____ CAI _____ Learning Programs in Lib/Lab _____ Handouts in Room 217 _____ Meeting with instructors _____ Meeting independently with other tutors _____ Conferences with SLC staff other than immediate supervisor _____ Attendance at special SLC training sessions _____ Attendance at outside conferences _____ Other

Was the tutor conscientious about following the necessary SLC recordkeeping procedures (e.g., submitting weekly contact sheets on time, registering his tutees with the Center, keeping a record of ID numbers and EOP/athlete status)?

Very conscientious   Conscientious   Erratic   Undependable

Additional Comments (Continue on reverse side if necessary):

Figure 7. Form for Student Evaluation of Drop-in Tutoring

1. I saw _____ for help in _____ .
   (tutor)   (course/skill)

2. I (___ am, ___ am not) an EOP student.

3. I received individual help. ___ yes ___ no. Approximate time spent with tutor _____ .

4. I received group help. ___ yes ___ no. There were ___ other students present. Approximate time spent
                                                      (number)
   with group _____ .

5. a. The tutor's patience was (___ excellent) (___ good) (___ fair) (___ poor)
   b. The tutor's knowledge of the subject was (___ excellent) (___ good) (___ fair) (___ poor).
   c. The tutor's explanations were (___ below my level) (___ at my level) (___ above my level) of understanding.
   d. The tutor's ability to help me to understand the material was (___ excellent) (___ good) (___ fair) (___ poor).

6. I used the computer terminal. ___ yes ___ no. Approximate amount of time _____ . I found the terminal (___ very
   useful) (___ useful) (___ somewhat useful) (___ not useful).

7. I felt the service was (___ excellent) (___ good) (___ fair) (___ poor) (___ did not get any).

COMMENTS/SUGGESTIONS (Please use back if necessary): _____

If you would like a reply, please indicate your name, address, and phone number. _____

_____ Thank you for helping evaluate our services.

**Figure 8. Sample Letter to Student and Postcard for Evaluation of Tutor-
ing Services**

Dear Student:

   We need your help in evaluating our tutoring service. The information you provide is required in our budget process and also to
help us make our service more responsive to your needs.

   Please take a few minutes to fill out the enclosed postcard and
return it.

   Thank you for your cooperation.

                                                        Sincerely yours,

Student Evaluation of Tutoring Service
         I came for assistance in _____
                                         (course or skill)
I saw _____for _____ hours.
                    (tutor's name)
Please rate the following using this scale: Excellent = A
                                              Good = B
                                              Satisfactory = C
         Drop-in tutoring ___   Poor = D
         Individual tutoring ___   Did not use = N
         Group tutoring ___
         Library-Laboratory ___
         Computer terminal ___
I learned about the Center through _____
I was referred by _____
Would you have preferred more appointments than you were able to get?
Other comments:

including learning-center directors. Regardless of how the systems
are labeled—management by objectives (MBO), planning-
management-evaluation (PME), or whatever—they are ways to assess such results as performance outcomes, quality of services, and
learning outcomes that maximize cost-effectiveness, and they are
also ways to serve the "humanistic needs" of the people who must
implement programs. In developing the management plan, the
MBO goal is to interrelate functions at every level of the organization and improve communication. MBO steps are as follows: (1) establish a plan, (2) work the plan, (3) evaluate it, and (4) revise it
using a management information system. In other words, the di-

rector sets objectives, determines the tasks to be done, monitors the tasks, and evaluates the results. Usually there are definite time lines for each task.

Some illustrations of how these principles can be applied to learning-center activities may clarify the procedure. When one learning center applied for a Special Services federal grant, the director wrote the following objective for the tutorial program: "By June 1978, the proportion of students who achieve improvement of one letter grade between midterm and final examinations in the course(s) for which they were tutored will double (from approximately 30 percent at present to 60 percent)." To implement this objective, he recommended adding an assistant director to the Academic Reinforcement Center to evaluate student progress and tutor effectiveness and to develop a plan whereby "faculty master tutors" from certain academic disciplines would conduct a training program required for all new student tutors and for continuing tutors who ranked between the 25th and 75th percentiles on the tutoring-effectiveness measure(s). Tutors who ranked below the 25th percentile would not be rehired. The tutorial services and the tutor-training programs were to be evaluated each semester. (In this case, the goal for student grades was not met. It would be more reasonable to establish a lower objective or a range, such as an increase of between 15 and 30 percent of tutored students receiving one letter grade higher.)

Charmian Sperling of Mount Wachusetts Community College (Gardner, Massachusetts) lists the following as one of the goals for basic skills instruction (developmental courses): "Students will demonstrate proficiency in setting goals and monitoring their progress relative to goal attainment." The proposed goal attainment course will be team-taught by a basic skills instructor and a teacher/counselor and focus on affective issues such as coping behavior, self-concept building, goal setting, and attainment. Small seminars of fifteen or fewer students will be modularized so that particular modules can be utilized with those students for whom they are most relevant; others will provide core material. The modules include goal setting, motivation, efficient time management, concentration and memory, studying textbooks, taking lecture notes, studying for and taking exams, test anxiety, coping with frustration and failure, using reference materials, theme and report writing, and interpersonal relations. One-to-one counseling is included as part of the course. To maximize transfer to other course work of the skills learned in this course, core modules will be planned to coincide with relevant events, such as time management at the outset of the semester, exam skills before midterms, and so on."

Developing an efficient management information system is important to the administrator not only for evaluating and monitoring programs but also for making routine decisions on such in-house operations as hiring, publicity and budget preparation, and budget management. I have used the model shown in Figure 9 to make decisions about hiring tutors and other staff members and when to publicize the services. It was also invaluable in preparing the annual budget. Figure 9 shows how a set of procedures facilitates the collection, processing, and flow of information for administrative and staff decisions and actions. The information was compiled weekly from learning specialists' and tutors' student-contact sheets (Figure 5) and reports from the receptionist, based on a count of the general record cards (see Figure 4), on the numbers of students requesting service and on the waiting lists for the different programs. When the workload for particular components dropped, I sent out publicity to attract more students for those programs. Conversely, when the specialists' and tutors' schedules were filled, I canceled publicity and decided whether the waiting list merited hiring standby tutors. Useful references on systems analysis applied to learning centers include Christ (1971, 1977). Recent references on MBO in college include Adams and Stevenson (1976), Deegan and Fritz (1975), and Heaton (1977).

Guidelines for an Effective Learning Center

The following criteria for evaluating a learning center are based on a review of the literature (Bloom, n.d.; Christ, 1971; Davis and others, 1975; Gourdine, 1976a; Reed, 1974; Schell, 1976) and my own experience. The criteria are subsumed under six headings: institutional commitment, implementation and administration of policies and procedures, staffing, resources and materials, and outreach and cooperation with the faculty.

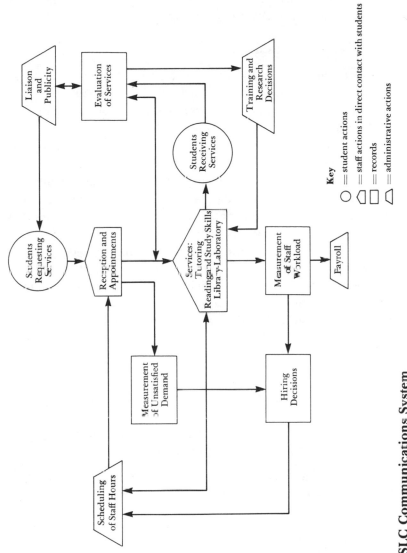

Key

○ = student actions

◁ = staff actions in direct contact with students

▭ = records

◁ = administrative actions

Figure 9. SLC Communications System

Institutional commitment is reflected in the objectives set for the program, the selection of a strong director, budget, facilities, space and resources allocated to the program, and support for decisions necessary to run the program effectively.

Institutional Commitment

- The program should have clearly stated objectives, and these should be widely disseminated to the faculty and students.
- The program should be allocated adequate resources in money, staff, space and materials to support the objectives.
- A program director should be chosen who is skilled in program management, respected by the academic community, and committed to improving students' learning. The program director must be accountable to the institution but also must have the freedom and power and the administrative support to develop and maintain the standards of the program.
- The institution's commitment must be manifested not only through funding and resources but through acceptance by faculty members, counselors, academic advisers, and other members of the student personnel staff and by students.
- The program should be centrally located in an attractive facility with adequate space for services. (Decentralized services such as writing or math labs located in academic departments also need adequate space.)
- The program should be institutionalized so that services are offered to all students who need them.

Implementation and Administration of Policies and Procedures

- A simple, yet adequate, data-collection system should be established and maintained for use in administrative decision making, evaluation studies, budget preparation, and so on. The director must also develop clear, efficient procedures for scheduling group sessions and appointments with staff members. Unnecessary paperwork and confusion that could alienate students should be eliminated. Simple recordkeeping procedures are needed to determine the hours worked by staff members for payroll purposes and for workload measures for administrative decision making and budgeting. Duties and work records are also needed for staff evaluations.

- Consideration for staff-client compatibility should be included in the procedures, with opportunity for students to select and/or change specialists or tutors.
- Flexible scheduling of service hours should be arranged so that service is available during noon hours, evenings, and weekends.
- Workable staff/student caseload ratios should be planned.
- Clear entrance and exit criteria should be specified for students.
- The delivery system for services should be flexible. It might include one-to-one interviews, dyads, groups of different sizes, drop-in services, and self-contained study groups in which the tutor acts as consultant or facilitator.
- Procedures should be established for systematic and ongoing evaluations of the effectiveness of the program and its functions. Evaluation processes should include evaluation by student users, program staff members, and faculty members as well as assessment of the impact of the program on student achievement and retention. Procedures for changing policies must be specified in advance of the need.

Staffing

- Clear criteria should be established for the selection of supervisors, specialists, and tutors who are knowledgeable, empathetic, and reliable. Tutors should be adequately compensated through salaries or academic credit. It is important that the center's staff and supervisors be representative of the ethnic populations the center serves.
- A well-planned staff-training program should be developed and an ongoing, supportive supervisory environment maintained. (Part-time staff members should be paid for attending training and supervisory sessions.)
- An evaluation system for rating of staff members by supervisors and a regular feedback mechanism for informing staff members of their progress should be developed.

Resources and Materials

- A library of learning aids, self-help materials, audiovisual aids, and other materials for student use should be provided as well as staff backup materials including textbooks and materials on teaching skills and tutoring techniques. These materials should reflect student needs and faculty expectations.

Outreach and Cooperation with the Faculty

- Acceptance by the faculty and its cooperation with the center's programs and goals are essential if the program is to be effective in assisting students.
- Close working arrangements between center staff and faculty will enable members of the center staff to obtain information from the faculty that will help them in their work with students. Liaison also enables learning-skills specialists to disseminate successful techniques developed by center staff members. Successful programs usually have a full-time academic liaison person who expedites cooperation and resolves potential problems and conflicts.

5

Overcoming Problems
of Learning Services

Directors and staff members of academic support services, whether large, comprehensive learning centers or small, departmental skills components, continually face problems in defining their roles in the campus community, in relating to faculty members and administrators, in clarifying and communicating their functions to students, and in forming their perceptions of themselves.

Relations with the Faculty

Of these problems, the most difficult concerns the service's role in relation to academic departments. Developing and maintaining the support of other faculty members is crucial (Davis and others, 1975; Reed, 1974). To be effective, learning-skills components and skills courses must be accepted as a regular part of the

151

college curriculum, clearly a prerequisite or support for sequences of beginning courses, and the programs of which they are a part should offer some services for advanced students. Both programs and courses should be open to any student who needs or feels he needs assistance. Despite the demonstrated need for special support services, some professors still harbor negative attitudes. They think that remedial instruction is not the proper province of colleges, and, therefore, that if such programs must be offered they should be temporary, as they are peripheral to the main mission of the institution. Traditionally, remedial instruction has been viewed as the least prestigious work in academe, and the duties generally relegated to new instructors or graduate students. A common stereotype is that if we must accept underprepared students, they should be placed in special programs and the services restricted to them—as if the rest of the student body might be contaminated if it, too, were offered special academic support services. When the question of opening the program to regular students is raised, the inevitable answer given by administrators is that the service is too expensive—even when the cost per student hour is lower than that of regular courses (Kingston, 1959; Shaw, 1961).

In other words, many administrators and faculty members view the learning-assistance program as serving a practical, political function in the college—that is, as a token of "what we are doing for" minority students, the physically disabled, or some other special group. Heard (1976, p. 6) warns, "If the learning center does come to fulfill only the role of a microcosmic showplace college in isolation, then we have failed."

Underprepared college students want to be treated like everyone else, but at the same time they need and want intensive help. Providing an atmosphere that fits both needs poses a dilemma for learning services. Because intensive remedial programs are costly, administrators may order that special services be limited to the lowest achievers. Indeed, federal and other grant-funding agencies often mandate that services be restricted to targeted groups. This policy makes it difficult, if not impossible, for the program to avoid a remedial stigma. As a result, the students who need help the most may avoid the program. Colleges try to resolve this dilemma in several ways: some maintain separate but equal services for regular and disadvantaged students; some provide certain services, such as reading and study skills help, to any student while restricting subject-area tutoring to students on financial aid; others provide free tutoring to EOP students but charge other students.

If a center becomes identified with the lowest achievers, professors who deny that remedial services are appropriate for college students may express negative attitudes toward students who use the services. If all students have access to the program, other professors may feel that the center threatens their roles and responsibilities (Reed, 1974). A needs-assessment survey of the faculty may help the learning-center director gauge these opinions and plan ameliorative strategies.

Academic support services define their function as providing skills and tutorial services to students to support their academic work, but differentiating support services from regular classroom instruction may be difficult. Warnath's warning to counseling centers is also appropriate for learning skills centers. Warnath (1971, p. 65) points out that professional counselors do not occupy a precise and unambiguous role on campus because professors have difficulty discriminating what professional counselors do from the many other advising and counseling functions that teachers and other professionals perform. The learning-skills specialist's role is even more ambiguous. It is not easy to explain the difference between skills work and the content taught by instructors in their courses.

Warnath's admonition (1971, p. 41) that "the presence of a counseling center on campus (no matter how poorly staffed) may have the effect of increasing the depersonalization of contacts between students and faculty" is equally applicable to learning centers. "A busy faculty member, when faced with a student who wants to work through some personal feeling or vocational plans, can rid himself of the responsibility by referring him to the counseling center." How much easier it is for the same professor, when confronted with a student who has a series of questions about a homework assignment, to refer that student to a tutor or learning-skills specialist!

Warnath cautions that if a student refuses to accept a referral from a faculty member, it may mean that the student is left with the problem that inspired the referral plus confirmation of his suspicion that faculty members do not care about individual students.

However, students may find it less threatening or risky to seek help from a tutor or learning-skills specialist than to confront a faculty member with their questions about the course or the assignment. After all, faculty members grade students, and tutors do not.

There is also a danger that support services will attract students in greater numbers than do dedicated course assistants or instructors during their office hours. When students stop seeking help from their instructors, the instructors assume the students are not interested, the instructors, in turn, lose interest in trying to help. The result can be mutual distrust between students and faculty or between learning-skills staff and faculty. To avoid competing for students, the skills specialists must develop close working relationships with faculty members in academic departments and must work toward reciprocal referrals.

Sometimes students try to manipulate learning-skills staff members and play them off against instructors (or vice versa), and sometimes students develop dependent relationships with their skills specialists or tutors. Either of these activities will reduce the effectiveness of an academic support program. Steering between these extremes requires delicate balance and diplomacy. The learning-skills staff must constantly educate both students and faculty regarding the proper roles and functions of the support service.

If a learning center is to serve a preventive as well as a rehabilitative role, it must establish and maintain credibility with the faculty. Too often support-service staff members find themselves trapped in a situation in which they are so completely immersed in student problems that they lack time and energy for anything else. As Richard Berry, a Berkeley counselor, recently remarked, "I'm so busy trying to pull drowning students out of the stream one by one, I don't have time to look up and see who's throwing them in." Planning time for staff members to do more than pick up and try to resuscitate the student victims of academe is a major function of the learning-center director.

Direct person-to-person contact is the best way to build relations between the faculty and the learning-center staff, but it is also

essential for the center to have a strong and supportive faculty/
student advisory committee to aid in establishing and maintaining
liaison with various academic departments and instructors. Learning centers can coordinate their efforts with faculty members' in
other ways too, such as through jointly sponsored programs, team-
taught classes, split appointments (in which a staff member spends
parts of his time in an academic department), cooperative research
projects, presentations to faculty meetings, teaching-assistant training workshops, and faculty consulting services. Below I describe
some of the strategies learning-center directors can use to gain the
confidence and cooperation of their faculty colleagues.

Faculty/Student Advisory Boards. Faculty/student advisory
boards should comprise faculty members from different disciplines
who reflect different points of view and students who are representative of the total student body. Do not select professors just because they support your program; include some conservatives as
well as some liberals, and invite both student-oriented and
research-oriented professors to sit on your board. Faculty/student
boards will be most effective if regular meetings are scheduled at
least once a term. Plan a specific agenda of issues and problems to
discuss after the board has been thoroughly oriented to your program's aims and services. (A discussion of the services and a tour of
the facilities are usually more effective in orienting faculty members than are lengthy, written reports, which few have time to
read.) The meeting agenda could include asking members' advice
on policies, new programs, and ways of improving relations with
other faculty members. Professors are not happy attending meetings where little occurs—they want a chance to use their expertise
and express their opinions.

It is advantageous for the center director to select a chairperson for the faculty board rather than try to chair the meetings
himself.

I found a strong board very helpful in supporting our center's efforts to develop new programs, to get grants, and to find
ways to resolve problems with other departments. A strong board
can help protect your service from problems with campus
middle-management administrators and help mediate some of the
inevitable conflicts that arise. Sometimes it is difficult to keep a
board meeting regularly, for faculty members have heavy demands

on their time which often make it hard to schedule meetings. So it is best to agree on the meeting schedule for the year well in advance—preferably at the beginning of the fall term—and keep the same schedule throughout the academic year.

Between regularly scheduled board meetings, the center director can call on board members individually to ask for their advice or suggestions on particular problems or projects. It is important to recognize that board members have to work under pressure too and not to expect them to become involved in lengthy, time-consuming projects—unless they volunteer. But despite the time constraints, boards can be very helpful. At one point our service was inundated with freshman chemistry students seeking tutoring help, and our board wrote to the dean of the College of Chemistry suggesting ways that our caseload might be reduced through faculty-group office hours, better scheduling of TAs' hours, TA training programs, and so on. The chemistry department implemented some of these ideas, and since then a number of chemistry faculty members have been very supportive in helping us get grants so that we can improve our services and develop learning aids for students.

There are those who suggest that the faculty members on the board be the most prestigious professors one can find. When the Upward Bound program was first instituted at Berkeley, many years ago, the director selected a prestigious faculty board that included several Nobel laureates. Subsequent directors have never regretted that decision, for the board has supported the program's efforts to raise funds from faculty contributions and has protected Upward Bound on many occasions from attacks by faculty members, administrators urging budget cuts, and other threats. In general, the board has ensured that the director retains sufficient autonomy for the program to function smoothly and survive.

Faculty-Sponsored Tutoring-For-Credit Courses. Seeking out professors who will sponsor tutoring-for-credit or practicum courses is another way to involve more faculty members in the center's work. We find professors generally supportive of these courses; for example, a professor of psycholinguistics has been particularly interested in enrolling his upper-division majors in the tutoring-for-credit course so they can get first-hand experience with students who have dialect, bilingual, or second-language problems. Faculty members in a number of departments—mathematics, education, chemistry, languages, and English as a second language—currently sponsor our tutoring-for-credit courses. Some professors prefer to offer such courses within their own departments as independent study courses; others agree to offer them through the education department or as fieldwork studies. Colleges vary in the amount of credit that a student can earn for tutoring-for-credit courses and in the number of hours a student must spend in this activity to earn credit.

Split Appointments, Team Teaching, and Other Arrangements. Split appointments are an excellent way of coordinating skills programs and academic departments. If an English instructor teaches regular English courses and also serves as director of the writing center, the inevitable faculty criticisms of learning services will be reduced. Team teaching, unfortunately, is relatively rare in colleges today and will become even rarer as budgets decline. Except for experimental courses, particularly in community colleges, team teaching in which faculty members are paired with learning-skills specialists seems to be most prevalent in professional and graduate programs where there are minority student groups who need improvement in writing skills. Nursing schools, public-health programs, law schools, and pharmacy schools are concerned about the quality of student writing. As a result, many have developed programs in which a faculty member team-teaches a course with a writing specialist (or two faculty members may pair up to teach writing). I have observed that faculty members in these teams seem to tire after a term or two and leave the writing teaching to the writing specialist while they return to teaching in their specialties.

Another cooperative arrangement is sequential teaching, in which different faculty members present their specialties in segments of the course or guest speakers are invited to give a lecture or two. Offering to talk to classes or departmental meetings is an excellent way to open up communication channels between the learning-center staff and the faculty.

It is wiser to let professors seek you out than to "offer to help them." Patricia Heard at the University of Texas Reading and Study Skills Laboratory (RASSL) includes the following announcement in her program's brochure: "*OUTREACH SERVICES* are provided to UT-Austin faculty and staff members who wish to consult about learning skills particularly useful to their students. The RASSL staff frequently present relevant study information upon request to UT classes and other student groups."

Outreach Roles. If the learning center is to function in a broader role on campus—as an ombuds-service or a catalyst for improving undergraduate instruction—then staff members must be trained and encouraged to view their responsibilities as extending beyond their work with individual students. Faculty members need help too, in coping with large classes of students from widely varying backgrounds. If I were starting another learning center, even one with a very small staff, I would spend most of my time— and see that my staff members spent more of their time—working to develop support programs with faculty members, rather than in individual conferences with students. If ways can be found to ease the burdens of faculty members and to help them develop more effective ways of helping students learn, many of the stresses that pressure students and create the large demand for learning-assistance services might be eased.

Learning-center directors who view the learning-skills specialist as a resource person for the faculty report that skills specialists can effect positive changes in faculty teaching strategies, exams, lectures, and other areas (Heard, 1976; Martin and others, 1977, pp. 18–22). One way skills specialists can serve as resource persons is to lecture on how to study a subject as part of a regular course. For example, they can talk to a French class about how to study foreign languages. Another method is to offer adjunct, or supplementary, skills courses that parallel regular classes. Adjunct skills courses require the skills specialist to attend the lectures of the regular class and work closely with the professor so the skills-training sessions dovetail with course requirements. If the skills specialist attends lectures, he will be better able to help students and also interact with the instructor. "As the resources person presents the major student question/concerns for the purpose of seeking guidance, the instructor has the opportunity to evaluate the effectiveness of his last lesson. It is not uncommon for an instructor to say something like, 'Oh! If they are confused about this point, then obviously they haven't yet learned . . .'" (Martin and others, 1977, p. 20). Since instructors rarely conduct detailed pretesting of their classes, they may assume that their students have knowledge and competencies that they in fact do not have. Hence, the skills specialist can alert the instructor to particular student needs and sometimes can make suggestions on what to do. As the New England Conference of Academic Support Services concluded (1977, p. 3), "Professors are often unaware of how helpful skills suggestions can be for some students in their classes . . . [Other professors] may recognize the needs of their students but not know how to deal with the work that is required."

Adjunct skills courses can be quite costly in the amount of time and effort that a skills specialist must devote, and so the question whether to offer them must be weighed carefully with the service's other priorities. One should select parent courses that have large enrollments, where many students have difficulty learning the content, where grading is tough—in short, courses where there is considerable evidence that students need help. In my experience, adjunct courses do not attract students when they are attached to courses where students average grades of B or higher, the enrollment is small, the instructor is accessible, the instructor uses mastery learning or personalized self-instructional methods, or teaching assistants or tutors are available to work with students in the classroom.

Although many learning centers offer sessions or workshops to inform professors of their services, and many invite professors to speak to their staff members, some learning-center experts feel that learning-skills support services should not offer formal faculty-development programs. "Faculty involvement should not be confused with faculty development; to do so is to jeopardize the integrity of the program. Learning centers . . . exist to develop and/or augment the skills of students, not to tell faculty members how to improve their instructional techniques. Moreover, college teachers are not only required to teach but advise, publish, and continually advance themselves professionally. As highly sophisticated specialists, instructors must be allowed to select those areas in which they feel a need for assistance. [Unsolicited] suggestions from learning-center personnel that instructors should alter their instructional content or techniques could be viewed as academic infringement—an anathema to faculty support" (Martin and others, 1977, p. 13). Martin and others conclude that faculty members often take a negative view of administrators' attempts to improve their teaching, and if the learning center tries to implement a program to "teach professors to teach," it may engender wrath instead of cooperation.

A learning-skills program that is accessible to both students and instructors can, however, become the natural resource for instructors seeking assistance in designing instructional packets, constructing better test questions, reorganizing their presentation of material, and developing alternative instructional modes for special groups of students. The key is that the instructor, not the learning center, should initiate the request for services.

Helping Develop New Teaching Methods. Sometimes instructors or academic departments want to test new teaching ideas, techniques, or policies but hesitate to experiment in their regular classes. A learning center that attracts large numbers of students can provide a convenient testing ground for assessing the effects of new techniques on student learning and attitudes. Centers can help, for example, in selecting a new workbook in basic grammar or in providing information on the readability level of proposed textbooks to assist selection committees in deciding on books that their students can read. Or centers can help in such policy decisions as whether to schedule TAs for evening hours in the library. (After we put tutors in the undergraduate library evenings and found that they did a brisk business with individual student requests, we were able to recommend this policy to the mathematics department.)

Many instructors are genuinely interested in developing new course materials, audiovisual aids, guides for their courses, and so forth but lack the time—and sometimes the skills—to do so. Implementing joint projects with instructors to develop and test study aids, materials and self-instructional programs, and even new courses that can be included in the regular curriculum are ways of enhancing a center's credibility. Some centers serve as "midwives" for new courses that other academic departments later adopt. New courses in precalculus (Berkeley and UCLA), credit reading-improvement courses (University of South Carolina), writing programs (such as that developed by the Undergraduate Writing Program at Stanford) that were originally developed by support programs have been absorbed by academic departments. If the learning center is not concerned with improving instruction, it risks becoming the wastebasket for ever increasing numbers of victims poor or inappropriate courses.

Helping faculty members develop new teaching approaches and materials is an area in which, I believe, the learning-center staff can have the most profound impact on student learning. Berkeley's Student Learning Center has worked with instructors on a series of small grants to improve instructional materials for over four years. We have developed a self-paced math course, selected and designed self-paced and audiovisual aids for a chemistry resources center, conducted minicourses in prestatistics, prechemistry, and problem solving, built computer-assisted-instruction units in probability, organic-chemistry concepts, and trigonometry, and written student guides for such courses as general chemistry, biochemistry, physiology, and mathematics.

Locating materials that professors can review, and possibly adopt, for their courses is another valuable function that learning centers can perform. Selecting appropriate textbooks, media, workbooks, and learning programs is a long and arduous task, as so many commercial materials are available in every field. In some departments, committees select introductory texts and use such criteria as readability in determining which books they will adopt. Reading-skills specialists can offer information on ways to assess text readability and can help professors locate appropriate texts for underprepared students (see Chapter Eight). Occasionally I have run contests inviting students to nominate "The Worst Textbook of the Year" and give their reasons. This takes some of the onus off the compulsive student who believes that textbooks are infallible and that he is to blame for not understanding. It also provides ammunition for professors to use in choosing textbooks. When one of our staff members was invited to testify before a departmental textbook-selection committee, he was able to persuade the professors to adopt a more readable, better-written introductory text, since their current text had recently won our "Worst Textbook of the Year" contest.

Another valuable function learning centers can perform for professors is to offer in-class diagnostic services. In open-admissions colleges, professors often face a wide range of students in their introductory courses and have no information on these students' skills. Juan Vazquez at the College of Alameda (Alameda, California) has developed a program in which professors can invite learning-center staff members to test their students for reading and other skills in their classrooms at the beginning of the term. Statistics on the range of abilities are given to the instructor, but *not* individual scores. Students are notified individually of their scores and needs and offered the services of the learning center.

Sharing handouts on how to study particular subjects is another way learning centers can help faculty members. If learning-skills specialists develop such handouts and offer them to professors to distribute in their courses, the professors may find the handouts helpful and/or suggest ways to improve them.

Other Methods. There are many other ways to reach faculty members. During the first year of the Learning Assistance Center (LAC) at California State University at Long Beach, Frank Christ and Margaret Devirian lunched each day with a different faculty member in the faculty dining commons. This greatly enhanced their image with many faculty members. (At present I am collecting data on whether learning-center directors who habitually bring bag lunches and eat in solitude in their own offices have more difficulty retaining their positions or more problems with faculty members and administrators than those who eat out. Although I do not have enough information to perform statistical analyses, at this point the brown-baggers who eat alone appear to have more problems.)

Christ and Devirian also arranged "county fairs," inviting professors from different departments to a demonstration of materials, programs, and equipment appropriate for their students. As a result, professors made many direct referrals to the LAC; some integrated skills modules into their courses and required students to use the LAC as part of their class assignments.

Planning an "open house" to which professors and administrators are invited to view the learning-center facilities and interact with the staff is a popular method for introducing your service to professors. If you do plan an open house—and you should try one if you have not—it is best to hold it when students are using the center. Inevitably, professors recognize some of their own students among the tutors or tutees, and seeing students at work gives them a more realistic picture of your program—particularly if you have a drop-in service.

Advertising for tutors, whether paid, for credit, or volunteer, is another way of alerting professors to your program, especially if professors are requested to write letters of recommendation for prospective tutors. In many centers, professors will volunteer to tutor.

The best advertisement for a center is a satisfied clientele. If students who use the program regularly are enthusiastic and successful in their academic work, they become effective intermediaries with professors as well as referral sources for other students.

Summary. In this section I have discussed a number of ways learning centers can gain credibility with the faculty, including the following:

- Developing a strong faculty advisory board.
- Making direct person-to-person contacts with the faculty.
- Holding open houses or faculty orientation programs.
- Advertising the service through recruitment of tutors and soliciting recommendations for tutors from faculty members.
- Requesting faculty members to sponsor tutoring-for-credit courses.
- Team-teaching with faculty members in courses combining skills and content or other arrangements such as sequential teaching.
- Offering to address classes on skills needed in the discipline.
- Offering adjunct skills courses that parallel regular courses.
- Providing an experimental laboratory for faculty members wishing to test new methods, materials, and procedures.
- Cooperating with faculty members in research projects on the improvement of instruction.
- Writing study guides for students.
- Assisting faculty members in selecting appropriate textbooks and other materials.

- Sharing handouts on "how to study" that faculty members may use in their classes.
- Offering skills diagnostic services within the instructor's class time at the beginning of the term.

Although it is important to make friends with some faculty members, the larger task faced by learning-center directors is to build feelings of mutual acceptance, support, trust, and respect. This is a lengthy and continuous process. Do not expect to convert all faculty members to your viewpoint; in fact, do not try. There will always be some professors who feel that students who need any help with their academic work do not belong in college. Work with those professors who believe that students' learning can be improved. Develop a tolerance for those colleagues who greet you *every* time they meet you with comments like "Still trying to save them?" or describe your efforts to help students as "love's labors lost."

Avoid the pitfalls that have resulted in the failure of many programs where the director and staff members are so busy seeing students that they isolate themselves from their colleagues and identify so strongly with students that they view professors as adversaries.

There are undoubtedly many other ways to build bridges of mutual trust and respect between skills specialists and academic faculty members, and some of these, such as serving on campus wide committees and performing other advisory services, are described in Chapter Three. But let us turn to another area that greatly affects the quality of the undergraduate learning environment and in which learning centers, at least those in universities, are increasingly involved. That is the area of training graduate teaching assistants. The techniques described for TA training also have implications for programs that employ paraprofessionals and part-time instructors.

TA Training Programs

Many learning centers are providing (or helping others provide) training programs for departmental teaching assistants, who in large universities often carry the main responsibility for teaching and working directly with freshman and sophomore students.

If I were to develop a program for training TAs in a large university or for orienting part-time paraprofessionals in a community college, I would focus the program on enhancing instructors' knowledge of peer-group processes and increasing their awareness of how to diagnose and work with problems that hamper students' learning, rather than attempting to improve their teaching skills directly. My rationale is that if TAs became cognizant of how to handle minor learning-skills problems and of their own nonproductive reactions to student difficulties, the number of students seeking help from costly tutoring, skills, and counseling programs could be reduced, and students' satisfaction with their courses would increase. If students learned to work and study successfully with their peers in this course, they might be able to apply the same approach to other classes. Counselors and learning-skills specialists would train the TAs and assist them in helping students work together effectively.

Undergraduates have problems in learning when taught by research-oriented, specialized, and academically talented TAs who are inexperienced teachers. This is an old problem for public universities, where graduate TAs have been an integral part of American higher education for over 100 years (Trow, 1966). Today, however, the problems are exacerbated as larger numbers of underprepared and nontraditional students enroll in university courses. So today the disparity is greater between the knowledge and expectations of graduate TAs and the knowledge and skills of students.

Training TAs in departments where required courses with large freshman enrollments generate the heaviest demand for tutoring, skills, and counseling help would seem a logical preventive measure. Such a training program might include group sessions with discussions and demonstrations of group processes, peer-learning techniques, and ways to create a supportive atmosphere for learning. Topics that might be presented are techniques for utilizing students enrolled in the course as peer tutors; ways to use dyads, as in a calculus course where students work together to solve problems; parcelled classroom arrangements, in which students are organized in groups (Hawkins, 1976); instructor-less study or writing groups; and peer-monitored assignments (Beaman and others, 1977).

TA participants in this program could make videotapes of their regular classes, discussion sections, or laboratory groups and critique them with other TAs, faculty members, and skills specialists. Role-playing typical situations that new instructors face in teaching and conferring with students would also be an integral part of the training program. The training would be geared to the constraints and content of particular disciplines—chemistry TAs who supervise laboratory sections perform different roles than English TAs. The main emphasis of the program would be to develop and test peer-learning models and student-involvement techniques, but TAs would be cautioned that no student who prefers to study alone should be forced to participate in group problem solving or study groups.

In addition to the training sessions, an individual counseling/consulting service would be offered for new instructors and TAs. Here they could discuss their questions and problems in complete confidence with a counselor or learning specialist. Since TAs are students too, they often find themselves in a double bind: their own study obligations are highest in their list of priorities, and their teaching obligations secondary. Often there are personality clashes between supervising professors (who may also be major advisers) and TAs. Outside help may aid in resolving such conflicts, which if unresolved could place unneeded stress on the TAs' students.

Counselors and learning-skills specialists might also assist TAs and faculty members in developing videotapes of particular teaching situations. Group and individual interactions that TAs typically encounter could be used in future TA-training groups; TA positions in many institutions turn over frequently, and each new group of TAs would profit from the training. These videotapes would reflect the course content peculiar to the department—math examples would be used with math TAs, writing examples with English TAs, and so on.

During the second year of the program, senior TAs and interested professors could run the TA orientation sessions. This would ensure that there would be residual effects from the first year and that the program could gradually become departmentally self-perpetuating. Each subsequent year, TAs who had been through the program the preceding year would be selected to conduct the program, and counselors and learning-skills specialists would serve as consultants to the trainers and work individually with staff members who requested special assistance.

The following criteria might be used to evaluate the program: (1) Reduction in the amount of tutoring, skills help, and counseling sought by students from classes of trained TAs, compared with students from untrained TAs' sections. (2) Students' greater satisfaction with their learning experience in trained TAs' classes than in control classes taught by untrained TAs, as shown in student evaluations (McClintock and Sonquist, 1976). (3) Increased student retention and improved learning of students participating in the peer tutoring or other student-to-student learning situations. (4) Improved academic performance of low-achieving students in the experimental classes. McClintock and Sonquist found that low-achieving students who attended out-of-class review groups with other students significantly improved their course grades, compared with low-achieving students who studied alone. Experimental evidence that lends further support to these techniques are the reviews of studies on PSI proctors by Goldschmid and Goldschmid (1976a, 1976b). (5) Improved TAs' satisfaction with the TA experience and improved self-evaluation of their effectiveness as teachers, compared with untrained TAs.

Specifically, students from experimental TAs' classes in which peer-teaching techniques were implemented could be matched with students from control classes for academic aptitude and relevant high school grades. The two groups of students could then be compared on the following measures, using an analysis-of-variance design: scores on a Likert scale or semantic differential measuring satisfaction with the course; academic performance in class (shown by grades on exams, projects, and so on); use of tutoring, skills, or counseling services (shown by number of students applying for service and number of contact hours); retention in college at the end of two terms and four terms; and number of students completing the course sequence (for example, those finishing a year of freshman chemistry). Three variables could be tested on the teaching assistants: satisfaction with own teaching experiences in the classes taught (shown by responses on a Likert scale); estimate of own effectiveness as a teacher (shown by responses on a Likert scale); and satisfaction with the training program (for TAs participating in the experiment only). It would also be interesting to ascertain whether the TAs in the training program shared ideas and techniques with TAs not in the program and whether a John Henry effect occurred (Saretsky, 1972)—that is, did TAs who were *not* in the program try harder? If found, this would be delightful. (In the John Henry effect, the control-group teachers work harder.)

Learning-skills specialists could demonstrate how to identify students with skills problems or emotional problems using role-playing or videotaped simulated scenarios. These training materials could be helpful to part-time instructors, as well as to TAs. Ways to refer students to support services could be demonstrated in a similar manner. It could be cost-effective for any institution that employs part-time instructors, and it also has implications for part-time students who work and therefore cannot make use of regular campus resources. Part-time students, especially adults, usually lack an appropriate study environment. If instructors encouraged students to gather in informal study groups and meet regularly outside class, the students could form their own study milieu.

The learning-skills specialists and counselors who provided the initial training would revert to the role of consultants after training was completed, and the responsibility for implementing and continuing the training would pass back to the academic department. The resulting decrease in the need for tutoring and support services would permit learning-center staff members to have more time to consult and work with the faculty.

Innovations of this sort are especially hard to implement in large, well-established institutions; however, there are always some faculty members who are deeply concerned that students learn and that TAs become effective teachers. A fringe benefit of the program described is that it would reduce the stress and time demands that teaching places on part-time TAs, whose graduate courses also drain their energy and time. If students complain less about grades and assignments and can work together cooperatively, TAs may be less pressured, and if peer-learning techniques are adopted, TAs can spend less time preparing for classes. This program might also provide an entree into faculty retraining in institutions that are hesitant about implementing new programs.

A word of warning: Before you plunge ahead on a formal TA training program, it is essential to have the full support of your institution's administration and some key faculty members. Despite the criticisms of college instructional methods by students and educators, such programs are rare even today, and there is much resistance toward them. Avoid treading on what faculty members consider their turf, and be alert to the fact that the boundaries of their turf change rapidly.

If the campus lacks formal TA training programs, the learning center may still conduct informal training quite successfully. A concerned professor may bring over his TAs, as a mathematician did to our center, so that they can observe tutors and skills specialists working with individuals, dyads, and small groups and learn techniques. Perhaps it is these informal, serendipitous arrangements that will produce the greatest change, for the larger, more formal programs are usually funded on soft money, and when the grants expire, so do the programs.

Resources on Teaching

A library of handbooks on college teaching is a useful resource for any learning center. These materials are valuable for tutor and staff training and as information sources for professors and teaching assistants. Some of the books we have found valuable are these:

Bernstein's *Manual for Teaching* (1976) is an excellent reference that summarizes much of the research on college teaching. It discusses objectives (including Bloom's Taxonomy), behaviorism in the classroom, and teaching techniques (lecturing, discussion, individualized instruction, PSI, audiotutorial, contracts, computer-assisted instruction, role playing, project-method, and many others). It also has sections on evaluation and on sociology of the classroom and an appendix of articles, student appraisal forms, and questionnaires.

McKeachie's *Guidebook for the Beginning College Teacher,* first published in 1969, is the classic guide to college teaching and is a must for any library.

Mann and others' *College Classroom: Conflict, Change, and Learning* (1970) describes teacher characteristics, teacher roles (specifically, the teacher as expert, formal authority, socializing agent, facilitator, ego ideal, and person), and the impact of these characteristics and roles on student learning. Eight categories of students are described: the anxious, dependent student, discouraged student, independent student, hero, sniper, attention seeker, silent student, and compliant student; the authors suggest that these categories be used as anchor points to understand the intricate communication processes in the college classroom. (A brief summary of this study appeared in *Psychology Today* — Ringwald and others, 1971.)

Faculty Development in a Time of Retrenchment (Group for Human Development in Higher Education, 1974) is a well-written monograph describing the issues in improving college teaching.

One might also look at *Change* magazine's special issues *Reports on Teaching,* which describe innovative approaches to teaching in different disciplines. The Center for Research on Learning and Teaching at the University of Michigan regularly publishes a bulletin, *Memo to Faculty,* each issue of which is devoted to a theme relevant to improving instruction. Past issues included titles like "The Lecture," "Grading by Contract," and "Student Reactions to Instruction." From 1976 until 1978, the center published *Criteria,* a newsletter for the evaluation, support, and recognition of college teachers.

Relations with Campus Administrators

Directors of learning centers most frequently express concern about relations with the faculty, but problems in gaining support from campus administrators run a close second in the hierarchy of problems centers face.

Studies of skills and tutoring programs have occasionally reported cases in which the director or the staff lacked commitment to helping students; however, lack of administrative support and restrictions on autonomy in directing the service are often cited as major problem areas (Davis and others, 1975; Reed, 1974). Since learning-center components usually assist underprepared students, especially those from ethnic minorities, their special services such as tutoring may become the focal point for political and social controversies between student groups, faculty members, and the external community. These quarrels create special problems for campus administrators, because institutions have become increasingly sensitive to attacks on their affirmative action programs, and the learning service is viewed as a major part of the affirmative action effort. Student groups are more likely to attack the tutoring and skills services than criticize the faculty if they think the college is not providing appropriate programs for their ethnic groups.

A learning-center director's autonomy may be threatened in many ways—by pressure from administrators to perform certain functions or hire certain people, by interference in decision making, by lack of support for programs and budgets. Some of my experiences may illustrate the range of problems. During the learning center's first year, we were investigated by the Student Task Force Against Bureaucracy at the same time the student budget intern was evaluating our recordkeeping and workload measures, asking questions that generated more paperwork. Ethnic-studies divisions complained that they were not getting enough funding for their peer-tutoring programs and insisted that a centralized service could not meet the needs of their students. The Committee Against Racism, a student/faculty group, expressed concern that minority students were not receiving enough tutoring help, while student groups wrote angry letters demanding that tutors from their ethnic groups be hired in each and every subject.

Budget committees wanted our staff to conduct more group tutoring programs and spend less time in individual work with students, as an economy measure. At the same time, EOP students complained that they were being forced into groups when they wanted and needed more individual tutoring appointments. This issue took several quarters to resolve.

Student budget interns eliminated the salary of our part-time speech therapist, the only speech person on campus. They argued that speech assistance belonged under the health service, whose director rejected the idea flatly, citing a policy of not treating students for preexisting conditions. (We were able to collect contributions from an alumni group to retain the speech position for a few hours a week, but the position was not re-funded when the donations ceased.) Unfortunately, students with speech difficulties tend to be less vocal and assertive in their demands for special services than other student groups.

In addition to pressures from various campus constituencies whose demands and disputes affect the learning service, the expectations and misperceptions of the functions of the service by administrators may exacerbate the center's difficulties. Some administrators, reflecting the views of their more conservative faculty constituency, may stereotype special assistance programs for students as remedial and feel that such programs are unnecessary. Other administrators may reluctantly concede the need for learning-support services but insist that services be limited to open-admissions or special-admit students. They justify this policy on the basis of budget limitations or lack of staff positions; however, restricting a service to those who need it most ensures that the program will be stigmatized by both students and faculty members as a salvage operation for academic misfits.

Current funding policies for many federal and state monies earmark them for the "disadvantaged student" or other special groups. Even in these specially funded programs, efforts must be made to provide comprehensive programs and to avoid "tracking."

Centers in highly selective institutions may, of course, find that their administrations hold the opposite view. That is, administrators may view them as helping regularly admitted students and suggest that services for the lowest achievers be limited unless funded from extramural sources.

Unrealistic Administrative Expectations. Administrators may have unrealistic expectations about how much an academic support service can accomplish in improving students' skills and how long it will take. Some seem to expect that a student who is reading six years below grade level will be able to make up the deficiency in one semester while carrying other college courses.

If a learning center has the responsibility of assisting students who are accepted as "special admits" in a selective college, then it is vital that the director sit on the admissions committee and have input into the procedures for determining which applicants will have the regular admissions criteria waived. As Sam Silas of William Paterson College states (in a personal communication), "It is absolutely essential that the learning-center director and the admissions office share similar views on the admission of students. The admissions officer can make or break your special-admit program, and it certainly does not hurt if . . . the director and the admissions officer are the best of friends."

Some of the many variables that affect the success of a special-admissions program are the recruiting process, the precollege counseling and advising services, the orientation program, and the involvement of the faculty. The college recruiters (or admissions counselors) must try to recruit students who, though they come from disadvantaged backgrounds, have the motivation and ability to learn quickly and some chance of succeeding in the institution's academic programs. Counselors and academic advisers can help prospective students choose appropriate courses and plan majors as well as aiding them in understanding how the skills services can help. There must be close coordination among the various components of the special-admissions program.

Misconceptions about the motivation of students with a history of low achievement also create difficulties for a learning service. Some administrators and professors expect the freshmen with poor college preparation to volunteer for special help and those with high achievement records not to. In reality, however, the reverse is true; weak students avoid the service, while stronger ones use it willingly. Often administrators are unaware of the shame, stigma, and despair that accompany poor achievement. So when administrators hear criticisms about their college's failure to uphold its commitment to disadvantaged minority students or other special groups, they investigate the learning center's services. If the center's services are not tightly coordinated with recruitment, admissions, counseling, advising, and faculty programs, the finger of blame points to the learning center. The dean may set up a faculty committee to investigate why so few special-admit students are completing degrees. The scenario that follows has been replayed in many institutions; the result is that learning services or reading and study skills services are eliminated or assimilated by other departments. The faculty committee interviews faculty members and other student services, and its final report may conclude with a statement like "The director and staff of the present learning service do not hold as a priority instruction in basic skills for special problems, and they have had no systematic success in handling them. In our opinion, basic remedial service must take precedence over polishing and refining the skills of already prepared students."

Such conclusions sound the death knell for any hope of mainstreaming special-admit students and ensure the ghettoization of learning-support services. Since regular students are perceived as *not* needing reading and study skills help, those who do are considered different, dumb, and remedial. (A postscript: Three years after the faculty committee's report quoted above, administrators in the same institution addressed strong letters to the chairperson of the developmental skills department, which had replaced the learning center, complaining about the heavy attrition rate of special-admit students, and the cycle began again.)

Faculty referrals of students in academic difficulty are another source of problems for learning services. To be sure, the service is the appropriate place for such referrals, but, as Felton and Biggs (1977) point out, administrators and professors often display a "tertiary responsiveness" to student problems. They are concerned about treating symptoms only when the symptoms have surfaced dramatically—that is, when the student is ready to drop out of school or is placed on academic probation. (Certainly, many aspects of our current system encourage this problem, since students rarely come to the attention of professors or administrators until they are at a crisis point.)

Therefore, an important goal for learning centers is to help professors and advisers identify students with learning difficulties early and make appropriate referrals. For instance, if a college has a policy that students who do not earn a C average at the end of two years are placed on junior-standing probation, and if advisers refer these probationary students to the learning center, it is difficult to help them. Probationary students who have accumulated many course credits with low grades find it statistically impossible to get off probation unless they earn straight As—a highly unlikely event for students who, at best, may have earned a B or two, but never an

A. If students with marginal grade-point averages were identified earlier, before earning low grades became habitual, it would be easier to help them. But preventive programs are usually considered too expensive or too intrusive by those who are convinced that young people can "grow out of their problems" if left alone. Students themselves often share this belief and express certainty that somehow their academic problems will disappear—next semester.

Problems with Student Personnel Administrators. Learning services that are supervised by student affairs administrators may face constraints resulting from the second-class citizenship conferred by academics on programs that they consider nonacademic. Warnath (1971) explains how the roles of student personnel administrators shifted in the 1960s from student concerns to budgets and facilities management. In effect, student affairs administrators have become business maagers as their programs for students expanded and as radical, minority, and other student groups bypassed the dean of students, going directly to the college president with their complaints. Warnath (p. 103) describes the situation: "In increasing numbers, presidents seem to be coming to the conclusion that their student personnel deans are unable to give them assistance in working with important student problems. Even more distressing is that student personnel deans are ignored as sources of simple information about students and their concerns."

Hodgkinson's survey of college presidents' attitudes toward deans of students (1970, p. 49) lends further support to Warnath's position. Hodgkinson reports that top administrators frequently view student personnel administrators as an arm of the central administration, programmed to conduct messages down the chain of command. No longer are deans of students expected to synthesize information from students for interpretation up the organizational pipeline for action by the top-level administrators.

The gap between the ideal of student-centered functions, which are the focus of the professional counseling psychologist or student personnel specialist, and managerial functions has widened to the point that few people on campus take seriously the contention of student affairs deans and vice-chancellors that their first priority is concern for the welfare of students.

In sum, the political reality of the academic scene is that the

learning service can count on little assistance from student personnel officers. "The amount of power the . . . center draws from student personnel is usually zero. In fact, for the center staff to make
effective contributions to the academic community and to the student body, they must frequently disclaim their connections with the
student personnel structure. . . . Unfortunately for the effectiveness of the total student personnel program, deans of students may
feel threatened if members of the center become too closely identified with the academic. If the dean of students senses that he
is . . . viewed as having a low position in the campus community, a
counselor who appears to identify with the academic community
through teaching or research or both runs the danger of stirring
up the resentments of the person on whose team he is supposed to
be playing" (Warnath, 1971, pp. 43–44).

The staff members of learning centers may be hampered,
then, by the credibility of the administrator to whom they report,
and because they work closely with academic departments, they
may pose a threat to student affairs deans or vice-chancellors. If
these administrators are sensitive to the ambiguity of their own
roles, they may overreact to faculty criticism of the learning center
and block new projects, limit travel or general budget funds, and
indeed appear quite punitive to the learning center.

Whether a learning service is under the egis of academic or
student affairs administrators, one of the most exasperating situations for a learning-center director occurs when his attempts to get
grants for his program are thwarted by campus administrators *before* being transmitted to funding agencies. Administrators have
discouraged grant seeking frequently enough that the reasons for
this action deserve mention. In some prestigious institutions, only
tenured faculty members are eligible to become principal investigators on grants, a frustrating situation for the learning-center
director who hopes to expand his program through outside funding and who is concerned—and sometimes defensive—about the
possible loss of autonomy in the program if someone else directs
the grant project and controls the funds. One rationale for this
policy is that funding agencies weigh heavily the academic experience and credentials of the principal investigator in making
awards. Therefore, it is really to the center's advantage if a top

academician or administrator can be convinced to sponsor a grant proposal, rather than for the learning-service director to attempt to fight for it through academic and administrative committees.

Some administrators are against grant seeking because federal programs entail much red tape and have strings attached or because they feel that placing a program on "soft money" will jeopardize the college's financial commitment to the program. These can be valid arguments. Less understandable, however, are the objections of administrators, particularly those in small public colleges, who argue that seeking special funds for learning-center services would tarnish the image of the institution because it constitutes an admission that the college accepts low-achieving students. It is sometimes possible to dispel this negativism by getting information about learning-center programs in other colleges, particularly colleges with strong academic reputations.

The Tenure Problem

After young learning-center directors have successfully established a service, they often seek academic tenure because it offers security and recognition. If they have taught undergraduate and graduate courses for a few years, they may feel they qualify and may ask for a tenure review. But in most colleges, getting tenure requires more than college teaching experience. Achieving tenure has never been easy, and it is particularly difficult in prestigious universities today. The proportion who gain tenure among those who aspire has been as few as one in thirty-five in some universities in the past, and all colleges are more cautious today in granting tenure, as financial problems and an aging faculty restrict the number of positions. Learning-skills professionals are often naive about the formalities of the tenure-review process. Indeed, in most colleges, the procedures are largely unwritten and rarely discussed. Although the tenure process varies from institution to institution, most universities require that a departmental committee review the candidate's qualifications in research, publications, teaching, and public and professional service.

The tenure committee tries to predict the candidate's future —to determine whether he will be an active scholar/researcher with innovative ideas twenty or thirty years from now. The question addressed by the members is "Will the candidate continue to grow and develop?" Since the committee members have no crystal ball, they must scan the candidate's previous publications, rate of productivity, growth, and scholarly qualifications, basing their final judgment of future potential on past performance.

In research universities, publications are judged very severely by tenure committees. The sheer number of publications by a candidate may mean little, while the quality and academic respectability of the journals in which they appear may be weighted heavily. Departments usually insist that publications appear in "refereed" journals—that is, journals where editorial boards of professional peers screen the articles to be published. Although most education journals today are refereed, they differ in reputation. Both the quality of the journal and the range of readers are important and the criterion often used is whether the journal exposes one's ideas to other acknowledged experts in the field who can judge their worth. For example, a tenure committee might view one article in the *Harvard Educational Review* as roughly equivalent to ten articles in the *Journal of Reading*. So it is important that the candidate find out from his faculty colleagues which journals they respect.

In some universities, textbooks are not considered in the candidate's publication dossier, because textbooks and articles in the popular press are considered remunerative and as part of one's teaching contribution, not as scholarly publications. Similarly, if one takes the time to rewrite one's doctoral dissertation into a book, one should not expect the review committee to be pleased. The committee may view this activity negatively, reasoning that the candidate is reworking old ground rather than advancing into new frontiers of knowledge.

Involvement with professional associations—serving on committees, holding offices, presenting papers, and so on—may be considered favorably by a review committee, but the committee members' attitude will depend on whether they recognize the organization as professional and scholarly. One can be nationally known in one's own field while one's work and qualifications remain unknown to one's peers on the faculty.

Another facet of the tenure evaluation is the collection of data on one's effectiveness as a teacher. Of course, having students evaluate your courses is one way. Another, and perhaps more important way is to work directly with other faculty members— teaching classes jointly, working on projects with them, and generally becoming accepted as an integral part of the department. This is difficult to do if the candidate also has heavy administrative responsibilities or spends a great deal of time counseling students with learning problems.

If one manages to earn the committee's favorable recommendation, there still remain other hurdles in gaining tenure. Most colleges require that the approval of the department in which one teaches be unanimous and also that the approval of campuswide committees and administrators be secured. When departmental approval must be unanimous, one faculty member who feels the candidate's work is "not significant" or "too applied" can block the appointment.

Novice administrators often underestimate the length of time it takes to become tenured. Most universities allow seven or eight years for the candidate to go through the process, with a midcareer review in the fourth year, if requested. Some candidates who have been approved by departmental and campuswide committees are still denied tenure because of lack of available positions or money. In that case, they may have to reinstitute the whole process at a later date.

Because the role of the learning-skills specialist differs from that of the typical faculty member, it may be hard to convince one's faculty colleagues that one is an acceptable candidate for tenure. Even if the learning-skills specialist has excellent professional and teaching qualifications, his interests may be considered too specialized or too applied to be acceptable.

This is not to suggest that learning-center staff members and directors never attain tenure, but it is a difficult, lengthy process in universities. As a result, many who try become discouraged and give up. It is undoubtedly easier to gain tenure *before* becoming an administrator. Admittedly, few graduate students, when planning their future careers, consider becoming a learning-center director. Upon graduating, however, they find greater opportunities and

higher salaries in learning center administration than in most
teaching positions. Thus, they opt for administrative jobs without
thinking about tenure. Other alternatives might be to find a new
position in which tenure is included along with administrative
duties (although such positions are difficult to find) or to return to
full-time teaching and research. A final caveat is that even if the
center director does have tenure, it will not immunize him from the
other problems discussed in this chapter.

Problems in Self-Perception

Learning-service personnel often share with counselors
some characteristics that appear to foster low morale, and they
often react to the inherent realities of their positions with what
seems to be a persecution complex. In particular, they may react
negatively to the slow pace of academic change and may tend to be
naive about (and often uninterested in) the sources and uses of
power. Warnath (1971, p. 43) describes the limitations of people
who self-select counseling roles:

> The counselor does not make a good politician. Those qual-
> ities which characterize the effective counselor—openness, a desire
> to encourage the optimum use of individual talents in others, and
> an opposition to arbitrary or imposed authority—unfit him to
> manipulate people or events to achieve some personal or organiza-
> tional goal. To those familar with the use of power, he appears
> naive in his direct use of confrontation or resistance. However,
> even if he has developed a political sense, a member of the counsel-
> ing staff is in an extremely vulnerable position from which to be-
> come a political force on campus. . . . Power resides in departments
> and schools in rough approximation to their status in that particu-
> lar academic community. . . . Since the counseling center is margi-
> nal to both academic and student personnel structures, what power
> or influence any one person in the center has may have to be drawn
> from an extremely small organizational supply.

The learning-skills specialist who lacks political acumen
often asks, "Why do we have to continually justify our service to
faculty members and administrators, explain our existence, and
evaluate and document our effectiveness, when other departments
do not?" "Why do they make our task so difficult by setting impos-

sible goals and hurdles for students?" "Why must we be so careful to maintain a low profile?"

The answers lie in the institution's real, not professed, commitment to students, especially to the low-achieving and underprepared students whom it admits. Most colleges perceive support services as incidental to their main business of educating future scholars and leaders of society.

We who help students cope with academe are endlessly confronted because we work where others, including professors, have failed, and if we succeed, our success calls attention to their failures.

Specialists who work with student learning problems rank low in academic prestige. For example, students and professors rank psychologists working with learning problems much lower in the hierarchy than psychologists working in clinics with patients' emotional and personality problems or those engaged in research. The complaints of learning specialists are related not only to the values of their colleagues in other disciplines but also to their own internalized acceptance of their low status. Some protest and confront faculty members, others side with students and become antagonists. Some revel in the positive evaluations they get from students and lose sight of other roles. For example, if a student says to a tutor, "I wish Professor Snodgrass could explain the problems as clearly as you do—you should be teaching the course!" it may be ego-building, but it gives one a false sense of importance. As Heard (1976) relates, compliments to the learning-center staff members may sidetrack them from performing functions as watchdogs, ombudsmen, and trendsetters.

Preventing Outreach from Becoming Overreach.

Balancing the needs of individual clients against outreach activities designed to improve general student learning may, unfortunately, increase student demands for service in an already overloaded program. If learning-skills specialists speak to faculty or student groups one week, there are inevitably more referrals the next week. At least that may be the initial result. If the talk is structured as a general invitation to "come and let us help you, whatever your problems may be," the result will be an increase in clients. If, however, the skills specialist discusses ways a student can help himself, then referrals will decrease.

Similarly, members of the skills staff can spend a lot of their time preparing for presentations to classes. For example, the Reading and Study Skills Laboratory at the University of Texas at Austin received about a dozen requests for a staff member to address classes in the foreign-language department. The skills specialists decided that it was more efficient to develop a videotaped presentation on how to study foreign languages than to have staff members invest large amounts of time preparing for each class presentation.

When skills specialists are dispersed, as in a decentralized learning service, heavy student demand may not be a problem. However, difficulties arise when students who are not registered in a course or department with a learning-center component need assistance. For example, a mathematics laboratory may restrict its services to students enrolled in certain basic mathematics courses and not permit others, such as adults who need a quick review in algebra before enrolling in statistics, to use its services.

Balancing out the amount of time and effort staff members spend in preventive activities and in direct work with students often poses difficulties for the learning-center director. In the final analysis, how this dilemma is resolved depends on whether the mission of the service is viewed by faculty members and administrators as serving a limited target population.

The problems discussed in this chapter do not exhaust the difficulties faced by learning centers. There are many others that characterize any department, including problems in staff relationships, expansion, and retrenchment of the program. However, too often directors believe that their problems are unique to themselves and their institutions. Rarely do they realize how ubiquitous these problems are throughout academe. Higher education has its rituals, and, although administrators and professors may vary from college to college, they hold similar values, goals, and beliefs and may enforce similar procedures. Perhaps if learning-center directors become aware of those conflict areas that are inescapable in academe, they will be able to cope more effectively with the problems inherent in academic positions.

6

Evaluating Learning Services

Over the past three decades, a voluminous literature on educational evaluation procedures has been published, and in this era of educational accountability there is great pressure on new programs to provide evidence of their value and long-range effects. Yet postsecondary institutions have few systematic evaluation programs that are not mandated by government grants or other outside funding sources. Ball and Anderson (1975) found that most government departments and private industrial and commercial enterprises were receiving some sort of evaluation but that colleges rarely indulged in formal program evaluation. Hodgkinson and others (n.d.), in a survey of 375 colleges and universities rated as having innovative instructional programs, found additional evidence that rigorous, analytical evaluation procedures are infrequently institutionalized at the college level—even when some sort of evaluation is required as a condition for program funding. Seventy-five percent of the innovative institutions indicated that evaluation by individual faculty members using locally developed measures was the main pattern for course evaluation. About half the innovative institutions reported using evaluation for long-range planning, and 41 percent said they used it for faculty promotion and tenure. Only 4 percent reported using evaluation for improvement of instruction or for faculty development. The most frequent problems encountered in using evaluation results were evaluating the effectiveness of new programs, developing cost-effective evaluation measures, and interpreting the results of the assessments.

So even though the authors of most of the books on evaluation are university faculty members and have developed sophisticated methodology and procedures, the use of evaluation techniques seems to be restricted to special research projects reported in the professional journals. It is not an integral part of academic decision making in colleges and universities.

Perhaps skills programs are an exception. Because they are viewed as peripheral to the main mission of a college, they are requested to demonstrate their effectiveness in aiding students. In contrast, professors rarely question how effective the general-chemistry lectures are in meeting their objectives, or the courses in basic biology or conversational French. Since these are accepted parts of a college education, they no longer need to prove themselves.

In planning an evaluation study for a skills program, one must first be very clear about the reason it is being done. Certainly evaluation studies can yield information used to make more-effective in-house decisions and improve a program, but often the evaluation questions are asked by the campus administration or faculty. Ball (n.d.) developed a model and used it to assess the evaluation studies of the colleges and universities participating in National Project II—Alternatives to the Revolving Door, a project that assessed programs for the disadvantaged. Ball proposes that evaluation studies have six basic functions: to contribute to decisions about installing programs; to contribute to decisions about program continuation, expansion or contraction, and accreditation; to contribute to decisions about program modification; to obtain evidence favoring a program to rally support; to obtain evidence against a program to rally opposition; and to contribute to new knowledge. Ball cautions that one should first consider the appropriateness of the program to be evaluated before planning studies that may contribute to new knowledge. In other words, studies that might be acceptable as doctoral dissertations may not be appropriate program evaluations. For example, one might design a study to identify the differences in body language between black and Chicano clients; such a study might contribute to new knowledge but have little direct application to the program under investigation. If, however, one studied the ways clients from different ethnic groups viewed the program's registration procedures, the results might both suggest ways to improve the program and contribute to new knowledge. The reason for the evaluation dictates the most effective design and the kinds of data to be collected. See Appendix H for Ball's article describing his evaluation model and its rationale. I think this model will be very useful in helping learning-center directors recognize the often hidden agenda in requests for evaluation information, as well as helping them design more effective studies.

Other sources that will help the novice evaluator include Anderson and Ball (1978), Beatty (1971) for an inventory of measures of affective behavior, Bloom and others (1971), Popham (1975), Scriven (1974) for a model that can be used to evaluate educational materials and products—to mention just a few. Readers unfamiliar with experimental design might look at Campbell and Stanley (1963) for information on experimental and quasi-experimental studies and Webb and others (1966) for some interesting information on unobtrusive measures that might be useful.

In this chapter I discuss the criteria that can be used in assessing learning-skills programs, their advantages and disadvantages, and some techniques for gathering data.

Regardless of the purpose of the evaluation or whether it is done by outside evaluators or internal staff members, it is essential that records be set up, maintained, monitored for accuracy, and ready for inspection before an evaluation can begin.

Evaluation Criteria

Student Use of the Service. The number of students who use a service (or enroll in a skills course) and the number and kind of student/staff interactions are essential basic data for any evaluation study. If the program provides different kinds of services, such as tutoring, group study skills programs, and counseling, the record-keeping system should reflect student contacts in each type of service. Records should be kept on the student's name, college, sex, major, type of problem, type of service used, and number and kinds of contacts—group meetings, self-paced instruction, individual appointments, and so on.

Because the methods of counting student contacts vary, it is impossible to compare figures on student use from learning centers in different colleges. Some programs base their figures on compilations from student sign-in sheets and total the number of contacts, while others count the number of different (unduplicated) students seen and record hours for each. Some compile records of the total number of unduplicated students seen each term, while others report totals for the year. Thus Program A may report that it serves 900 different students a year (that is, 300 per quarter) while Program B reports serving 600 students per year (based on the annual total). However, it is possible that both programs serve the same number of different students per year (if, for instance, one third of Program A's students receive help for more than one quarter). Some learning centers count a talk given at orientation to 500 students as 500 student-contact hours and add them to the number of students seen by their staffs in individual appointments. Others count this presentation as one staff hour of outreach and do not include it in their tally of student-contact hours. Ideally, someday there will be standardization on these kinds of reports, but meanwhile it is very important for the program director to decide on a simple, workable system for compiling student-use data and stick to it.

The number of students who seek help in a voluntary program and the amount of time they spend in the program are important criteria. Wood (1961) proposed that attendance be used as the criterion for evaluating voluntary, noncredit reading programs, arguing that if students persist in a program voluntarily, they must be gaining something from it.

Demand for the service can be reflected in several ways. For instance, if courses or programs fill each term, that can be considered a positive sign. If students must wait to enroll in the course or program, then the numbers on waiting lists reflect student interest and perceived need. Attendance is a useful criterion in assessing a required course, as is the percentage of students dropping out of the course.

Student Satisfaction. Most academic support services and remedial courses try to collect information on student satisfaction, and in some institutions collecting data on client satisfaction is mandated for budget-review procedures. Students' evaluations of the service can be obtained by handing out or mailing questionnaires or by telephone or personal interviews. It is preferable to have someone not directly connected with the program conduct the mailed survey or interview clients; if outsiders conduct the survey, students may respond more freely, and the service is less likely to be criticized for being too subjective. Sometimes this can be done through another department; for example, the counseling-center staff may agree to interview clients of the learning center. Or students may be willing to conduct and analyze a survey by mail or to interview student clients as a project for credit.

Generally students who use learning centers and similar services rate them as beneficial. How positive their reactions are depends not only on the service they received but on how the questions on the survey are worded. For instance, most students will check favorable responses to questions like "How much did the reading program help you?" or "To what extent were you able to apply the study skills taught in the course to your regular course work?" Questions like "How do you feel the program might be improved?" will yield more-critical comments. In surveys of this sort, it is best to ask for an overall rating of the program and then ask specific questions aimed at finding out whether the student was able to use the skills, not whether he liked the instructor, the tutor, or the course. Questions like "What do you think you might have done if you had not been tutored?" with alternatives like "Done the same things," "Seriously considered dropping the course," and "Definitely would have dropped the course" yield useful information.

A less obtrusive indicator of student satisfaction is whether students encourage their friends to use the program. This information can be obtained easily by asking clients to indicate how they heard about the service when they sign into the program and by asking them on the postquestionnaire whether they would refer their friends to the program.

Too often student evaluations of courses and programs are limited to assessing whether students enjoyed the experience and liked the instructor. It is particularly important in assessing skills programs to determine whether students learned skills and were able to apply them to other courses. One way to elicit specific information about transfer of skills is to use the critical-incident method (Flanagan, 1954). In this technique, students are asked to respond to questions about their frequency of use of skills and to describe specific examples of how they applied them. For example, if one asks, "To what extent have you used speed-reading techniques in your other courses?" the student might reply, "Very frequently." Then one could say, "Give an illustration of how you have used this skill most recently."

When college learning-skills specialists think of evaluation measures, they usually consider questionnaires, statistical analyses of grades, and other things, but they rarely think of case studies. Yet a well-written, realistic case study gives administrators and faculty members an understanding of the problems of students and the processes used to resolve them that they cannot get from lengthy statistical reports (if they even read them).

Testimonials from students who have been helped by the program are also useful both for publicizing the program among potential clients and for conveying the message to faculty members and administrators.

Inviting faculty members and administrators to a discussion with students who are using the service is another effective way of communicating the nature of the program and how students respond to it.

Grades and Grade-Point Averages. Evidence that students improve their grades, their grade-point averages, or both as a result of a skills-improvement program is the kind of hard data that administrators like to see. However, demonstrating grade improvement may be difficult if one's program is limited to the weakest students. In this age of grade inflation, it is essential to have a comparison group if grade-point average is used as an assessment criterion. In a special tutoring program, for example, the tutored group may attain C averages, which may seem to represent adequate progress, but the nontutored students may average B. Finding a comparison group may be difficult even in a voluntary program, for those who volunteer for tutoring may be more highly motivated than those who do not. If the program or course is required, then one cannot match tutored students with a comparable group. There are ways, however, to handle this problem statistically by calculating predicted grade-point averages based on students' high school background and test scores at entrance.

A further difficulty in using grades as a criterion is that the program the student has taken may not be related to his work in other courses: One would not expect that a reading-improvement course would necessarily help students enrolled in mathematics and chemistry or that a student tutored in chemistry would improve his grades in English. It is often possible to find grade changes when students are enrolled in a voluntary adjunct skills course that is directly integrated into a regular course (see Chapter Twelve).

Changes in the qualifications of students recruited and accepted by the college from year to year can influence the apparent results of a skills program. If a better-prepared group enters one year, their grades may be higher than the grades earned by weaker students in a previous year, regardless of the skills program. Changes in academic policy and instructors' grading patterns can also affect the overall grades students get, regardless of how successful they are in improving their skills.

Another caveat in using grades as a criterion is that often the grades used for evaluation are limited to those earned by the student in the same term that he is taking remedial/developmental instruction. It is important to follow up students after they have completed the skills program and look at their subsequent grades and grade-point averages. In other words, give the students an opportunity to internalize and apply the techniques that they have been taught, and their skills gains should be reflected in their future grades in relevant courses.

In assessing the effects of brief, noncredit minicourses that teach one skill among many required in a regular course, it is wiser to examine the students' performance on that aspect of the course, rather than final grades. For example, one might use course quizzes or the items on the final exam that relate to the skill taught.

Retention in College. Another criterion for assessing skills programs is whether their students persist in college longer than comparable groups who do not take skills work. Retention studies require careful and long-term follow-up of students. Usually data are collected on a term-by-term basis, or, for students enrolled in a sequence of courses, such as chemistry, mathematics, or English, persistence in the sequence is examined. Since many college courses are subject to grade inflation and since academically weak students typically complete fewer credits, it is generally best to examine group differences after a two-year period; this allows students time to complete a number of courses and to advance through the sequence.

If one can show that students who take a skills program do persist in college longer, one can use this information for budget justification. For example, Richard Cummins at the University of Montana pointed out to his dean that if the reading and study skills program resulted in retaining only 10 percent of each year's freshmen for six quarters from the group who normally drop out, the institution would gain $550,000 in registration fees, and if the number of exit-prone students who graduated increased by just 5 percent, the university would gain an additional $277,500.

There is considerable precedent to show that effective student services do increase retention. For example, Frank and Kirk (1974) found that a higher percentage of students who voluntarily sought counseling help completed degrees than students with equivalent backgrounds who did not use this service, and there are many similar studies on skills programs. If the students selected for the program are much lower than the rest of the student body in background and ability, however, retention rates will invariably be low.

Test Scores. Using differences between students' pre- and posttest scores on standardized tests to assess a program requires a knowledge of the limitations of these instruments: (1) They rarely reflect the objectives of a specific skills program; they test more general skills. (2) Standardized tests are reliable, which means that they have been designed to be relatively impervious to change, particularly over a brief period. (3) It is hard to evaluate change on standardized tests when the scores of the group tested are not normally distributed. If only the bottom 25 percent of students are required to take a reading or mathematics course, then one can expect the students' scores to improve as a result of chance regression effects alone. In situations like this, control groups are needed. Similarly, if students are sectioned into high and low groups on the basis of a pretest, the high group's scores may decline on the posttest if pretest scores cluster near the test ceiling. (4) The raw scores on alternate forms of a test are rarely equivalent. For instance, on our local norms in the Nelson-Denny Reading Test and the Xerox Listening Test, Form B is easier than Form A. To use these tests as pre- and posttests, it is necessary either to compute standard scores for the group and use statistical analyses or to counterbalance the forms of the test (that is, give Form A to half the group for the pretest and Form B to the other half, and then on the posttest give Form B to the first half and Form A to the second). (5) Standardized tests have very limited application in assessing individualized skills programs. If students work on different skills, at different levels, and at different rates—for example, some on spelling, others on vocabulary, reading rate, or critical-reading exercises—one test, unless it is a lengthy battery, will not reflect their gains. One can use criterion-referenced tests to determine improvement on particular skills, or one can use units completed, but then one must report results in percentages—for example, 70 percent of those working on spelling completed exercises at the eighth-grade level. (For a discussion of this problem, see Maxwell, 1972).

Despite these limitations, standardized tests are often mandated as a condition for evaluating federally funded programs. When they are, one should use other criteria as well in judging the effectiveness of a skills program, for the tests give just one bit of information—how students' scores compare with those of a norm group.

Faculty Attitudes Toward the Program. Assessing faculty attitudes toward the skills program is another way of evaluating its effectiveness. Instructors can be sent short questionnaires, but these should be sent only to those instructors who know about the program—unless you are doing a needs assessment, in which case you might contact all instructors or a random sample. Faculty members also might be interviewed by phone or in person and queried for their responses to the program and their suggestions.

A somewhat more objective criterion of faculty members' interest and involvement is the number of students they refer. This information can be gathered from the faculty member (and is easier to obtain if one has referral forms) or from the students when they arrive at the service or course.

Staff Attitudes Toward the Program. Another important source of information for making decisions about a program is evaluations by staff members, including skills instructors, tutors, learning specialists, receptionists, and clerical workers. The director or chairperson might hold post-mortem group sessions at the end of each term and have the staff members discuss their experiences and their suggestions for improving the program. In addition, I would suggest that a questionnaire be sent to each staff member to fill out privately, which would include items about each of the program's objectives and ask the staff member questions like "How well are we meeting this objective?" and "What should we be doing?" Staff members should also be asked to rate their in-service training experiences, their supervision, and other aspects of their work, including scheduling and receptionist activities. Providing one's staff members with sufficient time to think about the problems they have in working with students and to identify the most frequent problems students present can result in useful ideas for developing better in-service training programs and for generating new programs or improving old ones.

Impact of the Program on the Campus as a Whole. If one of the program's objectives is to serve as a catalyst for improving undergraduate experiences, then some criterion must be found to reflect this. For a learning center, one indicator of success would be that courses or programs developed by the center staff are accepted by an academic department and become institutionalized—for example, a trigonometry review course or a unit on reading for ESL students.

A less obtrusive indicator of the impact of the program would be that the director is invited to sit on campus committees, particularly those that make important policy decisions concerning students, or that administrators or faculty members solicit the director's advice.

The image of the program held by the student body may also reflect the impact of the program. Surveys of seniors and their attitudes about their campus experiences could include items about learning services. (It can be very useful to know that 90 percent of seniors know about your program and that 70 percent have used it and regard it favorably—or that they do not feel that it is a useful service.)

Outside Evaluators

Hiring an outside expert (or a team of evaluators) not directly connected with one's program adds credibility to the evaluation report submitted. Administrators may accept the expert's recommendations a bit more readily than those of the program director. A person not directly involved with a program may observe aspects of the service that can be improved which are overlooked by the staff.

Outside evaluators proceed in different ways. Some prefer to review the program's objectives and data before they visit. Others use Scriven's goal-free methods (1974)—that is, they prefer not to know the objectives of the program in advance, but rather to come in and observe what is actually happening in the program, claiming that this is a more objective way of proceeding. Regardless of the evaluators' philosophy, they usually talk to staff members, the director, students in the program, and administrators in the college and observe the program in action. Evaluators perform different services. Some will aid the program director in planning an evaluation study, and most are requested to write a report. Evaluators also can help troubleshoot in the event of staff problems and can recommend ways that innovations can be implemented.

If a program director is interested in improving the efficiency of the program but is unable to get an outside evaluator, he may be able to get management assistance from the college's business unit or school of business administration. Sometimes this assistance is called a management audit or a system analysis. A management audit can be particularly helpful in a time of crisis. For example, Haase and others (1977) describe how a management audit of a college reading program helped the program's administrator resolve staff morale problems resulting from the denial of university credit for reading program courses and recent budget cuts.

The Evaluation Report

After conducting an evaluation study, the next step is to write a report. The way the report is written and prepared depends on the purpose of the evaluation. That is, if the report is designed to answer questions about one's program raised by administrators, it should be written in a format that administrators will read. Too often evaluation reports are so comprehensive, detailed, statistical, and lengthy that they confuse issues rather than clarify them. Some directors feel that preparing lengthy statistical reports will impress faculty members and administrators. My experience has been that one will arouse interest and get a response more quickly if one prepares a clear, readable, concise summary of the findings and recommendations, not longer than four pages. Save your means, multiple regression analyses, and covariance for your dissertation or the papers you submit to professional journals. Write a summary in plain English of the work you have done. Percentages may be far more effective in presenting your results to an administrator than means and standard deviations. For example, if you have studied three groups of EOP students—those who came in regularly for tutoring in biology, those who came in occasionally for tutoring, and those who received no tutoring, it is better to state your findings as "90 percent of the students who were tutored regularly attained grades of C or higher in Biology 1, compared with 40 percent of those tutored occasionally and 60 percent of those who received no tutoring" than as "The mean for the regularly tutored group was 2.697 (S.D. = 0.2435), compared with the occasionally tutored group mean of 1.883 (S.D. =0.2276) and the nontutored (control) group mean of 2.483 (S.D. = 0.3354)." Which statement conveys more useful information?

Popham (1975) suggests using bar graphs and dancing girls to highlight evaluation results in presenting them to administrators. I have not tried the dancing girls, but I have been tempted on occasion to hire violinists and weeping mourners to provide melancholy background music for our lengthy budget hearings.

Evaluation, then, should be an ongoing process to inform the central administration about one's program, and to aid the program director in making effective decisions, among other purposes.

7

Understanding Psychological Characteristics of Underprepared Students

To provide effective instruction to individuals who need to improve their learning skills, teachers need to understand the effects of motivation, learning styles, and the stages of normal intellectual development on college students' learning and performance. Motivation is often considered the prime factor in working with students, so much so that other difficulties may be overlooked. There is a mystique that if students are motivated, they can accomplish anything.

Unfortunately, it is not that simple. For college success, motivation is necessary but not sufficient. Certainly those who would succeed in college must be motivated to perform the tasks and assignments required, but they also need the skills and knowledge necessary to understand their courses, and they must be able to learn quickly, for colleges restrict the amount of time one has to complete learning tasks. Colleges have been criticized for dividing knowledge into semester or quarter segments and insisting that students complete their work during the term, but two mitigating factors should be considered: (1) students are permitted to retake most courses if they are unsuccessful in their first attempt; and (2) students usually expect to finish courses with their peers and are thus reluctant to recycle, or repeat, their classes. Students who cannot read, write, or add may be highly motivated to become physicians or lawyers, yet they have no chance of passing basic liberal arts courses. If, instead, they were to enter a strong basic adult literacy program in a community college that phased into a sequence of vocational courses, they would have a much better chance of succeeding. Unfortunately, the social and political pressures to redress historical grievances of disadvantaged minority groups have resulted in the admission of students who lack the most rudimentary learning skills into some of our most selective institutions. Although this policy has been termed "equal opportunity," in reality it means "guaranteed failure" when the student is not prepared for the work required and lacks the aptitude. The tragedy is that such students are not willing to change their goals and return to institutions that might offer more appropriate preparation.

In addition to background, aptitude, ability to learn quickly, and motivation, students need persistence, flexibility, and a willingness to cooperate with instructors' demands and institutional policies if they are to succeed in college. These latter characteristics are often subsumed under the term *motivation*.

Intrinsic and Extrinsic Motivation

Current motivational theory recognizes two kinds of motivation—intrinsic and extrinsic. Intrinsic motivation is the desire to perform a task because of the satisfaction derived directly from working on the task and the value associated with solving a problem or accomplishing an enterprise. Extrinsic motivation is desire to perform a task because success will lead to an external reward, such as money, grades, increased social status, or praise.

Some people attain great satisfaction or pride in accomplishing difficult tasks and seem to be motivated toward competency or mastery over their environment, not just toward external rewards. If people with high intrinsic motivation lack the background, skills, or aptitude to achieve a goal or solve a problem, they become frustrated and need to find ways to overcome their deficiencies or change their goals.

Psychologists currently contend that there is a negative relation between extrinsic and intrinsic motivation (Staw, 1976). If people act because of the promise of strong external rewards (or the fear of punishment), they are likely to assume that their motivation is wholly extrinsic. However, if external contingencies are not strong, people assume that their behavior is due to their own interest in the work. Therefore, if people are asked to perform an inherently interesting task but are lavishly rewarded for their efforts, they may infer that the task was really not very interesting or satisfying and that they were just working for the reward. As an illustration, a tight grading policy may turn what was an interesting learning task into dull work, and, in the future, students will refuse to perform the activity without clear rewards. Or students whose main reason for attending college is the financial aid they receive may develop little interest in continued learning. External rewards weaken students' general interest in learning and decrease their willingness to continue learning after they complete college.

If, however, most people perceive a task as dull, it may be necessary to provide external rewards to get them to accomplish it.

Professors generally assume that students are intrinsically motivated—that is, they are in college because they chose to be and want to learn. Professors holding this viewpoint will be less concerned with administering grades as penalties and more likely to plan assignments that are varied and interesting. When intrinsic motivation operates, there is less need to monitor students' behavior, because the students feel responsible for their own work.

However, many students enroll in college for purely extrinsic reasons—family pressures, future social and economic opportunities, and so on. These students view grades as what matters most, consider college courses mileposts to pass, and see their role as finding the easiest, least painful way to get through college. They may view all course work as dull and may take advantage of professors who try to make courses interesting and who do not administer grades in a punitive way.

Our present reward systems to lure disadvantaged students into college are based on the premise that if one provides extrinsic rewards for learning (adequate financial aid so that students need not work), students will eventually develop a preference for the learning activity itself, and external rewards will no longer be necessary. This rarely happens, whether learning is associated with M&Ms or $s. Students will respond as long as the rewards are given but will not sustain learning on their own.

How Motivational Differences Affect Course Selection

As an academic adviser for many years, I observed that freshmen differed greatly in their expectations of what college offered and in their willingness to take required courses. One variable related to this diversity was the preparation and prior achievement of the student. The brightest, best-prepared students who were committed to a particular major were cautious about the number of courses they wanted to take as freshmen and concerned about making high grades. They usually insisted on taking the required courses as soon as possible. I am convinced that although they might have grumbled a bit, they would willingly have taken a course labeled "Nongourmet Cooking: Eating Crow 1A,B,C" if it had been required for a pre-med or psych major that they coveted.

Average students without a clear educational goal and those who had a career goal in mind but were vague about what it entailed would reject required courses as "irrelevant" or "unnecessary" but take them within a reasonable time limit. I recall one young man who said he wanted to be a lawyer but fought taking the required political science course for two years (signing up and dropping it). Some years later, when he was in law school, he came back to tell me that now (at last) he saw the relevance of the political science course and appreciated its importance.

Academically weak students, particularly those whose interest in a major field was built largely on fantasy, demanded their right to take a course overload, wanted to take upper-division courses immediately, and did everything in their power to avoid required courses—even those that related to their professed majors. Some succeeded in avoiding them until their senior year, hoping the rules would change and they could graduate without them.

I believe that many of these same observations hold today. The students weakest in writing still try to put off the required basic writing course as long as possible—even though it underlies success in other fields.

Underprepared students often see college only as a steppingstone to a better job and have difficulty understanding why they should have to take required breadth requirements or courses outside their field of interest. Helping them develop a broader perspective on the value of learning to the individual's satisfaction with life is a broad goal toward which both support staff and faculty must work.

Characteristics of Successful High-Risk Students.

Although it is impossible to predict with much accuracy which underprepared, or high-risk, students will succeed in college, a number of studies reveal some patterns of motivational characteristics that relate to college success. Potentially successful high-risk students seem to be distinguished by a general adaptive factor that involves goal aspiration, goal orientation, goal involvement, willingness to study hard, ability to solve personal problems, and a feeling of support from significant others, such as parents. Weigand (1949) gathered information about these characteristics through interviews with students who had entered college with high school grade-point averages below C. He found that potentially successful students had more favorable attitudes toward school and were less apathetic toward their previous school experiences. Successful students stated that they themselves had selected a goal or major and felt that their own interests had influenced the choices they had made. In contrast, unsuccessful students felt that their goals had been selected for them and gave more superficial reasons for wanting to attend college (for example, because their friends were going). Successful students were convinced that college was important and, despite hardships, found ways of studying. They felt they studied harder than the average student did or "should." Although successful students reported having as many financial and personal problems as unsuccessful students reported, they seemed better able to cope with their problems and to take positive action to alleviate them. Unsuccessful students either took no action or took action that did not alleviate the stress. The parents of successful students were more consistently supportive and interested and offered a more democratic type of supervision than did unsuccessful students' parents, who did not encourage them even when they were not failing.

Even though Weigand's study was done some thirty years ago, long before Patricia Cross discovered the "new students," I have found nothing in my experience or the literature that would refute his findings, and I feel that they are valid today. Researchers, particularly doctoral students in counseling, continue to probe for newer and more effective ways to describe the students who succeed despite inadequate backgrounds and poor test scores.

Characteristics of Unsuccessful Students

Similarly, there have been many studies on the students who fail in college. Pitcher and Blaushild (1970) list ten reasons for academic failure: lack of potential; inadequate conception of the work involved in succeeding; importance of other activities over study; interference from psychological problems; failure to assume responsibility for own learning; inhibition of language functions (poor reading, writing, and speaking skills); lack of understanding of standards for high-quality performance; selection of inappropriate major; vagueness about long-term goals; and selection of wrong college.

Pitcher and Blaushild, analyzing data from 600 college failures from 250 colleges who attended the Berea, Ohio, Educational

Development Center for a ten-week educational rehabilitation program, concluded that these underachievers in college had been underachieving all their academic life. Their problems had not begun in college. Pitcher and Blaushild also concluded that these students' problems were often due to upward-striving parents who considered anything less than full attainment of goals to be failure, to the conflict between the developmental stages of late adolescence and college structure, and to the disparity between most high school programs (where anti-intellectualism is rewarded) and college (where intellectual activities are valued). They found that the failure rate was highest in those state institutions which must, by law, take all graduates from accredited high schools and which solve the problem by dumping academically weak students quickly.

Studying the characteristics of the low-achieving college student was a popular research activity of counseling psychologists in the 1950s and early 1960s. Researchers were particularly interested in the "underachiever," defined as a student whose ability scores were high but whose grades were low. As research data accumulated, some studies showed that even students scoring poorly on standardized tests were "underachievers" too. Kornrich (1965) selected 51 articles from the more than 500 published studies for his book *Underachievement*. These papers range from research reports, case studies, and position papers to theoretical articles. For example, in an article "The Underachievement Syndrome," Roth and Meyersburg (1963) described constructs that characterize the poor college achiever:

- The student's poor achievement does not arise from incapacity to achieve.
- Poor achievement is an expression of the student's choice.
- The student's choice for poor achievement operates in the preparation he makes for achievement.

Specifically, they found that the way a student studies—the subject areas he concentrates on or avoids, the amount of study time— reflects a decision that leads to low achievement. Poor achievers spend much of their study time with friends, relaxing, watching television, or fantasizing. They prepare only partially for exams, and when they study, they are not sure what they are studying about. I have known many students with these symptoms. For example, Peter, an engineering student, complained that he had studied over fifty hours for a physics examination but could not recall the topics covered in the textbook or lectures—or even the chapter titles. It was as if studying for him meant staring at a book, trying to memorize each detail—a kind of penance serving.

- Low achievers have a history of poor achievement and poor or nonexistent study habits.
- Low achievement may be expressed as an overall limited achievement in all courses or as achievement in deviant channels.

When the student's overall achievement is low, Roth and Meyersburg conclude that the student's energies are directed toward maintaining the status quo. One example is the student who resists learning new subjects "that I haven't had before" and refuses to take new subjects. Those who achieve in deviant channels expend their efforts in extracurricular activities, like Jim, a student who was too busy organizing the card section for the fall football games to study, or Kwami, who spent so much time and energy trying to organize his own alternative school that he could not attend class or write papers. Others show a strong resistance to authority, like Rondi, who read books avidly for her own pleasure and interest but refused to read any of the works assigned by her instructors—even those she had started on her own volition.

Roth and Meyersburg also postulate that the patterns for poor achievement are enduring and do not undergo spontaneous change. However, they think counseling can serve as an impetus to change low-achievement patterns.

The low achiever tends to have family problems, is impulsively disparaging of self, is vulnerable to disparagement by others, tends to lack insight about self, lacks a clear set of personal goals and values, has frequent depressions, and is anxious. The psychodynamics of low achievement, as one might expect, are complex. Devalued by parents, these students learn early to get gratification from their peers, and they sometimes get attention from their parents for their embarrassingly low grades.

Students who are failing come in for counseling reluctantly if at all, when sent by advisers, revealing states of deep depression or denial. Poor achievers are not the college counselor's favorite clients, and the research on the efficacy of counseling and/or psychotherapy in improving the academic achievement of failing students reveals that counseling may not help. Kirk (1965, p. 181) describes the counselor's quandary: "Universally in these cases [students on academic probation], the counselor reports that it was a matter of extreme difficulty to obtain any direct discussion of the problem with the counselee, however obvious and apparent the problem, and however voluntarily the counselee had sought counseling. Moreover, the recurrent report is that it was extremely difficult to obtain a description or discussion of any of the counselee's feelings, or even, in many cases, situations or vicissitudes which might be expected to occasion strong counselee reactions." She adds that the clients show no surprise when they learn they have done extremely well on ability tests and that their excuses for their poor grades are "unrealistic, superficial, and largely implausible." The counselor must work very hard with these students, and the prognosis is poor.

It is sad that at about the same time that college counselors concluded there was little they could do to help underachieving, failing students, colleges and universities were forced to recruit and accept large numbers of educationally disadvantaged students and favor students with histories of underachievement for scholarships. Thus institutions of higher education admitted students with the poorest chances for success, those who would be least responsive to traditional educational programs and counseling. In other words, the U.S. government replaced the overprotective parents who classically had forced their children into college.

Are these "new" students really so different from those who have failed in college in the past? Although labeled "culturally deprived," "high-risk," "disadvantaged," or "underprepared," they have the same traits and characteristics as college failures in the past.

Unmindful of the vast literature on college failures in the past, a new group of experts arose, studied the new disadvantaged students, and discovered that they shared certain "unique" problems. The "uniqueness" of the problems, however, resulted from the experts' failure to look at other college groups or at the history of the underachiever. So we find summaries like Klingelhofer and Hollander (1973) stating that the educationally disadvantaged shared the following traits: deficiencies in conventional academic skills (reading, writing, and mathematics); lack of proficiency or practice in analytical approaches to problem solving; difficulties in working toward abstract goals or for symbolic rewards; strong leanings toward occupations in the applied professions rather than becoming scholars or researchers; bewilderment and feeling out of place at the onset of the college experience; and limitations on freedom of choice of situation or program.

As remedial programs expanded, counselors wrung their hands, and skills specialists wondered why academically weak students would not stick to self-paced and machine programs that had been designed to help them with basic skills. Why were they unwilling to work alone on these devices if they were so highly motivated to reach their goals—or were they?

Two new areas of emphasis by psychologists and epistemologists that promise to aid our understanding of young adults may lead to some answers to the preceding question and the general quandary about underprepared students. First is the work of William G. Perry, whose longitudinal study on the stages of intellectual and ethical development of college students extends the methodology and insights of developmental psychology into this crucial age group. Second is the extensive research on cognitive styles, particularly studies of field dependence/independence.

Perry's Scheme

Perry's work (1968) culminated in a scheme that lays out the stages of intellectual and ethical development of students during their four-year college experience. Interviews with Harvard and Radcliffe students through their college careers provided the data for the study. Interviewers asked students each year to reflect on their college experiences and recorded their conversations verbatim. Perry's analysis of these interviews involved a nine-position scale: In Position 1 the student sees the world in polar terms of we-right-good versus they-wrong-bad and feels that there is an ultimate truth, known by the instructor, and that there are right and wrong answers for every question, as on a spelling test. In Position 2 the student begins to perceive that differences of opinion and uncertainty exist but accounts for them on the basis that teachers are poorly qualified or that teachers know the answers but "want us to find them for ourselves." In Position 3 the student finds diversity and uncertainty pervasive but concludes that it is because we have not found the answer yet. In Position 4 the student accepts diversity and uncertainty as real and legitimate and accepts the belief that anyone has a right to his own opinion or sees the teacher's position as merely a special case of what the teacher wants rather than an authoritative viewpoint that has more validity than the views of others. By the time the student reaches Position 7, he is beginning to make an initial personal commitment to a viewpoint in a field of knowledge, and by Position 9 he "experiences the affirmation of identity among multiple responsibilities and realizes commitment as an ongoing, unfolding activity through which he expresses his life-style" (Perry, 1968, p. 10). Progress through these stages from dualism to commitment is not in smooth, automatic steps. Some students delay, deflect, and regress.

Perry concludes that the educational impact of diversity is best when it is intentional—that is, when it is deliberately planned to help students stand back and gain perspective. This can occur when individual professors are committed to different viewpoints and the student is exposed to this clash of ideas, provided that the diversity of views is based on disciplined independence of mind rather than the haphazard clash of dogmatic professors. There are problems, one being that students may become cynical and gameplay, trying to throw the professor's views back at him and refusing to think on their own. Yet one of the most frustrating kinds of learning experiences for students is when the instructor is completely neutral, presenting different viewpoints and theories but never expressing his own commitment. Perhaps this approach is necessary too, for it forces students to think for themselves rather than merely trying to please the professor.

Perry's scheme is being applied to both college teaching and student counseling in the hope that if instructors are knowledgeable about the stages of intellectual development, they might provide greater opportunities for student growth (Widick, 1977). The basic conditions for promoting growth are situations in which the student is both *challenged* and *supported*. Challenge is provided through presenting diverse viewpoints and experiential learning, while support is offered simultaneously through structured instruction and a personal atmosphere, including individual conferences between instructor and student.

In one study, Touchton and others (1977) offered a career-planning course for undergraduates at the University of Maryland in which three groups were taught by different instructors using the same materials and content. The experimental group was taught by instructors trained in Perry's scheme and in techniques of providing dualistic students with appropriate challenge and support. The second group was taught by teachers knowledgeable about Perry's scheme but not given the techniques for implementing the scheme. The control group was taught in normal fashion by instructors who were not familiar with Perry's scheme. The investigators found that 71 percent of the experimental group scored as dualists on the pretest (that is, they placed in Position 1 on the Perry scheme), but only 21 percent were dualists on the posttest, suggesting that for a significant percentage of the group, the complexity of thinking about occupations increased. In the group taught by instructors familiar with the Perry scheme but not using the techniques, 65 percent scored as dualists on the pretest and 24 percent on the posttest. The control group showed no change toward diversity of thinking: 47 percent were dualists at the start of the course, and 47 percent completed the course as dualists. In this study, students in the specially oriented courses showed significant movement toward a more complex intellectual stage in viewing career choices. (For another application of the Perry scheme, see Widick, 1977).

The Perry scheme has not, to my knowledge, been used in planning developmental or remedial skills courses, but it should have useful applications in this area. Developmental skills courses are meant to help students move to a position at which they can accept and learn intellectually demanding course material. Instructors in these courses use many of the elements suggested by Perry, but often rigidly or haphazardly—that is, some instructors emphasize a supportive counseling/teaching strategy, and others restrict the course to a very structured set of experiences. Students need both. To implement these ideas in developmental skills courses, one might challenge students by planning diverse activities such as having them share experiences and ideas with classmates, using a variety of materials and approaches to learning, varying practice to include discussion and written experiences, and providing a large amount of direct experience. For instance, students might keep logs and interview older students about their reading and study experiences and techniques and the demands faced in advanced courses. They might also ask their instructors about their perceptions of how students should study. Students can be supported if the instructor structures the class carefully and adheres to due dates for work, lesson plans, and contracts for students.

For example, Kathy Steele and Jeanine Webb at the University of Florida use several questions concerning what they consider important criteria to help interested professors improve their course outlines: (1) *rationale*: Why should the student take this course? (2) *student outcomes*: What do you expect students to achieve? (3) *topics*: What are you going to teach? (4) *assignments*: What must students do to complete the course? (5) *assessment procedures*: How many and what kinds of tests will you require? Projects? Papers? (6) *grading policy:* How will you determine the grade? (7) *instructional materials:* What materials are required—textbooks, lab manuals, and so on? (8) *policies:* What are your rules about class attendance, class participation, office hours, use of facility, and so on?

Personalization can be enhanced if students are free to disclose their problems and conflicts to the group; to this end, students might make an oral as well as a written contract stating their commitment to the course and agreeing to maintain confidentiality about what other students reveal in discussions. Personalization can also be enhanced by encouraging small-group interactions, dyadic interactions, individual interviews with the instructor, and written and oral comments by the instructor about the student's log book and other work.

It would seem that these approaches are particularly important in improving study skills courses, whose main goal is to get students to change their study behavior, rather than merely learn techniques. However, the model can be applied to all the other skills areas as well.

Cognitive Styles

There are many ways to learn. Each person has consistent ways of organizing and processing information or preferred ways of organizing all he or she sees and thinks about. Psychologists call these ways "cognitive styles." Cognitive styles are conceptualized as stable attitudes, preferences, or habitual strategies that determine a person's typical mode of perceiving, remembering, thinking, and problem solving. Current research suggests that a person's cognitive style affects the way he or she learns in college and has implications for teaching strategies. Psychologists currently believe that cognitive styles are not simple habits, but develop slowly and experientially, and are not easily changed by instruction. Cognitive styles differ from intellectual abilities, which concern content, or *what* is learned; cognitive styles concern *how* it is learned. Usually, cognitive styles are thought of as bipolar traits, either end of the scale representing appropriate adaptation in some situations, with individuals distributed along the points of the scale.

Messick and Associates (1976) describe nineteen dimensions of cognitive style that psychologists have researched. These range from scanning (differences in the extensiveness and intensity of attention deployment) to reflection versus impulsivity and risk taking versus cautiousness. These dimensions closely resemble what earlier psychologists called "learning style" or "learning set" or various personality traits that have been found to relate to college learning. For example, Smith and others (1956) and Maxwell (1978) have reported that aspects of learning style (namely, impulsivity versus constriction and stability versus anxiety) relate to improvement in reading rate and scanning speed. (See also Blanton and Bullock's (1973) review of the research on cognitive style and reading behavior.)

Verbal-learning researchers also have explored the characteristics of persons whose preferred way of learning is to master facts, in contrast to those who prefer to learn concepts. Siegel and Siegel (1965) developed a scale that measured educational set and tested a person's predisposition to learn facts without being driven to interrelate them into any contextual whole versus his predisposition to learn concepts. They compared scores of fact seekers with scores of those who preferred learning broader concepts. The fact-dominated students believed that a fact has an integrity all its own; the concept-oriented students rejected acquisition of facts except as units of information that are interrelated. Testing students in two biology classes, the Siegels found that concept-oriented students learned both facts and concepts better in the section whose instructor was more sensitive to conditions conducive to intrinsic motivation and attempted to interest and motivate students than in the class where the students were motivated only to pass the course. In the extrinsically motivated class, concept-oriented and fact-oriented students performed equally well on exams.

Field Dependence/Independence. Currently, the dimension of cognitive style that seems to have the greatest implication for educators is field dependence versus field independence. Field-dependent people tend to be more sensitive to people and social situations, whereas field-independent people respond well to situations that require them to use analytic and problem-solving abilities. Cross (1976) has found many similarities between field dependents and the "new students." New students spend their leisure time with people and report that their most important college learning experiences relate to getting along with others. Like field dependents, they are attracted to college majors and careers that emphasize interpersonal relations, are compliant with the wishes of others, are passive, and favor traditional women's roles. Field dependents tend to be poor at analytical problem solving, and New Students score low on instruments measuring preferences for analytic and critical thinking. Both groups tend to be guided by authority figures and extrinsically motivated.

Field dependence/independence seems to influence selection of majors. In a recent longitudinal study, Witkin and others (1977) found that college students who persisted in college and graduate work either remained in majors consistent with their cognitive styles or transferred to them. A significantly greater proportion of field-dependent (people-oriented) students majored in education than of field independents, who preferred majors in science and engineering. Most women are field-dependent, and women are underrepresented in science and engineering fields. Although I find this an interesting study, I am concerned that such findings as these may be used to counsel freshmen into careers consistent with their cognitive styles, a premature application of the findings. Since most women are field-dependent, much more information is needed on the developmental stages that college women go through before concluding that "people who need people" (that is, field dependents) should not enter science, engineering, or mathematics. Rather than screening out applicants with the "wrong" cognitive style, I would like to see studies on the learning conditions and demands that attract different types of people to different majors. For example, in one of our programs, we trained women and minority freshmen as tutors in the sciences. They continued in these majors and stated that the tutoring experience and role gave them status with their friends and an opportunity to help others. (These are *not* the usual reasons science majors give for selecting their fields.)

There appear to be more field-dependent than field-independent people in college today, judging from the numbers who enroll in popular social science and education courses (even though the job market for social scientists and teachers is glutted). Perhaps, however, other factors account for the popularity of these courses, such as that they tend to be easier and less demanding than science and engineering courses.

Locus of Control. Locus of control is another cognitive style that research suggests bears a real and consistent relationship to academic achievement and aspiration. According to Rotter's (1966) construct that individuals differ in their beliefs about whether external or internal factors affect rewards, individuals who are categorized as having a sense of internal control believe that rewards follow, or are contingent upon their own behavior. Conversely, those who have a sense of external control believe that rewards are controlled by forces outside of themselves and thus may occur independently of their own actions. Disadvantaged students are often said to have a sense of being controlled by external events; they feel powerless over their own lives. Since they feel unable to manage their environment and to obtain rewards by their own behavior, they may attribute their failing grades to teachers' discriminatory attitudes against them rather than to what they did or did not do. A number of programs have reported that counseling helps underprepared students develop a realistic sense of both personal and collective power, which seems to be a necessary prerequisite for succeeding in academic courses (Cooke, 1977; Klingelhofer and Hollander, 1973; Whyte, 1978).

Self-Concept. So much has been written about the negative effects of early school experiences on the psyches of disadvantaged students, who are now eagerly sought as college students, that the research on self-concept deserves mention. Concern about changing the negative self-concepts of underprepared students has become almost a cult among teachers and writers, with the result that the complexities of the relationship between confidence in one's ability and performance are often overlooked. Despite the eloquent and passionate writing of such authors as Holt (1964), Cross (1976), and Roueche and Snow (1977), there is little evidence to support the contention that underprepared college students consistently have lower self-concepts than their more able peers. In fact, there is compelling clinical and empirical evidence that just the opposite is often true (Beery, 1975; Klingelhofer and Hollander, 1973). Intellectually capable and well-prepared students who lack confidence in their ability to succeed in college fill the caseloads of college counseling centers while many underprepared students are very confident in their ability to succeed in college. When asked what grades they expect to earn in college they will respond "A's" although they never have earned grades that high in public school. Perhaps this response reflects a sort of denial or bravado (although it is often dubbed unrealistic), but it is very hard to convince weak students with high expectations that they will need intensive help if they are to meet their goals.

Many of these students confident of their ability to study and learn are those who earned high grades in academically weak high schools. They consider themselves well prepared for college and reject help until they find that they are failing. The policies established to prevent high school dropouts (particularly in inner-city schools) have resulted in automatic promotion and grade inflation.

As a result, we can expect to see many more of these ill-prepared students with good high school grades entering our colleges.

Disadvantaged minority students (especially blacks, the group that has been studied most often) have much greater confidence in their ability to handle social situations than do white college students, and it may be this social confidence that leads them to be overconfident about their academic prospects. Certainly students who have been on the borderline of failure for years, usually lack confidence in their ability to learn, but so do students who are high achievers. One consistent finding in studies of self-confidence is that women, as a group, have the most seriously damaged or lowest concepts of self. In reviewing a large number of studies of self-concept, Klingelhofer and Hollander (1973) conclude that at the college level, low self-concepts do not seem as typical of black women, but white women, lower-class women, white Southern women, and other minority women all contribute to a "morbid picture of low self-esteem, lack of self-confidence, and an unwillingness to take risks or be venturesome, which suggests the impact of cultural conditioning" (1973, p. 52). The women's movement faces a large task in raising the consciousness of women to recognize their own worth.

Hill's Cognitive-Style Mapping. A different approach to cognitive style that has aroused considerable interest in many colleges is the cognitive-style mapping that Hill (n.d.) has used to match students and curricula at Oakland Community College in Michigan for the past decade. Hill's model, extracted here, includes three sets of elements: (1) symbols (twenty-four elements), (2) cultural determinants (three elements), and (3) modalities of inference (five elements). Hill claims that 3,260 different profiles of individual maps are possible at a given level of learning and that each will produce information for prescribing a personalized program that will maximize the student's academic success.

Dimensions of Hill's Cognitive Style Map

1. Symbols and Their Meanings

Two types of symbols, theoretical and qualitative, are created and used by individuals to acquire knowledge and derive meaning from their environments and personal experiences. Theoretical symbols present to the awareness of the individual something different from that which the symbols are. Words and numbers are examples of theoretical symbols. Qualitative symbols present and then represent to the individual that which the symbol is. Feelings, commitments, and values are examples of the meanings conveyed by qualitative symbols. Theoretical symbols include:

- T(VL)—Theoretical Visual Linguistics—ability to find meaning in written words
- T(AL)—Theoretical Auditory Linguistics—ability to acquire meaning through hearing spoken words
- T(VQ)—Theoretical Visual Quantitative—ability to acquire meaning in terms of numerical symbols, relationships, and measurements that are written
- T(AQ)—Theoretical Auditory Quantitative—ability to acquire meaning in terms of numerical symbols, relationships, and measurements that are spoken

The four qualitative symbols associated with sensory stimuli are:

- Q(A)—Qualitative Auditory—ability to perceive meaning through the sense of hearing
- Q(O)—Qualitative Olfactory—ability to perceive meaning through the sense of smell
- Q(T)—Qualitative Tactile—ability to perceive meaning through the sense of touch, temperature, and pain
- Q(V)—Qualitative Visual—ability to perceive meaning through sight

The qualitative symbols that are programmatic in nature are:

- Q(PF)—Qualitative Proprioceptive (Fine)—ability to synthesize a number of symbolic mediations into a performance demanding monitoring of a complex task involving small, or fine, musculature (for example, playing a musical instrument, typewriting)
- Q(PG)—Qualitative Proprioceptive (Gross)—ability to synthesize a number of symbolic mediations into a performance demanding monitoring of a complex task involving large, or gross, musculature (for example, throwing a baseball, skiing)
- Q(PKF)—Qualitative Proprioceptive Kinematics (Fine)—ability to synthesize a number of symbolic mediations into a performance demanding the use of fine musculature while monitoring a complex physical activity involving motion
- Q(PKG)—Qualitative Proprioceptive Kinematics (Gross)—ability to synthesize a number of symbolic mediations into a performance demanding the use of gross musculature while monitoring a complex physical activity involving motion

- Q(PTF)—Qualitative Proprioceptive Temporal (Fine)—ability to synthesize a number of symbolic mediations into a performance demanding the use of fine musculature while monitoring a complex physical activity involving timing
- Q(PTG)—Qualitative Proprioceptive Temporal (Gross)—ability to synthesize a number of symbolic mediations into a performance demanding the use of gross musculature while monitoring a complex physical activity involving timing

The remaining are defined as:

- Q(CEM)—Qualitative Code Empathetic—sensitivity to the feelings of others
- Q(CES)—Qualitative Code Esthetic—ability to enjoy the beauty of an object or an idea
- Q(CET)—Qualitative Code Ethic—commitment to a set of values, a group of principles, obligations and/or duties
- Q(CH)—Qualitative Code Histrionic—ability to exhibit a deliberate behavior or play a role to produce some particular effect on other persons
- Q(CK)—Qualitative Code Kinesics—ability to understand, and to communicate by, nonlinguistic functions such as facial expressions and motions of the body (for example, smiles and gestures)
- Q(CKH)—Qualitative Code Kinesthetic—ability to perform motor skills, or effect muscular coordination according to a recommended, or acceptable, form (for example, bowling according to form, or golfing)
- Q(CP)—Qualitative Code Proxemics—ability to judge the physical and social distance that the other person would permit between oneself and that other person
- Q(CS)—Qualitative Code Synnoetics—personal knowledge of oneself
- Q(CT)—Qualitative Code Transactional—ability to maintain a positive communicative interaction which significantly influences the goals of the persons involved in that interaction (for example, salesmanship)
- Q(CTM)—Qualitative Code Temporal—ability to respond to or behave according to time expectations imposed on an activity by members in the role-set associated with that activity

II. Cultural Determinants

There are three cultural determinants of the meaning of symbols:

- I—Individuality—uses one's own interpretation as an influence on meanings of symbols

- A—Associates—symbolic meanings are influenced by one's peer group
- F—Family—influence of members of the family, or a few close personal friends, on the meanings of symbols

III. Modalities of Inference

The third set of cognitive style data includes elements that indicate the individual's modality of inference, that is, the form of inference used:

- M—Magnitude—a form of categorical reasoning that utilizes norms or categorical classifications as the basis for accepting or rejecting an advanced hypothesis
- D—Difference—a tendency to reason in terms of one-to-one contrasts or comparisons of selected characteristics of measurements
- R—Relationships—the ability to synthesize a number of dimensions or incidents into a unified meaning, or through analysis of a situation to discover its component parts
- L—Appraisal—the modality of inference employed by an individual who uses all three of the modalities noted above (M, D, and R), giving equal weight to each in the reasoning process

Hill's symbols are of two kinds, theoretical and qualitative. There are four theoretical symbols: auditory linguistic, verbal linguistic, auditory quantitative, and visual quantitative. A counselor determines how much the individual student relies on theoretical symbols rather than qualitative symbols by analyzing his or her scores on traditional standardized tests (specifically, reading, listening, and mathematics tests given in both written and oral form). Then, through interviews, questionnaires, and other means, the counselor analyzes the qualitative symbols, the cultural determinants, and the modalities of inference.

After the testing, interviews, and other activities, the counselor prepares a map from the data, verifies it, and interprets the results to the student. Then the counselor and student work out a study program so that the student can maximize his strengths and select the most appropriate mode of learning, class, and instructor.

Hill assumes that the teacher's style should mesh with the student's. This implies that the cognitive maps of faculty members are available to the counselor. Others (Cross, 1976, for example) question whether it is desirable to place students in learning environments that match their preferences rather than challenging them to adapt to conflicting environments by encouraging them to enroll in courses in which their learning styles do not mesh with the teachers' styles.

The complexity of Hill's cognitive-style mapping system and the amount of time it takes to use raise questions about its appropriateness for most college situations. Certainly this system, as it is presently structured, would require the support and commitment of the administration and the majority of the faculty in an institution. It would be costly and time-consuming to implement and difficult to train faculty members and counselors to use. Martens (1973) has written a booklet in programmed-learning format to help faculty members and counselors learn Hill's terminology and understand and apply his complex cognitive-style mapping code. Reading Martens' book and learning to map a few students might alert instructors to the range of differences in learning styles among their students, and even if formal mapping of all students and faculty members were not carried out, the information gained would be useful.

One obstacle to putting Hill's system into practice is that college courses are traditionally bound to formal, theoretical, symbolic verbal and quantitative modes of instruction, and students must either have these skills or be able to acquire them quickly. I doubt that textbook publishers would be inspired to produce materials in economics or political science that would allow students to scratch, sniff, and remember concepts and theories, although there are books like that on the primer level. Moreover, it is hard to imagine that instructors would have the incentive, energy, or creativity to adapt their instruction to so many different learning styles. It is not easy to convince some instructors that some students learn better if given the opportunity to work on group projects, much less to expect those instructors to design learning activities that would meet the needs of the thousands of combinations and permutations of the cognitive-style maps postulated by Hill.

In one attempt to apply Hill's system, faculty cooperation was found less than ideal. In 1975 the American College Testing Program (1977) began studies at Michigan State University and McComb College (also in Michigan) to evaluate Hill's model. The researchers tried to develop and validate a test battery measuring Hill's constructs and to train faculty members in using cognitive mapping (Henderson, 1976, Orr, 1976). Of the twenty faculty members who volunteered to participate in the first year of the study, only seven remained for the second year.

During the second year, the project attempted to explore the aptitude-treatment-interactions within a series of independent researches with the goal of finding out whether students learn better and/or feel better about learning if their learning experiences are tailored to their needs. Seven implementation studies were planned and six were carried out. One of the studies at Michigan State University was not completed because the counseling-center directors who developed the plans were unable to obtain the necessary cooperation from the counselors in the center. Of the other six studies, none confirmed the existence of significant relations between cognitive style and educational outcomes. However, there were many problems in carrying out the project, such as lack of control data with some groups, students' complaints that they were required to spend two weeks of class time taking the tests, and shifts of trained faculty members to administrative posts. The final report spoke to the need for establishing measures that reliably and validly measure elements of cognitive style and the difficulty of completing such field research projects at the college level.

I believe it would be more helpful and realistic to determine which of the many variables involved in cognitive-style mapping are crucial to learning a particular subject. Then a simplified assessment of students' cognitive styles could help them identify their strengths and weaknesses and plan appropriate study strategies capitalizing on their strengths. For example, in a history course, a student who is strong in qualitative visual symbols might be encouraged to draw pictures or make multicolored charts of lists of facts to be learned; the student who scores high in "histrionics" might dramatize a debate between two political theorists.

Currently, a number of researchers are striving to develop simpler instruments for measuring cognitive style. Canfield's Learning Styles Inventory (1976), presently being validated, is one new test. Cooke (1977) reports that the Canfield inventory allows instructors to find out information about students at the beginning of the term that they otherwise might not learn until the end of the quarter, if at all. She states that instructors find it useful in planning appropriate learning experiences for open-admissions students. A much easier instrument to administer and score than the Hill cognitive-style model, the Learning Styles Inventory contains the following scoring categories:

I. Conditions: Concerns for the dynamics of the situation in which learning occurs.
   A. Affiliation: Relations with others
      P—Working with peers
      T—Knowing the teacher personally
   B. Structure: Logical, well-defined, and clear study plans
      O—Organization: Course work logically and clearly organized, meaningful assignments, and a logical sequence of activities
      D—Detail: Specific information on assignments, requirements, rules, and so on
   C. Achievement: Independence of action, pursuit of own interests, and so on
      G—Goal Setting: Setting one's own objectives, pursuing one's own interests and objectives
      I—Independence: Working alone and independently
   D. Eminence: Comparing self with others
      C—Competition: Desiring comparison with others
   E. Authority: Desiring classroom discipline and order; desiring informed and knowledgeable teachers.
II. Content: Major area of interest
   N—Numeric: Working with numbers and logic, computing, and so on
   Q—Qualitative: Working with words or language, writing, editing, talking, and so on
   I—Inanimate: Working with things, designing, constructing
   P—People: Working with people, interviewing, counseling, selling, helping
III. Mode: General modality through which learning is preferred
   L—Listening
   R—Reading
   I—Iconics: Viewing illustrations, graphs, and movies
   D—Direct Experience: Handling or performing (as in shop, laboratory, field trips, practice exercises)

An Implementation of Hill's Cognitive-Style Mapping. Harryette Ehradt of Mountain View College in Dallas, Texas, writes me that her campus is using a modified Hill model to measure students' cognitive styles and to use the data for instructional design/ development and as a diagnostic tool in the classroom. Since 1972, over 8,000 students have been mapped with a locally developed instrument that takes forty-five minutes to administer. Some instructors who understand the mapping process map the students in their classes informally (that is, they use their own powers of observation and question students but do not use the self-assessment instrument). Students may request the procedure and take the instrument by computer or in an informal situation with a counselor or paraprofessional or on audiotape. Instructors may request computer printouts of the cognitive maps of their students and receive help in developing instructional techniques to enhance their students' learning, and the student and the instructor can jointly decide on the most effective materials and setting for that student. Students who have been mapped believe that the process gives them valuable information about how they learn and enables them to choose course sections and learning materials. An integral part of the program is a publication called the *Mirror*, which students can read to obtain information about courses and materials that match their learning-style profiles. At present, courses at Mountain View College are offered in the standard lecture format and also in such alternative modes as audiotape, audiovisual tutorial, video presentation, computer-assisted instruction, peer instruction, and written programmed instruction. Materials in the satellite learning laboratories provide support for these courses.

About 30 percent of the faculty are using some form of cognitive-style mapping, and the majority believe that mapping helps them understand how they can change various aspects of instruction to improve student learning.

The Mountain View College reports suggest that mapping is most crucial for students who have been frustrated in previous learning situations—minority students, students from low socioeconomic backgrounds, and students with learning disabilities.

Another approach to applying cognitive style research is exemplified by a project to help students become more sophisticated consumers of their own education. This program—designed by Patricia Cross, coordinated by the University of Nebraska, and funded by the Fund for the Improvement of Post-Secondary Education—offers freshmen a three-credit elective course called "Learning Analysis". In the course, students analyze their own learning styles and explore how well they learn from presentations by faculty members who use different teaching methods and styles. The students are tested to determine their cognitive styles and are required to evaluate the amount they learn from different professors by weighing the advantages and disadvantages of the different learning situations. Preliminary results suggest that many students found the open classroom method uncomfortable and preferred traditional lecture-demonstration or experiential group discussion methods. These findings are consistent with the field dependent learning styles that characterized most of the students (Trani and others, 1978).

Implications for Practice. Although researchers may not have developed instruments for testing cognitive style that meet statistical tests for reliability and validity, one cannot conclude that differences in cognitive style do not exist. If schools had waited to teach reading until researchers had explained the process of reading and agreed on the best method of teaching it, you would not be reading this page today. Good teachers have always recognized that students differ in learning style and have tried to accommodate these differences. Some students prefer listening over reading, others learn better with pictures and graphs, and some even learn better with textbooks. Helping students discover what learning strategies work best for them is the essence of an effective skills program. Until instruments are perfected that will yield specific and valid scores, we may have to be content to use simple inventories and our best clinical judgment, tempered by experience and common sense, to help students learn.

The studies on cognitive style reflect the changing nature of college instruction, particularly in basic skills. People who need people (field dependents, if you prefer) do not work well in a personally isolated situation, as in traditional reading labs. They do respond to the same materials when they can work with others—with tutors, in small groups, or in dyads—and these peer-teaching methods currently seem to be popular in every skills area.

Short of revising their courses to be personalized self-instructional (PSI) programs, often a costly and difficult process, what can instructors do to more effectively teach students with different learning styles? There are some simple steps faculty members can take to make even a straight lecture course more palatable and effective: (1) Encourage students to work and study together. Group learning may take many forms. Students can work mathematics problems in dyads within the classroom, form study groups that meet outside class hours, or take turns serving as tutors. Instructors can facilitate work outside class by distributing names, addresses, and phone numbers of students who are interested. Obviously, students who do not want to be included should not be forced to study with others. (2) Give assignments with suggestions on different ways the task may be completed. For example, instead of requiring all students to write papers, suggest that some may prefer other ways of showing that they have mastered the information—for example, class presentations, tape-and-slide programs, individual appointment sessions, pictures, collections, or dramatizations. (3) Encourage students to determine the modality in which they learn most effectively, and then see that opportunities are provided to meet these needs. For example, see that the course content is available in the form of tape recordings, audiovisual aids, and so on. (4) Ask textbook publishers to provide audiotapes, filmstrips, and other aids for those students who learn best from them. With such materials, learning centers can offer flexible, personalized services that respond to individual students' unique learning styles and abilities.

8

Improving Writing
and English as
a Second Language

No educational subject has engendered greater concern among faculty members and more national publicity in the past few years than the deteriorating writing skills of college students and college graduates. Indeed, the writing problem is viewed as a national crisis. In this chapter, I examine the writing problems of students, their nature and background; the strategies and programs colleges are currently using to improve writing; and some of the approaches that seem most promising.

Evidence of the decline in writing ability comes from many sources. Examples of horrible student writing are easy for professors to collect, exhibit, and give to newspaper reporters or write articles about for popular magazines. However, the decline in essay-writing scores of high school students on the recent National Assessment of Educational Progress (1975) provides more-objective evidence that writing skills are getting worse. These test results show an overall decrease in the quality of essays written by thirteen-year-olds and seventeen-year-olds in 1974 compared with those written in 1969. The percentage of seventeen-year-olds writing high-quality essays dropped 10 percent during this period, although there was no evidence of deterioration in the mechanics of writing, including grammar and punctuation (National Assessment of Educational Progress, 1975, p. 1). There was a significant increase in errors involving awkwardness of expression, run-on sentences, and incoherent paragraphs. The changes reflected the tendency of students to write as they speak. There are more poor writers, and their scores are lower, than in 1969. The National Assessment of Educational Progress report (1975, p. 1) states that "poor writers seem to be getting poorer in those skills that are specific to written communication, but seldom called for in conversation; that are acquired largely through broad reading and considerable rewriting; that are most seldom taught, and when taught are most difficult to teach, especially to poor readers and people who have little use for written communication."

The continuing drop in average scores on college entrance examinations, including the SAT, the ACT, and the CEEB (College Entrance Examination Boards), provides additional evidence of the pervasiveness of the problem. Experts have attributed the decline in scores to the increasing number of low-achieving, disadvantaged students admitted to colleges since the mid sixties and to a potpourri of other causes. (See Chapter One.)

The clearest evidence of the deteriorating writing skills of college students is the implementation of remedial writing courses in colleges throughout the nation. Students are swamping classes that offer composition skills, and many graduate and professional schools are now requiring composition courses, if they have not had them before.

A small minority of English professors protest that the writing crisis is a media-generated issue and that student writing today is probably no worse than before. For example, Lloyd-Jones (1976,

p. 70) argues that the media have decided Americans' poor writing is news and that there is no crisis: "A crisis is a good turning point. Perhaps our need for good writing has increased so that our inadequacies are more poignant. Still our DIS-ease about writing is probably chronic rather than acute." He criticizes tests and other indicators of a decline in writing skills on the ground that they emphasize grammar and mechanics, which are superficial aspects of writing, and he points out that professors have secretaries and editors to make "silent changes" in their works and politicians hire ghostwriters, but "only in classroom exercises do Americans consider help with mere mechanics to be cheating" (p. 70).

English instructors struggling to teach open-admissions students, however, claim that their students' papers need more than editing. The Association of Writing Supervisors at the City University of New York attacked the CEEB Test of Standard Written English as being far too sophisticated in content and having grammatical questions too obscure and difficult for the average CUNY freshman, who has eighth-grade reading skills (Committee of Standards and Testing of CAWS, 1976).

History of the Writing Problem

The issue of writing problems among college students is not new. In 1874, when 97 percent of the nation's high school graduates entered college, the Harvard faculty, distressed by the poor writing skills of upperclassmen, sought to remedy writing deficiencies by instituting freshman English. The original purpose given for the almost universal instituting of freshman English in colleges across the country, following the Harvard model, was to "make up" for what students "failed to learn" in high school. In essence, freshman English is and always has been considered a remedial course.

The first remedial writing course at the University of California at Berkeley, Subject A (a prefreshman English course), began in 1898. At that time the university required high schools to certify each applicant's proficiency in "oral and written expression," and students not certified were required to take Subject A, a noncredit composition course. There have been many disputes about the course and its effectiveness, and students resented the extra fee they paid from 1922 until 1976 to take it, but it lives on, known to generations of Berkeley students as "bonehead English."

College professors often expect remedial writing courses to perform miracles, as shown by the goals set for these courses. For example, a faculty-senate report (Turner, 1972, p. 19) described the role of the ten-week University of California remedial writing course just mentioned: "Subject A has been given the enormous burden of (1) preserving a high (that is, university) level of literacy in society; (2) preparing students to work at a high verbal level in other university courses; and (3) introducing students to the kind of communication in which university work is performed. These include both the 'complex competence required by society and the university' and the 'literacy level' which, at its minimum, will allow for communication in one mode of language, used at the university and elsewhere." Note carefully the assumptions in this statement, which speaks of both university-level communication and that of society in general and implies that one ten-week course will both solve the students' basic communication problems and introduce them to the complex discourse used by university professors. The differences between literal literacy and academic literacy currently create instructional dilemmas and sometimes confuse the issues. I will delve more deeply into this later. But first let us look further at the historical background of today's writing crisis.

Over the years many critics have insisted that freshman composition fails to teach students to write, and an endless parade of professional educators has urged that it be abolished, but the course remains a requirement in almost every postsecondary institution. But what is taught under the rubric of freshman composition varies widely. Kitzhaber (1963) surveyed composition courses in four-year colleges and concluded that their quality and content were exceedingly diverse. He described English courses as "meretricious" in content and philosophy, taught by unprepared graduate assistants and new faculty members, and using a wide range of materials (from *Reader's Digest* to the classics) and approaches which reflected the idiosyncratic biases of the departments offering them. Although Kitzhaber's survey was made in 1960, he castigated composition instructors and their approaches with phrases that ring true today: "Teaching young people to write well has always proved so frustratingly difficult, and the methods used so time-consuming and laborious for teachers and students alike, [that] the problem has seemed to be a kind of standing affront to the American reputation for efficiency. Surely, they have thought, there must be some easy, quick, and fairly painless way to do the job; and they have looked eagerly, if often naively, for pat solutions" (Kitzhaber, 1963, pp. 73–74).

Indeed, instructors have tried many panaceas for teaching writing, including the following:

- Having students memorize "laws of discourse" to discipline their mental faculties so they could compose well with a minimum of practice (1880s and 1890s).
- Requiring that students write five themes a week, on the assumption that practice was everything (1890s).
- Emphasizing the writing of the paragraph as a miniature composition (1890s).
- Espousing the view that the only way to teach composition was to require students to read "good literature" (late 1890s).
- Emphasizing grammatical correctness as the supreme virtue in composition, so that writing was taught through exercises in grammar and sentence diagraming (1900 through 1940s).
- Teaching composition through general semantics (1940s).
- Combining speech, reading, writing, and listening into communications courses (1940s and 1950s). Communications courses had virtually disappeared from four-year colleges by 1960, although the courses remain in high schools and community colleges.
- Relying on the new educational technology—teaching machines, televised programs, overhead projectors, and computers—with the hope that it promised a way to teach more students with fewer teachers (1960 to present).

No one approach has solved the problems, nor does it seem likely that any strategy or philosophy will provide a remedy (Kitzhaber, 1963). Each method helps some students and fails with others. Writing needs persist; teachers must teach composition if students are to develop effective writing skills.

If we examine the antecedents of today's college problems, we find many changes in high school preparation. During the past two decades, writing courses in both precollege and college programs seem to have deteriorated. For example, Hall (1977) contends that since the early 1960s, goals and written work in both public and private secondary schools have steadily declined. Secondary education has succumbed to four tempting, but destructive, principles: "Learning should be fun," "If it's new, it's good," "Let the students choose," and "I teach what I want." Creativity was stressed instead of grammar, punctuation, paragraphing, and style. Science-fiction courses were offered in place of modern or traditional literature. Fads predominated, and the one-term course made it difficult, if not impossible, for teachers to help students master the readings and perfect their writing. Many observers have pointed out that students read and wrote about their own feelings and experiences, rather than about literary topics, and that the elementary and secondary preparation of students lacked a core, or common denominator, of subject matter. In contrast, college students of previous generations were expected to have read prescribed works in British and American literature.

Good writing requires practice and adequate feedback, which many high school teachers have deemphasized. In fact, students may substitute such electives as journalism, speech, and drama for the traditional high school composition and literature courses. When given an option, students who most need writing practice choose subjects that do not require writing. In addition, students are rarely able to assess the quality of their own writing; they are usually not taught how to evaluate their work and are unaware of the criteria teachers use in grading it. A student who, in high school, receives an A for describing his feelings about an experience may later not understand when a college instructor grades the same kind of theme F because the assignment was to write an expository essay with a thesis statement. Further, multiple-choice and other objective test questions in high school have replaced term papers, which gave students an opportunity to acquire both the information and the writing practice that college instructors expect. Homework is no longer routinely assigned unless the student is enrolled in a rigorous college preparatory program or private school, and even there middle-class parents help their children with homework assignments. Although some schools still have free periods during which students may study, the discipline problems endemic in many high schools have resulted in counselors' assigning students to additional classes to avoid the problems of monitoring study halls.

In short, high school students have little need to practice writing. Few papers are assigned, and for those few, work is often done hastily and with minimal effort. Students who have managed to avoid writing in high school have usually avoided reading, and their lack of reading exacerbates their writing problems. Heys (1963) found that high school juniors who read more and wrote less improved their writing more during the school year than those who wrote a theme a week without doing the extra reading.

Students who receive high grades in high school English may be unaware of their writing problems. Because of grade inflation, more A's and B's and fewer lower grades are given today. Consequently, students entering college with good grades in English may not have been required to write in high school and may have minimal skills.

Not all prospective college students, however, are complacent about their writing skills. In 1976, the press reported that only 34 percent of the entering freshmen responding to the American Council of Education questionnaire thought their high schools had prepared them very well for college English courses, although only 13 percent planned to ask their colleges for special assistance in writing.

The rarefied atmosphere of colleges and universities, where faculties assume that students can write well, is a contrast to the experiences students have had in high school, where the previously mentioned constraints restrict their development of confidence and skill in writing. Increasingly, college students are required to take remedial writing before they can undertake regular freshman composition courses. The percentage of entering students required to take remedial writing depends on the writing-quality standards of the college, which vary widely. However, the University of California at Berkeley, which draws its students from the top 12.5 percent of high school graduates, requires remedial writing of about the same percentage of students—50 percent—as the Bronx Community College, which draws 75 percent of its students from the lower half of New York City high school graduating classes.

Not only have high school English programs deemphasized traditional college preparatory composition and reading courses, reducing the preparation of traditional college freshmen, but the open-admissions system has brought into our colleges large numbers of students totally lacking in preparation for college and possessing the barest of literacy skills.

Descriptions of the City University of New York open-admissions program (1970–1976) document the clash of cultures that occurred when traditional college faculty members were confronted with students with severe linguistic shortcomings (Bossone and Weiner, 1973; Castro, 1974; Gross, 1978; Rosen and others, 1973; Wagner, 1976). Over 4,000 students with high school averages below 70 (that is, below a C average) enrolled in CUNY colleges, and all the colleges faced major problems. All established or greatly increased their remedial writing programs. For example, the City College of New York, an institution that prided itself on its high academic standards and its reputation as the Harvard of the proletariat, was compelled to develop new courses in basic writing. Where formerly 30 percent of its freshmen had been required to take composition, in 1970, 90 percent were unprepared for college English. Instructors, recruited from foreign languages and history, could not cope when confronted with classes of superannuated eighth-graders who could not write. Some students were highly motivated, most were apathetic, but some were overtly hostile toward the instructor and the subject. Instructors resisted teaching the courses, and students resisted the instructors. As Gross (1978) describes the scene, the instructors were intellectually unprepared and emotionally unwilling to teach these students, but some tried very hard. Basic writing, they found, proved to be a most difficult subject to teach, requiring a stretching of the imagination, a tolerance rarely asked of intellectuals, and an understanding of students whose characteristics were vastly different from those of students they were accustomed to teaching.

Although open admissions at CUNY is now dead, the writing problems of college students have not disappeared. Increasing numbers of adults, themselves the victims of inadequate teaching, enter college along with federally funded, misprepared eighteen-year-olds. Colleges are confronted with multiple goals—teaching students basic literacy skills, teaching them competency skills, and teaching them to express complex ideas in academic prose. The alternative is to develop curriculums that do not require writing.

Students' Writing Problems

The college student with minimal writing skills and little previous exposure to books and reading has been called the "Basic Writing student." Shaughnessy (1977, p. 7) describes how such students view writing:

> For the Basic Writing (BW) student, academic writing is a trap, not a way of saying something to someone. The spoken language, looping back and forth between speakers, offering chances for groping and backing up and even hiding, leaving room for the language of hands and faces, of pitch and pauses, is generous and inviting. Next to this rich orchestration, writing is but a line that moves haltingly across the page, exposing as it goes all that the writer doesn't know, then passing into the hands of a stranger who reads it with a lawyer's eyes, searching for flaws.
>
> By the time he reaches college, the BW student both resents and resists his vulnerability as a writer. He is aware that he leaves a trail of errors behind him when he writes. He can usually think of little else while he is writing. But he doesn't know what to do about it. Writing puts him on a line, and he doesn't want to be there. For every three hundred words he writes, he is likely to use from ten to thirty forms that the academic reader regards as serious errors. Some writers, inhibited by their fear of error, produce but a few lines an hour or keep trying to begin, crossing out one try after another until the sentence is hopelessly tangled.

Many college students who do not have severe grammatical or other basic writing problems do have difficulty with academic writing assignments. Lamberg (1975) has identified the major problem areas in students' attempts at academic writing:

- They lack self-management skills. Symptoms include a history of incompletes in courses, turning in papers late, and not knowing specifics of assignments, such as due date or amount required.
- They lack a strategy for composing and have no set of procedures for working through a writing assignment from beginning to end. Symptoms include great difficulty in getting started and performing tasks at inappropriate times (for instance, reading references before deciding on a topic.)
- They fail to understand and follow directions. They may write good papers but not follow the instructor's assignment; for instance, they write a paper based on reading when the assignment calls for an original essay.
- They write poorly organized papers and sometimes fail to select a topic.
- They have many errors and patterns of errors; in other words, they lack a system for proofreading.
- Their papers lack introductions.
- They have problems in understanding and accepting the teacher's criticisms.

Unfortunately, these errors tend to persist, for they are seldom addressed in courses where writing is assigned. Thus writing instructors face a dual task—inculcating literal literacy into Basic Writing students and helping those who have some writing competency develop skills in writing more formal academic prose. Each of these tasks must be considered in relation to the expectations of faculty members who teach advanced courses.

Faculty Expectations. It is not possible to understand students' writing problems without considering the expectations of college professors. Every professor, whether in a university or a community college, expects students to be literate. Many students have learned in high school to camouflage their lack of reading and writing skills, so that it is often difficult for professors to identify weaknesses until students turn in papers or take exams. Then the writing dificiencies are obvious. Depending on the perceived degree of inadequacy of the writing, professors may react by labeling the student dumb or by feeling that their own teaching efforts are wasted—or they may do both.

Faculty reactions to poor student writing are seldom gentle and often brutal. For example, *Harper's* recently published comments of Yale professors on student papers ("Learning to Live with Criticism," 1975, p. 8), including the following: "Where did you get these ideas: From *Sesame Street*? An illiterate high school teacher?" "This is very badly written—incorrect, lumbering, repetitious, with no sense of proportion, no regard for the assignment. Do not do this to me again." "Perhaps the only thing worse than the style of this piece is your proofreading job. Then there was your style— wooden, choppy, insolicitous [sic] use of language, all manner of dangling and split flora and fauna. Generally it sounded like [sic] you glued this piece together (and then left the paper out in the rain)." "Grade F. If you had given me only fifteen pages of bullshit, I could have given you a C. But for fifty-five pages I have to give you an F."

So even in highly selective colleges, professors are dismayed at the caliber of their students' writing. But when confronted with the writing of open-admissions or special-admit students, they are traumatized.

Shaughnessy (1977, p. 8–9) describes the faculty view of student's grammatical and spelling errors and how it colors professors' perceptions of students:

> So absolute is the importance of error in the minds of many writers that "good writing" to them means "correct writing," nothing more. "As long as I can remember," writes a student, "I wanted to be an English teacher. I know it is hard, keeping verbs in their right place, s's [where] they should be, etc., but one day I will make them part of me."
>
> Much about the "remedial" situation encourages this obsession with error. First, there is the reality of academia, the fact that most college teachers have little tolerance for the kinds of errors BW students make, that they perceive certain types of errors as indicators of ineducability, and that they have the power of the F. Second, there is the urgency of the students to meet their teachers' criteria, even to request more of the prescriptive teaching they have had before in the hope that this time it might "take." Third, there is the

awareness of the teacher and administrator that remedial programs are likely to be evaluated (and budgeted) according to the
speed with which they produce correct writers, correctness being a
highly measurable feature of acceptable writing.

Dedicated English professors who taught basic writing
courses faced not only the negative attitudes of their professional
peers but the misconceptions and expectations of students with
severe language disabilities (Shaughnessy, 1973, 1976). As Gross
(1978, p. 16) states:

> [We] strained so hard to be successful that we didn't have
> time to question the expectations imposed upon us by minorities
> and, more important, by ourselves. When our conservative col-
> leagues screamed that the standards were falling, we answered by
> saying that the record wasn't in yet. When we failed to bring stu-
> dents up to the appropriate level of literacy, we blamed our-
> selves—we hadn't been adequately trained or we lacked pa-
> tience or we'd set standards too high.
> But in fact we had false expectations. Open-admission stu-
> dents came with a sense of fear and self-doubt confronting a stan-
> dard language which was rendered even more complicated by their
> need to master, at the same time and in the same place, the separate
> language of biology or psychology. Their entire miseducation and
> bookless past rose to haunt them, and all the audiovisual aids and
> writing laboratories and simplified curricular materials we tried
> could not turn the trick.
> The mistake was to think that this language training would
> be preparation for college education when what we were really
> instilling was a fundamental literacy that would allow social accul-
> turation to occur. We were preparing our students to be the par-
> ents of college students, not to be students themselves. And the
> impossible burden that we assumed was one properly meant for the
> community colleges.

While CUNY instructors were struggling with open-
admissions students, departments of English at most state universities still taught literature and literary criticism and regarded composition teaching as a distraction or a chore to be relegated to
graduate students. Lyons (1976) captures well the attitudes of
many English professors when he describes them as viewing themselves as transmitters of the civilizing arts, counting themselves as

among the company of the elect, and looking "with condescension on the lowly teachers of basic writing skills." He points out that the English department at the University of Texas assigned teaching assistants to teach 75 percent of the total enrollment load of English courses at a cost of 27 percent of the department budget. The department voted down a proposal that would have required each professor to teach one section of freshman composition every year and a half. The departmental report cited as the reason "Not every English professor is suited to teaching freshman composition, just as not every English professor is suited to teaching linguistics. . . . Doing a competent job in teaching freshman composition . . . requires two skills: the ability to reach freshmen and linguistics. Some of us have only one skill, but not the other; some of us have neither skill and openly acknowledge the fact" (Lyons, p. 34).

This argument is not unusual. Some English professors state flatly that they do not know how to teach students to write. Saul Bellow, in an interview following the awarding of his Nobel Prize, commented that he could not teach a student to write, he could only help the student realize that he was not crazy if he chose to write.

With the exception of a few composition and rhetoric faculty members, professors seem to share the belief that good writing can be taught in a course, but "by somebody else, not me!" Besides this attitude, there are practical problems faced by those who want to teach writing but are limited by large classes and other constraints on their time. Consequently, support services in writing have mushroomed.

Some writing professors take issue with the trend away from teaching writing. Miles (1975, p. 14) expresses the position that teaching writing is the responsibility of each faculty member: "We know that good writing, like good thinking, cannot be taught 'once and for all.' It's not a simple skill like swimming; indeed, even a swimmer can be coached to get better and better. Thinking is one of the most complex abilities, and writing is evidence of it. So students need help with writing at many stages, from third grade to eighth, to tenth to high school, to college and beyond, and from subject to subject. Whenever a new stage of thought and a new subject matter comes along, the accumulated abilities of the student need conscious and thoroughgoing adapting to the new material and maturity. *Therefore, the concept of 'remedial work' is misdirected; the teacher who sends a student back to brush up technical details is trivializing his own serious job of helping the young writer adapt his present active skill and latent knowledge to important new demands."* Karliner (1974, p. 12) expresses a similar position in regard to the unrealistic results professors expect from remedial writing courses: "Writing competency is a skill which needs continual reinforcement. It is impossible to expect that one or two quarters in the freshman year will make good writers out of students who have never written before and who will not be required to write again in their college careers. If professors require little or no writing, award A's to poor writers when they do require a paper, and provide no constructive feedback when writing is found to be inadequate, then it is foolish to expect that most undergraduates will develop their writing skills further from their freshman year to the time of graduation."

Faculty-Generated Writing Problems. As both Miles and Karliner view the writing problem, they reprimand professors who overlook the complexity of the writing/thinking process and the time and practice required for a student to develop mature, scholarly writing abilities. It is the rare undergraduate who can write a paper of the caliber acceptable for publication, and that should not be the criterion by which student work is judged. (It is, however, a goal that prospective graduate students should work toward.) As Carkeet (1976) explains, often the dual role of the college English professor as both a literary scholar and a teacher of writing promotes the dangerous possibility that one will evaluate classroom writing style by what are ultimately bizarre and untenable criteria—the criteria for literary scholars. Professors in other subjects also sometimes apply professional standards to the writing their students produce.

The kinds of writing assignments that professors give also create writing difficulties for students, and at Berkeley we have found in our learning center that the most frequent problem students express is inability to understand assignments. Connelly and Irving (1976, p. 670) state: "Students who are given writing assignments they do not understand in disciplines they do not know tend in their uncertainty to write reports. Furthermore, these reports reveal the writer's uncertainty not only in poor organization, but also in more elementary compositional errors. We are convinced that the students' compositional incompetence is not the only cause of bad writing. The single most widespread external cause of bad writing is bad assignments."

Miles (1967) studied the stylistic errors in students' writing and their relation to the type of assignment given. She found that the topics assigned tend to be subjects in the grammatical sense— "my summer vacation," "my home town," "the Vietnam War," and so on. She points out that a predicate increases or decreases the size of the subject, forcing students to give reasons and shape their ideas. For example, if a student is asked to write on the topic "What will happen to my home town if the drought continues for another year" instead of "My home town" or on "What I'd do to decorate my room if I had a thousand dollars" instead of "My room," the "if . . . then" predicate demands a cause-effect assertion. The appropriate predicate can also direct the students' writing to other organizational patterns, such as "either/or." This strategy has implications for all types of academic writing. I can remember well my own frustrations when faced with a doctoral prelim question that stated simply, "Discuss IQ": Where do I start? How much should be included? How can I narrow the topic? What does the professor expect?

The problems professors generate by their poor writing assignments and poor essay-exam questions are not new. (In fact, I sometimes wonder whether the professors who are most critical of student writing have repressed their own writing struggles.) Few people can write well and fluently under time pressures and deadlines. For many of us, writing is an agonizing and time-consuming task that requires many revisions. Yet we expect students to produce several papers in a ten-week term. Students unskilled in writing but determined to survive have found ways to cope. Some hire the same secretaries who type and edit professors' papers during the day to type and edit theirs at night. Others ask a spouse, friend, or parent to edit their papers. Still others hire ghostwriters. Though research and paper-writing services are illegal, they are still available for students with money.

Since instructor-induced writing problems have long been

part of academic life, it is not surprising that there have been many
attempts in the past to improve the writing of both instructors and
students. For example, in 1950 the Berkeley English department
conducted an experimental program among 1500 undergraduates
who were taking courses in fifteen departments. Teaching assistants from the English department read and marked papers for
professors in other departments, and the papers were also graded
for content by departmental readers. Three methods of aiding
poor writers were tried: (1) Requiring the student to rewrite his
paper after a conference with the TA. (This proved effective but
time-consuming.) (2) Setting up voluntary conferences between the
instructor and students with low grades. (This was less effective
because students participated less when they were not required to
attend conferences.) (3) Having the English TA present a class lecture with the instructor or reader after each set of papers was
graded; together they analyzed particular errors, indicated ways of
clarifying answers, and stressed principles of organization. (This
was the simplest procedure, and it was more effective than the
other methods in improving students' writing. It was most effective
when there was close cooperation between the instructor and the
English TA.) Fifty percent of the students who earned grades of D
or worse on their first exams and papers improved as a result of the
program. The researchers stressed the importance of training
readers in different disciplines to evaluate student composition and
to aid and advise students in ways to improve their writing/thinking
skills.

        After a study with such positive results, one might expect
that the program would be implemented on a wider scale and that
student writing would continue to improve. This did not happen. A
decade later, another committee on prose improvement reported
on yet another experiment to remedy the fragmentary, impres-
sionistic writing that they attributed to true/false questions and to a
"serious weakening and diminishing of writing throughout the
country." In this study too, English TAs graded the essays of students in other courses and conferred with instructors and readers
in an effort to improve writing. Although the final report does not
describe the impact of the program on student writing, it does

focus on how instructors were helped to understand how the intent of the question determines the structure of the answer.

Thus, at Berkeley—indeed, at most institutions—student-writing crises seem to appear each decade. Experiments and innovations are introduced with great enthusiasm, succeed briefly, and slowly die; the writing problem emerges again and another innovative cycle begins.

Despite these efforts, professors naively continue to write poor questions and assignments and criticize student writing harshly, and writing crises recur.

What Is Needed? To improve their composition skills, students need a supportive environment, a clear idea of what is expected, and information and ideas to write about. They desperately need adequate feedback from the instructor or from someone else, such as an aide. Underprepared students generally need highly structured programs in which they can be taught the grammatical and organizational skills that they have not learned. They need good, explicit teachers, not programmed texts that fractionate the skills and assume that they are capable of mastering prose writing on their own. They do not need sociological and psychological excuses for their poor composition skills or professors who cop out by stating, "It's not Joe's fault that he has no background in writing and was enrolled by mistake in my advanced Chaucer course when he should have taken remedial writing. Even though he can't write a sentence, I won't fail him, since he's a victim of his poor background."

Instructors continue to need educating in more precise and reliable ways of judging and evaluating student prose. Models for such judging and evaluating are described in Diederich (1974) and Godshalk and others (1966). Instructors also need help in phrasing more adequate questions and assignments.

Strategies for Improving College Writing

Of the many strategies for improving student writing currently used in colleges and universities, the ones that have the greatest potential for success are those that provide intensive in-service and pre-service training for high school teachers and college instructors.

   In-Service Training for High School Teachers. College professors usually blame high school and elementary school teachers for the sad state of student writing, rarely acknowledging that public school teachers are trained in college English departments. Articulation between high schools and college programs, although never strong, has weakened in the past decade. Realizing this and the futility of finger pointing, some universities are making greater efforts to provide effective in-service training to elementary and secondary school teachers.

   The Bay Area Writing Project (BAWP), directed and developed by James Gray, is one model exemplifying an attempt to improve university–public school articulation as a way of preventing college students' writing problems. The following assumptions form the basic philosophy of the BAWP (Gray and Myers, 1978):

- The writing problem is shared by the universities and the schools; it can best be addressed by cooperatively planned and cooperatively funded university/school efforts.
- Most teachers have not been adequately prepared as teachers of writing.
- Although there is a body of knowledge about the teaching of writing, much of it is recent, and most teachers are unaware of it.
- Curriculum change cannot be accomplished by transient consultants who appear briefly, never to be seen again, or by change agents who insist that everyone see the problem in the same way. The best teacher of teachers is another teacher who has had success in a similar situation.
- Curriculum change cannot be accomplished with a packet of "teacherproof" materials. Teacher involvement in the selection and creation of materials is critical to a successful program. Gimmicks do not work.
- Successful teachers of writing can be identified; the best practices of successful teachers can be effectively demonstrated to others.
- Teachers of writing must themselves write.
- Field-based research could make a significant contribution to the improvement of instruction.

Jointly sponsored by the University of California at Berkeley and adjacent public school districts, the BAWP began as a consortium of fifteen colleges and universities in the San Francisco Bay Area and has recently expanded to encompass thirty sites throughout the United States and a European program. The program's goals are to improve the quality of writing in the schools, promote and guarantee the continued education of classroom teachers and instructors, seek significant information on the teaching of writing, perform research and disseminate its results, and create a center for the teaching of writing. Originally, the six strands of the program comprised (1) an intensive summer program in which twenty-five experienced high school English teachers were trained as teacher/consultants to offer in-service composition programs to groups of teachers, (2) a consortium of four college and university composition teachers who met regularly throughout the year on freshman writing problems, (3) a pre-service component in which supervising teachers for teaching-credential candidates were drawn from the cadre of trained teacher/consultants, (4) a program coordinated with the University of California Upward Bound component whose English instructors were also drawn from the teacher/consultants, (5) a training program for college remedial writing specialists given by members of Berkeley's Subject A (remedial writing) department, and (6) regular meetings with school administrators to discuss common problems and encourage them to review their schools' writing programs and commit their districts to a three-year writing-improvement program that would include regular writing assessments of students at all levels (Glass, 1975; Gray and Myers, 1978).

English teachers have responded to the Bay Area Writing Project with an almost evangelistic enthusiasm. Perhaps one reason is that the program gives hope to the overworked and sometimes downtrodden classroom teacher, but it also involves teachers directly in solving a long-standing problem and does not submit them to the traditional ritual of educational reform—that is, to call in the experts, who will tell the teachers what they are doing wrong. The BAWP has expanded from a local writing project to a statewide one and, most recently, to a national one. A Carnegie grant enables an outside evaluator to assess the program, and one criterion that will be used is whether fewer University of California students of those from high schools whose teachers have been touched by the BAWP are held for the remedial writing course than were their predecessors. The BAWP is receiving such an enthusiastic response from school districts, teachers, and universities that it will be interesting to follow its future development.

In-Service Training for College Instructors. Universities are increasing their programs for present and future college teachers of composition. In the past, few university English departments offered formal training programs for teachers of composition at any level. The English department at the University of Iowa was reputedly the first to give graduate degrees in the teaching of composition, in a program developed by John Gerber when he was chairman of the department in 1953. For a number of years, the University of Northern Iowa and Florida State University have offered master's degree programs in teaching writing in community colleges. Currently, many other institutions are offering or planning to offer courses and degree programs to train college instructors of writing and of English as a second language.

The University of Iowa's Institute of Writing is one example of current efforts to improve college English instruction. Directed by Karl Klaus and funded by the National Endowment for the Humanities, the institute is scheduled to open in 1979. Forty-four current or prospective directors of freshman English will attend a six-month intensive training session at the University of Iowa, where they will study linguistics, writing theory, and other topics. They will each develop a model program for their institution, observe other programs and labs, and receive consultation. They will also write scientific papers, social science case studies, and historical accounts to help them better understand the kinds of writing demands students encounter in courses other than English. The deans and department heads who supervise the participants will attend short sessions before and during the institute. Each college must guarantee that the directors sent will continue in their positions and that the pilot programs they bring back will be implemented. The home school must also agree to establish an interdepartmental committee on writing and participate in a follow-up evaluation of the implemented program in the year after the institute session.

It is clear that we can expect a great deal more emphasis on training new composition teachers and retreading old ones in the near future. Some hand-wringing about the futility of trying to teach basic skills to college students will undoubtedly continue, and there will be setbacks similar to the Mellon Foundation's recent decision to give up trying to fund projects to develop solutions to the writing crisis because the foundation found no experts who agreed on how it might be done or even whether it could be. One thing is certain: For the next decade, colleges will accept many students with poor writing skills. Faculty members must learn how to teach them.

Today's most promising programs suggest directions that other colleges will follow. Most of the ideas are not new, but they are being tried with more vigor than was true in the recent past. These programs include student-centered teaching approaches, mastery learning, modular instruction, writing labs, peer tutoring, structured programs combining reading and writing, and interdisciplinary team-taught courses. Many of these are specific courses or intensive programs aimed directly at improving student writing. But they cannot succeed in a vacuum. All faculty members must be involved in the development and improvement of student writing skills.

Special Workshops and Small Classes. Placing students in special remedial writing courses, often without credit or with partial credit, has been and continues to be the traditional method of dealing with poor writers, and this approach has rarely been questioned. In the past, some attempts were made to modify these special writing classes. For example, at the University of Maryland in 1964, probationary freshmen whose high school grades were below C were enrolled in special freshman composition classes during a summer session. They had regularly scheduled conferences with their English instructors and also received additional tutoring and skills help from writing and reading specialists. In addition, they were offered an optional four-hour workshop in organizational skills: differentiating among facts, opinions, and generalizations; limiting the topic and framing an adequate thesis statement; recognizing premise-conclusion and cause-effect relations; and outlining and organization. Students attending three or four hours of the workshop showed significant improvement in writing out-of-class themes (80 percent improved their grades, compared with 44 percent of the students not attending the workshop) and in-class themes (66 percent improved their grades, compared with 46 percent of those not attending the workshop). Interestingly, those attending the writing workshop averaged lower scores on the ACT-English entrance examination than the control group and earned significantly higher final grades in freshman English (Maxwell and Zitterkopf, 1965).

If a four-hour workshop can significantly improve poorly prepared writers' composition performance, one wonders why more cannot be accomplished in the traditional semester composition course. Of course, in this instance, students who attended the workshop were motivated, but the study does suggest that perhaps English courses waste a lot of time.

Modules and Mastery Learning. Mastery learning is a way of teaching that requires that learning objectives be specified and student achievement of the objectives be measured. Seeking to eliminate the stigma of bonehead English and the need for placement tests before students enter a writing class, Mills (1976b) developed a three-level mastery course in writing for community college students. The program offers individualized instruction in sentence, paragraph, and essay writing and uses self-instructional study units, self-pacing, open entry and exit, and tutoring. Fourteen instructors, working in teams of two, teach nine sections of fifty students each. Students are pretested and assigned to individual programs in one of the three strands—sentence, paragraph, or essay writing. Tutors earn one credit unit for each fifty-four hours they spend in class tutoring and one unit for meeting with the class instructor for one hour. Students in the class are also asked to tutor others. Mills reports that their writing improves as they begin to work even more seriously on their assignments so they can be effective tutors.

Although the program is highly structured, it is also flexible in that students choose their own essay topics and the skills and exercises they work on are continually being adapted to meet their needs. As students complete units and mastery tests, they gradually move on to advanced writing skills by building from simple to complex skills—for example, integrating their work on sentence writing into units on paragraph preparation. Mills developed her own self-paced materials for students in this course (Mills, 1974, 1976a).

Many colleges have adopted programmed materials and incorporated tutors into writing courses (Stryker, 1977), but teaching students with such a wide range of skills as Mills describes in one classroom is still rare. A more common practice is to section the weakest into separate classes and give them intensive practice—a custom that makes the teacher's work easier but makes it harder for the students to maintain motivation.

Student-Centered Approaches. Instructional methods reflecting today's student-centered emphasis are being widely publicized. For example, team learning or collaborative learning methods have long been used by innovative teachers in elementary and secondary schools but are rarely observed in college writing courses (Bruffee, 1973; Dugger, 1976; Hoover, 1972). Hawkins (1976) describes the details of how to set up and implement a group inquiry method for teaching freshman composition, calling his approach "the parceled classroom." In this method, the remedial writing class is divided into small working groups of four to six students. The aims of the program are described as encouraging students to take responsibility for their own learning in the classroom, encouraging students to participate actively in the learning process through working in small groups, and enabling the teacher to function as a facilitator of learning during the small-group work by listening, questioning, and observing. The teacher circulates freely among groups, observing, asking questions, and troubleshooting. The groups select their own names (for example, the Gerunds) and choose their own reading assignments, essay topics, and other work, such as grammar exercises, study of expository structure, and paraphrasing. During the typical fifty-minute work period, the first ten minutes are spent on passing out papers and making general announcements; then the groups work on their writing tasks for twenty to thirty minutes, and during the last ten to twenty minutes they share their written work. Each student takes a turn in distributing his paper to the group and having it critiqued.

Hawkins feels that this approach works best when there is a reasonably heterogeneous group and when students are reasonably willing to work and motivated to improve their writing, and he reports that poorly prepared students often do very well in parceled groups. However, he cautions that students with skills below the eighth-grade level should not be placed in a group where other students are working on more advanced skills, but given individual tutoring if a group is not found that is closer to their needs. Most students seem to prefer this approach, although it does not work for all, Hawkins reports.

Gibbs and Northedge (1976) use a similar approach to improve students' essay-exam skills at the Open University in England. There is increasing experimental evidence that group projects and peer monitoring improve the performance on final examinations of students who have done poorly on earlier exams (McClintock and Sonquist, 1976).

Other approaches that can be characterized as student-oriented and are ways of reducing student apprehension about writing are free-writing and teacherless-writing programs. Brown and Associates' *Free Writing: A Group Approach* (1977) and Peter Elbow's *Writing Without Teachers* (1973) provide many suggestions for implementing such programs in the writing classroom. (Daly and Miller, 1975, developed a test for identifying students who are apprehensive about writing.)

The success of such student-centered methods depends on the capability and skills of the teacher, and not all instructors are able to work effectively with several small groups in the same classroom.

Materials used in teaching writing also reflect a growing concern for motivating as well as instructing students. Not only are such materials becoming easier to read, but humor is used more frequently. For example, Bernstein's (1971) *Miss Thistlebottom's Hobgoblin's; The Careful Writer's Guide to the Taboos, Bugbears, and Outmoded Rules of English Usage* helps the student whose writing has been constricted by overzealous high school English teachers. And Crews (1977) uses such characters as Stanley, the campus revolutionary, and Norbert, a young man with a growing interest in mysticism, to liven up his grammar handbook. Also included is Dr. Dollar, author of such bestsellers as *Be Fat and Forget It*.

Writing Labs and Peer Tutoring. Writing labs represent another approach that is hardly new, for the University of Iowa has had one for fifty years. However, most colleges have or are developing writing laboratories or centers, which provide individual help to students with writing difficulties (Moore, 1950; Sandberg, 1967; Smith, 1975). Depending on the institution, the writing laboratory may be staffed with professors or experienced graduate students. Increasingly, undergraduate tutors are providing individual work with students, although they are usually supervised by a teaching assistant or a faculty member. Smith (1975) extolls the virtues of a peer-tutoring program in a writing center, enumerating the advantages to both the tutees and the peer tutors. He feels that students relate better to peers, who are less threatening to students than professors and teaching assistants are, in that they are more likely to tell students, "This part of your paper doesn't sound right; let's see if we can make it clearer," than to criticize them for too many dangling modifiers.

English instructors are sometimes reluctant to have their students tutored, particularly those instructors who think tutors are doing students' work for them—and sometimes instructors are correct in thinking so. But some instructors who see themselves as adversaries of students will criticize tutors as unqualified and view students who receive tutoring as cheating. Smith (1975) points out that antagonism may be reduced if instructors are educated to the fact that tutors may save them many hours of individual work with students who have severe writing problems as well as serving other students whom instructors do not have time to see. He stresses the importance of each tutor's maintaining regular contact with the instructors to ensure coordination of efforts and reduce negative attitudes.

Despite Smith's enthusiasm about the use of students as writing tutors, tutoring programs have limitations. Karliner (1974) describes with candor the problems of directing a remedial writing program serving 1,100 students a year with seventy undergraduate tutors and nineteen unenthusiastic teaching assistants, all of whom needed training themselves in the mechanics of English. She emphasizes that tutors and teaching assistants tend to focus solely on ideas and organization, "paying scant attention to gross mechanical errors and the more subtle problems of clarity, brevity, and precision which might be called style" (p. 12). Stating that it takes about two quarters to train a tutor or a teaching assistant, she begs for more-experienced staff members to assist in the training and concludes that the use of untrained, inexperienced undergraduate and graduate students as the primary instructors is "a stopgap measure, which, while perhaps financially advantageous, is educationally bankrupt" (p. 12).

Team-Teaching Interdisciplinary Courses. Team teaching is frequently described in professional journals in connection with writing programs at open-admissions junior colleges in which teams of faculty members from different departments teach together. At the Upward Bound Veterans Program at Oscar Rose Junior College in Oklahoma City, for example, "horizontal faculty teams" meet regularly and coordinate curricular and extracurricular activities for a group of students. For instance, they plan interdisciplinary programs such as a campus production of *The Taming of the Shrew.* Students in reading and writing courses study and write about the play, personality-adjustment classes analyze the characters' role stereotypes, and the mathematics instructor devises lessons around the "cost" of the production. The goal of the project is to introduce the students to the world of excellence as described in "Alternatives to the Revolving Door" (1976b, p. 5): "The language of Shakespeare or Arthur Miller may bear little [relation] to the modestly turned paragraphs required by a freshman English instructor, but it bespeaks a level of achievement and genius which helps place freshman themes and college in a more complete perspective. Competency is one thing; art is another. It is a mistake to believe that students do not recognize this." If the faculty members work well together, such integrated programs encourage student interest, participation, and responsiveness.

Structured Programs Combining Reading and Writing. Some writing experts (for instance, Bossone and Troyka, 1976; Brooks, 1973; Eanet and Manzo, 1976; Edmonds, 1976; Mills, 1976b) are designing structured, systematic programs and materials for students with severe writing difficulties and are making progress in remarrying the long-divorced skills of reading and writing. One of the best studies I have seen was done at CUNY by Bossone and Troyka (1976), who developed a structured writing program and tested it on 1,000 college students enrolled in remedial writing courses and 1,000 high school students with severe writing problems. Eighty percent of the experimental group improved in essay writing, compared with 45 percent of the control group, taught by experienced remedial writing instructors. The experimental college classes were taught by graduate interns who used specially developed lesson plans that integrated reading and writing in sequential lessons with prepackaged materials for student use. Teachers were free to adapt the materials and lessons to the needs of their classes. Experimental-group teachers received ongoing in-service training throughout the experiment. The practice materials were designed to coordinate reading and writing skills. For example, in one unit students were required to identify topic sentences and supporting details in the reading materials and then write a four-paragraph expository essay containing an introductory paragraph with a clear thesis statement, two body paragraphs with clear topic sentences, and a concluding paragraph. Despite strikes and other problems, most students completed the program, and the experimenters report that the responses of both teachers and students to the experimental materials were positive.

The results of this study clearly point to the need for better materials integrating reading and writing skills and better pre-service and in-service training for teachers in remedial composition courses. The authors conclude that "improvement in composition is not impossible to measure or achieve—that tests, test conditions, and methods of instruction, when employed properly, can reflect and contribute to writing improvement and that research dealing with remedial writing does not have to remain an unexplored territory" (Bossone and Troyka, 1976, p. 91).

Including Remedial Writers in Regular Courses. Some institutions have routinely incorporated "remedial writers" into regular freshman composition courses. If students are offered intensive outside tutoring, they seem to fare as well in the regular courses as they do in special remedial courses and are less angry and apathetic about the experience. No one has yet shown unequivocally that assigning poor writers to remedial classes produces better writers than assigning them to regular courses and concurrently giving them individual help in the basic skills they lack. Class size, instructor's acceptance, and the extent to which poor writers differ from others in the class seem to be crucial to the success of such a program.

Educational Technology. The glowing promise of educational technology as a way to improve student writing skills has yet to materialize. In fact, self-paced materials, programmed texts, teaching machines, and computer-assisted instruction are criticized widely, and there is little evidence of their success (Bossone and Weiner, 1973; Smith, 1975). Complaints focus on the facts that such materials are limited to technical details of grammar, spelling, and punctuation, are dull and boring for students, and are merely mechanized workbooks. In general, college English teachers resist educational technology.

Computer-assisted instruction has not fulfilled the dreams of those experts in 1960s who made statements like "As computer-assisted instruction becomes a reality, the ultimate in directing learning will be achieved" (Coulton, 1966; Fuller, 1962). Although computer hardware has steadily decreased in price, the development of effective programs, particularly in writing, has lagged. Furthermore, students who have the greatest need for skills drills are not responding to the existing computer programs. Perhaps this is due to the poor quality of the programs, or perhaps it reflects the antagonism many English and composition instructors feel toward and express about computers.

There is little evidence that students who need intensive help in writing improve with computer-assisted instruction. In a study of CUNY open-admissions students enrolled in remedial writing courses, Bossone and Weiner (1973) reported that the few students who used the computer programs intensively improved in knowledge of the elements of grammar and sentence structure but not in ability to write longer essays than they had previously written. Many students rejected using the computer. For the most intensive remedial courses, neither computer-assisted instruction, programmed learning, nor regular classroom instruction emphasizing linguistics was effectitve in improving students' writing skills. Students who needed a small amount of help improved; those who needed intensive help did not.

Similarly, the large, heavily funded TICCIT computer project developed at Brigham Young University (Provo, Utah) under National Science Foundation funding has been phased out because of the high costs of maintaining it when the grants ran out. TICCIT writing programs are sophisticated, have been thoroughly tested, and are complete courses. In analyzing student use, investigators report that remedial students preferred to "cling to their instructors" rather than use the computer and that the students who were most likely to complete the computer writing courses tended to be highly motivated, high-achieving students who wanted to finish the courses quickly. Recently, the English department, faced with a cutback of funds from $90,000 to $30,000, decided to abandon the computer program, print up the materials, and hire teachers to present the course to students (Hansen, 1976).

A number of other colleges are using computer-assisted writing programs, but most of these programs are designed to supplement composition courses rather than to be complete courses. For example, there are computer-assisted-instruction programs in writing at Stanford (Nold, 1975) and in the University of Illinois PLATO system.

Computer scoring of essays still has very limited applicability for improving college writing. Themes can be scored on six elements by computer: fluency (total number of words used), spelling, diction (measured by word length), sentence structure (sentence length), punctuation (number of unusual punctuation marks), and paragraphing (number and average length of paragraphs). Today's essay-scoring programs do not match the aspects of language that are interesting to teachers judging students' writing, nor do they match the present capability of the computer in assessing these limited factors (Slotnik, 1972).

Less expensive autotutorial and programmed learning materials have very limited appeal to those students who need great improvement in writing. Much depends on the cooperation of the instructor, for when audiovisual and programmed materials are assigned by instructors as part of the regular course assignments, students are more likely to use them regularly. Few students voluntarily complete a self-help program on their own.

Audiotapes and self-instructional minicourses for teaching basic grammar, spelling, punctuation, and other writing skills are available from several companies. For example, Educulture Tutorial Systems (3184J Airway Ave., Costa Mesa, California 92626) publishes seventeen modules on basic English, spelling, and vocabulary exercises in audiotutorial form and a twenty-four-module minicourse in rhetoric and critical thinking. Westinghouse Corporation also publishes tape-cassette and programmed lessons in basic grammar and sentence structure, as do many other publishers.

Alternatives to Traditional Composition. Some colleges are trying to deemphasize writing skills, traditionally given high priority, by permitting students to create with other media in place of themes. Courses in semiotics, defined as a special kind of literacy that requires students to compose with drawings, collages of photographs, and other elements with the goal of equipping students to cope with newer media of arts and communication are increasing in popularity and replacing traditional literature courses in some English departments.

Integrated Approach to Writing. Faculty members in smaller colleges and universities have traditionally placed more emphasis on undergraduate teaching than have their counterparts in larger institutions, where, with few exceptions, freshman English is usually taught by inexperienced and untrained graduate assistants. So it is not surprising that in smaller colleges where full professors regularly teach freshman composition, there is a greater emphasis on collegewide writing programs and competency examinations. For example, for over ten years Marshall University has offered a program in which senior faculty members teach freshman composition and monitor each graduate teaching assistant so that the program "is not completely turned over to novices." Students with low ACT scores are required to take a three-unit remedial English course that stresses grammar, rhetoric, logic, and reading before they can enroll in the regular freshman English course. If students earn grades of C or lower in the English-composition series, they must pass a two-hour writing-competency test before graduating

(Ardinger, 1976). Students with problems in writing (and those who fail the competency test) are encouraged to use the writing laboratory, which provides individualized help. In addition, the English department offers advanced writing courses, honors programs, and awards to motivate students toward excellence. Although faculty members in this program admit that it does not guarantee literacy, as some students may evade the most carefully planned procedures, they believe it guarantees students the opportunity to learn to write well.

As writing problems become more pervasive, coordinated faculty efforts directed at the campus as a whole are increasing. For example, Guralnick and Levitt (1977) present a case study of how the English department at the University of Colorado responded to faculty rage and despair at the diminishing quality of student writing. The department—

- reinstated the freshman composition requirement, which had been dropped in the mid 1960s.
- raised the entrance standards for admission to the university by setting progressively higher cutoff SAT scores. (Minority students were exempted but required to take intensive remediation courses in the summer session before enrollment.)
- developed a "college seminar program" in which faculty members from all disciplines teach writing to small groups of students. (Each department in the Arts and Sciences College agreed to offer two writing courses a year.)
- reduced the class size of regular composition courses.
- required a diagnostic writing test, designed by the English department, for all entering students.

Trends and Implications. Several major directions show promise in improving the current writing situation. None of them is really new or different; we might say they have been rediscovered.

First, colleges and universities are making serious attempts to develop preventive programs by coordinating their knowledge of teaching writing with teachers in the public schools. After more than a decade of neglect, during which high schools determined for themselves which courses would qualify a student for college, colleges are awakening to the inadequacies of high school courses and are realizing that closer articulation with their feeder schools is vital.

Second, college professors in many disciplines are pitching in and teaching writing courses. The job is too large for English departments to handle alone.

Third, there is an intensive search for methods and materials that will help students with minimal writing skills. There is a growing recognition that composition can be taught, and studies of the characteristics of students who have avoided writing in the past and of how to teach them are appearing more frequently in the literature.

Fourth, there is more emphasis on training writing instructors, including teaching assistants, at both two-year and four-year institutions, as well as helping faculty members in disciplines other than English teach and evaluate student writing.

Karliner (1974, p. 12) summarizes the current "state of the art" well: "The teaching of composition is universally acknowledged to be difficult. There are no easy answers and no panaceas. What has been found to work is expensive: a low ratio of students to instructors and good, experienced instructors who have as their major commitment the teaching of composition. Even a massive infusion of money intelligently used to attain these objectives, however, will not provide a miracle."

We have not lacked the techniques to teach composition, but we have lacked the commitment. Although remedial composition has been an integral part of higher education for over a century, professors and administrators in many universities still seem to view it as temporary, allocating few resources to it and giving it low priority. The long-range solution is to recognize writing as a discipline, one that is essential for people at all levels from grade school students to graduate professors. Teachers must be trained to teach composition; faculty members must also assume some responsibility in ensuring that students improve their writing. The alternative can only be a continued deterioration of the writing skills of our media-oriented youths and adults and the hastening of the arrival of a postliterate society.

English as a Second Language

Thus far in this chapter, I have discussed the writing problems of students for whom English is a first language and the programs that colleges have developed to help them. Students whose primary language or dialect is not standard English have even greater difficulty.

There have been many recent changes in college writing programs as the number of students whose native language is not English (or is not standard English) has increased. First, colleges are offering English as a second language (ESL) courses to disadvantaged U.S. students as well as foreign students. Colleges have long offered special courses in English as a foreign language to help international students; the realization that many students born and educated in the U.S. lack adequate communication skills in English is relatively recent. Current surveys show that one out of ten students in the U.S. comes from a home where English is not spoken. A second change is the application of linguistic research, especially contrastive language analysis, to ESL programs in an attempt to understand and ameliorate the problems non–English speakers have in learning to read and write English. A third, related change, following the research by linguists on the structure and grammar of black dialect, is the recognition that for speakers of black dialect, standard English is a second language. Fourth, there have been changes in the methods of teaching languages, including a trend away from using the audiolingual method exclusively and toward hiring more peer tutors and teacher's aides to work individually with students. Fifth, bilingual programs in the public schools, mandated by federal law, are proliferating, in contrast to the situation fifteen years ago, when teachers were forbidden to teach classes (other than foreign-language classes) in any language but English. Colleges too are realizing that many of their adult students are from bilingual or bidialectal backgrounds and need special help in learning to write effective essays in standard English.

In teaching students who have problems in writing standard English, one must differentiate between those who have used English all their lives but whose families and friends habitually speak another language, such as Chinese, Spanish, or black dialect, and those who have come to the United States within recent years as immigrants. Brooks (1978) reports that although these two groups can be taught in the same class, it must be done tactfully and with the open admission that students will apply in different ways the information they are given. Some will be meeting it for the first time, and others will be learning a different form from the speaking habits they have already acquired. Some will be learning new insights into why they write the way they do.

Students enrolled in basic ESL courses, whether native-born or immigrant, share certain traits. The little English they know has been acquired in listening and by talking. They have rarely had formal training in English grammar. The first step in helping these students is to listen to their speech and see whether they make the same errors in speaking as in writing. For example, find out whether they write "He would of gone" for "He would have gone."

Another factor that is important in understanding the language difficulties of students who were born in the U.S. is whether they were deprived of standard English models at a crucial time in their development of language skills. Students who as children spoke another language or were cared for by someone who did not speak English tend to retain their confusion—and sometimes the syntactic structures of the other language—for many years in their writing and sometimes in their speech. Students who immigrated to this country before completing the equivalent of high school differ from the international students who are sent here by their countries to attend college. International students have usually mastered the formal writing and rhetorical skills and patterns of their native language. Students who move before completing high school have a double problem—learning a new language and at the same time developing formal writing skills in English.

Some international students have great difficulty learning English, and it is hard for an American instructor to determine whether the student has specific problems in learning English or general language deficiencies that affected his reading, his writing, or even his speech in his native tongue.

Contrastive Language Analysis. Having determined something about the linguistic background of the student, one will then find it useful to understand some of the differences between the student's mother tongue (whether a foreign language or a dialect) and standard English and to understand the cultural differences that affect writing and speech.

Knowledge of the lexical, syntactical, semantic, and rhetorical differences between English and other languages enables the ESL teacher to interpret student writing errors and to help the student recognize the systematic differences between his language and English. This understanding makes learning easier for the student. (For some examples of differences between English and Spanish, Asian languages, and black dialect which cause confusion for the ESL student, see Appendix E.)

Cultural Influences on Student Writing. In addition to courses in the history, sociology, and literature of particular cultural groups, many ethnic studies departments have developed their own basic composition courses. As a result, colleges frequently offer special writing courses for Asian-American, black, or Chicano freshmen that are taught by professors in the respective ethnic studies departments, not the English department. These ethnic studies faculty members stress the importance of understanding the cultural influences that lead to writing problems as well as the structural differences between students' other languages and English. For example, Watanabe (1972 p. 1) explains that the appalling reading and composition problems of Asians and Asian-American students are symptoms of a much larger problem; "an antipathy toward articulation and an aversion for assertion." Watanabe states that the Asian student needs more than a mechanical mastery of language skills—he needs both a thorough knowledge of the "unique cultural influences impinging on the Asian and an understanding of how the Asian experience in America has discouraged the development of a strong sense of self, which in turn has restricted the form and function of self-expression in English."

When asked to write an argumentative paper or take a position on a controversial issue, the Asian student tends to write a long, involved, convoluted essay, typically in the passive voice. The exasperated English instructor is likely to scrawl on the student's paper, "Why don't you get to the point?"—or stronger words.

Watanabe points out that it is difficult, if not impossible, to change the Asian student's preference for the passive voice in English unless one realizes that the preference stems from the student's wish to "suppress his individuality as Asian culture directs" (p. 1). Noting that the doctrine of filial piety shapes communication in the Asian home, Watanabe stresses that argument is almost unheard of in traditional families: Clearly defined roles of dominance and deference to one's elders virtually rule out argument and debate. By developing composition courses in Asian studies, ethnic instructors can connect the students' cultural identity to their expression in language and help them understand the reasons behind some of their difficulties in English composition.

Grammatical Needs of the Asian-Language Speaker. In contrast to Watanabe, Brooks (1978) is convinced that the view of the passive Asian student who cannot be persuaded to make a firm statement in writing is in large part a myth. She thinks this view developed because the student selects the wrong verb, particularly in conditional clauses, thus conveying an impression of indecisiveness that can be corrected by giving him some clearer insights into how the English tense system works. She thinks that what linguistically inhibited or disadvantaged students need in order to improve their writing is to be taught English grammatical rules and shown some simple applications. No one has taught them, for instance, the conditions in which the definite article is used in English. Brooks recommends that they be given training in use of the definite and indefinite articles, subject-verb agreement, and tenses, including specific instructions to stick to the present tense as much as possible, using other tenses only when a clear time indicator is present or when another tense is required by the sequence of tenses. She recommends exercises on the *-ed* ending on verbs; teaching students to check their papers for overuse of the conditionals *would, could,* and *might* and to omit these words or substitute *will, can,* or *may;* training in proper use of "if" and "when" clauses; and training in simple idioms (for example, providing lists of two-word verbs and be/have combinations). (See also Lay, 1975.)

If, after grammar lessons and correction of unconventional forms, the students are still having problems expressing themselves, Brooks (1978) suggests that we start to probe the murky depths of cultural and psychological differences.

For additional information on Asian-American cultural differences and linguistic abilities, see Lesser (1976), Sue and Frank (1973), Sue and Kirk (1972), and Watanabe (1973).

The Spanish-Speaking Student. Spanish-speaking students come from homes representing a range of proficiency in English. In some families, no English is spoken. Other families speak dialects of American English and Spanish — barriology or pochismo, for example. Even if the student attended public school, if his parents and friends do not speak English, he is likely to have difficulty in reading and writing.

Spanish poses some special difficulties for the student learning English as a second language. The fact that Spanish and English are written with the same alphabet is a major problem in that a student may be able to pronounce English words and sentences but have no understanding of their meaning. The Latino student in the classroom often mimics the actions of other students and remains quiet, so that the teacher does not recognize quickly that the student does not understand English.

English and Spanish differ in sound patterns, spelling, word order, stress, and intonation. These differences may interfere with the development of English speech, reading, and writing skills. (See Appendix E.)

An illustration of what occurs when a student tries to translate English literally into Spanish occurred when a psychologist asked a Chicano he was testing, "How many ears do you have?" When the student replied, "Eighteen," the psychologist referred him to a hearing specialist. One way to interpret the student's answer is that he was trying to translate the question literally and logically. In Spanish, *¿Cuantos años tiene Usted?* (literally, "How many years do you have?") means "How old are you?" One expects to be asked one's age more often than the number of ears on one's head.

Black Dialect. Black Americans speak many dialects, not a single dialect, and usually their speech reflects the dialect spoken by white people in their geographic region. Because speakers of black dialect are exposed to standard English through television, radio, movies, and daily life experiences, they usually understand it well, although they may not be able to produce it themselves. The greatest impediment to teaching black students standard English is the teacher's attitude. Regardless of their ethnicity, teachers tend to come from middle-class backgrounds and have strong attitudes about what is "correct" English. So teachers often punish students who speak and write in dialect for using poor or incorrect English, thus alienating them from attempting to learn standard English.

Studies have shown that black dialect does not interfere with reading comprehension; the major concern of college instructors is that black dialect interferes with writing formal essays. Shaughnessy (1977) describes in detail how to help speakers of black dialect learn to write standard English prose.

Can Writing Errors Be Reduced? Duffin and others (1977) analyzed the writing errors made by a group of ESL students enrolled in a basic writing skills course at the University of California at Davis. The classes were small (from four to six students). The students had very weak writing skills. Half were Latino, 14 percent black, and 11 percent Chinese or Vietnamese. Errors made on entry essays were analyzed into nine major categories. During the course, the investigators found, students made significant improvement in reducing errors in organization and focus (−83 percent), omission of articles, diction, omission of inflections, and pronoun usage. The areas that were most resistant to change were those classified as mechanical conventions; spelling errors decreased by only 1 percent, and word choice, intrusion of articles, and some sentence-structure problems showed minimal improvement. Although all students made some of the same errors, the most frequent errors made by non–English speakers tended to be those predicted by contrastive language analysis. For example, Japanese and Korean speakers had problems with plural and possessive inflections and wrote "many homeworks" (Korean) or "much competititons at UCD" (Japanese). (Such noun countability errors decreased by only 22 percent during the term.) These findings support the theoretical inferences linguists have made about the types of grammatical difficulties that speakers of English as a second language and dialect speakers should have.

The investigators observed that most of the improvement occurred during the first three weeks of the quarter. After that, student interest and motivation flagged, and there was little improvement. Since the course was noncredit and required, the investigators believed that competititon from other courses accounted for the decline in improvement and the dropoff in attendance.

Most ESL courses stress pronunciation, writing, and conversation skills. Reading improvement and study skills are rarely included in college courses, although the students need them desperately. As a result, learning centers find that a number of students who have completed the ESL-requirement sequence of courses seek help because in reading and paper writing they still cannot compete with other students in their college courses. There is often a gap between what can be done for these students in ESL classes and the skills they need for the next-level course. Learning centers may be expected to help fill that gap.

Cultural Rhetoric. A second-language or dialect speaker who has thoroughly mastered English grammar, spelling, and sentence structure may still have problems in organizing his ideas and writing essays. Each culture has its own ways of organizing and perceiving speech and has its own rhetorical conventions. For example, Japanese discourse resembles a decreasing circle eventually arriving at a central point. Speakers of Semitic languages, such as Arabic, organize and perceive language in terms of parallels. They make Statement A and then rephrase it into a parallel Statement B. Spanish and Russian speakers use a digression pattern, roaming far from the point before returning to it. Dialect speakers also use rhetorical patterns that differ from those of standard English.

In teaching composition to non–English speakers, the instructor must help them see the maxistructure of formal English writing as well as understand the parts of sentences (ministructure). Unless students can see the broader rhetorical conventions of English and compare them with the conventions of their own language or dialect, they have difficulty organizing essays.

Sandberg (1976) experimented with training Malaysian ESL students in speed-reading techniques and mapping (Hanf, 1971) to teach them the structure of English prose. After the training, all the students were able to skim at 600 words a minute or faster, although their speeds before training had been 300 words a minute or slower. By reading selections rapidly, the students could read each essay three or four times, each time for a different purpose, move more quickly to writing tasks, and leave the instructor more time to spend on other skills during the class period.

Idioms. Idioms give all non–English speakers problems, and ESL teachers usually emphasize idiomatic expressions and provide drill and practice using materials like McCallum's *Idiom Drills.* A dictionary of American idioms, such as Boatner's (1966) book for deaf students, can also be very helpful to ESL students.

Peer Tutoring and Other Techniques. Although most ESL programs involve class sessions and many instructors still use the audiolingual approach and require language-lab attendance, some programs are currently expanding peer tutoring and using teacher's aides who work directly with students. As Houston (1976) points out, peer tutors help create a healthy learning environment and reduce stress, whereas traditional classroom structure creates a ghettoization of non–English speakers and places the ESL teacher in an authoritarian role. Houston's thesis is that peer tutors supplement the electronic learning devices and humanize the student's learning experiences.

There are a number of books and other materials to aid the peer tutor in ESL, including Black (1975), Fox (1973), Jolly and Jolly (1974), and Paulson and Bruder (1976). The Laubach Literacy Foundation publishes many materials useful for ESL tutoring, as well as training materials for its program's volunteer tutors. The Center for Applied Linguistics, 1611 Kent St., Arlington, Virginia, publishes a newsletter in applied linguistics called the *Linguistic Reporter* and a *Selected List of Materials for Teachers of English to Speakers of Other Languages.* The *Journal of Basic Writing,* published by the Department of English, City College of New York, 138th St. and Convent Ave., New York, New York 10031, contains practical articles on teaching writing to dialect speakers and students for whom English is a second language.

9

───────────

Enhancing
Reading Skills

───────────

Reading scores and SAT verbal scores—and the two are related—are good predictors of both undergraduate and graduate achievement. Hence, the steady ten-year decline in SAT verbal scores, coupled with a similar decrease in Graduate Record Examination scores, has raised serious questions in the minds of professors and administrators about the deterioration of students' reading skills. To be sure, colleges have been accepting a larger pool of applicants under open-admissions policies for over a decade, but there is other evidence that reading ability is declining nationally among high school students and young adults.

Scores on standardized reading tests administered to large numbers of high school students have fallen too, and the National Assessment of Educational Progress (1976) found that although both thirteen- and seventeen-year-olds showed a slight improvement on literal reading skills between 1970 and 1974, their scores on inferential comprehension declined. Inferential reading abilities are critical for success in traditional college courses.

Many reasons have been postulated for the decline in reading scores—the curricular chaos in the public schools, the impact of television and other media, and broader social changes, including the increase in single-parent families. Young people have been living social science, not reading about it. Both public school and college curriculums have been affected by new media, and it seems quite likely that the public may *not* view reading as being as essential in schoolwork or adult life as most educators have led us to believe.

Despite the lofty goals of the Targeted Right to Read program and the billions of dollars invested in improving reading programs for disadvantaged children over the past two decades, many students who graduate from high school today and seek college admission have very limited reading skills. The assumption underlying government funding of compensatory education programs seems to be that if children get a good start in reading, they will continue to improve as they move up into higher grades. In fact, however, disadvantaged students' reading and other achievement scores begin to drop off sharply when they leave elementary school. The fact that reading is a developmental skill and that different levels of education require different reading skills needs broader recognition and implementation. In other words, the skills that make a child an outstanding third-grade reader will not get him through law school. Although reading programs are found in more and more high schools, their services are usually limited to the lowest-achieving students, and the majority of students receive little attention.

There is a touch of irony in our self-proclaimed national reading problem, in that educators from other countries view the United States as having a national obsession with the teaching of reading. For over 150 years, methods of teaching beginning reading have been the subject of political battles, both local and national. The question whether reading should be taught using the "phonics" or "whole word" method has been bitterly fought in local school-board elections, and the arguments are political, not pedagogical. As a nation, we have been determined that our children all learn to read (at least that is the view we espouse), and everyone else too. Yet there are several million adult illiterates in the United States today, and the National Assessment of Educational Progress reports that 42 percent of black seventeen-year-olds are "functionally illiterate"; that is, their reading skills are below the fourth-grade level. These figures may seem appalling, but they represent a significant improvement over the 1970 testing. Despite the stories on the shameful state of literacy and the need to "go back to basics" that appear in our newspapers, often when school boards run into financial difficulties, citizens raise money to support athletic programs with much fanfare, while funds for special reading programs are quietly eliminated from school budgets.

From a worldwide perspective, the U.S. is a leader in education, with an expensive, compulsory education system. Yet U.S. adults read fewer books than adults in other English-speaking countries, and we do not begin to approach the literacy rate of little Iceland, which is reputed to be the only country in the world where all adults can read and write. (However, Iceland has a homogeneous population with no immigrants, a sharp contrast to our large, ethnically diverse, and changing population.)

One major question in determining whether we do indeed have a "national reading problem" has not been researched. That question is whether students and adults cannot read or will not read. Efforts to eradicate adult illiteracy have usually produced minimal results, even when the receipt of welfare checks was made contingent on the person's attending literacy classes—an experiment that was tried in Cook County, Illinois, and failed (Cook, 1977). Many U.S. citizens do not want to learn to read and see neither the value of reading nor the need to read. Why should one try to read a bus schedule or map when one can question the driver? Why read the telephone book if you can dial Directory Assistance? Why read college textbooks if you can get the information from other sources in less time and with less energy?

Most colleges now have extensive audiovisual-equipment centers, so that students with minimal reading skills can learn many subjects without reading or writing. Perhaps that is one reason that the correlation between reading-test scores and grades in community college courses has been declining since 1970. Spring (1975) tested the reading ability of a group of community college students and found that poor readers did not think their textbooks were difficult (even when the texts tested high on readability measures). The majority of the students she studied, both good and poor readers, reported that they found other ways of getting the information they needed to pass their courses than reading textbooks. They talked to their instructors (either in class or in office hours), asked other students, and learned from audiovisual aids.

It may be that the present "reading problem" will become a bogus issue if students are able to function effectively in college courses without having to read. Certainly students' grade-point averages, particularly in social sciences and humanities courses (where grade inflation has been greatest), have improved while their reading scores have declined.

That college students have reading problems is not a recent realization in American higher education (see Chapter One). However, the number of students with reading difficulties is increasing, and their problems are more severe, judging from the expansion of reading programs, the decline in test scores, and the changes in college curriculums.

A Brief History of College Reading Programs

As the field of psychology developed during the latter part of the nineteenth century, early psychologists—William James, Huey, and others—were fascinated with studying the process of reading. The development of high-speed photographic techniques intrigued the early psychophysicists, who performed many studies on the way adults perceive words, at first using crude observation and later using instruments like the tachistoscope. By the 1930s, remedial reading programs were an accepted part of the public school curriculum, and by the end of the 1930s, many colleges and universities, including some of the most selective institutions, such as Harvard and Dartmouth, established reading programs for their students. For example, Stella Center founded the Reading Laboratory at New York University's extension department in 1936, and Francis Triggs established a reading clinic at the University of Minnesota in 1938, while Harvard's program started that same year. Much of the impetus for such programs came from Strang's *Problems in the Improvement of Reading in High School and College* (1938), which alerted educators to the need to teach reading beyond elementary school. In 1941 Robert Bear of Dartmouth published a pamphlet called "How to Read Rapidly and Well," and college reading programs expanded rapidly from then on. (I suspect that one important factor helping create the need for reading services was the widespread adoption of general survey courses, such as "Survey of Western Civilization" or "History of Man," in which students covered the complete span of history in one year, with lengthy texts and long reading lists of original sources.)

Perhaps a look at the history of the Harvard reading course, which became the prototype for many university programs, will clarify the factors that led to the establishment of reading programs and the needs that those programs were designed to fill.

In 1938 Harvard, as a result of faculty concerns with the reading disabilities of a few of its students, established an experimental "Remedial Reading Course." Each fall, freshmen were tested, and those who scored lowest were informed of their plight and allowed to volunteer for the course. Around thirty students regularly enrolled in the twenty-session class. In 1946 Harvard's counseling center, the Bureau of Student Counsel, took over the program, and when the bureau administered a standardized reading test to the remedial class, it found that every student scored higher than 85 percent of the college freshmen in the country. As a result, the program was revised, the term *Remedial* was dropped from the title of the course, which was renamed "The Reading Course," and 800 students and two law professors signed up (Perry, 1959).

To handle the multitudes of Harvard students who wanted to improve their reading, Perry devised a new kind of reading test to screen for students most likely to benefit from the course, specifically those who "if they can be persuaded of their right to think, even though reading, they can then develop a broader and more flexible attack on the different forms of study and put their skills to work on long assignments" (p. 195). The test consisted of thirty pages of detailed material, a chapter from a history book entitled *The Development of the English State—1066–1272*. Students were told to see what they could get from the text in twenty-two minutes of study. When tested with multiple-choice questions, they were able to answer "every sensible question we could ask concerning the details," Perry reports (p. 196). However, when 1,500 entering Harvard freshmen were asked to write a short statement on what the chapter was all about, only 1 percent could do so, even though there was an excellent summary paragraph marked "Recapitulation" at the end of the chapter. Virtually all the freshmen read with what Perry calls an "obedient purposelessness" (p. 197) that would be most counterproductive in reading course textbooks. As a result, Perry devised an additional screening test in order to limit the number of students admitted to the course. This test consisted of a history exam question with two answers purportedly written by two students. One answer was a "chronological reiteration of the chapter by a student with an extraordinary memory for dates and kings and no concern for the question or any other intellectual interest" (p. 197). This answer might be graded a C− for effort. The other answer was shorter, contained no dates, and directly addressed the issues posed by the question. Probably this answer would be worth an A− or B+. Students were asked to judge which answer was better. One third picked the C− answer, and these students were permitted to enroll in "The Reading Course."

Perry's article "Students' Use and Misuse of Reading Skills: A Report to the Harvard Faculty" (1959) has become the document cited most frequently by college reading specialists to convince faculty members that a develomental reading program is needed and desirable in their institution. If Harvard students are not capable of reading college textbooks well and Harvard has a reading course, the implication is, then Winnemucca University students deserve one too. Faculty members in every institution, who see themselves as Harvard types regardless of their background or the students they teach, concede.

More recently a *Time* article ("Help for the Brightest," 1976) described the Stanford University Learning Assistance Center, which enrolls 50 percent of Stanford freshmen in its reading and study skills courses. This news item has served a similar function to Perry's article—it called the nation's attention to the fact that students in our most highly selective institutions are volunteering for help in reading and study skills. It seems that every generation, at some point, discovers that students cannot read as well as they would like or as well as professors expect.

Not only have some of the most academically prestigious institutions had reading programs for many years, remedial reading programs at public institutions have an even longer history. (See Chapter One for examples of college admission requirements in earlier times.) Many colleges were established for the primary purpose of teaching basic skills to minorities and other disadvantaged groups, and over twenty-eight years ago, Oscar Causey founded the Southwest Reading Conference (which later became the National Reading Conference) and brought college remedial reading specialists together annually for a conference at Texas Christian University. From its inception this conference has concerned itself with improving programs and practices for the below-average college reader. For example, in 1956 Bliesmer presented a paper describing materials and techniques for teaching college students whose skills were below the sixth-grade level (Bliesmer, 1957).

So college reading programs are not a product of the 1960s. They existed many years before. However, they have greatly expanded as the number of nontraditional students has increased.

The Range of Students' Reading Problems

To reiterate, more entering freshmen with minimal reading skills are seeking a college education today. However, to put the problems of underprepared students into perspective, one needs to be aware of the reading difficulties that college students in general experience and the situations that create these problems. Freshmen find that the amount of reading assigned by college professors exceeds anything they were exposed to in high school, and the difficulty level and conceptual complexity of the assigned reading are also greater.

College reading specialists work with a wide range of students—from those with the highest ability and excellent preparation to those who are considered poor college risks. Some clients are self-referred, others are sent by professors or advisers, and some are required to take the program because they got low test scores. Whether students are very well prepared or unprepared for college, their skills problems are inextricably linked to fears about succeeding in college. Typically clients who volunteer for reading-skills service complain about their inability to complete reading assignments (and their need to increase their reading speed) and their inability to understand and learn from their textbooks (and their need to increase their comprehension and memory). These complaints of inadequate speed and comprehension may mask students' anxieties, conflicts, and anger at the expectations and demands of their professors.

In this section, I describe some of the kinds of student problems I have encountered frequently during the thirty-five years I have worked in this field, and I discuss their implications.

Early each fall, anxious new freshmen and transfer students seek help from the voluntary reading service in large numbers or enroll in reading courses. Although these clients tend to be very well-prepared, capable students, they fear that their backgrounds and skills are not adequate for the demands of their new environment. After a week or two, their symptoms often disappear as they discover their classes are not as hard as they expected. As their confidence increases, they may drop the reading program.

Another group that seeks help early is bright, competitive students who are quite self-confident about their abilities but want to improve their efficiency in reading so that they will have more time for extracurricular activities or can earn higher grades with less effort.

However, as the term passes, slow, very conscientious readers fill the schedules of reading specialists as the dreaded deadlines for examinations and term papers approach. For the slow, contemplative reader, attaining a liberal arts degree or completing a preprofessional program equals four years of nonstop reading. From the freshman year on, students are confronted with a veritable wall of books to consume each term. Reading lists, particularly in humanities and social science courses, range from lengthy to impossible. My surveys at the University of California at Berkeley suggest that reading assignments in undergraduate courses range from 300 pages a night in some history and political science courses to 10 pages a week in mathematics, although math students may spend twenty hours or more on those 10 pages. The sheer amount of reading staggers freshmen unaccustomed to lengthy assignments, unsure of how to approach them, and unclear about what they are expected to learn from them.

For example, Gordon, who aspired to become a history major, failed an exam in a "History of American Diplomacy" course despite carefully reading Winston Churchill's five volumes of memoirs. He complained that the professor had asked only questions about the Yalta Conference and he had been unable to recall anything about it. While reading the five books, Gordon was adrift in a sea of words, rudderless and directionless, doggedly consuming each page. The instructor's lectures on the theoretical framework of history, its mega- and metastructure, might as well have been delivered in Urdu as far as Gordon was concerned. He did not realize that he should concentrate on the international diplomatic issues and events in his reading, and he belatedly came to the reading program to try to salvage his grade.

Corinne was another slow reader who, after spending a year in Japan, returned to college, enchanted with Japanese customs and determined to major in Asian culture. Enrolling in a course in Japanese history, she soon found the reading list impossible. Thirty lengthy tomes were assigned, including translations of the diaries of Dutch missionaries. Since she was a conscientious student, she asked the professor for suggestions on how to approach the reading assignments. The professor, assuming that her problem stemmed from her lack of background in the subject, assigned ten additional books to "prepare her" for the course. She came to the reading lab in tears, desperate to find ways to increase her reading speed. With the help of a librarian who recommended a short outline of Japanese history, we helped her plan a program around her assignments, emphasizing skimming and scanning skills. Had she enrolled in a speed-reading course that required additional reading, she probably would have withdrawn from college—or so she said.

The amount of reading required in many courses may discourage students, who—if they cannot find ways of coping—fall into deep despair, stop attending the class, and drop out of college. Some students, however, find ingenious ways to survive. They ask classmates (or the professor) which chapter is most important to read and what it says. Others use notetaking services, study guides, or outline series and ignore their texts and other reading assignments. The more gregarious form "reading conspiracies," divide up the reading assignments, and meet regularly to discuss the ideas they have read. College reading assignments that are extremely long account for the popularity of speed-reading courses on campuses.

But are the long assignments really necessary? Amann (1977) argues that professors and librarians are abusing books by assigning and displaying so many of them that students feel intimidated and ignorant. Thus professors, by giving lengthy reading assignments, may create in students an aversion to reading. (In analyzing the reading autobiographies of my graduate students over the years, I find that few retained their love of reading for pleasure after graduating from college. Many say they refuse to read anything unless it is required.) Spending four years compulsively reading dull, pedantic books and speeding through those that are most interesting may turn the most ardent bibliophiles into bibliophobes. Interviews with professors suggest that they, too, are not immune to reading aversion. As they age, professors admit that they read fewer professional articles outside their immediate areas of interest and become more selective in reading articles within their specialties, because of the poor quality of professional writing or the paucity of new ideas. Sometimes even professors admit that their pleasure reading tends toward the light and frivolous.

Why, then, is so much reading assigned? Certainly the information explosion has affected every discipline, and academe's publish-or-perish economy requires that someone consume the products. Students are the designated, and often reluctant, consumers. Even professors who themselves are slow readers assign long reading lists, for they may forget the limitations of their students. But underlying these realities is something more basic: the veneration of academics for the printed page. Course committees evaluate courses on the basis of their reading lists. The longer the reading list, and the more prestigious the authors, the more likely the course committee is to rate the course as academically impeccable.

Unnecessary, lengthy assignments, when given without clarification of how to approach them, are the faculty-generated causes of the problems that many of our reading clients present. Some students, however, have long-standing problems that are exacerbated by the stress of college.

Recidivists in Reading. One group of reading clients consists of those I call recidivists in reading—that is, students who have had many years of remedial reading help. Some have had special reading assistance since first grade and have grown dependent on reading teachers. They seek out the reading program as soon as they are admitted to college. Indeed, they may even select a college because it has a strong reading program. Although their reading skills may be quite adequate for college work, their confidence is low, and they attribute any prior academic success to their reading instructors' help. Weaning these students from their dependency on special help requires effort and tact. Sometimes they work out well as student aides in the reading program, if they can be convinced that they can help others, but often their attitudes and dependency symptoms preclude this solution. Then the reading specialist must slowly but persistently reduce the number and length of appointments and support the student in working on his own.

Other students who have had prior intensive reading help seem to cling to their classification as problem readers, and the thought of changing threatens them with a loss of identity. For example, Jeff was diagnosed as dyslexic at age 5½ at a hospital clinic and has used this label to manipulate his parents and teachers. The physician who diagnosed his case told his parents not to frustrate him, and Jeff has used this admonition to get his own way. His parents provided him with intensive help throughout his twelve years in school, and his scores on a standardized reading test placed him in the 90th percentile in comparison with other freshmen in his college. However, once admitted to college, he announced to all his instructors that he was dyslexic and sat back while they reacted. They reacted by holding meetings with the counseling staff and reading specialists to discuss what could be done for Jeff. Meanwhile, Jeff refused to work on spelling, which was the last vestige of his disability, refused to follow suggestions to dictate his themes and papers, and refused to attend classes or to accept tutoring help. He failed all his courses.

Some recidivists are intellectually capable, motivated students who, despite years of special help, enter college with very limited reading and writing skills. These clients are usually referred to reading specialists by writing instructors, because they are poor spellers and exceedingly slow readers. Some were diagnosed as dyslexic in elementary school; others, usually from lower socioeconomic backgrounds, claim they did not learn to read until age nine or ten. If these students had good, intensive remedial programs before entering college, there is usually little more a reading specialist can do to help them. Condemning them to the treadmill of additional remedial courses does not help. Indeed, it may increase their frustration and require so much effort that they fail in other courses, such as science and mathematics, in which they have the skills and ability to succeed.

If these weak readers are bright, knowledgeable, and motivated and can learn quickly through listening, they can develop alternative ways of coping with reading assignments and written papers. I suggest that instructors treat these students as if they were blind, permitting them to hire someone to read their textbooks to them and to dictate their papers for someone to type. These strategies work quite well, take the pressure off the students, and sometimes even result in improvement in reading and writing. One freshman who used these strategies made the honor roll, and other such students have completed doctoral dissertations despite their verbal handicaps. However, it is very hard to convince instructors that a perfectly healthy young adult with normal eyesight has a reading/spelling handicap that cannot be cured.

It is sometimes hard to discriminate between students who have a history of genuine dyslexia and those who develop the symptoms while in college, diagnose themselves, and come to the reading center for confirmation. This syndrome is most likely to occur when a student is under great stress, as when he is faced with a lengthy, difficult reading assignment or the intensive reading required when preparing for doctoral preliminary exams. Paul's case is illustrative. Worried about his prelims in computer science, he described his early problems in learning to read. His mother, an elementary teacher in Paris, arranged for him to be tutored in phonics for three years, a failure experience that he recalled vividly. When he was preparing for his doctoral exams, all those early

fears and feelings of inadequacy returned, and he convinced himself that he was suffering from "word blindness." Students with this
kind of problem take diagnostic tests willingly and respond to
counseling and reassurance. However, it is sometimes hard to help
them understand that although they have had difficulties with
reading in the past, their skills are adequate now, and they can
cope with their present college requirements. If given support,
these students can discover ways to succeed in the tasks they
currently face.

Other slow readers do not seek help because they feel that
they cannot afford to spend the time on activities not directly related to their courses. If they do enter a voluntary program, they
may get discouraged quickly and drop out, particularly when they
observe that others are faster and better readers than they are. If
slow readers are identified early and given a reading course, they
can be helped, but success depends on the type of course. For
instance, if very slow readers are placed in a completely self-help,
machine-oriented speed-reading program, the experience can be
demoralizing. Each question the student misses reaffirms his negative self-image. Such students, if they remain in school, cope by
avoiding courses that require lengthy reading assignments and
choosing subjects like art.

The Untaught. The adult student who has managed to avoid
reading almost completely but wants to return to college poses a
very difficult problem. Some students in this group can read but
have not practiced, so that reading is a laborious, time-consuming
activity—in short, sheer agony. Others have not learned to read
and learned little throughout school—members of the automatic-
pass generation. They may disguise their problems well, they are
not likely to volunteer for special programs, and instructors may
not discover their weaknesses until late in the term.

Wanda's case illustrates the problems that students with minimal skills face when enrolled in a selective university through a
special-admissions program. Although Wanda had graduated from
high school, she could barely read, and she had great difficulty
figuring out new words. During her first year in the university, she
earned a C average, aided by tutors who read her textbooks for her
and briefed her on their contents. However, she was unable to get

tutoring in her sophomore courses and was left on her own to cope with reading assignments. She came to the reading center for help. She explained that she had never had phonics and could not decode new words, although she was able to recognize words at sight that she had learned before. Diagnostic tests confirmed that she had very poor decoding skills. She was given an intensive individual phonics and reading-enrichment program. In ten weeks she was reading material at the eighth-grade level independently and had decided to spend another term in intensive reading activities before resuming her college courses.

These are a few of the kinds of students who seek help in reading. Some are anxiously confronting new and higher demands on their skills; others have long-standing and very basic difficulties. In order to help, reading-skills specialists need to understand both the student's problems and fears and the college's expectations.

Methods and Materials

College reading programs and courses vary greatly in format, content, methods, and materials. However, they have some characteristics in common. Virtually all of them use standardized reading tests for selection, placement, and/or evaluation (Fairbanks and Snozek, 1973; Geerlofs and Kling, 1968; Roueche and Snow, 1977). (See Chapter Two for a discussion of reading tests and Appendix A for a list of frequently used tests.) Reading courses generally focus on improving students' reading rate and comprehension skills. They may include intensive vocabulary work, paced practice on exercises with comprehension quizzes, and supplemental practice on reading machines. In most programs textbook-reading skills are taught in study skills courses, but they may instead be included in reading-improvement courses. (See Chapter Nine for a discussion of textbook-reading methods.)

There are many workbooks and other aids for improving college reading skills. Unfortunately, most are based on easy articles from magazines and newspapers, on the premise that to increase reading rate, a student must practice on simple material. However, the programs' stated objectives are to prepare students to read more effectively in their other college courses—that is, to read long textbook chapters on political science or psychology and reference materials, a far cry from the level and length of the popular articles used for practice. (It takes a gifted teacher to show students how they can transfer and relate the skills learned in reading easy material to their other college reading.)

The typical format for college reading workbooks is paced reading practice on short passages and magazine and newspaper articles, with multiple-choice or true/false questions to measure understanding the main idea, remembering supporting details, vocabulary in context, and conclusions. Some examples are Pauk's *Six-Way Paragraphs* (1974b), Sack and Yourman's *Developmental Speed Reading Course* (1965), and Spargo and Williston's *Timed Readings* (1975). Materials for community college reading programs tend to be easier, although they emphasize the same skills. Kai and Kersteins (1968) and Joffe's series (1970–1971) are examples of some of the better materials published.

Modules for practicing particular subskills in reading are quite popular. Many of these materials try to make explicit the nature of the reading/thinking process—for example, they show students how to identify a main idea rather than merely telling them to find one. Many of the modules are accompanied by tape cassettes that give the student explicit instructions and illustrate what he is expected to do. Examples of these modules are the *McGraw-Hill Basic Skills Series,* Educulture's modules on reading skills, and those published by Westinghouse.

A more general audiotutorial program that is being widely used is Glock and others' (1975) PROBE, which, although written at about the ninth-grade level, provides intensive practice in comprehension skills students need to read college textbooks effectively.

A few workbooks do have longer passages from college textbooks, such as Maxwell's *Skimming and Scanning Improvement* (1968c), Rauch and Weinstein's *Mastering Reading Skills* (1968), and Spache and Berg's *Art of Efficient Reading* (1966).

Reading specialists in senior colleges and universities often complain about the lack of material suitable for above-average students and for graduate students. Some of the older books written to improve the reading skills of liberal arts students are still appropriate, such as Adler's *How to Read a Book,* a companion piece to the Great Books program and published regularly since 1940, and there are Case and Vardaman's *Mature Reading and Thinking* (1959), Center's *Art of Book Reading* (1952), and Richards' *How to Read a Page* (1942). Since these books provide instruction on how to read the classics, philosophy, and literature, their information and strategies are as valid today as when they were written.

In practice, most reading instructors develop their own materials for teaching advanced students—that is, they select textbooks, articles, or paperbacks and write their own questions. Many programs also use the college edition of *The Atlantic Monthly,* which contains questions and exercises on the articles in the issue. Community college reading instructors more often use the special edition of *Reader's Digest* for the same puposes.

At the other extreme we find a growing supply of materials for teaching the very poor readers enrolled in community college reading programs. One example of such materials for this adult basic education (ABE) group, which includes ESL and learning-disabled students, is Brown and Hulbert's *Letters, Sounds, and Words* (1976), an excellent workbook for students whose reading skills are below the fourth-grade level. Dupuis and Askov (n.d.) have compiled an excellent annotated bibliography of reading materials for ABE students that includes critical evaluations by ABE instructors.

Reading laboratories are invariably equipped with electronic devices that purport to increase reading speed. The piece of equipment most frequently reported by surveys is Educational Developmental Laboratories' Controlled Reader, a machine that projects a filmstrip a line at a time (or the filmstrip can be shown with a sliding shutter that forces the reader to move his eyes rapidly from right to left). This trains the reader to reduce his eye fixations and emulate the eye movements of a skilled reader. The machine can be adjusted for speeds up to 1,200 words per minute, and students take multiple-choice comprehension quizzes after reading the filmstrip. Hard copies of the articles are also available so that students can preview the selection before reading it on film and can practice reading other articles in the booklets to make sure that they can transfer to the printed page the speed gains they make with the machine.

Pacers, tachistoscopes, and other reading devices designed to help readers increase their speed of perception are also found in reading laboratories. There are many types of mechanical aids for students to use in self-help programs. I believe that their value depends to a large extent on the way reading specialists incorporate them into students' programs. Some reading specialists are committed to the use of machines and design their programs so that students accept and use the machines. Other reading specialists reject machines, maintaining that reading can be taught only through counseling and working individually with the student and his textbooks. Implicit in the attitude of those who refuse to use machines is a feeling that if a machine is any good, then it should be capable of doing the job alone. Of course, machines and the programs written for them both have limitations.

What reading instructors need is a realistic understanding of the advantages and limitations of mechanical devices, the research on which they are based, and the ways they can be used to aid students. Sue Davidson Johnson at California Polytechnic University at San Luis Obispo gives her student facilitators and paraprofessionals an intensive training program on how to help students make appropriate use of the mechanical devices. First, the trainees read information about the equipment and the related research, and they complete comprehension exercises on this material. Second, the trainees learn to design appropriate programs for students, basing their designs on formal and informal tests. Third, they are trained to warn students of the types of problems they might encounter as they use the machines and to tell students how to cope with problems as they occur. Fourth, they monitor students using the machines. After this training, the trainees understand how to use the machines in an individual program, know the research and philosophy behind the use of machines, know how to operate and demonstrate each machine and what kinds of programs can be used with it, and are aware of the problems that students might experience in using the machines and how they might be forestalled. They are trained to answer student questions like "How long do I have to work on this machine to get results?" or "Why did you put a machine on my program?"

I have visited many reading centers and observed that a high percentage are underused by students. Often the reason is that the person who designed the program has left, and his replacement disclaims any knowledge of machines, does not know how to turn them on, and claims that students find the program dull and do not persist in it. At other centers with the same kinds of students, the lab programs are heavily used. I conclude that the success of a self-paced laboratory depends on the people who run it. If they are uninterested and do not train students to use the equipment, answer their questions, show them how the devices will help them, and keep a continual check on their progress, then students will not use the program. (One indicator an administrator can use to identify the attitude of a reading staff toward machines occurs at budget time. Reading specialists who have well-organized, comprehensive self-paced programs for students and find students responsive will request additional machines. Those who reject using machines will request additional professional positions.)

Another kind of material found very frequently in reading labs is the multilevel kit—for example, Science Research Associates' *Reading Laboratory III-A* or *Reading for Understanding* cards. These short exercises are graded in difficulty and can be timed. Students use them individually. (I can attest to the ubiquity of SRA kits in high school reading programs, having observed students using them in a remote high school in the southern highlands of Papua, New Guinea.) More than 60 percent of the country's reading labs use SRA kits (Fairbanks and Snozek, 1973; Geerlofs and Kling, 1968). Many students who were exposed to SRA kits in elementary and high school refuse to use them in college. However, these materials are particularly useful for two groups: (1) international students who need improvement in English vocabulary and reading skills and practice in taking multiple-choice examinations and (2) students reviewing for professional and graduate school adminissions examinations. Students who use the cards to simulate an objective examination and who work under time pressure find practice on the cards very helpful.

Remedial reading instructors often design modules for teaching particular skills by combining selected exercises from different workbooks, reading machine programs, and multilevel kits with audiotaped instructions. Students diagnosed as deficient in a specific skill, such as reading for main ideas, are assigned a module with exercises and activities that are appropriate to their particular problem. See Sowande (1977) for a description of how the Hunter College (New York) program uses such reading modules.

Speed Reading

Speed-reading courses continue to be popular and will undoubtedly always attract students as long as publishers print a half million books a year, professors assign unconscionably long reading lists, and teachers insist that one must read every word to comprehend the message. Many people seem convinced that the measure of one's intellect is the number of books one has swept one's eyes through. As early as the 1940s, articles about speed-reading courses reported astronomical reading rates when the students' final grades were based on how fast they read. Experts in the reading profession, including myself, have verbally battled commercial speed-reading courses since the 1950s, but these programs continue unabated. Our criticisms of the commercial programs were directed against their exorbitant claims and guarantees to teach people to read at speeds as high as 20,000 words per minute. (For references on the speed-reading controversy, start with Evelyn Wood's article on the Reading Dynamics program [1960]; then see Spache, 1962; Taylor, 1962; Maxwell, 1968a, 1969; McLaughlin, 1969a; and Carver, 1971.) One of my personal concerns about commercial speed-reading courses was that they did not screen their students, so that the weaker students who took the courses ended up in my office feeling even more inadequate and insecure about their reading and intellectual abilities. The very feelings that had led them to take the courses in the first place were heightened rather than reduced. Another problem was that some students entered speed-reading courses with poor comprehension and finished with higher speeds but even lower comprehension—they apparently had learned only to turn pages faster. Some students were convinced that they must read everything "dynamically" or they would lose the skill they had paid so dearly to acquire. This attitude was fateful for students with weak high school backgrounds who compulsively speed-read their chemistry textbooks and later wondered why they failed chemistry.

But there are many people who are helped by a speed-reading course that gives them the freedom to read rapidly and to learn to trust their own judgment for identifying those ideas worth reading slowly and ignoring poorly written trivia. The information explosion, which I have long considered diarrhea of the presses, is the raison d'etre for speed reading. With so much to read in every field, mature readers must read selectively and skim. Reading specialists have maintained that an important goal of reading-improvement courses is to train students to read flexibly—that is, to vary their speed and depth of comprehension with their purpose. Improvement in flexibility has been hard to demonstrate, however. Kershner (1964) discovered that adults who read rapidly do not vary their speed with the difficulty of the reading matter. Slow readers display more flexibility in that they read difficult material more slowly than easy material. A problem in teaching students to vary their speed with their purpose is that they may not understand the purposes that mature readers have. After all, the freshman is reading textbooks mainly to learn the material that the instructor thinks is important enough to include on examinations. Novices in any field lack the background to make the sophisticated judgments that experts can on what is important (and should therefore be read carefully) and what can be skimmed or skipped. So speed reading—although I prefer the term *skimming*—represents a mature reading skill involving making critical judgments about the material one reads.

Today's college speed-reading courses differ little from the commercial ones. Both use standardized reading tests at the beginning and end of the course, paced practice, and easy materials. The major difference is that the commercial programs are far more expensive.

Recent research suggests that if students in speed-reading courses are given information on the nature of the reading process and current theories of memory and retention, not just paced practice, they will show greater improvement. For example, Cox (1977) taught some students information-processing theory in a speed-reading course and showed them how to apply it to difficult books. These students—the experimental group—varied their speed and purpose according to the difficulty of the material and the amount of information they needed in order to identify, understand, analyze, and outline key ideas from an advanced political science book. In other words, students were taught to develop their own advance organizers for keying into major concepts. Cox's control group, taught with a diagnostic-prescriptive approach using the same reading materials, but without receiving training in information processing, scored significantly lower on tests of reading flexibility at the end of the course.

Hansen (1977) taught speed reading to a class of honors students and matched them with a control honors section who did not receive speed-reading training. She found both quantitative and qualitative differences between the experimental and control classes. Analyzing the college-textbook materials used for the pre- and posttest measures, she found that slower readers were more likely to recall temporal relations (that is, they were able to follow the chronological sequence of events) than speed readers, but that speed readers excelled on recalling concepts involving reasoning, coordination, relationships, comparison, and contrast. She found no evidence that her speed-reading group was just skimming for main ideas. They were reading the posttest material two or more times for different purposes and recalling more units.

Another interesting approach to speed reading is that of Sandberg (1976), who taught speed reading to Malaysian students in an ESL class and found that it enhanced their ability to see the overall organizational patterns of English prose by permitting them to read the passage more than once for different purposes. He states that the ability to read rapidly with good comprehension requires skill in selecting the important concepts carefully and rejecting those that are insignificant.

Slower readers, particularly those with poor comprehension and vocabulary skills, spend a great deal of time decoding individual words and struggling with the syntax. Although some poor readers can remember details, many cannot synthesize into principles and concepts the information they read. It is unfortunate that more efforts are not being made to introduce younger students to skills in skimming and scanning, not as a substitute for careful, slow reading but as a tool they will surely need in determining for themselves what should be read slowly and carefully. It is particularly important that students have a variety of reading skills in their repertory when confronted with material that they consider difficult and dull. In a recent high school group I taught, I asked how many students read material that they considered dull and difficult more slowly than material they found interesting. Ninety percent replied that they read difficult material slowly and procrastinated a long while before tackling it. The belief persists that one should read dull and difficult material very slowly, despite Adler's (1940) suggestion that the more difficult one finds a selection, the faster one should read it, at least the first time through. Too many students equate reading with serving penance. They feel that if they sit staring at the book hard enough, the facts and ideas will rise and come into their heads, but by approaching reading slowly and negatively, they recall little.

Some college reading programs are capitalizing on the fact that there is no stigma attached to taking a speed-reading course by calling both their developmental and remedial sections "speed reading." Because virtually no one is completely satisfied with his reading rate, these courses attract a wide variety of students. One method is to enroll students in a speed-reading course and then test them and divide them into sections on the basis of their comprehension scores. At California State University at Hayward, students in the lowest speed-reading section have clear standards to meet in order to pass the course. They must be able to read selections from each of fourteen disciplines, pass a criterion referenced reading test on each, and write a summary of each selection that someone who has not read the selection can understand. Although the reading materials may be somewhat simpler than the average college textbook, students are exposed to ways of reading and the organization and terms of different subjects, which they certainly would not voluntarily select.

Harmful Myths Abouts the Reading Process

In their attempts to help college students improve reading skills, reading instructors may operate on a set of beliefs (myths) about reading development and may misinterpret research on the reading process. These attitudes lead to poor instructional strategies and poor materials.

1. The view of reading skills as an absolute hierarchy with clearly defined steps, ranging from decoding to critical reading, affects the materials chosen and the strategies used. College reading instructors holding this view may assume that poor readers must start at the first-grade level and recapitulate in sequence all the skills taught through elementary and high school.

2. Bloom's taxonomy (Bloom and others, 1971) is misinterpreted so that the various objectives are fractionated by students' levels; that is, poor readers are expected only to recognize specifics and terms, while readers at the Grade 13 level are expected to analyze, synthesize, and evaluate materials. There are many examples of this error; for instance, some workbooks for the poor reader contain only questions on facts, while workbooks written at a higher level contain only interpretive and application questions.

The idea that one cannot teach students to read and think critically until they can function at a high school level is pernicious and persistent. Interpretive and application questions and statements can be written for students at any level (Herber, 1978, has many examples). Similarly, Bloom's taxonomy can be applied to materials at any grade level and should not be used to restrict the teaching of principles and generalizations or universals and abstractions to advanced readers.

Good teaching and explicit guides are needed to help weaker readers develop these thinking/reading skills, but restricting questions to the most literal will not help them, nor will a series of questions tapping various intellectual abilities and skills at random—that is, an exercise that starts with difficult interpretive questions and intersperses factual questions. If the poor reader is to learn, then exercises should begin with literal questions or statements and progress to interpretive and then to application questions.

An exception of course, occurs when a student is weak in one particular skill, such as reading for main ideas, and needs extra practice in this skill. He may need intensive practice on materials that require main-idea identification, but he also should have the opportunity to transfer this training to regular textbook material and to develop critical reading skills.

3. The misuse of diagnostic and prescriptive teaching is

another reason many students fail to show gains, get discouraged, and drop out of college reading programs. The problem here is that students are tested and found to be deficient in some basic skill (phonics or word-attack skills, for instance) and then are prescribed intensive training—in phonics, say—to remedy their weakness. The teacher then requires college students to work on the very skills and exercises associated with their failure to learn to read adequately in elementary school. Such exercises tend to be dull and meaningless, particularly if the student is expected to work alone on self-paced exercises. An educationally more productive approach is for the instructor to analyze the student's strengths and interests and to offer materials and methods that capitalize on them. When students cannot hear the differences between phonemes, teaching them to recognize whole words embedded in an interesting context yields faster results and fewer dropouts. As students see that reading does not have to remain a painfully slow decoding process and begin to make progress, then special help in their weaker skills can be given. Some experts have made this point more harshly. For instance, Robert Samples recently commented in a speech that teaching phonics to dyslexics is analogous to treating anemia by bleeding the patient.

The rules of pronunciation and spelling that poor readers have learned in intensive phonics programs often hamper them in advanced reading and writing because they have not internalized English spelling patterns or learned to go beyond the rules. Consequently, when faced with the many variations and exceptions inherent in English words that are not covered by rules, these students are very frustrated.

4. The widespread use of standardized reading tests has limited college reading courses in two ways. First, reading and writing are divorced and taught by different specialists, often in different departments. Second, the majority of workbooks used in college reading courses resemble the reading tests—short passages followed by multiple-choice or true/false questions. To be sure, other college courses have multiple-choice examinations too, but the reading selections on which course examinations are based are chapters in textbooks, not paragraphs.

5. Materials used in reading courses, if not limited to short passages of several paragraphs, are articles from popular magazines. They are rarely selected to challenge students intellectually; rather, they often appear to be the easiest, non-thought-provoking material that the author could find. So deeply committed are some reading specialists to making the reading task easy and interesting that they seem unconcerned with helping the students grow intellectually or with relating the course material to other college subjects. It is almost as if some reading specialists were determined to teach leisure reading, but at the same time to destroy the fun by giving tests, thus ensuring that reading would not replace television viewing for their students. There is minimal evidence that students can transfer skills gained from practice with nonbooks and simple articles to reading the textbooks in their courses. Textbooks and other assigned college reading materials pose problems for students because they often contain abstract concepts, copious information, and new terminology. In introductory courses, textbooks are written to provide students with an overview of the structure of knowledge and of the specialties in a particular discipline. Since the course content may be completely new to the student, understanding and mastering the concepts and terminology require great effort.

Readability: Have We Gone Too Far?

In recent years there have been concerted attempts to make college textbooks simpler and more readable, and as a result many of today's college texts are easier than those of a decade ago.* But making books more readable can be a two-edged sword. Some books are still written in an unnecessarily pedantic style; but an attempt to simplify complex ideas and technical information, reducing them to a very low level, is a disservice to both the student and the subject.

One function that college reading specialists frequently perform is conducting readability analyses on textbooks and informing

*An earlier version of this section appeared in the *Journal of Reading*, March 1978, *21*, 525–530.

instructors of those that are too difficult for the reading abilities of their average students. There has been a recent resurgence of interest in the readability of textbooks, particularly in community colleges where the abilities of students range widely.

History of Readability Measures. What makes a book readable has been a topic of concern to educators, authors, and publishers for many years. Following the successful development and implementation of mental measurements in World War I, psychologists and educators began to search for an objective way of quantifying readability. Thorndike's publication of lists of the most frequently used words in the English language in 1921 greatly influenced educators to restrict vocabularies in basal readers and other books used in elementary schools. Gray and Leary (1935) surveyed 300 librarians, publishers, professors, and readers who asked librarians for assistance, asking them what made a book readable. Although only 5 percent of the responses cited features that could be measured objectively, these formed the basis for the later development of readability formulas.

However, it was Rudolf Flesch who popularized the concept of readability through his books and articles and ushered in the era of plainspeak, which has had a profound impact on authors, publishers, journalists, and educators. Plainspeak has become the lingua franca of the educated—the language in which they speak and write when they are communicating with others outside their specialties. Although plainspeak lacks the richness, metaphors, and complexity of classical prose writing, it does make it possible to express ideas to the educated and noneducated alike (Flesch, 1943, 1948, 1951, 1958).

Essentially, Flesch's books spawned a writing revolution. Authors became painfully aware of the length of the sentences they wrote and the number of polysyllabic words they used.

Applying Flesch's Readability Formula was time-consuming and somewhat difficult in the days before hand calculators. Consequently, many other researchers developed simpler formulas using similar variables—sentence length (or number of independent clauses) and some measure of word length (number of syllables or number of three-syllable words, for example). Among the many attempts to simplify Flesch's formula were the Farr-Jenkins-

Patterson Formula (Farr and others, 1951), the Lorge Formula (1959), Gunning's FOG Index (1952), Fry's Readability Formula (1968), and McLaughlin's SMOG Grading (1969b). The Dale-Chall Readability Formula, which is still widely used, involves sentence length and the number of words not appearing on a list of 3,000 common words (Dale and Chall, 1948). All the scales were validated against some measure of reading comprehension.

Flesch (1948) also developed a Human Interest Scale, which includes, among other variables, the number of personal pronouns and personal references in a 100-word passage. The criteria he used weighted drama and fiction as the most interesting and science writing as the dullest.

Although all the readability and reading-interest measures mentioned above can be applied objectively to written material, they consider neither the semantics nor the syntax of the passage, and they have other serious limitations. However, they are useful as quick and easy ways of judging a book's difficulty level and its appeal to students, provided that their limitations are recognized.

Limitations of Readability Formulas. Back in the 1940s, when I was a graduate student working on a project to determine the readability of soap ads by testing consumers, we circulated statements like the one reproduced below on the exceptions to the Flesch Readability Formula.

Very Difficult Prose

Them dirty lousy politicians is getting altogether too high and mighty, the way they is always arranging to take advantage of the little businessmen by raising up the tax payments and collecting more money from the little fellows. They ain't nothing much can be done about this here business, because them politicians has certainly got the inside connections and they always work through undercover arrangements. It's mighty funny that the generals and the admirals and the presidents of the big corporations aren't paying out no oversized tax installments but only just the little businessmen who aren't getting much money nohow.

- *Flesch Rating*—7 plus
- *Audience*—Top 4½ percent of population
- *Education Required*—College graduate (sixteenth-grade reading level)
- *Similar Publication*—*Yale Review*

Very Easy Prose

You ask me, do you, how fares the morpheme? I tell you it is the warp and woof of style. Use it awry and your style is inept. Like Pater, you must grasp its forte. The suffix adds crisp closure to a word. The prefix shapes the things to come. By their apt use, you do but whet your style. Your prose takes on a new semantic sheen. Your yen for verbal zest now finds an open way. You see your style is now less trite. Your peers will laud new éclat. You will preempt a place among our mentors.

- *Flesch Rating*—Less than 1
- *Audience*—90 percent of the population
- *Education Required*—Fourth grade
- *Similar Publication*—Comics

The above passages do not indicate that the Flesch formula is without value. They may suggest that a correlation of .70 between difficulty ratings of texts using Flesch's formula and difficulty ratings of texts by expert judges provides something less than perfect prediction. They may also suggest that the blind and mechanical application of any available reading-difficulty formula can produce vastly misleading results. Finally, they may suggest that any predictive formula merely sets the stage for actual tests of comprehension with adequate samples of the reading audience.

Applying the Fry Readability Formula, SMOG, or most of the other current readability tests to the above passages yields similar results. I have found some newspaper articles with high (difficult) readability scores, but the scores are the result of the words used. For example, an article on Florida alligators, which includes the words *Florida* and *alligators* in every sentence, tested at Grade 11 on the Fry scale. I have had difficulty locating current articles and passages of general interest that test as high as the twelfth-grade level on readability measures. Even general articles in *Science* magazine, although conceptually sophisticated, tend to have short sentences and few polysyllabic words. Fry's book *Reading Instruction for Classroom and Clinic* (1972), which I use in my graduate courses, tests between the eighth- and ninth-grade levels of readability, though the students do not complain that it is too simple.

The widespread acceptance of readability formulas as guides to writers provides ammunition for critics of our present educational system, like Lyons (1976), who states that college freshmen today are reading books that would have been considered high school freshman texts a generation ago.

None of the readability formulas described above includes the reader in the assessment of how readable a book is. However, in 1953, Taylor, a journalist, did consider the reader when he developed the "cloze" test as a measure of readability. *Cloze* is a more elegant term for "fill in the blank." In applying cloze, students are given a passage with every fifth word deleted and asked to write in the missing word. Studies by Bormuth (1962) and Coleman and Miller (1968) show that cloze scores correlate with reading comprehension and other measures of readability. However, applying cloze procedures requires testing students and computing their scores and is more time-consuming than applying other readability formulas.

Misuses and Abuses of Readability. Routinely applying rigid and limited readability formulas to all reading material assigned students reveals a failure to recognize the limitations of the formulas. Recent reading journals contain advertisements by a company that performs "computerized multiformula readability analyses" using the Spache, Harris-Jacobson, Fry, Dale-Chall, Flesch, and Farr-Jenkins-Patterson formulas. I hope someone will send them William Faulkner's *Absalom, Absalom,* which contains a sentence of 1,300 words. That might crack the computer's floppy discs or exhaust its memory.

Psychologists, who have had an interest in readability for many years, now diligently compute and report the Flesch readability scores on introductory psychology textbooks as well as studying the relation of Flesch's human-interest scores to student satisfaction with texts (Croll and Moskaluk, 1977; Feldstein, 1977; Gillen, 1973, 1975; Hofmann and Vyhonsky, 1975; Stevens and Stone, 1947; and many others). Of course, the readability of a college textbook is important in selecting a text, since college students in different institutions vary greatly in their reading skills and backgrounds, but other factors should also be considered, including the content, the appropriateness of the concepts, and the goals of the instructor. Textbook selection is a difficult task for college instructors teaching introductory courses, as there are many texts on the market. In introductory psychology, for example, there are currently 147 textbooks. No doubt it is tempting for instructors to look only at the texts rated most readable.

Authors often feel that they are victims of arbitrary applications of readability measures. An anonymous article by two authors of a "widely used introductory psychology text" (Anonymous, 1977) illustrates the dilemma authors and publishers face when editors retain a "reading expert" to evaluate their manuscripts. In this case, the reading expert reported that the mean readability score of their book was at the college sophomore level on the Dale-Chall scale and castigated the authors as follows (p. 50): "Because the average reading level of community college students would be closer to the tenth-grade level, the text would frighten many (but not all) of our freshman students who are often introduced to social science via psychology." The expert listed the following words as too difficult for college freshmen, since they were not included on the Dale-Chall list: *reinforcement, bar-pressing, eventually, discriminative stimulus, elicited, satisfied, telephone, sex,* and *psychology.* The authors retorted that it would be an impossible challenge to write a textbook on psychology without using the term *psychology* and conceded that *reinforcement* and *discriminative stimulus* were difficult terms but maintained that these terms represented concepts they considered important to the course. They further challenged the reading expert's statement that today's media-oriented freshmen would find words like *bar-press, eventually, satisfied,* and *telephone* difficult and wagered that freshmen could readily offer two definitions of the word *sex.*

Exceptions. Although we have come a long way in producing more readable textbooks, magazines, and other written materials, there are still areas in which learning materials for students are far more difficult than they need be. For example, some automobile-mechanics textbooks for community college students are written in a style and with a complexity more suitable for upper-division engineering students. The problem is not limited to materials for students. Legal contracts and law books still tend to be written in a complex style, although efforts are being made to simplify them, and tax forms and propositions on election ballots are often written at a very difficult level.

However, research suggests that there is a limit to the extent to which material can be made readable to all. In a study by Kincaid and Gamble (1977), standard and more readable automobile-insurance policies were presented to three groups of readers— good, average, and poor. The good readers understood both the regular and written-down versions, the average readers understood the readable version but not the regular version, and the poor readers understood neither.

Psychologists and scientists have long debated the extent to which scientific writing can be made more readable. Hebb and Bindra (1952) pointed out that making something easier does not always make it more interesting or desirable. Suggesting that there may be an optimal level of difficulty that makes material maximally readable and admitting that scientists tend to write long sentences and use many long words, they warned that they found one text unreadable because it was aimed at the lowest quartile of the freshman class. They further recommended that the Flesch scale be used occasionally to bring word and sentence difficulty *up* to an adult standard.

Reading experts often attack science and mathematics textbooks as too difficult for the students who use them—but the simplistic readability formulas they use are not designed for specialized texts. Each field has its own terminology, whether it is physics, horse racing, or helicopter maintenance, and readers must master the vocabulary to understand the concepts in the discipline. Books that are judged difficult according to readability measures usually become easy *if* the student understands the terms. Wouldn't it be more rational to teach students the specialized vocabulary they need than to simplify the book? Shouldn't reading specialists take some responsibility in helping other faculty members teach the terminology of their subjects rather than throwing up their hands in horror at the vocabulary load of mathematics, biology, or physics?

Reading instructors usually assign light fiction or easy magazine articles to their remedial classes. In my experience, even very poor readers, when given the choice, read to solve problems rather than reading lengthy novels or even short vignettes (such as tales of the ghetto), which most of them could write themselves.

Reading tasks that allow them to achieve an answer to some problem or to undertake some activity often provide greater motivation for poor readers than does reading fiction.

Perhaps our obsession with readability and our confinement of reading instruction for "poor readers" to a narrow niche of high-interest, easily read materials (or watered-down literature) contributed to the decline of thirteen- and seventeen-year-olds' inferential reading skills between 1970 and 1974, as reported by the National Assessment of Educational Progress (1976): "All ages are doing exceptionally well on items that are straightforward, basic, literal; they are doing very well on minimal levels of reading tasks. But as soon as the tasks start to get harder (that is, as soon as the passages become longer or the questions require more manipulation), the results seem to drop off rather quickly."

Unfortunately, the environmental, social, economic, and political issues which our country faces and on which our citizens vote are *not* literal, straightforward, and basic. Students must be taught how to think critically about complex problems, weigh evidence, use logical processes, and problem-solve—and must be expected to. Rather than crusading, as many reading groups are doing, to simplify all textbooks, reading specialists might better serve their students by teaching them how to read more difficult, intellectually challenging works, including mathematics and science materials.

How Effective Are College Reading Programs?

College reading programs have been part of the academic scene for over forty years, but they share with other student services and most academic courses the problem of having little hard evidence to support their effectiveness. Critics accuse them of being failures, pointing to the fact that although 80 percent of community college students in some states enroll in remedial/developmental reading courses, only 20 percent of these same students go on to take further courses in English. The problem is, of course, that the weakest students are required to take reading, and if they aspire to traditional academic majors, they have little chance of succeeding even with several reading-improvement courses.

Many of these reading courses represent a token effort, at best, to remediate serious, long-standing linguistic deficiencies.

What is clear is that college administrators, most faculty members, and certainly college reading specialists believe strongly that their reading programs are necessary and that the programs help students who would not otherwise succeed in college. Students, too, expect colleges to offer reading-improvement assistance and have faith that the special programs will improve their skills.

Aukerman (1964) asked a national sample of college presidents whether they felt their colleges' reading programs were necessary. The presidents were almost unanimous in agreeing that they were. To a further question on whether their reading programs helped students succeed in college, the majority replied yes but qualified that answer by saying that they had no definite figures to support their opinions. Similar surveys of faculty members suggest that they too are supportive of reading programs, particularly if they have known students who have used the service.

Students strongly favor college reading services, as the American Council of Education's (1978) freshman survey, which was recently reported in the news, shows. Forty percent of the Class of 1981 gave "to improve my reading and study skills" as an important reason for attending college.

Many researchers have studied the effects of taking a reading-improvement course on students' grades. Although poorly designed and poorly controlled studies seem to outnumber the others, some of the carefully planned studies show positive results. Entwisle and Entwisle (1960) reviewed the research and concluded that students who take reading and study skills courses improve their grade-point averages about half a letter grade. Recent reviewers are less optimistic, for fewer than half the studies reviewed show significant results in changing grades (Anderson, 1975; Fairbanks, 1974; Huslin, 1975; Santeusanio, 1974). Fairbanks, however, analyzed the characteristics of programs that were successful in improving students' grades and found that successful and unsuccessful programs differed in a number of ways. Specifically, the successful programs involved students in their own diagnoses, were voluntary, combined reading and study skills with counseling, placed more emphasis on developing the skills of recognizing main ideas and differentiating fact from opinion, included more class time for individual practice, and lasted forty hours or longer.

An increasing number of recent studies support Fairbanks' conclusions that counseling-oriented, multiple-skills, voluntary, individualized, and long programs are related to student grade improvement (Burgess and others, 1976; Haburton, 1977; Turner and others, 1974). One example of such programs is the Teacher Mentor Counselor program at Brooklyn College (Obler and others, 1977). This was a special services program for underprepared minority students that functioned, in effect, like a separate college: It offered interdisciplinary remediation in reading and implemented counseling and tutorial services directly in the classrooms. The program stressed close communication among instructors, counselors, tutors, and remedial personnel, who met together three times a week. Average contact between students and staff through classes and individual appointments was eleven hours a week. In comparison with a control group who received the same services but whose counselors, remedial specialists, and instructors did not interact, the experimental group showed significantly more credits attempted and completed, higher grade-point averages, and a significantly higher rate of retention in college. Obler and others conclude that integration of services appears to be a more successful model for educating academically deprived freshmen than separate auxiliary services.

Although it is impossible to separate out the various components of an integrated program to determine which aspects of it make a difference, the combination of instruction, counseling, reading and study skills services, and tutoring within one program and the interaction of the various staff members seem to be the conditions necessary for a successful program.

One important factor in the success of reading programs, of course, is the training of reading specialists. Despite the long history and recent rapid expansion of college reading programs and courses, few graduate schools offer programs to prepare college reading specialists. With as many as 80 percent of the students in some large community college districts enrolled in developmental/ remedial reading, job opportunities are plentiful; yet trained, experienced people are scarce. In the early 1960s, the national sample of college presidents in Aukerman's (1964) survey expressed the need for more trained people to teach college reading courses, and, if anything, that need is greater today.

The main educational priority of graduate schools of education is to prepare teachers and researchers in elementary and secondary education. They are rarely interested in training college teachers, except those who will teach teachers. Unlike specialists in other college fields (counseling, student activities, and so on), college reading and study skills specialists have not been very successful in attaining graduate degree programs, certification, standards, or the other hallmarks of a profession. Yet almost every college and university offers reading and study skills programs, and these are often taught by education and psychology graduate students. Sometimes they get practicum credit for teaching (see Maxwell, 1966b, for a description of a practicum course), but more often it is a part of their role as teaching assistants.

The University of Minnesota was probably the first institution to offer a master's degree in college reading and study skills (Raygor and Vavoulis, 1973; Vavoulis and Raygor, 1973). The Minnesota curriculum is based on a survey of college reading experts who rated the applicability of various graduate courses for training college reading specialists. The courses selected are counseling, diagnosis and treatment of college learning difficulties, foundations of reading, the teaching of reading in secondary schools, measurement and statistics, language and literature, and psychological foundations. Students are required to take a series of practicum courses in the Reading and Study Skills Center and must develop competencies in counseling, instructional skills, measurement skills, and research.

The University of Florida at Gainesville has had a master's program to prepare community college English instructors since the early 1970s. This curriculum emphasizes how to teach reading as a basic skill, in contrast to how to teach critical reading or how to teach literature (Cranney and others, 1973). In the reading section of the program, students are given a three-week experience in analyzing and improving their personal reading skills, and they keep logs of their experiences. They are also taught to use learning contracts as a part of a reading program.

Other universities are starting or expanding graduate programs for instructors in college reading skills, developmental skills, or both. These programs often include courses in the teaching of both reading and writing, and they may also stress administration courses. The University of Iowa, the University of Northern Iowa, Murray State University (Murray, Kentucky), and Appalachian State University (Boone, North Carolina) are among those that offer graduate programs for community college developmental skills instructors.

Special courses in how to teach college reading are also increasing. For example, Lila Bruckner at the University of South Carolina teaches a course called "Teaching and Administering the College Reading Program." Her syllabus describes the course goal as giving graduate students the background and skills necessary for instructing and administering reading programs at the college level. Students are required to diagnose and treat the learning needs of one student enrolled in a college reading center for one semester and present a case study to the class at the end of the term. They must also take a test battery, score and interpret the results for each other, plan how they would spend $5,000 to equip a reading laboratory, construct instructional material, design a learning-activity package, and develop a lesson plan for a particular skill and teach it as a minilesson for the rest of the class, using audiovisual aids. In addition, students compile annotated bibliographies of reading and study skills materials and observe other reading centers.

Although one might assume that most persons teaching college reading skills today have at least had education courses in remedial reading for younger children, surveys suggest that this is not true. College reading specialists come from varied college majors, ranging from optometry to counseling to classics. Even among specialists with advanced degrees in English, fewer than half feel that their graduate training prepared them well for their college positions (Schnell, 1974). Most community college reading teachers in Schnell's survey felt that they would have benefited from internships with experienced practitioners and more training in psychology and counseling, content-area reading, study skills, psycholinguistics, and how to hold in-service workshops.

Because there are few courses to prepare college reading instructors, there are few books on how to teach college reading. Most of the books are either guides to particular student materials, such as Miller's *Teaching Efficient Reading Skills* (1972), Raygor's *Guide to the McGraw-Hill Basic Skills System* (1969), and Schick and Schmidt's *Guide to the Teaching of Reading* (1973), or bibliographies of materials and programs, such as Ahrendt's *Community College Reading Programs* (1975), and Kersteins' *Junior-Community College Reading/Study Skills* (1971), which is an annotated bibliography of studies and program descriptions. Textbooks on how to teach high school reading include chapters on college reading, and often these texts are used in courses for college reading specialists. Among the more popular texts of this type are Fry's *Reading Instruction for Classroom and Clinic* (1972), Herber's *Teaching Reading in Content Areas* (1978), Robinson's *Teaching Reading and Study Strategies: The Content Areas* (1975), and Karlin's *Teaching Reading in High School: Improving Reading in Content Areas* (1977).

Professional associations such as the National Reading Conference, the College Reading Association, and the Western College Reading Association provide most of the in-service training for beginning as well as experienced college learning-skills counselors through their annual conventions and their publications. The International Reading Association's *Journal of Reading* publishes papers of interest to college reading instructors as well as those in high schools. (For a list of professional organizations, see Appendix D). Summer workshops offered by universities and regional groups also offer information for the beginner. However, many of us agree with Crafts and Gibson (1975), who charge that graduate schools are shortchanging college reading specialists by not providing more programs to fit their needs and interests.

In conclusion, reading programs succeed when the skills are taught in relation to the content of other courses in which students are concurrently enrolled and when the reading program is an integrated part of a comprehensive effort including counseling, tutoring, and instruction.

Many of the skills that can be taught successfully at the college level could be implemented in earlier grades and should be offered more widely in public schools. Such skills as selective reading, skimming and scanning, speed reading, and critical reading are necessary for college success. Since a larger proportion of our population is attending college, high schools have a responsibility to help more students prepare for continuing education.

Without concerted effort from both college instructors and public school teachers, the inevitable result will be a continuing deemphasis on reading as a tool for learning, and, in their desperation professors and students will turn increasingly to nonprint media as substitutes for reading.

College reading specialists, despite the forty-year history of the field, continue to be largely self-taught. Few graduate programs are currently available to train them, although there are many positions. As college reading specialists are forced to work with weaker and weaker students, they need training in remedial techniques. I know of few college reading specialists who can work with students who read below the sixth-grade level (and those who can are too busy with other students and other duties to spend the large amount of time necessary to help very weak students). It would benefit both the institution and the individual student if students with very weak reading skills were not encouraged to apply to—and not accepted into—colleges whose curriculums all assume that students can read and read well.

Enrollment in college reading programs is based on budget and facilities available, not on student need. As in other skills areas, reading programs are most successful with students of average or near-average ability in relation to other students in the institution. Highly anxious, well-prepared students and those who have had reading help in the past are the most frequent volunteers for reading programs. Academically sophisticated students are often painfully aware of their reading limitations and worry that they cannot complete the lengthy reading lists assigned. They may have unrealistic ideas about the level of performance professors expect or may set impossibly high standards for themselves. But professors contribute to such students' problems by requiring long reading lists without specifying their purpose or describing how they should be approached. Amann (1977) suggests that the needlessly long reading assignments lead to apathy and laziness in today's college students, result in superficial reading habits, and may create an aversion to reading.

The weakest college readers rarely volunteer for reading help unless they are identified early and counseled about their skills deficiencies and shown that they can improve. Most community colleges require poor readers to take remedial/developmental reading courses. These courses rely heavily on self-help materials, reading machines, and workbooks. Again, students who show the greatest improvement are those with average or borderline skills relative to the other students in the class. In these reading courses, class sizes tend to be large and students' skills very weak. Reading instructors usually carry a heavier course load than instructors in other subjects, and their students need intense personal attention. Unless poor readers are highly motivated, can sustain their motivation, and can work relatively independently on self-paced materials, their chances of improving their skills significantly so that they can advance to higher-level courses are minimal.

10

Building
Study Skills

Colleges have offered programs to orient new students to the rituals of college study since the 1920s. Today's study skills programs and courses differ little in content from those taught in the past. The skills typically stressed are time management (setting priorities, scheduling one's time), taking lecture notes (and sometimes improving listening skills), textbook-study methods (usually SQ3R), preparing for and taking examinations, and improving memory and concentration. Depending on the length of the program, units on research-paper writing, career planning, adapting to academic regulations (and learning them), and improving personal and social adjustment may also be included. Study skills courses are often offered separately from reading and writing courses, and in universities they may be presented as noncredit minicourses, supplemented by individual appointments with

302

learning-skills counselors. Community college programs concentrate on improving students' skills in basic reading, writing, and mathematics, but sometimes they offer courses in study skills improvement for students who plan to transfer to senior colleges.

If a student earns poor grades in college, parents and professors often conclude that he has "poor study habits"—a euphemism for not studying or investing minimal time and effort in study. Before assuming that the student needs a study skills program, the learning-skills counselor should determine whether the student has studied at all. It is currently fashionable to label college students with poor grades "learning-disabled." However, I find that many of the students referred to me as potential learning-disability cases share one characteristic—they managed to avoid studying, reading, and writing in high school and do not study in college. They are quite capable of improving, once they can be convinced that intensive studying and practice are necessary. The virtual elimination of high school homework during the past decade has widened the gap between the skills needed to succeed in high school and those required by colleges and has created more learning problems for college students.

However, a few students do need to improve their study efficiency. These are students who devote endless hours to studying but get little payoff in either learning or grades. Discriminating between students who know how to study but do not and those who need to develop more effective study methods is crucial but sometimes difficult. Unfortunately, using standardized study-habits inventories rarely helps the skills specialist make this discrimination, because they are attitude tests, and most students know what answers are expected. (See Chapter Two and Appendix A for descriptions of study-habits inventories.) The instructions given to students taking study-habits inventories are to answer the questions honestly. Students who are worried about their study skills problems usually answer honestly, but those who are uninterested may not. If students are administered the same inventory with different instructions, such as "Answer the questions as you think a straight-A student would," they typically make very high scores. Indeed, if students given such instructions do not score in the upper decile on the inventory, there is reason to suspect that they do not know how to study. Accordingly, study-habits inventories as routinely administered are not very effective for determining who should be required to take a study skills program, although they may be useful in counseling students who are motivated to seek help voluntarily.

So one basic question is whether students know the most effective study skills but do not use them or whether they lack basic information about how to study. Robyak and Patton (1977, p. 200) state that "prior research has supported *neither* the notion that students do not know efficient study skills and must be taught them nor the notion that the content of a study skills course accounts for the effectiveness of the course. On closer inspection, the grade-point average that usually follows the completion of a study skills course may be a more accurate reflection of the degree to which students learn to use effective study skills rather than the degree to which students acquire knowledge of them. Thus a student's increased *use* of study skills may be more closely related to improved academic performance than the student's increased knowledge of study skills." In their research, Robyak and Patton found that the student's personality type seems to determine whether he will increase his use of the study skills taught in a course. Students rated as "judgers" on the Myers-Briggs Type Indicator used significantly more study skills after taking a course than students rated as "perceivers." (Judgers are characterized by a propensity to come to a conclusion and reach a verdict; perceivers tend to expect new developments to occur and to await new evidence before doing anything they fear is irrevocable.) As a result, counseling seems to be important in helping perceivers understand their resistance to studying and their tendency to procrastinate, while judgers respond well to a structured study skills course.

I have observed that some instructors teach study skills courses as if they were formal academic subjects, lecturing on methods and topics and assigning projects without first determining whether students already know the skills. If students are familiar with the skills, the course may waste the instructor's time, the students' time, and the institution's resources. Inevitably students find the course boring and irrelevant, particularly if the exercises are based on content that is not directly applicable to their other subjects. However, if students know the skills but do not use them, then counseling techniques and practice on relevant materials should be included. To identify students who need the course, successful programs use screening interviews and do not rely exclusively on study-habits inventories. In summary, study skills courses tend to be most successful in improving student achievement when they blend counseling, structured presentations, and intensive practice on course-related materials.

Time management is usually the first topic taught in study skills courses. Working out a practical study/class/work/recreation schedule that will enable students to maximize their learning and still have time for other activities is an important aspect of college adjustment. Recently, study skills specialists have applied time-management techniques developed for business executives to students' scheduling of study—setting priorities on work that must be accomplished, planning ahead for deadlines, and so on. Helping students set long-range and short-range educational and personal goals and determine their life priorities are also popular services offered by skills specialists. Books by Koberg and Bagnall (1976) and Hanks and others (1977) are useful references for these personal life-planning and problem-solving approaches.

Many study methods identified by acronyms are described in the manuals and materials used in study skills programs. Each represents someone's interpretation of the basic laws of learning, expressed in a formula. For example, here are two methods designed to improve students' listening and notetaking skills: The 5 R's—Record meaningful facts/ideas; Reduce by summarizing, clarifying, and reinforcing; Recite by covering the notes and recalling aloud; Reflect by thinking about meaningful categories; Review by going over your notes regularly (Pauk, 1974a). WRECK—Wonder, that is, approach notetaking with a curious frame of mind; Record by writing down as much of what the lecturer says as possible, excluding repetitions and digressions; Edit as soon as possible, condensing notes in a separate notebook; Correlate by comparing your condensed notes with notes and information from your textbook; Keep and review your notes periodically to ensure retention (Fred Duffelmeyer, Drake University).

The textbook-reading method taught most widely in study

skills programs is the SQ3R method, developed by Frank Robinson of Ohio State University (Robinson, 1946/1970). Almost every study skills book published since the 1940s suggests (with or without credit to Robinson) that students use SQ3R or presents some modification of this strategy. The acronym SQ3R represents the four steps in the method: S for Survey (read topic headings and summary), Q for Question (turn topic headings into questions), R for Read to answer the questions, R for Recite (try to recall the answers to the questions without looking back at the text), and R for Review (check back in the text to clarify the answers you may have missed or are confused about). Smith (1961) added a fourth R: 'Riting (take notes on your answers to the questions).

The SQ3R method has often been criticized by skills experts because it has not been systematically researched as a total method, although there is research to support each of the separate steps. But the critics miss the point. For the fearful student, faced with a long, difficult text to read, the SQ3R method provides a technique for getting started. Moreover, it makes explicit the steps that a skilled learner automatically follows. So even if students grumble that it takes too long or that underlining passages in their textbooks is quicker and easier, they will find that, when all else fails, using SQ3R will help them gain a better understanding from their reading. I have found that many students modify the method but that when they are desperate—that is, when faced with an examination that will determine whether they pass or fail a course or when in a situation in which they must make a high grade—using the original SQ3R without modification pays off.

Other reading methods have been developed to help students learn from essays, cases, and other works. For instance, Mayfield's FAIR (1977) is a special strategy for reading law cases. F stands for Facts, A for Action taken in the case as well as action taken in the lower court, I for Issues the court is deciding and the court's holdings on these issues, and R for the court's Reasons for its decision. Students are instructed to write the appropriate letter in the margin as they are reading a law case and underline the appropriate word or phrase for a quick review later. (Having known several law students who discovered this technique for themselves and sailed through law school with minimal study, much to the consternation of their classmates, I am delighted that it has been written down and is being taught to others who may not discover it unaided.)

Hanau's book *The Study Game: How to Play and Win with "Statement-Pie"* (1972) is widely used in study skills courses in health-science programs. Combining cartoons, gamesmanship, and full-page "rest periods" with a method for studying textbooks and taking notes that requires students to engage in hard thinking and questioning, her book presents a challenging reading method in a context designed to interest and relax students. Statement-Pie requires students to identify the Statement in a text or lecture and separate it from the PIE, which means classifying ideas into Proof, Information, and Examples.

To help students master these methods, instructors frequently use peers as study skills counselors. Study skills programs have historically accepted student aides and trained them as peer counselors because of the large number of students who need skills help, the shortage of trained professionals, and the budgetary limitations that afflict most programs. Students respond well to peer helpers, and those who have completed the skills program themselves provide a convenient and motivated pool of applicants for peer-counseling training programs and part-time positions. Articles by Jackson and Van Zoost (1974), Johnson-Davidson and McCarty (1977), Newman (1971), Ross (1972), and Yuthas (1971) describe typical programs that use peer counselors. Adams and Stevenson (1976) present guidelines for planning implementing, and evaluating peer counseling programs.

There are hundreds of study skills books and materials on the market, ranging from scholarly tomes to multimedia, activity-based, self-instructional programs such as Christ and Adams' *You Can Learn to Learn* (1978). Pauk's *How to Study in College* (1974a) remains one of the most popular manuals, but there are books to meet almost any need and learning style, and a quick glimpse at some of the titles suggests the range and the way styles have changed over the years. Whipple's *How to Study Effectively* was published in 1916, and before her work, books on increasing one's will power or developing self-control and on improving one's memory were popular. Some books stressed making studying easier; others tried to convince students that studying is difficult but able to be mastered. Among the books that have been widely adopted are Smith's *Learning to Learn* (1961), and Gilbert's *Study in Depth* (1966). More recent works include Use Your Head (1974) and Use Both Sides of Your Brain (1976) written by Tony Buzan, a teacher of study skills courses on British television for open university students. One book that has maintained its popularity over many years and through many editions is Voeks' *On Becoming an Educated Person* (1970), a series of sensitive essays on adjusting to college.

Current authors are writing study skills books that tend to be a bit more realistic about faculty foibles. For example, Walter and Siebert's *How to Be a Better Student and Still Have Time for Your Friends* (1976) gives students specific instructions for "shaping up your instructor and teaching your teacher how to teach." In addition to the usual skills suggestions, the authors present guidelines for making friends, improving your personality, and avoiding the games that losers play—all this plus cartoons from *Peanuts*. Bandt and others (1974) present a sophisticated model for analyzing one's learning style and developing appropriate skills as well as suggestions for improving personal adjustment.

Wood's (1977) *College Reading and Study Skills* (I prefer the original title, *Some Ways to A's*) gives very explicit directions for reading different types of textbooks and preparing speeches and term papers, with precise illustrations of how one should go about these tasks. The book has a readability level of about ninth grade and should be helpful for community college students who are beginning academic programs.

Yet another study method is presented in Davidson's *4T's: Teacher/You, Text, Talk, and Test—A Systematic Approach to Learning Success* (1977). Davidson points out that most study methods are single techniques that the student applies to all texbooks, whereas her approach stresses helping each student build a personal system consistent with his special needs and skills and decide how much effort and time he needs to spend studying for each course and whether he needs to develop new skills. Once a student has set up a system for evaluating instructors' demands, analyzing his own skills, needs, and time, and implementing a study plan, he presumably will be able to adapt the plan to his courses in subsequent terms. (Essentially this is a task-analysis approach in which students analyze the skills required by the instructor's assignments. See also Adjunct Skills Courses in Chapter Twelve.)

Behavior modification techniques, from their inception, have been applied to improving students' study skills. Groveman and others (1975), reviewing the literature on self-control approaches to improving study behavior, suggest that programs include structured group counseling, self-monitoring, progressive relaxation, self-instruction, and self-reinforcement. The goal of the structured group program is to teach students how to use behavior modification techniques to control their own study behavior. In self-monitoring, the student records the target behavior (for instance, the number of minutes he spends studying chemistry each day) over a prescribed length of time—a day—and tries to increase his time per day over the period of a week. In progressive relaxation, tense individuals learn relaxation/desensitization techniques along with effective study skills methods; the combination seems more effective than relaxation or study skills training alone. Stimulus-control methods encourage students to improve concentration by conditioning themselves to study for longer periods. For example, students are asked to find a comfortable place to study each day—perhaps their desk or a spot in the library—and to record the number of minutes they spend actually concentrating. If they find themselves daydreaming, they are told to get up and leave. At first, students may find they are able to concentrate for very short times, even less than a minute, but gradually, students should be able to condition themselves to concentrate on study for longer periods.

In self-instructional methods, students are trained to say positive things to themselves, such as "I know that if I study diligently I can improve my grades, so I'd better get busy," and eliminate negative thoughts. Another method, called "self-reinforcement," requires students to select a reward for completing a study goal. When they complete their work, they reward themselves. Wark (1967) and Wark and Johnson (1969) report case studies in which self-reinforcement techniques were used. Problems may arise in self-monitoring rewards, as in the case of Jack, who rewarded himself for reading a difficult chapter by watching his favorite television show but then remained glued to the set and was unable to get back to the rest of his work. I have found very few students who can change their study behavior by aversive control methods—that it, by punishing themselves if they do not finish studying in the time they allocate. Reward is more effective for most people than punishment.

Appleton (1967) suggests that study problems and difficulties in concentration stem from the need to turn away from pleasurable activities and study alone. He postulates that denial of affect is required at exam time in order to study and that other defense mechanisms such as isolation and intellectualization are useful for sustained concentration. He notes that one way students have found to "augment sensory input as well as providing companionship" is the study date. But for most students the lonely, arduous task of studying for examinations demands both high motivation and the elimination of such distractions as socializing.

Test-Taking Skills

To do well on an objective examination, students need good reading ability and vocabulary skills so that they can interpret the questions and recognize information and concepts stated differently than when presented in textbooks and lectures. Essay examinations, in contrast, require that students recall information from reading and lectures, integrate, synthesize, and organize it, and the ability to express one's ideas well in writing. Although performance on the two kinds of examinations is correlated, some students excel on one kind and do poorly on the other. One way to help such a student is to review his completed examination paper (after grading by the instructor) and analyze the types of errors he makes (Maxwell, 1967).

Most study skills manuals include a chapter on preparing for and taking tests, and there are a few books especially on this topic. For example, Millman and Pauk's *How to Take Tests* (1969) is a useful book written jointly by a study skills expert and a statistician. It contains principles, examples, practice problems from different types of tests, and strategies for taking tests. Another concise book is Dueker's *Writing Better Bluebooks* (1967) for helping students with difficulties in essay-exam writing. I have also found *Multiple-Choice*

Questions: A Closer Look, a booklet by the Educational Testing Service (1963) on how to construct multiple-choice tests, useful in working with students who have difficulties with objective test questions. Having students construct their own multiple-choice questions is another way to improve their test performance.

Probably the best strategy for strengthening students' test-taking skills is to simulate the test situation. The practice test sessions are inevitably judged the most helpful part of the course that our center offers to students preparing for graduate and professional school admissions tests.

Exercises that increase test-wiseness also improve test performance. Research suggests that the examinee's capacity to utilize the characteristics and format of the test or the test-taking situation to receive a high score is independent of his knowledge of the subject matter that the items purport to measure. Moore (1971) found that thirty to forty minutes of practice on different kinds of analogy questions significantly increased a group's performance over the performance of a group that did not practice. If it is possible to improve one's performance on analogy items through practice, it should be possible to improve one's scores on other types of items.

Because acceptance by graduate and professional schools is contingent on a student's passing admissions examinations, and because competition for entrance is keen, many students enroll in special programs to prepare themselves for these tests. The claim by test publishers (College Entrance Examination Board, 1968) that a preparatory course cannot significantly raise one's score has not discouraged applicants. Each student who has done poorly on the Law School Aptitude Test (LSAT) and plans to take it again is convinced that he can beat the odds and become that one person out of 300 who will improve by 150 points. Also there are an increasing number of studies that show that *intensive, lengthy* test-preparation programs result in higher scores. (Marron, 1965; Whimbey and Whimbey, 1975).

So intense is the competition among students applying for advanced training that most learning centers in senior colleges offer review courses to prepare for admissions exams. Review courses help students overcome anxiety, orient them to the types of problems on the test, and instruct them on how to use the answer sheet and how to break down difficult problems and solve them. Information on how the test will be scored and the meaning of standardized scores is also given, and students take a mock version of the test under timed conditions. Colleges offer their own review courses for two reasons: They reduce students' anxieties about the test, and they save students money, for the commercial test-preparation programs are very expensive and of variable quality.

Test Anxiety

Should exams, which cause students so much anguish, anxiety, and frustration, be abolished? Should all knowledge be arranged in small pieces and fed to students so success is assured if they complete enough steps and branches of a program? Are ease of learning and security in one's knowledge essential concomitants of successful learning? Or are there satisfactions and values to be gained from the struggles and uncertainties of the present examination system?

Ideally, testing should be a positive learning experience, one in which students recognize their goals, are assured of their knowledge, and feel competent. However, students rarely feel satisfied after taking final examinations or standardized tests. In fact, exams are dreaded and feared—or, at best, tolerated as an inevitable part of a college education. A few students, however, do view examinations as a challenge and a way to express their knowledge or pit their skills against the examiner. There are even students who write to the Educational Testing Service and describe what an ecstatic experience it was to take the Scholastic Aptitude Test. Naturally, these are the people who do well on tests.

Many of us as students, however, have had the experience of suffering a bout of amnesia in the middle of an examination. This is a most frustrating experience indeed, especially when an hour or two after we turn in our bluebooks, the ideas we were struggling so hard to recall pop back into our heads.

Psychologists have performed many experiments on test-anxious students. Results tend to be equivocal. Often these experiments do not consider individual differences, viewed as error variance by experimental psychologists. Clinical psychologists and counselors have also "treated" many students with exam panic and found that it is easier to define the conditions that produce exam panic than to cure it, but they continue to try to develop techniques for treatment.

Always endemic among college students, exam panic currently seems to be reaching epidemic proportions, judging from the number of programs offered by counseling and learning centers. It is therefore essential that anyone who works with college students be aware of its dynamics.

First, it is important to realize that many students are genuinely afraid of failing, in fact paralyzed by anticipated failure. Not just underprepared college students who have failed in the past, but also those who have excelled in school fear failure. Of course, our school system encourages this fear from the first grade on by reinforcing the idea that to be a worthwhile person, one must succeed in school (Beery, 1975; Marzolf, 1962). Unconsciously or consciously accepting society's values, thus equating one's worth with being bright and getting A's, sets the stage for continued frustrations as one ascends the educational ladder.

Students may rank in the top 5 percent of their high school graduating classes, yet find themselves in the middle ranks in college, earning B's and an occasional C. In graduate or professional schools, former straight-A students find themselves in competition with the top students from other colleges and may earn lower grades despite intensive study. A B average to a former A student can be more humiliating than an F to an average student, but such is the selective sieve we push our students through. As public colleges and professional schools implement affirmative action regulations and accept large numbers of educationally disadvantaged students, the struggle to maintain prior academic standards and, at the same time, prepare these students for high-level careers places great stress on both the faculty and the disadvantaged students.

If students feel that grades reflect their self-worth and attach great significance to them—that is, equate failure with letting down family, friends, former teachers, or other significant persons—they will be susceptible to exam panic. Individuals handle this tendency in different ways. Some become superstrivers and fiercely compete, others suffer deepest despair, and some avoid situations in which they will be tested. Sometimes fear of failure is genuine, as in a student who has not prepared for the exam; sometimes it represents an overreaction, or what might be termed a neurotic anxiety. Freud stated that anxiety occurs in three forms. One is a free-floating general apprehensiveness, ready to attach itself for the time being to any new possibility that may arise—a condition he termed "expectant dread." Students with this type of apprehensiveness will undoubtedly be anxious about reading, homework, exams—anything that they feel represents a threat.

A second kind of anxiety is firmly attached to certain ideas. These ideas may have some connection with danger, but the anxiety felt toward them is greatly exaggerated. This kind of anxiety Freud terms a phobia, and there are some students with exam phobias. Each time such students are faced with taking an exam, they have an anxiety attack. By developing a phobia, they protect themselves from the anxiety and either feel very uncomfortable during the exam or find an excuse to avoid taking it. Thus exam phobias externalize neurotic anxiety and protect the person's ego. If students panic each time they take a test by blanking out, then they will either avoid courses requiring exams and write reports instead or drop out of school, thereby preserving their feelings of intellectual adequacy, since no one can discover their real intelligence or ability (or self-worth) if they suffer from text anxiety.

A third, more severe neurotic anxiety similar to that which occurs in hysteria may manifest itself as an attack or a condition that persists for some time, but always without any visible external danger sufficient to justify it.

Treatment for severe cases of text anxiety is very difficult and can be lengthy. Like some of Freud's anxious patients, the afflicted students express their subconscious sense of guilt in a negative reaction to therapy. If one gives a person a solution to a problem or symptom, one expects at least the temporary disappearance of the symptom, but this does not happen in these cases—the client gets worse! Even a few words of hope and encouragement may aggravate the condition. Thus one might conjecture that some students do not want to be "cured" of their exam phobia despite its painfulness and the handicap it creates for them. This observation leads to the diagnostic question, What benefits or advantages accrue to students with exam panic? What do they gain from being helpless victims rather than masters of the test?

College students who are secretly afraid that they do not have the intelligence ascribed to them by teachers and parents may refuse to put their full efforts into studying. Not studying gives them an excuse if they fail; if they had invested time and effort in studying, then failing would confirm that they were not really very bright. They protect themselves from this exigency by procrastinating, studying too little and too late, developing myriad excuses for failing, or—if, despite all, they do pass—dismissing responsibility for their grade by saying that the test was easy. I once asked Peter, a Berkeley junior in physics who claimed that he had not had to study in college, whether he had ever failed a course. "Yes, once," he replied, "when I lost my math textbook the first week of the course. I looked for it the night before the final, and I'm sure that if I could have found it, I would have passed the course." Since Peter had lost his textbook, he had a convenient excuse for not studying and therefore did not lose face for failing.

Research Findings. Wine's (1971) review of the literature on test anxiety provides some additional clues to the dynamics of test anxiety. Wine reports that highly test-anxious students perform poorly on tests that are admittedly stressful and evaluative. Poor performance is most likely when the exam is difficult, when it is different from other papers or exams in the course, when it is closely timed, and when competition is high.

Highly anxious test takers divide their attention between themselves (their own internal cues) and the task; they spend time doing things that are not related to the test. For example, they worry about how well they are doing, reread the same questions, ruminate over choices, notice where others are on the test, and observe that their peers are finishing faster. These superfluous activities guarantee poor performance on tests that require one's full attention.

Testing two aspects of text anxiety, worry and emotionality

(autonomic arousal of anxiety), Wine found that worry tends to be constant over time, whereas emotionality peaks just before the exam and falls off rapidly after the exam. This suggests that it is worry, not emotionality, that interferes with test performance. *Worry* has been defined as cognitive concern about the consequences of failing, the ability of others compared with oneself, or one's own performance. These cognitive processes occur while the student is taking a test and demand his attention. They represent learned interference responses. Emotionality is not related to test performance; worry is (Wine, 1971).

Wine presents evidence that the highly test-anxious person is very responsive to social cues, including verbal cues, modeling, persuasion, and pressures to conform, and to different types of test questions. Her research suggests that people can be trained to be selectively more attentive to particular stimulus dimensions and less attentive to others (that is, to attend to relevant stimuli and ignore the irrelevant). She tested attentional training, attentional training plus relaxation training, and a "self-exploration" approach with test-anxious students in a six-hour experiment. Test-anxious subjects in the attentional-training condition improved significantly on self-report measures of test-related anxiety and on two standardized performance measures. Attentional training plus relaxation produced the same changes as attentional training alone. Subjects in the self-exploratory condition did not change significantly on any measures.

Not only did students in the attentional-training condition improve their performance, they described having a lower test-anxiety level. Wine suggests that text anxiety may be defined on the basis of where one directs one's attention and treated through techniques that direct attention to the task itself rather than the consequences of failing at it. This conclusion supports clinical observations that test-anxious students and underachievers are more sensitive to external stimuli and more easily distracted.

Alpert and Haber (1960) describe two types of test anxiety: facilitating and debilitating anxiety. They hypothesize that anxiety is debilitating only to students who have learned a habitual class of interfering responses to the test. Without these responses, test anxiety leads to task-relevant responses and good performance.

Students for whom anxiety is debilitating tend to blame themselves for their failures, their levels of aspiration become progressively lower over trials, they become more pessimistic about their performance, as the trials progress, and they devalue their performance and generally describe themselves in more negative terms than do students for whom anxiety is facilitating. Further, students with debilitating anxiety are highly responsive to reinforcement when the response being reinforced is negative self-reference, but they do not condition to verbal reinforcement of positive self-reference (Alpert and Haber, 1960).

Supporting the idea that anxiety may have different effects on different individuals' performance is a study by Clark (1977), who used a single question to determine the anxiety of students who had taken the LSAT. She asked them: "What degree of anxiety did you consciously experience during the test? (1) very little; (2) noticeable; (3) considerable; (4) severe; (5) incapacitating." Students who had scored highest on the LSAT described themselves as having been noticeably anxious, while those who had scored lowest stated that they had been severely anxious, had been incapacitated by anxiety, or had felt very little anxiety. This last response suggests that some students with low scores felt numb during the test, suggesting a hysterical repression of anxiety. Or perhaps it suggests that they could relax because they knew they were flunking. People are anxious in the face of uncertainty: "Will I pass the LSAT or will I fail?" A student who can see, during the test, that he is doing poorly will no longer be anxious because he knows the outcome.

When extremely test-anxious students are taking a test, they tend to spend more time than others worrying about how well they are doing—so much that they have trouble concentrating. They reprimand themselves with negative thoughts like "I should have spent more time studying." Studies have also shown that they develop a kind of tunnel vision, a narrower attention to test cues, which leads them to overlook the important clues and misread key words. For example, a student recently failed an exam despite writing an excellent answer describing the *ecological* factors in the social development of certain animals. Unfortunately, the question asked for the *evolutionary* factors.

Perhaps my poem will help those who have never experienced exam panic understand it:

> *Test panic's a worm*
> *that erases the blackboard of my mind*
> *and writes, "Worry!"*
> *So I worry*
> *about those I'll let down.*
> *What will they say?*
> *What will they think?*
> *What will I do*
> *if I fail?*
> *Panic's now a python*
> *crushing my chest*
> *gnawing my gut*
> *turning my adam's apple to stone.*
> *While my bluebook waits,*
> *time*
> *runs*
> *out.*

Trait Anxiety and State Anxiety. Psychological experimenters studying anxiety-proneness (called trait anxiety) and the intensity and frequency of manifestations of anxiety states (state anxiety) have often used performance on tests as a variable. They postulate that people with a high degree of trait anxiety are more likely to respond with high levels of state anxiety in situations that threaten their self-esteem, and college examinations are such situations. The measures of trait anxiety (Spielberger and others, 1970) are relatively stable and have relatively high reliability, while state anxiety is less stable. Early research suggests that trait anxiety seems to have no direct effect on test performance but that state anxiety occasionally interacts with trait anxiety to result in lower achievement. Gaudry and Spielberger (1970) find students whose grades are on the border of failing to be more susceptible to state anxiety than high achievers. More recent studies show that the relationship between state and trait anxiety and performance on examinations may be different from the theories postulated earlier. King and others (1976) report that trait anxiety may directly affect exam performance as well as influence achievement through state anxiety. Lange (1978) reviews studies that suggest that we may have mislabeled test anxiety as a type of state-anxiety because in some people it is an enduring trait.

Characteristics of High-Achieving Low Testers. The most pernicious and hardest-to-treat problems of test anxiety are found in those few students who have exceptionally high course grades but tend to fall apart when taking a standardized test.

Clark (1977) studied thirty-seven University of Maryland students who scored low on the LSAT although they had distinguished academic, employment, and extracurricular records. The group included four Phi Beta Kappas, one Fulbright scholar, one candidate for Rhodes scholar, six officers of the student government, and others with high academic standing. Their mean LSAT score was at the 23rd percentile, and their mean SAT verbal and mathematical scores were also undistinguished (32nd and 34th percentiles); however, their GPAs were are the 89th percentile on the university's norms. Ten were women. The twenty-nine who were accepted into law school are performing well in a preliminary follow-up study.

Clark differentiates these academically superior "low testers" from "overachievers," students whose grades represent extreme painstaking struggle and who may be said to be performing academically above their potential. She (1977, pp. 18–19) lists a cluster of traits that describe the "genuine low tester":

> 1. He is academically superior but has consistently done poorly on standardized ability tests.
>
> 2. The motivation to study law amounts to an all-exclusive long-lived passion. The student almost always feels there is no other career for him. Although he may have laid alternate plans, as the author [Clark] always tries to advise him to do, pursuing the alternate would be like going from first choice to last choice. He has always "known" he was going to be a lawyer since he first became aware he had a choice in the adult world.
>
> 3. He is usually rendered desperately anxious at the prospect of having to take the LSAT, often dreading it for his entire college career because of his shockingly bad performance on the PSAT and the SAT.

4. He has very rarely suffered any abnormal anxiety about his performance on tests in academic subjects. If there is something that can be studied and mastered, he can count on himself for superior performance, regardless of the amount of difficulty of preparation. Before the LSAT, however, there is nothing he can study; therefore, he feels the situation is out of control.

5. He is extremely competitive and has been so all his academic life, as far back sometimes as elementary school. He is a perfectionist with often impossible standards for his own performance. The fact that others do better than he on standardized ability tests sometimes "proves" to him not that there is something unrealistic about his attitude toward the test, but that the test is telling the truth: It is exposing him for what he really is; he really does not have the ability he needs; his superiority is a sham.

The student is apt to react to all this self-generated pressure, in addition to the genuine pressure of the testing situation, with paralyzing anxiety and rigidity, which sometimes progress to a kind of petrification in which no conscious anxiety is experienced and the complaint is that concentration on that kind of problem is impossible or that the test is boring.

6. The "gamesmanship" aspect of the test, which is a very important component in high scores, eludes him. For instance, the same perfectionism which drives him academically and which may help make him into a top law student and lawyer militates against his being able to choose the "right" answer to a mildly ambiguous question of the kind [the Educational Testing Service] (ETS) is so fond of asking in the rigid framework of multiple-choice. [Clark believes] that ETS is also testing for tolerance of ambiguity and unrealtiy. This student cannot tolerate either in this situation. The test is very real to him. He is forced to guess the answer to a question that his less brilliant neighbor has answered "correctly" without even detecting the ambiguities involved. He wants to write "but on the other hand" in the margin on an answer sheet that is being graded by machine, and for him this is a genuine dilemma.

Another important aspect of "gamesmanship" is being able to abandon a question and go on to the next, since the score depends entirely on the number right. This student perseveres. He cannot abandon a question. In law school and in life, this same quality may be part of what makes him superior.

7. Most of these students, with one or two notable ex-
troverted exceptions, are guarded and private people, well defended, socially adept (indeed, delightful), and helplessly ashamed
of their performance on such tests. It is singularly difficult—in
fact, has proved impossible—for this author to refer such a person
to psychological counseling, which might help mitigate some of the
unrealistic anxiety he experiences. He would not know what to say
when he got there that he has not already said to himself, and he is
completely, though in this area unrealistically, self-reliant.

These "low testers" are at a classic and painful competitive
disadvantage in the applications process, because all the low scores
are permanently on their records. ETS describes them as one kind
of "discrepant predictor." Since all the ETS "discrepant predictor"
studies show that the low-score, high-grade group does not significantly break the pattern of LSAT validity on law school
campuses, most admissions officers feel that no special attention
need be paid to these students. In addition, the committee that admits a "low tester" has inevitably displaced one who had a better test score—sometimes with unpleasant consequences for the
committee.

A former dean of admissions counseled admissions officers
late in 1973 that such brilliant "low testers" are likely to add an
important dimension to a law school and later to the legal profession itself and added that if the LSAT score is the only negative
factor in the admissions folder, "the probability of success may be
high enough to mandate admission." Yet admissions committees
cannot easily feel justified in reserving spaces for "low testers"
when the pressure from other applicants is so great.

When confronted with a student with problems like those
described above, learning-skills specialists should write a strong
letter of recommendation to the professional school's admissions
committee explaining the student's problem with tests.

Identifying Students with Test Anxiety. Students seem to have
few qualms about discussing their test anxiety. If a program to
alleviate test anxiety is advertised, students will volunteer, and they
frequently come in to discuss their test fears with instructors, counselors, skills specialists, friends, or anyone who will listen. Instruc-

tors can identify exam-panic victims easily, even in large classes, for they turn in blank bluebooks on exams. Learning-skills centers that administer checklists for students using their service find that a number of students will check test anxiety as a problem.

In addition, there are a number of scales that purport to measure the degree to which test anxiety affects student performance, such as Alpert and Haber (1960), Liebert and Morris (1976), Mandler and Sarason (1952), Spielberger and others (1970), and Suinn (1969).

The two test-anxiety scales most often used in learning centers are Alpert and Haber's Achievement Anxiety Questionnaire and the STABS (Suinn Test Anxiety Behavior Scale, 1969). Alpert and Haber's questionnaire yields two measures of test anxiety—facilitating anxiety and debilitating anxiety—and is based on the hypothesis that anxiety is debilitating only to students who have learned a habitual class of interfering responses. Without these interfering responses, the authors believe, test anxiety leads to task-relevant responses and good performance. For example, the test contains items like "Anxiety helps me do a better job on an exam."

Exam anxiety can camouflage other problems, and academically weak students are just as susceptible to it as those with strong skills. In diagnosis, it is important to consider the paradigm presented in Figure 2 (Chapter Two), for the skills specialist needs to determine whether the student's anxiety is due to lack of study skills or basic reading inabilities or is a learned way of responding to evaluative situations or a condition precipitated by poor instruction. In my experience, the most pernicious cases of exam panic occur in students whose anxiety masks a deficiency in reading for inference, a deficiency in logical thinking, or a refusal to read material carefully. Controlled, intensive practice on the skills these students have avoided is necessary, for neither deep relaxation, desensitization, intensive therapy, nor tranquilizers will result in improved performance, though these treatments may reduce the anxiety felt about tests.

Cramming. No discussion of exam panic is complete without mentioning cramming and the institutional procedures that create and perpetuate it. Cramming has been almost totally ignored by psychological researchers studying the learning process, and study skills manuals invariably admonish students that it is a poor way to study, citing research showing that lower retention results from "massed practice" than from "distributed practice." Cramming is usually considered a cause of exam panic; yet it remains a student ritual engaged in by 97 percent of the students attending our most selective colleges (Sommer, 1968). Despite the discomfort associated with cramming, students report that it is helpful and that they remember information better if they study intensely just before an examination.

Faculty members tend to view cramming as a natural result of student procrastination and the pressure students feel about earning grades. Students, however, report that cramming is most useful in courses that require considerable memorizing, particularly "Mickey Mouse" courses with multiple-choice examinations. Other reasons that students give for cramming include boring courses with poor teachers who give disorganized lectures, courses that require extensive outside reading, courses with no daily assignments and long intervals between tests, and courses in which the student has fallen behind in his work. (Note that only one of these reasons involves the student's work habits; the others are a function of the course and the academic system.) Students report that cramming is least useful in courses that require thought, problem solving, or creativity or are very difficult (Sommer, 1968).

Exam week is a stressful period for many college students, as evidenced both by self-reports and by observations. Men students wear old clothes and appear unkempt and unshaven; women take less care in their dress and appearance. Men students tend to eat less and lose weight; women report weight gains and delayed menstrual periods. Both sexes report sleep loss or problems in sleeping, worry more, are fatigued and nervous, and spend less time socializing. High-achieving students report less stress and fewer somatic disturbances, although they may cram too, but lower-achieving students more frequently have both stress symptoms and health problems during the exam period (Sommer, 1968).

The many "how to study" manuals that cajole, threaten, and lecture against cramming have not decreased the practice. Recent writers are starting to admit that cramming is an inevitable study strategy, are discussing it openly, and are even providing suggestions on "If you must cram, then . . ." (Wood, 1977). High achievers usually have crammed for high school examinations and developed skills for doing it effectively. Underprepared students, particularly those who have studied rarely or not at all, have not mastered the art of cramming, and if they cram, they are more likely to develop symptoms—either physical or nervous—and do poorly on the exams.

If today's colleges demand anything of students, they expect them to develop skills in working under time pressure and against deadlines. Unfortunately, if academically weak students who have not developed regular study habits try to emulate students who are skilled at working under pressure and do well in courses when they cram, they will fail.

Treatment Methods. If testing has eliminated inadequate study skills and poor reading as possible causes of exam panic, and you find that the student can perform adequately in the subject as long as tests are not involved, you may wish to consider using relaxation therapies.

Behavior therapists have tired of personally administering the relaxation instructions to each student and have tape-recorded relaxation suggestions. One can buy these tapes commercially or record one's own. Scripts for deep muscle relaxation are included in Wolpe and Lazarus (1966) and in Bernstein and Borkovec (1973), Budzynski (1976), and Jacobson (1938). If you make your own tape, find someone with a relaxing, soothing voice to make the recording. We have used tapes for a number of years in our program and find that relaxation exercises help some students relax enough to study or read. One should warn students not to fall asleep while listening to the tapes; otherwise many of them do.

Most published accounts of treatment of test-anxious subjects describe various systematic desensitization techniques and report reduction in self-reported measures of text anxiety (for example, Kahn, 1976; Mitchell and Ng, 1972).

Gourdine (1976b) described a program in which peer counselors (resident assistants in a dormitory) were given a two-hour training program in using relaxation/desensitization procedures on

text-anxious students. The peer counselors were taught (1) to identify text-anxious students through group or individual sessions;
(2) to administer a study skills inventory to them to determine
whether inefficient study skills were causing the student's problem,
and if so, to refer them to the learning center; (3) to administer
the Suinn Test Anxiety Behavior Scale to those not in need of
study skills assistance and score and interpret it; (4) to provide
relaxation/desensitization training to the students by monitoring
their use of five forty-five-minute tapes (for example, peer counselors were taught to inform students scoring below the 50th percentile on the STABS that they probably would not see changes in
their attitudes toward test taking but would learn deep muscle relaxation techniques); (5) to follow up the students to determine
whether there were changes in their attitudes toward exams and
whether they felt more confident and showed less avoidance of test
taking.

In this project, peer counselors were taught to use Meichenbaum's insight therapy (1973) and to teach students to identify
their counterproductive self-evaluations (negative thoughts about
themselves) and substitute constructive thoughts—for example, to
focus on how to complete a task rather than to count their errors.

Exam panic is a complex problem, and there have been
many attempts to reduce its effects—individual and group counseling, lecturing, explaining the causes, behavior modification, relaxation therapy, and even Zen meditation (Shapiro and Zifferblatt,
1976). Students themselves in group sessions often suggest activities they find relaxing—exercise (including swimming or other
sports), drinking alcohol, sexual activity, smoking marijuana, and
other stress-reducing activities not mentioned in study skills books.

Learning centers can take these steps to ameliorate the test-
anxiety problem, aside from providing a strong study skills and
test-taking skills program: (1) Working with professors in improving examinations, (2) Encouraging professors to experiment with
anxiety-reducing ways of administering tests. For example, Charles
Mest of Honolulu Community College devised an inexpensive and
ingenious way to administer multiple-choice examinations to his
psychology classes. He connected two Carramate slide projectors to
a computer terminal. One projects the test question and the answer

choices, to which the student responds by typing the letter of his answer on the keyboard and also his degree of certainty. If the student misses the item, the other Carramate projects additional information about the concept, and the student gets an opportunity to try another question on the same material. This procedure enables students to take the test whenever they feel ready and saves the professor valuable class time that would otherwise be spent giving the exam. Besides, the students receive their test results immediately after the test. (3) Training peer counselors to administer test-anxiety scales and help students use self-administered relaxation tapes (Gourdine, 1976b). (4) Establishing a study table and panic clinic during exam week where commuter students can receive tutoring, study, snacks, and health care twenty-four hours a day, as California State University at Northridge did (Enright, 1976). (5) Providing a handout on exam panic—a list of general tips on how to prepare for tests and how to avoid panic. For other suggestions on changing test anxiety, see Lange (1978).

A word of warning: Few members of a campus community see their role as correcting the conditions that impose the stresses which result in text anxiety. However, there are a number of professionals who view test-anxiety reduction as their special province. These vary from campus to campus. Sometimes physicians in the student health service offer group relaxation training as a way of reducing the number of stress-generated illnesses they treat. Elsewhere, it is the counseling or psychiatric service that maintains that only it can offer test-anxiety help to students. On some campuses, test-anxiety reduction is assigned to learning-skills specialists, or student peer counselors may be briefly trained to work directly with test-anxious students. In initiating any program in test anxiety, it is vital for learning-skills staff members to determine which campus department or service claims this role, and if none does, then to take steps to gain the cooperation of counselors and other relevant professionals as the program is developed.

Summary. Some anxiety seems to be an essential precursor of learning. Freud suggests that even the more traumatic anxieties associated with examinations may serve a useful function in later life. In *The Interpretation of Dreams* he discusses at some length his recurring "examination dream" and notes that it occurred at times when he was anticipating performing a responsible task the next day, failure at which would bring him disgrace. He observed that he always dreamed about exams that he had passed brilliantly, never about ones he had failed. Hence, he interpreted the "examination dream" as a way of consoling himself that things would work out well. In effect, his preconscious mind was saying, "Don't be afraid of tomorrow; think of the anxiety you felt before your exam in history (for instance). Yet nothing happened to justify it, for now you are a doctor."

Perhaps the role of the learning-skills specialist can best be described as supporting students who are experiencing anxiety, reassuring them that it is normal to feel anxious about examinations, and helping them focus their attention on the test questions and the tasks entailed in preparing for the test. Further, one can help students avoid slipping so deeply into the quicksand of their own anxiety that they cannot function. We should not present them with an unrealistic model of the supercool, nonanxious genius. Surely, the force feeding of facts leads to boredom, indigestion, and regurgitation. There is no challenge or feeling of accomplishment unless one struggles to attain a goal, and struggling involves uncertainty and anxiety. Students show their contempt when courses are made too easy for them.

As for preventing cramming, students' suggestions are as valid as any I have heard from professionals. "Cramming doesn't work," they say, "when the course demands thought, problem solving, and creativity." Instructors and learning-skills specialists, take heed.

11

Developing
Mathematical Skills

The increasing need for college remedial courses in mathematics, prompted by the decline over more than a decade in entering college students' mathematical ability, apparently results from four interrelated factors. First, the reforms of the 1960s in mathematics education, particularly in college preparatory mathematics, made it possible for many universities and four-year colleges to implement calculus (traditionally a sophomore-level course) as the first general math course for liberal arts freshmen. Second, this curriculum change was followed by the recruitment of lower-ability minority and economically disadvantaged groups, many of whom lacked traditional college preparatory mathematics courses, with a concomitant lowering of admission standards and prerequisite requirements. Thus four-year colleges and universities accepted a different pool of students and lowered their entrance standards, but kept general calculus as their required freshman math courses. Third, the expansion of theoretical knowledge in mathematics and its rapid application to many academic disciplines and professions created a need for a larger proportion of college students to take mathematics and statistics courses. Fourth, the technological advances in computers and the resulting proliferation of data processing in all fields make it essential that college students have a more sophisticated understanding of mathematics.

Headlines proclaim that the rise in the need for remedial courses is taxing colleges throughout the country as professors find that students have skills gaps in elementary arithmetic. Many are unable to work with fractions, compute percentages and square roots, or understand proportions or other simple mathematical relations (Maeroff, 1976).

The mathematical scores of entering freshmen on college entrance tests have been declining for many years, paralleling the decline in verbal scores, but only in the past few years have professors and administrators become vocal in their complaints of the increasing numbers of "math illiterates" who enter their institutions. (They are particularly vocal in universities and private, selective colleges.) As college budgets tighten, the major issues seem to be the cost of offering many sections of remedial mathematics courses, which require a low faculty-student ratio, the stretching out over two or three terms of course content what was formerly covered in one term, and the expense of providing tutors. Related questions such as whether remedial courses in mathematics should carry credit and what they should be called are still being debated.

One indicator that the decline in math ability is leveling off is that entering freshmen in 1976 averaged the same mathematical SAT scores as those in 1975. This does not mean, however, that the problems will disappear.

Standardized test scores of secondary students provide additional evidence that the mathematics problem will continue, although it may not get worse. Nationally, mathematics scores of high school students have declined, as indicated by the National Assessment of Educational Progress and longitudinal studies on the national norms of such tests as the Iowa Tests of Basic Skills and the Comprehensive Test of Basic Skills (Conference Board of the

Mathematical Sciences, 1975; Munday, 1976). Despite the "back to basics" movement currently in vogue in many public school districts, it will take time for any effects to be noticed at the college level. There are too many generations of students with weak mathematics skills who are seeking to enter college and too few well-prepared students for most colleges to reject the weak.

Factors in the Mathematics Problem

To view the present problem in perspective, it is necessary to examine the changes in college preparatory mathematics programs, societal demands, and the changes in the college-student population.

Changes in Mathematics Education. The decline in mathematical ability is particularly interesting because for twenty years mathematics has held an unprecedented favorable position in the public schools as a result of the technological competition between the United States and Russia, which was intensified by the launching of the first Sputnik. The National Science Foundation, other federal agencies, and private foundations have invested heavily in innovative mathematics programs, particularly in the elementary grades. Many large-scale efforts were made to reform the teaching of mathematics, reconstructing its scope and sequence through the introduction of set theory, the application of learning theories (particularly those of Bruner and Piaget), and a heavy emphasis on teacher training and the development of new classroom materials. Yet today mathematics teaching is a "troubled profession with strident criticism from colleagues and the press" (Conference Board of the Mathematical Sciences, 1975, p. ix). Critics attack the reform labeled "new math" as being the source of the problem and castigate the reformers for developing programs they describe as excessively formal, deductively structured, and too theoretical. They claim the new math ignores the application of mathematical concepts to other fields. Yet the new math is far from being one system, for over 800 textbook series are used in public schools, each of them attempting to combine the traditional mathematics and its own conception of nontraditional mathematics in a meaningful fashion. With such diversity, the concept of new math is vague. The mathematics curriculums in the public schools have been described as a vast array of patchwork programs, since decisions on content are made by local school districts.

The numerous studies comparing students taught with traditional and modern math textbooks have yielded equivocal results, attesting to the complexity of teaching and learning mathematics. However, there is a trend that suggests that students taught with traditional books perform better in computation while those taught with modern math texts perform better in comprehension (Conference Board of the Mathematical Sciences, 1975, pp. 102–118). (The recent development of inexpensive hand-held calculators, while not rendering computational skills completely obsolete, still requires that students understand the logic and processes involved in making appropriate applications of mathematics.) Despite the monies spent on innovative programs, surveys suggest that the way most elementary teachers teach mathematics has changed little, if at all, in twenty years.

Originators of the new math argue that the new math was never really implemented in elementary schools and point out that seventeen-year-olds surpassed adults in computational skills on the 1972–73 National Assessment of Educational Progress math test as evidence that their programs did not adversely affect arithmetic skills. They admit that minimal effort was made to systematically train elementary teachers to use the new math and that the authors of the programs generally overlooked classroom teachers, who were expected to understand the new material (including number bases other than ten), which the experts now admit was both confusing to most teachers and inappropriate for elementary students. Further, the programs erred in attempting to exclude parents, who were told not to try to help their children with the new concepts. This decision alienated parents, who concluded that their children were not being taught fundamental concepts and skills (Kolata, 1977).

The modern mathematics movement had its greatest impact on college preparatory mathematics, particularly courses in high school and to a somewhat lesser extent those in junior high. The 1959 report of the Commission on Mathematics of the College Entrance Examination Board was probably the greatest influence in bringing about these changes. The report recommended that secondary school mathematics instruction must present new content, organized in a way that helps bring students more efficiently to the frontiers of pure and applied mathematics. It recommended that topics from logic, modern algebra, and probability and statistics be included in high school and that plane and solid geometry be merged in a single course. Trigonometry was to be integrated into second-year algebra, and the curriculum was to be unified through emphasis on the deductive method, the process of pattern searching, and structural concepts like set, relation, and function.

Calculus as the Beginning Math Course. As a result of these recommendations, many high schools revised their college preparatory programs, and students soon began entering college having completed more-advanced math courses than their predecessors. State universities and selective colleges were able to drop their traditional remedial math courses and also abandon the college algebra, trigonometry, and analytic geometry sequence, which had been the freshman series. There were many well-qualified applicants, and those who were not prepared could easily be diverted to the junior colleges and state colleges that were changing from teachers' colleges to liberal arts institutions. Most state universities made general calculus the beginning freshman math course in the early 1960s, and it remains so today.

Changing College Population. Toward the end of the 1960s, the same institutions that had changed their freshman math courses were admitting increasing numbers of educationally disadvantaged students, minority applicants, and women. These students not only lacked the intensive, theoretical college preparatory math courses but generally came from high schools with very weak mathematics programs, and most had not been exposed to the new math. Entrance requirements were eased so that students could enter with only two years of high school math.

Minority students, with the exception of Asian-Americans, tend to perform poorly on mathematics tests and are less likely than white males to complete the full four years of college preparatory mathematics. Black students score lower on mathematics aptitude tests at both the elementary and secondary levels than on verbal tests. Puerto Rican students score lower on mathematics tests than on reasoning tests (Lesser, 1976; Stodolsky and Lesser, 1967). Black students and others from low socioeconomic backgrounds average 100 points lower on the SAT math section than white males and others from higher socioeconomic levels (Wirtz and others, 1977).

Women students share some of the same problems in math with minority students. Women have always averaged lower scores on college-level aptitude and achievement tests in mathematics than men (Admissions Testing Program of the College Entrance Examination Board, 1976; Ernest, 1976; Munday, 1976). In elementary school there is little difference between boys' and girls' mathematics scores. In junior high, however, girls' scores begin to drop, and by the time women enter college, their mathematical SAT scores average 50 points lower than men's.

Whatever the reason—social pressure, counselor's advice, or something else—women take fewer mathematics courses in high school than men. Sells (1976) reported that 57 percent of the male freshmen entering the University of California at Berkeley in 1973 had completed four years of high school mathematics and only 8 percent of the female freshmen had done so. By not having taken enough mathematics in high school, women students were disqualified from fifteen out of twenty majors (or if they chose a major requiring mathematics, they had to take remedial courses). Lack of mathematics training and skills thus excludes women from entering many professions.

Many reasons have been given for the poor mathematics skills of girls, including early conditioning to believe that being good in math is unfeminine. High school counselors, who themselves are insecure about math, often discourage girls from taking math courses—so claim the feminists. (However, as a former counselor, I recall how very difficult it was to persuade young women to take math courses.) Teachers who do not care about math, dislike teaching it, and communicate passive attitudes toward it and the tendency to teach math, at least at the high school level, in rulebook form rather than presenting concepts and reasons are also listed as causes (Stent, 1977).

Recent efforts to encourage women to take high school mathematics courses and elementary school math programs for girls may be having some effects, for 40 percent of the freshmen women entering college in 1976 had four years or more of high school mathematics, compared with 61 percent of the freshmen men (Admissions Testing Program of the College Entrance Examination Board, 1976, p. 13). However, women's mathematical SAT scores remain 50 points lower than men's. (For a comprehensive review of the studies, programs, and problems of women in mathematics, see Ernest's *Mathematics and Sex*, 1976.)

The reasons used to explain women's poor performance in mathematics tend to be psychological, while the poor performance of minority students in mathematics is attributed to weak schools.

Women and minority students (whether men or women) share interests in social science majors and biology (if they have any scientific bent), and both these areas now generally require some training in mathematics or statistics. So many of the special fields that traditionally attract women and minority students have become mathematicized.

Summary. The rapid development of computers and of their applications in almost every field has created a greater need for mathematical skills. In fact, some experts claim that knowledge of computer algorithms has become the fourth basic "literacy" skill needed by college graduates. Mathematics will continue to be increasingly important as computer technology advances and its applications broaden.

So the problem is complex. In the 1960s universities and selective colleges instituted calculus, which requires a strong foundation in algebra and trigonometry, as the entry-level general mathematics course for freshmen, on the assumption that the new-math proposals had been implemented in college preparatory programs. However, by the end of the 1960s these same institutions were accepting large numbers of educationally disadvantaged, minority, and women students without college preparatory mathematics. Moreover, high school programs changed so that students were allowed electives, and those with weak skills opted out of rigorous math courses they needed. These "new students," once in college, found that they were not adequately prepared even for the programs that in previous eras had not required mathematics, much less the majors and careers in science and mathematics that many of these students sought.

Should Precalculus Be Classified as Remedial?

As large numbers of students with minimal high school mathematics backgrounds continue to be accepted into college, there is a great need for precalculus and prestatistics courses. I fail to see the logic of mathematicians who term these courses "remedial" when students are legitimately accepted into college without precalculus. How can one remediate students in a subject they have not studied before? If colleges and universities admit students without adequate preparation, it seems only reasonable that they should provide the necessary skills courses to prepare students for their courses. Indeed, this is what must be done, since few institutions today can restrict admission to well-prepared students. As the number of young, well-prepared high school graduates who chose to enter college declines, colleges will be compelled to accept a larger number of students with weak high school math preparation and offer remedial programs if the colleges themselves are to survive.

How the Nature and Teaching of Mathematics Create Learning Problems

For most people, mathematics is a difficult, complex subject to learn. It requires the ability to think abstractly and analytically, to reason logically and deductively, to translate words into mathematical symbols, to manipulate these symbols to solve word problems, and to integrate this information and apply it to practical situations. To solve math problems, one must use disciplined and structured thought patterns, develop flexibility in translating between words, symbols, and pictures, understand their relations, and develop a conceptual framework of the processes involved.

Researchers who have reviewed studies based on Piaget's theory of intellectual development conclude that about 75 percent of the seventeen-year-olds and over half the college freshmen in this country have not reached the level of formal operations, which is necessary to understand the abstract concepts required for modern college preparatory and college mathematics (Chiapetta, 1976; Lowery, 1974). One prerequisite for college mathematics is the ability to think precisely and logically, an ability many people apparently lack.

Another prerequisite is the ability to learn mathematical language. Learning the symbols and terminology of mathematics is one of the major problem areas students meet in trying to master mathematics (Horner, 1974; Kolata, 1968; Schey and others, 1970). Richard Good of the University of Maryland summarized the problem well in a personal communication many years ago: "Much of the difficulty experienced by students in mathematics courses is not really mathematical in nature, but rather due to poor acquaintance with the language in general. We use language to communicate ideas. However well expressed the input of a student may be, it is futile if he is unwilling to realize the precision of the words he hears or reads. Vice versa, when he expresses himself, either orally or in writing, his careless or disorganized output will not convey his meaning satisfactorily."

Others question whether it is even possible to communicate mathematical ideas to the general public, since mathematics relies on terms with such precise, technical meanings and on such clearly defined concepts, while English and other languages owe their expressiveness to the ambiguity and changing meaning of their words and phrases. Translating mathematics into English has been described as being more difficult than translating Chinese poetry (Kolata, 1968). Yet young children do learn both Chinese and mathematics.

Henkin (1975), examining the linguistic factors that influence one's understanding of mathematics, agrees that there is extensive naming in mathematics but notes that the basis of the logical operations in mathematics is the use of connective words such as *not, and, or,* and *if . . . then* and that it is the concepts these words represent on which mathematics is based. Elementary school children do use these words in their speech and can be taught to think about their implications for mathematics.

Critics of mathematics teachers have been strident and harsh. In 1968, in a statement at the conference of the Mathematical Association of America, Johntz said: "The reason there are so few mathematicians in the U.S. is that only a few people have been able to withstand from six to fourteen years of miserable mathematical education and come out of it with any interest at all. There is a prevalent myth which says that mathematical talent belongs to only a small percentage of the population. The truth is that it is extremely widespread among young children before they are corrupted. One source of corruption is rote learning promoted by textbooks which rigidify concepts based on one set of assumptions and teachers who suffer from ego-anxiety and are afraid of children's intellectual curiosity."

So elementary teachers have been attacked for being generalists and intimidated by mathematics, and high school math teachers have been criticized for being weak in knowledge, rigid, and dull. In the 1950s and 1960s, it was hard to keep highly trained math teachers in public schools because there were excellent opportunities in industry, business, and government for people with mathematics training. Even though the economic situation has changed, I do not see that conditions will improve, because schools are facing reduced funding, classes are larger, and teachers who remained in the public schools have security, so that there is little opportunity for new, younger people to enter the field. Nor is there much incentive for secure teachers to change their teaching methods.

The negative effects of the current stagnation of math teachers are made worse by confusion about how mathematics should be taught. For two decades, math teachers have faced political and administrative pressures to make what the Conference Board of the Mathematical Sciences (1975) considers false choices between the old and the new in mathematics, skills and concepts, the concrete and the abstract, intuition and formalism, structure and problem solving, and induction and deduction. The board recommends that the core of every mathematics program contain a judicious combination of both elements of each pair, the balance between the two being determined by the goals of the program and by the nature, capabilities, and circumstances of the students and teachers in the program (Conference Board of the Mathematical Sciences, 1975, p. 137). Teachers would then be freed from the constraints of one method, approach, or book and enabled to work directly with students, adapting to their special needs.

The board also recommends that mathematics curriculums include as essential features the maintenance of logical structure, the use of concrete experiences as an integral part of the acquisition of abstract ideas, the opportunity for students to apply mathematics in as wide a realm as possible, the development of familiarity with the use, formalities, and limitations of mathematical symbols, and the wider use of hand-held calculators and computers in secondary schools (1975, p. 138).

Perhaps these ideas will be implemented, but the present demand for "back to basics" threatens teachers with being constrained even more than they have been in the past.

College mathematics professors have had their share of criticism also, but as Willcox (1977) points out, teaching is ignored in graduate training in mathematics, as it is in many other fields, and mathematicians have acquired a widespread reputation as casual teachers, which Willcox thinks is undeserved. In contrast to other disciplines, mathematicians do not usually specialize at the undergraduate level; therefore any well-trained mathematics instructor can teach any undergraduate course. This makes it easier to assemble a team of mathematics instructors to experiment in different ways of teaching. As a result, there were many innovative mathematics programs in the 1960s and 1970s; however, despite apparent initial successes, most have disappeared. What has happened is that instructors evolve back to traditional prototypes—good teaching and hard work (Willcox, 1977).

Whether the cause resides in poor teaching, sexual stereotypes, social opprobrium, or the difficulty of learning math, the fact is that fear of math, rather than lack of ability, prevents many students, particularly women, from pursuing careers that require math courses. I can recall students twenty years ago who desperately majored in journalism, not because they were the least bit interested in writing but rather because journalism was the only major in the business college that did not require mathematics. So students will go to great lengths to avoid studying math, even when it is essential to their career goals. Fears and anxieties about math have existed for generations, but today there is more concern about these attitudes.

Jacobs (1977) describes the approaches being tried to increase women's participation in the study of mathematics as "math anxiety" and "math avoidance." In the math-anxiety approach, self-selected individuals work through their negative attitudes toward mathematics in a group therapy setting, sharing their negative feelings. After the group session, the leaders (usually a counselor and a math instructor) help the participants use intuitive approaches to solving mathematical problems and feel more at ease with mathematics. For example, the Math Anxiety Clinic at Wesleyan College (Stent, 1977) offers supportive workshops, classes, a psychology lab, and individual counseling. Students enrolled in the program keep logs describing how they feel about homework and the class. Many of the students do not use the psychological services, but are interested in the course because they want to improve their grades on the Law School Admissions Test and the Graduate Record Examination.

Another example of programs to reduce anxiety is a private group therapy program, Mind over Math, based in New York City. Two thirds of the clients were women with blocks about mathematics, and the techniques used are similar to those in the Wesleyan program   group therapy, efforts to demystify math, and practice. Mathematics specialists from these two programs have recently written books designed to help students conquer their math anxiety: *Overcoming Math Anxiety* (Tobias, 1978) and *Mind over Math* (Kogelman and Warren, 1978).

The other approach—that is, treating the problem as math avoidance—is exemplified by the Wellesley College program, which does not include psychotherapy and is described as experimental rather than remedial (Stent, 1977). Students who have average mathematics ability are encouraged to take the course, which stresses instruction by supportive faculty members. The goal is to help women broaden their career options by learning math and to show them how mathematics is applied to other disciplines.

Whether one calls it math anxiety or math avoidance—and I agree with others that treating the problem as math avoidance is more productive—fear of math is a widespread problem that every tutoring or skills program where students come for assistance will encounter. Fear of math is a major deterrent to completing self-improvement programs in mathematics, even when good programs are available and the student knows she needs the skills.

(Most math avoiders are female.) Providing a supportive environment as the student works on improving mathematics skills is essential, whether in a tutoring situation or a class.

Reading Mathematics

Virtually all the college math courses offered in the U.S. today—92 percent—use textbooks (Moskowitz, 1976). Not only the abstract symbols but the syntax and style of mathematical writing make textbooks hard to read, particularly for the student who is a poor reader. Mathematicians themselves describe the books as being unreadable to the uninitiated, with concepts buried in such a complex context that students do not understand the context and cannot find the concepts. Such a textbook can be disastrous for a previously unsuccessful reader (Jason and others, 1977). Reading specialists, who are also concerned about the readability level of math textbooks, find that they often test four to six grades higher in difficulty than the students are able to understand (Lees, 1976; Williams, 1975). Although the readability yardsticks (Dale and Chall, 1948; Flesch, 1951; Fry, 1972) are less relevant to mathematics texts than to those in other subjects, most reading experts agree that the nonredundant writing style and density of the abstract concepts in mathematics are difficult for students to grasp. There is an ongoing debate about whether it would be more desirable to rewrite the textbooks at an easier reading level or to try to improve students' abilities to read so that they can understand the texts. Or, perhaps, we need to do both.

There have been a number of attempts to improve the interest level of mathematics texts and to simplify them. For example, Swann and Johnson's *Prof. E. McSquared's Original, Fantastic, & Highly Edifying Calculus Primer* (1976) is a calculus cartoon book. Other popularized books helpful for students who have math anxiety/avoidance problems include *Statistics Made Relevant: Casebook of Real Life Examples* (Baum and Scheuer, 1976), *Math Without Tears* (Hartkopf, 1976), and *Lady Luck: The Theory of Probability* (Weaver, 1963). Dupuis and Askov's *Annotated Bibliography of Adult Basic Instruction Materials* (n.d.) lists and describes mathematical and computational exercises and other materials for the adult student with below-eight-grade reading and math skills.

Some authors are rewriting college mathematics texts to make them more readable for students whose background in both mathematics and reading is limited. For example, Fitts (1976, p. 3) illustrates the difference between his self-paced precalculus materials and the textbook used by other instructors in the same course:

Self-Paced Precalculus	*Regular Precalculus Text*
A *function* is a rule that tells you how to take a number (called the input) and figure out another number (called the output).	Let the symbol x represent a real number, taken from a certain set D of real numbers. Suppose there is a rule that associates with each such x a number y. Then this rule is called a *function* whose *domain* is D.
Logarithm is another word for the exponent in an exponential. For example, consider the exponential 10^3. The logarithm of 10^3 is 3. In mathematical shorthand, we could write log (10^3) or log $(1000) = 3$.	If y is positive, then there is one and only one real number x such that $10^x - y$. This number is called the logarithm of y, and is written x = log y. For instance, $10^3 = 1000$, and $3 = \log (1000)$.

(Students are warned that if they plan to take more than one year of calculus, they should take the course with the textbook that uses the more rigorous mathematical language.)

Teaching Problem Solving

A number of recent publications on how to teach mathematics, emphasizing the reading and learning skills involved, should be valuable for the new college remedial math instructor as well as the public school teacher (Call and Wiggins, 1966; Bye, 1975; Earle, 1976; Herber, 1978; Lees, 1976). For example, Earle (1976) outlines four steps that a learner must accomplish to master a math objective: (1) perceive the symbols, (2) attach literal meaning to the symbols, (3) analyze the relations, and (4) solve the word problem. He describes detailed techniques for teaching these steps, including presenting students with a structured overview of mathematical terms (in a graphic or tree format showing their relations) to aid retention and recognition of the terms, developing study guides, providing reference lists for supplementary work for students at different levels of achievement, and presenting a glossary of frequently used mathematical terms. One hopes that teachers would not give the lists of terms to students to memorize like spelling lists, and they would not if they read Earle's book.

Skills specialists who work with students with math difficulties usually stress procedures like the following: (1) Read the problem quickly and try to visualize it as a whole. (2) Read it again to see what you are asked to find. (3) Read it again to see what information you are given. (4) Analyze the problem to note the relation of the information given to what you are asked to find. (This is the most difficult step) (5) Translate it into mathematical terms. (6) Perform the necessary computations. (7) Examine your answer carefully; label it to correspond with what the problem asks and judge whether the answer seems plausible.

These instructions contain a number of tacit assumptions about the student's ability to understand and follow directions. They assume that the student knows what to look for in the problem.

Herber (1978) uses a somewhat different approach to teach students to solve mathematical word problems. He recommends that the student be given a reading guide rather than just being told to read to see what the problem asks him to find. Herber's reading guides are developed by the teacher to help the student comprehend at three levels: the literal level (what is actually stated—the facts), the interpretive level (what is meant—the mathematical concepts underlying the problem), and the applied level (the numbers involved in solving the problem and any previous knowledge or experience related to the task). The guide consists of a series of statements, not questions, at each level. The student shifts back and forth between the problem and the statements to determine which guide statements are facts that will help, which guide statements are ideas that are related to the problem, and which of the guide statements illustrate mathematical formulas that will lead to the answer. After the teacher has demonstrated how to use a guide with a related problem, students use the guide in small-group discussion sessions. Although this approach requires more work by the teacher in preparing the guides, it can be very effective in enhancing students' interest and learning, for it shows them precisely how to do the problems (as well as how not to do them, for incorrect or irrelevant "facts" and concepts can be deliberately written into the guide).

Another problem-solving strategy is to think aloud. Reading experts have long observed that adults, when reading very difficult prose, read slowly and vocalize. However, talking to oneself is viewed as strange behavior in our society, and so teachers often scold pupils, "Read with your eyes, not your mouth," or tell them to "do the problem in your head." Ferguson (1974) found that encouraging disadvantaged students to participate orally in interpreting mathematical relations was an excellent technique for getting them to understand highly symbolic mathematical language. Similarly, Bloom and Broder (1950) had described having low-achieving students solve problems aloud and then explained to them the ideal problem-solving approach and helped them recognize the difference between their approach and the ideal. This technique, they found, produced better problem solvers.

In analyzing the differences between good and poor problem solvers, Whimbey (1976a) found that poor problem solvers work too hastily, skip steps, lack the motivation to persist in analyzing the problem, reason carelessly, and fail to check their solutions. Good problem solvers are more active than poor ones: They visualize the idea, draw diagrams and scribble, talk to themselves, count on their fingers, and so on. Whimbey then developed materials and began to test students working in pairs. One student serves as listener and the other as problem solver who must solve the problem orally. The listener's role is to work actively with the problem solver and to check each step as the problem solver verbalizes it for accuracy and sense. The listener and the problem solver alternate roles as they work through Whimbey's exercises. When they agree that they have the solution to a problem, they look on the back of the page, which contains a description of each step and an explanation. If they have trouble with a problem, they can ask the teacher or a tutor for help.

Whimbey's materials are designed to help students develop the basic logic and problem-solving skills they need in order to learn basic courses in science and mathematics. His materials contain word problems, figure and verbal analogies, and problems in other formats traditionally used in intelligence tests. By going through the exercises step by step with a partner, students learn to solve word problems and other types of problems. Whimbey's materials are being widely used in courses in problem solving for academically weak students, but I have found that other students profit from them as well. Students thoroughly enjoy vocalizing their thoughts and working with a partner. Whimbey claims that students who complete these exercises show improvement on tests of scholastic aptitude as well as developing the analytic thinking skills needed for studying mathematics and science. For other references on this approach see Whimbey (1974, 1976a, 1976b, 1977) and Whimbey and Whimbey (1975). Other materials for improving students' logic and problem-solving skills are Adams (1974); Samson (1970), and Upton and Samson (1961).

The approaches of both Herber and Whimbey are consistent with current research and theory on the development of cognitive skills, in that they make explicit the steps a skilled learner uses in the process of solving problems. High achievers can make the inferential leaps from vague directions to the answer, but the weak student cannot. Both Herber's method and Whimbey's maximize learning for students whose preferred learning style is to talk and socialize. With these approaches they can do both and learn to think analytically.

Approaches to Teaching Mathematics

The most frequently used approach to teaching college mathematics is a lecture-discussion arrangement with fifteen to thirty students per class; however, about 40 percent of university mathematics departments also use large lectures (Moskowitz, 1976). Individual tutoring is provided by more than half the institutions and is more common in two-year colleges (65 percent) than in universities (51 percent). Two-year colleges are more likely to use PSI (Keller plan) delivery systems, mathematics labs, and mathematics teaching centers than four-year colleges and universities. Four-year colleges are more likely to offer mathematics courses as independent study programs than other types of colleges. Computer-assisted instruction is offered by 13 percent of the mathematics departments, with no differences between types of colleges. Fewer than 10 percent of the institutions use closed-circuit television to teach mathematics.

Math professors in two-year colleges show the broadest interest in materials. They use slides, audiotapes, self-contained modules, demonstration models, and programmed materials more than math professors in four-year colleges and universities. However, they are least likely to use computers or to be interested in using film loops. Professors in universities are more likely to use computers for their classes than professors in other types of colleges. About 75 percent of the mathematics departments have computers available for student use, but more than half of these departments report that their computer facilities are underutilized. Hand calculators are used by students more frequently in two-year colleges, although more than half the mathematics instructors in other types of colleges also encourage their use.

In Moskowitz's (1976) survey, 70 percent of the math departments indicated an interest in or were using self-contained teaching modules. What the instructors are most interested in getting is self-contained modules that contain practice exercises, are competency-based, use intuitive development, and motivate the student to begin solving a problem by applying principles.

Of the 639 mathematics professors responding to Moskowitz's survey, 41 percent indicated that their departments had problems with the precalculus course, and 33 percent felt the remedial math courses presented problems. The most frequent reasons cited for the problems with these courses were student diversity, inadequate preparation of students, motivation of students, large number of dropouts, and inappropriate placement of students. Thirty-four percent reported that the text materials available were inadequate for their remedial students.

The interest in self-contained instructional modules encouraged the Undergraduate Mathematics and Its Applications Project (1977) to produce a directory with descriptions of 424 mathematics modules used in college and university undergraduate mathematics courses. The modules are indexed by application, course, author, organization, and title, and math instructors are encouraged to test them and evaluate their effectiveness. This and subsequent volumes will save teachers much time.

So it seems there is increasing interest in self-paced modules, although mathematics instructors in some institutions reject the more old-fashioned programmed learning materials.

How effective is self-paced instruction in mathematics? Self-paced instructional materials have been widely used to help students master mathematical concepts in math labs and in community college classrooms, perhaps because math materials can be easily developed (at least in comparison with other subjects), more materials are available, and regular faculty members are reluctant to teach remedial courses. Whether a program is effective depends on the appropriateness of the materials for the skills of the students, the motivational level of the students, and the ways the materials are used. Studies on the effectiveness of using programmed materials to remediate students with math difficulties show equivocal results. For instance, Harris and Liquori (1974) found no significant differences between classes taught with programmed instruction and those taught traditionally, but Eraut (1967) found positive results in favor of programmed instruction. Many of the studies with open-admissions students in math classes where programmed instruction was used were never published because too few students were around at the end of the course to take the posttests.

A major difficulty of programmed learning for teaching underprepared students is that most of the students are weak in the reading skills that the programs require. When they cannot understand a problem or a set of instructions, they soon become frustrated and give up. However, when the materials are readable and are written at an appropriate level, and the students are tutored regularly or work in Keller-plan courses in pairs or groups, disadvantaged students persist in mathematics courses longer than those enrolled in traditional or in completely self-paced courses (Carman, 1975). Audio-tutorial programs can also help the poor reader learn math by providing reinforcement through hearing (McWilliams, 1977).

Self-paced calculus courses following the PSI model seem to be increasing, judging from the number of materials that are being published for this course. Footlick (1977) describes a PSI calculus course at Hamilton and Kirkland Colleges (New York) that combines peer tutoring, a text, and a study guide. Students are not only motivated but enthusiastic about the course, which has survived four years—a novelty in itself. The chance to work problems with peers seems to make the difference.

The self-paced precalculus course at the University of California at Berkeley has been helpful to students with very weak mathematical skills and those who are fearful of math. When the instructors are well trained and committed to individualizing instruction, both students and teachers enjoy the program. The Cummings Publishing Company's *Series in Mathematical Modules* is used, and students are encouraged to work on the problems in pairs and/or small groups; if they prefer, they can work alone. Instructors like the fact that it saves them preparation time and gives them the opportunity to work individually with students. Before the self-paced course was offered, the learning center had a large demand for tutoring from students enrolled in precalculus. The self-paced course has virtually eliminated the need for tutoring in precalculus, because the stronger students take the regular lecture-discussion courses, while those with weaker skills enroll in the self-paced sections. Students who need very intensive help in basic math, particularly special-admissions students, may have difficulty with the self-paced course, but if they can get help from a tutor during class or can work with the instructor, they rarely need additional tutoring. Evaluations of the course show that the academically weaker students perform better in the self-paced course and remain in the mathematics course sequence longer than equally weak students who take the regular lecture-discussion course. In addition, students with the poorest preparation in math are more likely to choose to enroll in the self-paced course.

Jason and others (1977) developed a learning system for teaching mathematics to underprepared engineering freshmen which is based on the conventional lecture method but is also responsive to the heterogeneous initial preparation of students. Called the "quasi-modular approach," it coordinates counseling and conventional classroom lectures with workshop sessions. Tutorial facilities are available for students on request, and help sessions are arranged for groups identified by their performance on weekly tests. Jason and others are careful to emphasize that their view is that the program is not remedial, nor is it based on the notion that students are slow learners; they believe it verifies that what these students lack in preparation is more than compensated for by their desire to overcome their deficiencies and tackle new topics. They argue that underprepared students respond well to lecturers who can relate to them and that instructors provide a humanizing effect and can help change attitudes and bring success. Further, the underprepared students need to see the instructor do the problem. (I would argue that college students expect lectures because that is the way most college courses are taught. If they are offered media and tutors instead of classes, they know they are being treated differently.)

The quasi-modular approach is comprehensive in that it offers the following features.

1. Two specially designed math courses are phased into the standard curriculum of the department to alleviate the negative connotations associated with remedial programs. One course begins with basic arithmetic and goes through elementary algebra. The second begins with intermediate algebra and provides a natural transition to college algebra.

2. Deficiencies in arithmetic skills and elementary algebra are approached through specially prepared modules, which "can be taught with some degree of sophistication" (p. 38). Finding that most of the self-learning kits were so elementary that students rejected them, Jason and others designed project-type problems having some research potential to introduce basic concepts. (An example is analyzing data from a survey on supersonic aircraft.) They define a module as a unit on some particular topic or a particular section of a chapter, such as fractions and decimals. Construction of the modules is based on three criteria: (1) examples must be challenging and not routine and drill-like, (2) modules must be used in the context of the topics taught in the course, to alleviate problems stemming from lack of background, and (3) the modules are designed to emphasize readability with less emphasis on mathematical precision, on the assumption that the students using these materials are self-confident in neither math nor English.

3. Instructors lecture to classes of forty-five students for thirty minutes. Then students are asked to solve sample problems in class and discuss math problems individually with the instructor or one of his assistants.

4. The duration of the remedial courses is flexible and tailored to individual needs. Students can take one to four quarters to prepare for calculus, depending on their background and progress. A counselor administers diagnostic tests when students enter the program, and the students are grouped according to the length of time they will need to complete the precalculus sequence. Students who score low on the diagnostic math tests are given intensive tutoring and attend special help sessions with the instructor during the first three weeks of the course.

5. Remediation in English is a concomitant but independent part of the program. The goal is to see that the student has both the writing skills and the reading speed that are satisfactory to the English department before he advances.

6. Students participate in a science-engineering club, which introduces them to professional people and careers in science and engineering, as well as providing a social environment. (For a more detailed description, see also Gaonker and others, 1977.)

Another advantage I see in the quasi-modular approach is that it not only teaches students the content they will need in a tightly coordinated sequence so that when they emerge they are prepared for advanced courses, but it introduces them to the lecture approach to teaching, a reality they must face throughout their college careers. This approach minimizes the problem of transferring the skills learned in a completely individualized self-paced course to advanced courses in which lecturing is the mode. Too often students enjoy the freedom of the self-paced course and do well, only to fail the next mathematics course in the sequence because it is not offered in a self-paced format.

Such programs as the minority engineers program at Stevens Institute of Technology, Hoboken, New Jersey (Mullins, 1977), handle the extra assistance academically weak students need in a more traditional manner, called the "extra class option." Students whose performance is below average must attend additional lectures and guided study sessions. They can review the week's lecture in mathematics and receive assistance in problem solving, and the smaller class size offers more opportunity for slower-paced students to get individualized assistance from the professor.

Because mathematics instructors probably have greater access to computers than instructors in other disciplines do, one would expect that computer-assisted instruction (CAI) would be popular in teaching basic mathematics. Certainly many CAI programs have been developed, tested, and dissolved, and computers are used to help students solve problems. Still, only about 10 percent of the institutions surveyed by Moskowitz (1976) used CAI to teach mathematics. Of the 424 mathematics modules listed in the Undergraduate Mathematics and Its Applications Project directory, only 3 were developed for CAI use.

Perhaps mathematicians are working out other ways to help students with computers, like Shapiro (1977), who found a novel use for the computer to help students and instructors (who might get irritated or bored correcting the same errors by the same student over and over). His Individualized Supplementary Calculus Instruction Program fits any calculus or precalculus course. Students use it when they cannot solve a problem or when they make an error. The computer retraces the student's work and helps him explore the methods used and locate the error, but it does not work the problem for him. Thus the computer functions as a diagnostic aid, not a teaching device, saving the student embarrassment and time.

In summary, college mathematics departments are still concerned about the problems students have in remedial mathematics and precalculus courses. The new materials that are being developed emphasize the process of solving mathematics problems and describe precisely the steps and cognitive skills needed to solve math problems successfully. There is also a trend toward writing mathematics materials in a more readable style. The most pervasive approach to working with underprepared students seems to be well-designed modules and other learning programs used with other students in pairs (Schermerhorn and others, 1975) or small groups or with peer tutors (Carman and Adams, 1972). In general, there seems to be a trend toward more traditional methods, such as incorporating lectures, tutoring, modules for self-study, and even extra sessions with the instructor.

12

Increasing
Science Skills

The problems students have in learning college science must be viewed in the context of the growing demand for scientific literacy, the rapid expansion of scientific knowledge, and its increasing application to other disciplines. Students today have a rising interest in science courses, particularly those focused on environmental issues and health-related fields. As job opportunities decline in such traditional fields as liberal arts and teaching, more students are exploring science-related majors. The greatest enrollments, however, are in freshman science courses, particularly physical sciences—a direct result of the expanding application of physical science to the "softer sciences," including biology and psychology. The creation of new fields like molecular biology, medical physics, and genetic counseling typifies this trend. Even mental-health majors are often required to take biochemistry courses. Moreover, the information explosion, which has virtually doubled scientific knowledge each decade, shows little sign of abating. As a result, freshman science courses require a higher degree of abstract thinking and problem-solving ability, and even laboratory experiments are more complex than those of the recent past (Haight, 1976).

In addition, affirmative action efforts to attract minority and women students to prepare for physical science careers bring large numbers of underprepared students into science courses. Despite strong affirmative action efforts for over a decade, women and minority groups continue to be underrepresented in physical science and engineering majors, and graduate programs continue to seek these students actively. (For recent reviews of the problems of recruiting and training minority students in the sciences, see Hurst, 1977; Majer, 1975; Rentention Task Force, 1977; Sullivan, 1977; Wilburn, 1977.)

Although scholarships are readily available for disadvantaged students who are interested in science, many of these students lack the college preparatory courses in mathematics and science that college courses demand. The elective system in high schools has exacerbated the problem for academically weak or uncertain students who, when given a choice, avoided the mathematics, chemistry, and physics courses that would have given them the background for college science. For example, college-bound students in many high schools are allowed to substitute advanced high school biology for chemistry, but in college they find that they must take college chemistry if they want to major in biology. Nationally, science achievement scores of high school students have paralleled the decline of scores in other subjects. (Scores on the CEEB science achievement tests have not declined, but only the best-prepared students take these exams.)

Women and minority students (with the exception of Asian-Americans) tend to get lower grades in high school science courses, to take fewer science courses, and to score lower on science achievement tests at college entrance than white males. So underprepared women and minority students are recruited into science majors while competition increases as other, better-prepared students swamp beginning courses.

Problems in Learning Science

How does learning science differ from learning other subjects? Perhaps Huxley's definition of science will clarify the difference between science learning and learning in other disciplines. Huxley wrote, "Science is the reduction of the bewildering diversity of unique events to manageable uniformity with one of a number of symbol systems so as to control and organize unique events. Scientific observation is always a viewing of things through the refracting medium of a symbol system, and technological praxis is always the handling of things in ways that some symbol system has dictated. *Education in science and technology is essentially education on the symbolic level*" (Huxley, 1962, p. 281).

To succeed in college science courses, students must be motivated to master the precise definitions of symbols and terms and the systematic problem-solving and laboratory procedures demanded by the professor. They must also think analytically, conceive abstractions, visualize the invisible, and understand and apply principles. For many students, science learning requires a much heavier investment of time and mental effort than is required in other courses. Students who have not had strong high school science courses must have persistence and a dogged determination to master college science courses. Unfortunately, our rigid college academic terms set time constraints on learning, which work against part-time students or those who learn more slowly, who often become discouraged and drop the courses. Students from academically weak high schools and students returning to college after years of working find science courses especially difficult to learn. Others, who have expelled science and its tool, mathematics, from their personal universes, often find that they must take science courses to qualify for their chosen careers. They both need and demand intensive support services as they study basic college science courses.

The Information Explosion. The information explosion in science has had major effects on college science courses. The sheer amount of information poses problems for textbook authors, instructors, and students. An organic-chemistry textbook in 1900 contained about 200 pages; today's text requires 1,500 pages (Haight, 1976). Wending one's way laboriously through such a lengthy and difficult text is a challenge for even the best-prepared and most highly motivated student.

Another illustration of the way scientific information has proliferated is that over two million organic compounds have been identified in the past 200 years, and the number of possible compounds is virtually infinite. Although there are systems for organizing this vast knowledge, mastering them requires dedication and time for the uninitiated.

Mastering Terminology. Learning the symbol system and terminology accepted by scientists is analogous to learning a new language. The vocabulary in courses like biology is immense and requires a skilled memory. When students must learn a large number of terms, memorizing the glossary is not an effective way to do it. Research suggests that students learn terms more readily from a chart that shows the relations among the terms. Providing such a chart is sometimes called "mapping" (Hanf, 1971) or presenting a "structured overview" (Ferguson, 1969). Although instructors sometimes present, or authors include, structured overviews that show the relations among terms in a discipline, students often merely memorize the chart without understanding it. Studies by Shepherd (1969) and Barron and Stone (1973) suggest that students who draw their own maps *after* reading science material perform better on recall tests than students who are given the structured overview prepared by the teacher or the textbook author.

However, when there is a large amount of material for students to assimilate, it is very tempting for a teacher to organize and present a graphic model showing the relations among facts and terms. For instance, one of our chemistry tutors filled three chalkboards with small figures illustrating the interrelations among all of the major, and most of the minor, concepts in freshman chemistry. It was an impressive display of her ability to organize the material, but I doubt that it helped those students who felt that they had to memorize all of it. It may even have caused them to feel inadequate, since they were nearing the final exam and were unable to synthesize and relate the course information as successfully as she did.

Visualization Skills. The manuals written to improve students' study skills suggest that students try to draw their own charts and graphs as well as studying those in their science texts. For example, Hanau (1972) tells physiology students to draw their own "visuals" of diagrams and anatomical charts. Researchers are confirming that the ability to visualize abstractions, such as molecules and atoms, and their relations is an important skill in learning science (Baker and Talley, 1972; Ozsogomonyan, 1977; Rigney and Lutz, 1976; Talley, 1973; Thelen, 1976). Visualization skills are particularly needed in solving problems effectively (Whimbey, 1976b).

Historically, chemists have used three-dimensional models to help them visualize molecules. In the 1890s, the German chemist Baeyer stuck toothpicks into breadcrumbs as he tried to visualize the shapes of sugar molecules. Today's chemistry instructors are more likely to use color-coded Styrofoam balls weighted with buckshot. Prelog recently won a Nobel Prize for his system of assigning descriptors for specifying asymmetrical organic molecules. He devised a two-dimensional notation system for describing, assigning, and deciphering molecules as a substitute for the classical bulky, three-dimensional, tetrahedral figures (Prelog, 1976). To understand this choreography of molecules requires talent in visualizing from the two-dimensional sketches.

Besides ability to visualize abstractions, college science increasingly requires sophisticated motor skills as equipment in laboratories becomes more complex. Programs have been developed to teach students to use compound optical microscopes, for example (Brandt, 1976; Simmons, 1976).

Reading Skills. Students need strong reading skills to succeed in science. They need to be able to read flexibly (that is, to vary their rate and approach according to the relevance and difficulty of the material), to learn from graphic aids, including charts, tables, and diagrams, to interpret and formulate questions, to read directions accurately, to evaluate scientific writing and draw conclusions, and, finally, to apply information from their reading to practical problems (Shepherd, 1969).

Reading experts generally agree that students have difficulty reading science because of the high density of facts and ideas. Science textbooks differ greatly from texts in subjects like social science and literature, where the writing style is more redundant and repetitious and fewer concepts are presented. Ferguson (1969) explains that poor reading habits are the main reason that students who are otherwise capable fail to understand science. He notes that students do not use the study aids built into their textbooks. They ignore the organization and the topic headings, and they read superficially. Science instructors should, but sometimes do not, analyze the steps of the scientific method to determine which reading skills are needed and then teach them. For instance, they should show students how to define a problem and how to determine its limits, how to collect evidence that bears on a problem, how to locate information that is appropriate to the problem, and how to integrate skills in order to construct hypotheses, test them, draw conclusions, and apply solutions (Ferguson, 1969; Keetz, 1970; Shepherd, 1969; Thelen, 1976; Watanabe and Gordon, 1977).

   The readability level of college science textbooks is a topic of great concern among college reading specialists, for the methods they use to determine the readability level of a book are designed in such a way that science books score as dull and difficult (and they usually are!). In addition, since most standardized reading tests do not reveal whether or how well students comprehend material in the sciences, other techniques must be devised to determine whether a given textbook is suitable for a class or for an individual student. Skills specialists (or the instructor) can construct simple, informal comprehension tests based on the text material. An even quicker and easier method is to construct a "cloze" test (see Chapter Seven) based on a passage from the text. To construct a cloze test, select a passage of about 200 words from the text, leave the first and last sentences intact, and delete every fifth word from the rest of the text. Give the passage to students with instructions to fill in the blanks. Students who supply the exact words in 50 to 70 percent of the blanks are able to learn from the text independently. When a student scores between 30 and 50 percent, the instructor should check to see whether the words supplied are synonyms of the deleted words; if they are not, the text may prove frustrating to the student. Under these circumstances, it would be best to assign an easier text or to provide intensive help with the concepts and terms. Students with scores under 30 percent should not take the course.

Reading-skills specialists often see students who have been referred by their science instructors for help in vocabulary development, only to find that the vocabulary that the students lack is the specific terminology for the science course they are taking. In this situation, reading-skills specialists feel ill equipped for teaching the physics or biology terms, which they think should be the instructor's task. The skills specialist must work both with the student, on general techniques for learning new terms, and with the instructor, to help him learn effective ways to teach technical vocabulary.

Problem Solving. In science, as in mathematics, many students have difficulty recognizing and applying the principles underlying the problems they are asked to solve. If a problem is stated in different words or if the syntax is rearranged, students may not recognize it even if they have solved a half dozen similar problems successfully. The arrangement of problems in a chemistry text, for example, may make solving them harder. If the problems are arranged in random fashion, with easy items interspersed among difficult ones and with problems involving different principles mixed together, some students will have difficulty working them. Although Haight (1976) speaks contemptuously of programmed learning materials in chemistry and states that chemists have taught with similar problem exercises in workbooks for over 200 years, an element of "let the student find his own way through the maze" is still implicit in the arrangement of problem sets in chemistry textbooks. Editors have told me that one of their most difficult tasks is to try to extract from authors an answer to the question "Which of the problem sets are the most crucial for a student to master?" Authors usually answer, "All of them." Gradually, however, some authors of chemistry textbooks are adopting programmed-instructional principles as Keller-plan courses increase in popularity. (For an example of materials for a Keller-plan course in chemistry, see Clouser, 1977.)

Because so many students have difficulty with the underlying mathematical concepts and logic necessary for mastering college-level science courses, academic departments and learning centers are offering special problem-solving pre-science courses and math review courses aimed specifically at the math skills needed to understand college chemistry and physics (see Chapter

Ten). In addition, many community colleges and some four-year colleges offer basic high school chemistry courses. Although chemistry review courses help a few students, I have found little evidence that these courses by themselves aid large numbers of students. The dropout rate in college science courses remains high. Few students complete the chemistry courses in proportion to the numbers who aspire to careers that require them, like medicine.

Chemistry remains the most difficult science course taken by a large number of students. Typically taught in large lecture sections that rely on television monitors so all can see, it is considered the main hurdle by prospective science majors and by students planning to enter health-related professions. Purdue University may have the largest number of students enrolled in freshman chemistry—over 5,300 each fall. The intrinsic difficulty of the course and the fact that, unlike many college courses, it has not been subject to grade inflation explain why so many students have trouble with chemistry. If you picture the largest lecture hall on campus, packed with students listening to chemistry lectures, you can see how traumatic this course can be for the student who feels and/or is underprepared.

Instructors face a dilemma in planning and teaching large lecture courses in introductory science. Although most of the students enrolled have no intention of becoming research scientists, some will go on to graduate school as majors. Those in the former group will probably never perform a scientific experiment again. Instructors must acknowledge their needs as well as those of students who will become scientists. Most colleges have not completely resolved the question whether there should be separate courses for nurses, dietitians, poetry majors, engineers, pre-meds, and others who do not plan to become chemistry majors. In many universities all students are required to take the same course, but some colleges offer chemistry courses without concepts from mathematics or physics. Other colleges consider these courses watered-down and inferior and refuse to accept them for transfer credit.

Instructional Problems. Science instructors have often been criticized for their emphasis on having students memorize pre-designed experiments, which violates the authentic discovery process a scientist must endure in practice, when hours or even years of tedious work precede a discovery and breakthroughs come very rarely (Skinner, 1968). In short, scientific methods have not been applied to teaching science, and the laboratory experiments required of students bear little relation to the work of the professional scientist. Hurd (as quoted in Thelen, 1976, p. 6) states it another way: "To teach only the findings of science is to teach an illusion of scientific knowledge." Yet these arguments are somewhat specious unless our objective is for everyone to become a research scientist, an idea that may have seemed the goal in the 1950s and 1960s, when scientific opportunities were expanding and research funds seemed unlimited. Today young scientists, like other college graduates, have difficulty finding appropriate employment.

What the critics do not acknowledge is that teaching the findings of science is a worthy and difficult objective in itself. Furthermore, it is a crucial need in an era when scientific issues have entered the political arena and citizens must weigh the differing opinions of scientific experts and vote on scientific issues.

There have been many other criticisms of the way science is taught. Skinner (1968) insists that the fallacy that any teacher can teach what a good teacher can teach and that any student can learn what a good student can learn has had detrimental effects on science teaching. He challenges the Socratic method, which he dubs the "cat and mouse game," and accuses its proponents of promoting science as a running debate. He claims that the Socratic method would be useful if one's goal were to produce good debaters rather than scientists. Skinner also challenges self-study materials, stating that they favor the good students.

There are some signs that science instructors are moving away from the traditional descriptive approach in teaching, with its concomitant rote memorization, and that they place greater emphasis on conceptualizing and on application of the scientific process by requiring students to generate hypotheses and view problems from more than one perspective (Haight, 1976). The difficulty they face is how to teach students these strategies— that is, how to get students from concrete operations to an understanding of the abstractions involved in scientific methods. Some educators proclaim that the majority of adults and adolescents have not attained the level of formal operations, described by

Piaget as essential to understanding the abstractions of scientific thought (Chiapetta, 1976; Haight, 1976; Lowery, 1974). Others argue that thinking at the formal-operational level develops at different rates for people exposed to different disciplines and that lack of exposure to scientific terminology and modes of thinking is an important factor in the problems students have in learning college science. Still others who are not scientists suggest that students' difficulties may be due not to inability to think in abstractions, but rather to lack of flexibility in shifting from the abstract to the concrete (Shaughnessy, 1977). This rigidity of thinking would make it difficult for the student to master chemistry and other sciences, in which shifts in thinking from abstract to concrete must be done frequently and quickly.

As in any area of college teaching, there are pockets of innovation in teaching the sciences, but they seem to involve only a small proportion of professors and students in any institution. Some colleges are trying interdisciplinary courses, such as the core program at Evergreen State College (Olympia, Washington), where students work on "real life" projects like water pollution (Benet, 1976). Others are experimenting with chemistry courses that are practical in orientation for the nonmajor, while some are using student-oriented inquiry methods (see Chapter Seven for descriptions of this approach). Keller plan and PSI seem to be maturing (Kulik and Kulik, 1974), as publishers are producing a wide variety of self-paced and audiovisual materials in science subjects.

Nevertheless, I have found in the research no compelling evidence that science instructors should alter their traditional lecture-laboratory teaching approach. Certainly there are ways of improving the delivery of science information through lectures and laboratory sessions, but the programs and strategies (described below) to help underprepared students succeed in science courses are, with few exceptions, designed to supplement, not replace, the lecture-lab teaching paradigm.

Programs for Improving Science Skills

Most learning-skills specialists—except those working in reading and study skills programs within engineering, medical, nursing, or other science-related professional schools—have not emphasized skills in science. They have instead focused on improving general study skills and reading in the social sciences and humanities. Perhaps they trusted students to transfer these skills to science, or, more likely, they felt unprepared to teach science skills, since few had formal training in science.

Recently, however, the number of learning centers and reading and study skills programs for science students has increased dramatically at both the undergraduate and graduate levels. Programs, particularly in large universities, are hiring science specialists or graduate students to supplement the standard instructional services provided by instructors and teaching assistants. Particularly in institutions where minority tutoring programs merged with reading and study skills services to become learning centers, services have expanded to include help in basic science courses and preparation for admissions examinations for medical school and other health-science professional schools. In some universities science tutoring and skills work are offered by the academic department, which hires skills specialists to work with students or assigns regular faculty members this duty.

Although a number of researchers have tried to evaluate the effectiveness of study skills programs on science achievement, most have failed to find positive results (Foxe, 1966; Keetz, 1970; Sheldon, 1948; Weinstein and Gipple, 1974). The paucity of results may spring from the problems in designing appropriate experiments and also from the assumptions underlying the experiments. For instance, if one assumes that a program of a few weeks' duration will yield significant grade improvement, one is ignoring the fact that students need time to practice and to internalize new skills. If they are concurrently enrolled in a demanding science course, they must master a large amount of information in the same short period when they are changing their learning skills. The criteria used in some studies militate against obtaining positive results, especially when the dependent variable is change in overall GPA or in course grades during the same term. A large percentage of the grades given in a science class are C's, and if grade improvement is used as the criterion, it is hard to demonstrate statistically that improvement has occurred as a result of a brief study skills program. For instance, the spread of points between a low C and a high C is greater than that between a high C and a B, so that students could conceivably improve substantially during the course but still receive a grade of C.

The earlier studies focused on the skills that seem logical, such as textbook reading and notetaking, and used materials that were related to the students' texts but generally easier. Current studies are focusing on the specific cognitive skills necessary to learn the actual course material and devising ways to explain and demonstrate these skills explicitly. As a result, these studies do show significant gains.

The following studies are representative of the kinds that have been done in order to understand and improve the science-learning skills of college students.

Chemistry Skills. Offer a study skills improvement program to students enrolled in freshman chemistry, and you will get many takers. Foxe (1966) invited students in a general-chemistry course at the University of Maryland to take a brief study skills program, and 427 of the 1,068 enrolled in the course signed up. In analyzing the characteristics of students who volunteered for the program, she found that volunteers were weaker in mathematics (on ACT scores) than those who did not volunteer and more anxious than typical college students. Her random sample of volunteers received six hours of training in time management and the following skills applied to chemistry: listening and notetaking, efficient textbook reading (SQ3R), improving memory and concentration, and preparing for and taking examinations. Although the experimental group made significant gains on standardized tests of reading and listening, there were no significant differences in GPAs or in chemistry grades between those taking the brief course and the controls. One reason may have been that the study skills program overlapped the midterm examination, so that there was little time for the skills program to affect chemistry grades that term, and no follow-up study was done to determine whether the program affected grades in subsequent chemistry courses. Foxe concluded that since students volunteering for skills help were weak in mathematics, it is important that study skills courses in chemistry emphasize mathematical skills as well as study skills.

A recent study approached teaching chemistry skills by analyzing the assumptions, strategies, and concepts underlying freshman chemistry and building a skills program based on them. Ozsogomonyan (1977) measured the effects of a brief review course in stoichiometry on the performance of educationally disadvantaged students enrolled in freshman chemistry. Stoichiometry, calculation of the quantitative relations necessary to balance chemical equations, is an important skill in mastering general and analytic chemistry. Three skills were emphasized: visualization of molecules, proportional reasoning, and a systematic approach to problem solving. Using models (Styrofoam balls weighted with buckshot and plastic balls that were color-coded, with the radius proportional to the ionic radius) and programmed materials, Ozsogomonyan taught the symbols on the blackboard before explaining the formulas. Students who took his program scored higher than control subjects on a test of stoichiometric principles at the end of the four-week program, on a posttest two weeks later, and also on the problems involving stoichiometry on the final course exam. However, the experimental subjects did not get higher grades than controls in their first chemistry course. Ozsogomonyan explains that the stoichiometric skills taught in his program represented just one part of the freshman chemistry course.

Physics. Larkin and Reif (1976) trained students in a general-physics course to understand various relations in physics, including interpreting without confusion the symbols in the relation and identifying the situations in which the relation could be applied. (A very simple example of such a relation is summarized by the equation $d = st$, which describes the distance d traveled during a time t by a particle moving with constant speed s along a straight path.) The students studied textbook descriptions and answered questions requiring them to demonstrate the specific abilities necessary to apply the relations: They were asked to state the relation, give an example of its application, list the properties of the quantities in the relation, interpret the relation by using information in various symbolic representations, make discriminations and comparisons, and use the relation to form other relations. Larkin and Reif found that the explicit description of a learning skill—in this case, understanding quantitative relations—is useful even without associated training in the skill, since the description can be used as a goal toward which both instructors and students can work. Further, they conclude that providing direct instruction in a quantitative skill is a reliable way to help students become independent learners. Students taught with Larkin and Reif's system learned more from their textbooks than students in an intensive self-paced physics course. In addition, students taught to understand and apply relations in physics were able to transfer this skill to concepts in a completely different field (inventory turnover in cost accounting). Larkin and Reif achieved their goal of training students to understand text material as well as an experienced reader does, one who reads with selective attention and remembers essential information. Basic learning skills of this type, which would have direct application to the improvement of students' learning and instructors' strategies, must be identified in other disciplines. (See also Whimbey and Barberena, 1977, on physics skills.)

Biology Skills. The trend toward integrating reading and study skills programs directly into the content of college classes is also represented by studies by Tomlinson and Green (1976) and Tomlinson and others (1974). In these studies, the reading skills students need to understand basic college biology were analyzed. The investigators then offered an adjunct skills course designed to follow the course content and to teach the skills as they were needed. The subjects were volunteers who scored low on the biology midterm examination and enrolled in the adjunct course for the rest of the term, remaining in the biology class as well. The skills taught included surveying, mapping biology concepts, analyzing text material for comprehension, systematic vocabulary study including using context clues and analyzing Latin and Greek roots, understanding graphs and diagrams, and developing self-questioning strategies at the literal, interpretive, and integrative levels. (See Figure 10 for an overview of the skills taught and their relation to the sequence of lessons). The study skills specialists attended the biology lectures and worked closely with the professor. Students taking the experimental adjunct skills course made significant improvement in their biology exams, including the final. They also retained their gains over the next quarter's course in biology, and they persisted in the freshman biology sequence longer than control subjects.

Figure 16. Analysis of the Science Reading Task. Outline of the task analysis done while planning this unit on science reading. Roman numerals represent the lessons in which the basic teaching of the various skills took place.

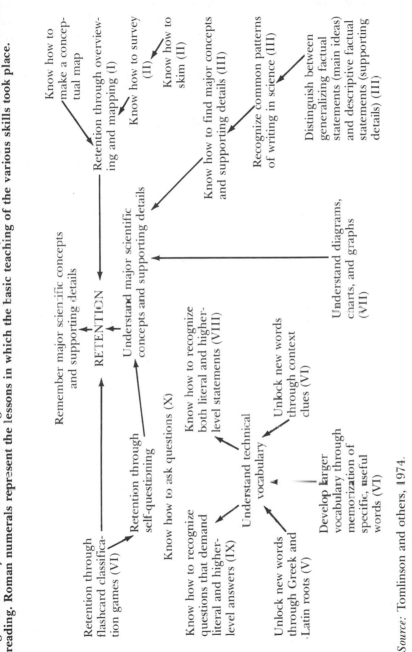

Source: Tomlinson and others, 1974.

It is more effective, particularly for the academically weak student, to teach in adjunct skills courses the skills needed for a particular course or to have the instructor integrate the skills directly into the course than to offer a general "how to study" course, which assumes that students can adapt and transfer to their science classes the skills learned.

Materials for Improving Science Skills

In contrast to the number of publications on improving general college reading and study skills, there are only a few books on how to study science (although many study skills manuals include a chapter on science). Adams' *How to Read the Sciences* (1970) is an excellent source for the average or above-average student; Fisher's *Reading to Understand Sciences: A Program for Self-Instruction* (1970) is more appropriate for the student with weaker skills. Hanau's *Study Game: How to Play and Win with "Statement-Pie"* (1972) is widely used in both undergraduate and graduate health-science programs. Many learning centers are developing their own guides to help students study textbooks, study questions, and other aids for students in science courses. The booklet by Watanabe and Gordon (1977) designed for students in freshman chemistry at Berkeley is one example. (Appendix F reproduces excerpts from this booklet). It contains a do-it-yourself diagnostic test to evaluate a student's readiness for freshman chemistry, suggestions on how to prepare for each lecture, how to listen and take notes, how to read the text, and how to use the laboratory, and a list of places around the campus where students can get additional help. Hubin and Riddell (1977) have written a similar guide to studying physics, excerpted in Appendix G.

Herber's *Teaching Reading in Content Areas* (1978), Chap. 3, is a useful source of information on how to write study guides for science textbooks to include the literal, interpretive, and applied levels of comprehension.

In contrast to the paucity of materials on how to study science, there are a vast number of modules and special programs to help students learn virtually every basic concept in lower-division science courses. These aids come in many forms—programmed learning, tape-and-slide presentations, audiotutorials, videotapes, films, and workbooks—and are written on many levels, from chemistry programs that do not even assume that students know how to divide, such as Kotnik's (1975) materials, to the academically most rigorous.

In selecting supplementary materials, one must consider the level of the course and the background of the students. Science courses vary greatly from institution to institution, although all cover the same general concepts. An aspiring beauty operator enrolled in a community college course to review chemistry in order to pass the state licensing examination in cosmetology is working at a different level than the anxious pre-med in a university chemistry course, although each may find learning chemistry difficult. The audiovisual aids and other materials that are useful for the community college student struggling with chemistry are generally far too simple for the pre-med student. Science courses vary also in the way the topics are sequenced, in their scope and depth, and in their philosophy, these features depending on the professor and the textbook. For example, if Professor Snodgrass does not lecture on Concept A until the fifth week of the term but does introduce Process C in the third week, a videotaped explanation containing both Concept A and Process C may confuse students unless they are alerted to the difference between the tape and the professor's lectures.

So many supplementary materials published for college science courses exist today that selecting those which are most appropriate for students in a given course is a lengthy process. Most colleges currently have media centers or instructional-resource centers to assist teachers in locating, using, and/or developing their own instructional aids. (Peterson, 1975, describes a model for such centers.) The learning-assistance center may also participate in helping instructors select and/or evaluate media and materials, or it may function as a place where students use the aids. If learning-center staff members have the responsibility for purchasing materials in science, they need input from science instructors on which materials to choose.

Educational technology, especially the technology used in self-paced instruction, has been widely accepted and used in community college programs. Many products have been developed and published for the large community college student market, but faculty acceptance of self-paced media programs at four-year colleges and universities has been a great deal slower, and on many campuses there is still considerable resistance to using devices to teach. However, as more materials appear that are suitable for students at four-year colleges and universities, and as learning-resources centers proliferate, acceptance and use of individualized audiovisual materials have increased. This has made it possible for students with nontraditional learning styles to succeed in college science courses, for there are many materials to help students who prefer to listen, view, observe movement, and observe colors in order to learn.

Community colleges have relied on audiovisual self-paced programs to teach underprepared students science concepts as support for traditional lecture-laboratory methods (Most, 1974; Sollimo, 1972; Walter, 1971; Young, 1971). As Kotnik (1972) observes, however, underprepared students are basically conservative people and are not going to use "those newfangled machines" voluntarily. It takes a supersalesman to convince them that they can learn from the machines (and even from the instructor), but once they have had success in learning from machines, they become dedicated supporters.

Audiotutorial Programs. Following the model developed by Postlethwait (1975), many instructors in college biology are using the audiotutorial method to present their course material. In this method, instructors receive scripts to tape-record for their classes to follow while working through the textbook, laboratory manuals, and other exercises. Postlethwait stresses that the tapes are more personalized and acceptable to the students if the instructor makes them than if a professional speaker does. There are a number of other published programs based on this model in chemistry and other science fields; for example, Schmidt and others (1976) have written a complete course called *Hands on Botany.* Although some students can learn more effectively by reading the material, others find that listening to the descriptions of procedures, theories, and facts improves their learning.

Computer-Assisted Instruction. Although there are some excellent science programs written in the CAI format, the computer as an instructional tool is not used as widely as the early enthusiasts predicted. It remains a very expensive way to deliver instructional support services, and the development of appropriate software has not been as rapid as it has in television and tape-recording equipment. Unless a college has a very heavy financial commitment to CAI, strong faculty acceptance, and a large number of students to use the programs, it is hard to demonstrate the cost-effectiveness of CAI in comparison with other ways of teaching. Experimental CAI programs tend to be abandoned as soon as the grant funding that supported them runs out. As a result, it is very hard today to obtain grant funding to install CAI programs.

The best-known and most elaborate college CAI programs are those in the PLATO IV computer system, developed with funding from the National Science Foundation at a cost of $12 million at the University of Illinois (Jenkins, 1976). The acronym PLATO stands for Programmed Logic for Automatic Teaching Operation. The PLATO chemistry programs developed by Stanley Smith of the University of Illinois are ingeniously designed and make learning chemistry exciting and fun. Taught on terminals sensitive to touch, PLATO programs enable students to manipulate the pictures of chemical apparatus on the special screen and simulate experiments using complex equipment by touching the screen. Both lecture and laboratory materials are presented on the CAI terminals, and students spend time working on the computer in addition to attending regular lecture and laboratory sessions.

However, the preliminary evaluation report on the PLATO system (Anastasio, 1972) leaves unanswered many questions about its practicality and effectiveness. Results from a more recent evaluation by the Educational Testing Service (as released to the press) show that students in PLATO chemistry programs had more favorable attitudes toward chemistry but did not learn more than students in traditional chemistry classes. The differences in achievement between the two groups were no greater than those usually found between classes taught by different instructors. Whether elaborate, costly programs like PLATO will continue to attract more colleges into their networks or whether the present financial problems that plague many colleges will mark the demise of the grand CAI programs will be interesting to follow. Meanwhile, microprocessors and minicomputers are becoming less expensive, but at this stage they lack the sophisticated software and the versatility of PLATO.

Computer-Managed Instruction (CMI). Another use for the computer in helping students learn science is CMI, in which the computer keeps a record of the student's progress, test results, and work completed. For instance, Purdue University's Chemistry Resources Center uses CMI to individualize instruction for the more than 5,000 students who enroll in freshman chemistry. After students are tested each week, the computer analyzes their scores and prints a detailed program sheet for each student, delineating the concepts he needs to work on. This gives the tutors and teaching assistants information on which to base their work with the student. With so many students and with a large collection of materials and media for students to use, the center finds that the computer is a necessary tool for arranging for students to find and use the appropriate materials.

Tutoring. Tutoring is probably the most frequently used method for aiding low-achieving students in science courses. When it is offered and is easy to obtain, tutoring attracts large numbers of students. Drop-in tutoring seems to be the most popular arrangement for working with underprepared students, particularly in the physical sciences.

In addition to providing encouragement and support to struggling students, science tutors clarify concepts and problems. Their major function, I believe, is to help students determine which facts and concepts are *not* important to learn in the vast amount of material presented in lectures, laboratories, and textbooks.

If student tutors are carefully selected and well trained, they help underachieving students improve their grades. (See Chapter Four for detailed information on tutor selection and training.) There is evidence that tutoring improves tutors' skills in science as well as tutees' (Drucker, 1976; Hedges and others, 1976).

As in mathematics (Chapter Ten), some combination of tutoring and programmed learning seems the most effective way to aid underachieving students in science.

Tutored Videotaped Instruction. Using tutors to supervise discussion groups who watch videotaped lectures of science and engineering lectures seems to improve student learning. A regular course lecture is videotaped and then replayed (either on the same campus or in a classroom some distance from the campus) for a group of students led by a tutor. The videotaped lecture is stopped when students have questions, which may be as often as every five minutes, and their questions discussed or the lecture information clarified. For example, Gibbons and others (1977) videotaped lectures in an advanced engineering course at Stanford and offered them to small groups both on campus and in an industry some miles away. Tutored videotaped instruction was found to be educationally more effective than regular classroom instruction, especially for marginally qualified students, because it gives them an opportunity to interrupt and ask more questions and, through organized discussion, to find the answers for themselves.

Gibbons and others report that the key factors in the success of tutored videotaped instruction appear to be the attitude, personality, and instructional style of the tutor, the size of the group (fewer than ten is preferable), and the commitments of the students to learn the subject. They advise that unedited tapes of real, unrehearsed lectures (provided, of course, that they are well organized) are more interesting to watch and encourage more active participation from students than tapes of carefully rehearsed, canned lectures.

Tutored videotaped instruction is cheaper than regular instruction, since it uses tutors and does not require additional professors. It allows instruction to take place at students' convenience and is an efficient way to use available resources. Students who require a longer time to assimilate new ideas and information can be accommodated. Furthermore, the technique might be useful in equating the instruction that evening and day students receive.

This study is especially interesting because it was described in the only article on education to appear in the 1977 *Science* magazine issue devoted to applications of electronics to different fields, and the article was the only one that did not mention computers.

Comprehensive Programs. As I have stated in other chapters, the success of an academic support service in aiding underprepared or underachieving students does not depend on the quality of the individual services alone, whether they be outstanding instructional programs, tutoring, counseling, or skills help. What it does depend on is the extent to which the various support programs are well coordinated with one another and with instruction. Science is not an exception. The programs that work best are comprehensive, are coordinated, and involve the student in many services.

Studies on the retention of minority students in engineering, such as the one done by the Retention Task Force of the National Research Council Committee on Minorities in Engineering (Retention Task Force, 1977), have implications for other low-achieving students as well. The Retention Task Force found that between 1973 and 1977, the graduation rate for all students in engineering was 77.8 percent, while for minority students in engineering it was 54.8 percent, and identified the following causes of attrition:

- Insufficient preparation in mathematics and the physical sciences.
- Inadequate motivation toward engineering as a career.
- Lack of adequate financial resources.
- Absence of self-confidence, which is closely tied to poor preparation in math and science.
- Personal or family problems, which often interfere with the academic performance of minority students.
- Excessive occupation with social and nonacademic activities, which demand so much of a student's time that studies are neglected. (However, organizations of minority engineering students appear to affect retention rate positively and offer students an opportunity to gain professional identity and peer support.)

Certain characteristics of engineering programs stimulate higher retention rates among minority students:

- The programs have well-integrated and coordinated components and provide a variety of services to better serve the needs of a diverse student body.
- Although most programs do not change radically from one year to the next, the most successful ones evolve constantly by identifying the successes and failures of previous years and integrating them into future planning.
- Programs operating within the engineering college are generally more effective than university-based programs in providing career guidance, academic counseling, tutoring, and similar services.
- Effective personal counseling is an important component of minority retention programs. The need for such counseling appears to be greater at predominantly white private colleges than at black colleges.
- Tutoring by minority upperclassmen has proved an effective means of encouraging freshmen and sophomores at many colleges.
- Most predominantly black engineering colleges have a critical need for larger staffs. Increasing the number of staff members in administration, tutoring, and counseling almost always improves the quality of the academic services.
- Many colleges in the Southwest need more Hispanic staff and faculty members to serve as role models for their large concentrations of Hispanic students.
- Personal interactions of students with instructors and staff members should be encouraged. The more time that minority students spend with college representatives, and the richer the quality of their interactions, the more successful the students have been in the engineering programs.
- Retention programs should be flexible enough to meet the needs of individual students. The broadly varying needs and abilities of minority engineering students will demand correspondingly varying degrees and forms of assistance.

Among the variables that account for retention and that institutions can control, the Retention Task Force cites the admission criteria and the quality of support services as most important.

If minority students are admitted whose academic preparation is weaker than is typical of the general student body, effective, comprehensive support programs are needed. The number of minority students needed in each entering class to achieve "critical mass" for providing enough intra- and interclass support should be determined. The Retention Task Force report also stresses the importance of demonstrating sincere institutional commitment if retention rates are to be improved. In particular, the faculty should be flexible with regard to course scheduling and placement during the freshman year to allow for the possibility of inadequate academic preparation.

Instructors' overemphasis on theoretical concepts will present "notorious" problems for engineering students and provide added difficulties for unprepared minority students.

A final finding was that a part-time job may adversely affect a student's performance, depending on the student's academic ability and dedication.

Currently throughout the country there are comprehensive programs to encourage and support minority students planning careers in science, mathematics, and engineering. One is Mathematics, Engineering, Science Achievement (MESA), which started in 1970 at the University of California at Berkeley and has expanded to ten universities and thirty California secondary schools. Students selected for MESA must be in the eighth grade or higher and enrolled in college preparatory mathematics (that is, first-year algebra), be members of an underrepresented minority group, and have an interest in exploring careers in mathematics-related fields, such as engineering, physical sciences, and architecture. MESA students must agree to study college preparatory mathematics, science, and English in high school and to maintain a grade-point average above B. MESA students are also required to attend regular meetings of the MESA group, participate in field trips, attend MESA tutoring sessions regularly with the purpose of achieving an A average, and write a resume, updating it each year. In addition to tutoring, the MESA program provides the student with academic counseling, college counseling, scholarship-incentive awards that enable students with high grades in advanced math and science courses to earn scholarship support while in high school, summer enrichment programs, career counseling, field trips to industries, universities, and other agencies that employ engineers and scientists, and summer employment opportunities. The MESA tutors are undergraduates from minority backgrounds, and most are graduates of the high school MESA programs. As they advance educationally to graduate school, they also provide tutoring for MESA undergraduates.

Programs like MESA offer strong social support systems for students from their junior high school years through college, through graduate school, and into their professional careers. At each stage, students become role models and helpers for younger people entering the program. In addition, the students themselves monitor one another's progress as they advance. The various student services are integrated, and the program elicits strong faculty support. For descriptions of other programs of this type, see the articles by Gaonker and others (1977) and Jason and others (1977) on the Acceleration Program in Science and Technology at Southern Illinois University, Edwardsville, and Mullins' description of the Stevens Technical Enrichment Program (1977).

Summary

The intrinsic difficulty of college science courses, which use abstract concepts, unfamiliar symbol systems, and technical vocabulary, poses special problems for the motivated but underprepared college student. The situation is exacerbated by the pace at which these courses are taught, the amount of information covered in traditional semester or quarter courses, and the lecture-laboratory methods used. Currently many colleges are offering supplementary self-paced audiovisual and other programs to help students learn, accompanied by tutoring from carefully selected and trained peers. As is true for other skills, the science skills programs that are most effective are comprehensive, coordinated programs in which tutoring, skills assistance, counseling, and social support groups are integrated into the course instruction.

Conclusion

Accepting Realities and Taking Action

The problems colleges face today in developing and maintaining effective programs for poorly prepared students must be viewed in the context of the changes that are occurring in higher education in this country, the individual institution's standards and goals, the diverse expectations and characteristics of the students themselves, and the attitudes, teaching strategies, and expectations of the faculty. Fiscal realities and the shrinking pool of highly qualified recent high school graduates who choose to attend college are other significant influences on the kinds of programs colleges offer and their effectiveness.

Although the definition of *underprepared* varies with the institution, one fact remains: colleges, whatever their standards, will continue to accept large numbers of poorly prepared students. Colleges today are in transition, faced with rising costs and the specter, if not the reality, of declining enrollments. As a consequence, students who have not been considered college material in the past are now being courted by colleges—working adults, middle-aged housewives, the elderly, the physically handicapped, and the economically disadvantaged. Former college dropouts are also being sought to return and fill college classrooms. Increasing federal and state financial aid programs permit these new kinds of students to pay for higher education. At the same time, the number of well-prepared students (that is, those in the upper quarter of their high school graduating classes) who enroll in four-year colleges continues to decline (Peng, 1977), paralleling the decline in scores on college admissions tests. The high-ability student has more options if he decides to attend college, for over 1,300 institutions of higher education award credit toward graduation for CLEP (College Level Examination Development) test scores. These factors combine to change the basic quality of freshman courses by removing high-ability students from these courses and increasing the number of students with lower ability and weaker skills. The open-admissions policies of the 1960s, based on social and political pressures to provide higher education to students from widely divergent and historically isolated backgrounds, have given way to admissions policies based on economic necessity. Faced with an adverse demographic condition (fewer eighteen-year-olds in the population) and rising costs, many colleges must admit students with lower skills and retain them as students if they are to survive as institutions.

While faculty members complain about the lower skills of entering students and the disintegration of academic standards (blaming the latter on the students), grade inflation continues, confusing able students and robbing lower-ability students of their incentive to learn. The failproof course has improved neither motivation nor learning.

Out of the efforts and experiences of open admissions and programs to help disadvantaged students enter the country's mainstream through attaining college degrees have emerged some principles and programs that suggest effective ways of helping underprepared college students. In addition, the failures of this period suggest paths to be avoided. The heritage of college remedial instruction has been mainly one of failures, and this fact has sustained negative attitudes among faculty members.

Myths That Hamper Remedial Efforts

College skills programs have been hampered by some enduring faculty beliefs that can be termed myths or partial truths. These ideas concern the characteristics of college students and the best types of treatment programs for those with low skills. As myths, they ignore the complexity of the problem, the motivations and expectations of students, and the kinds of resources it takes to improve students' skills. Some examples are these:

"If students have been properly taught and have properly learned the three R's in elementary school, they should need no further help." A corollary belief is that if students have passed freshman composition courses, they should need no additional help in writing, even when they arrive at the doctoral-dissertation stage. This belief ignores the developmental stages that all students must go through as they move up the educational ladder. Skills are not mastered once and for all. Each subject area and each level of college requires somewhat different skills or the refining and polishing of skills already learned. Writing skills, for example, cannot be separated from the topics one writes about. Freshmen should not be expected to write papers on theoretical topics at the same level of sophistication as seniors.

"Underprepared students will learn more if taught in separate classes and removed from the main body of students." The tenacious belief in the superiority of homogeneous grouping seems to affect teachers at every level, but fifty years of research refutes it (Wilson and Schmits, 1978). Ability grouping has consistently been found to reduce the achievement of low-ability students and to impair their motivation and attitudes toward education while inflating the self-esteem of high-ability students. Yet the practice persists. To be sure, at the college level there are limits on the range of skills and abilities that an instructor can teach in one classroom. However, there should be flexibility in placing students, so that those who have mastered the subject matter can move on to advanced courses, for there is nothing more devastating educationally than requiring students who know a subject to repeat it; nor can most students pass an advanced course if they lack the prerequisite knowledge. Therefore, placement in college courses should be based on knowledge of the subject, not on skills. If a student has the knowledge, he can be helped to develop the necessary skills through learning-center services.

"Students who need remedial programs will volunteer for them, and average students will not." College programs find the reverse is true. Those most in need of academic support services will not volunteer; in fact, they will avoid services planned to help them, while students who have stronger skills are often motivated to improve. The academically weakest students need to be identified early and strongly encouraged to use support services.

"Illiteracy is a disease that should be stamped out (or cured)." A corollary is that students who have limited writing and reading skills should be excluded from college. The perception of illiteracy as a pathological condition, rather than the natural state of the uneducated, protects faculty members who prefer to teach students whom they consider their intellectual peers and reject students who need to grow and develop their knowledge.

There are also a number of beliefs about the arrangement of courses and methods for underprepared students that have little basis in fact. For example, the assumption that slow learners learn best in small classes taught with group-discussion methods has not been verified by research. In fact, most studies show that high-ability students profit most from small discussion classes, while low-ability college students achieve better in larger classes taught by a well-organized instructor in an authoritarian manner (Bernstein, 1976).

The belief that slower learners can learn any subject if given enough time, espoused by many progressive educators, may be theoretically valid. But in practice, few students are motivated to continue working indefinitely on a skill or body of information. Most underprepared students expect to be able to keep up with their peers and learn material at approximately the same pace. Rarely are they motivated to work on a course for longer than two terms.

One other pernicious assumption held by some faculty members deserves mention. That is the belief that there is only one way to learn in college—that is, the way I myself learned, by studying alone in my room or the library without help from anyone. In truth there are many ways to learn, and students have been found to have different learning styles and different ways of studying.

Experimental Approaches

Since the early 1960s a number of reforms, alternative teaching methods, and curricular changes have been introduced in American higher education. In a thorough analysis of the changes in more than 400 colleges, Grant and Reisman (1978) concluded that none had found the panacea but that without the experiments, higher education today would not be as varied or as enriching as it is today. However, Grant and Reisman are convinced that loosening the curriculum by letting students take do-as-you-please courses and pick-and-choose programs is a costly indulgence for both faculty and students. The best ideas and practices have spread from the colleges that originated them to other colleges through peripatetic students who tell one another of the best buys in the academic marketplace. The authors criticize competency-based-performance programs and independent study approaches, which they claim offer neither independence nor study.

In their attempts to improve students' skills, colleges have also tried a number of experimental programs over the past two decades. Of these, two approaches are widely accepted today—mastery learning and peer learning.

Mastery Learning. Mastery learning and related individualized methods such as the Keller plan, personalized self-instruction, and computer-assisted instruction have been heralded as the ideal methods for teaching underprepared college students and have been called "the instructional revolution" (Bloom, 1976; Cross, 1976, 1977). Proponents claim that 95 percent of the population can attain high levels of intellectual accomplishment in a mastery learning course if appropriate feedback, sufficient time, and a clear criterion of what constitutes mastery are provided. Yet courses for underprepared students taught with mastery learning methods have yielded more failures than successes, and there is little convincing evidence to support the contention of those experts who travel around the country lecturing that the lecture method should be replaced by individualized instruction at every level and in every college course.

Evaluations of mastery learning programs show that the students who learn well are the same students who succeed in traditional lecture courses—that is, the best-prepared students. Underprepared students often perform poorly in mastery learning courses or drop out. Longitudinal studies of individualized courses have failed to show that any of the innovative, personalized methods is consistently superior to traditional teaching methods. What seems to matter most in improving the learning of underprepared students is the amount of exposure students get to the course material, the amount of time they spend in direct, structured learning situations, and the skills of their teachers.

Mastery learning methods as they are currently offered have not lived up to the expectations of their supporters.

Why have mastery learning programs failed so often with underprepared students? The answer apparently lies in faulty assumptions about the materials used, the learning process, and the characteristics of the learners and in the demands the method places on teachers. If the materials used are merely textbooks repackaged into a mastery learning format and do not recognize the deficits in the students' backgrounds, they place the learner in the same frustrating situation as traditional lecture-textbook courses do. If the materials require students to have good reading and writing skills that they do not in fact have, students find them harder than regular courses, in which one can listen to a lecturer explain information. If the program assumes that students are capable of working alone on the materials with minimal help from the teacher, it will fail, because underprepared students are rarely self-starters capable of sustained independent work.

Immediate knowledge of results, a feature of mastery learning, is purported to enhance learning. This assumption is being questioned by psychologists who in recent studies have found that under some circumstances and with some students, immediate feedback may have negative effects on learning (McKeachie, 1976). For example, low-ability students may not be able to think of alternative ways to solve a problem. If they learn through feedback that their first attempt is wrong, they lose motivation quickly and give up. High-ability students, in contrast, do not need feedback because they usually know whether their answers are correct. Immediate feedback is most effective in facilitating learning for students of average ability who can think of alternative ways to solve a problem and who are uncertain whether their answers are correct.

Ideally, under mastery learning, students work at their own pace and can take as much time as they need to attain mastery. In practice, however, very few students can sustain their motivation to persist in a course that takes them more than a year to complete. Students expect to keep up with their peers, and they judge their own progress in light of that which they observe in others.

Underprepared students may resist self-paced learning because, as traditionalists, they expect to be taught in lecture or discussion sections. Inevitably instructors find that for mastery learning situations to be most effective, teacher-directed activities with the class as a whole must be scheduled regularly or heavy attrition will occur. Individualized programs have often erred in assuming that underprepared students will be self-directed and can learn with minimal teacher involvement. They have underestimated the importance of the teacher and the class on student learning and overestimated the value of the materials.

Students who have succeeded in a mastery learning course may have difficulty in transferring their learning strategies to advanced courses taught by other methods. I have known students who wander from department to department looking for additional mastery courses and who seem unwilling, if not unable, to take courses taught by more traditional methods.

Faculty members in some disciplines, such as philosophy and literacy criticism, find it hard to plan and implement mastery learning courses because the concepts in their fields do not fit easily into the hierarchies assumed by a mastery learning system. Developing a mastery learning course in these subjects requires great effort and ingenuity. Creating and field-testing new materials is costly and time-consuming because it requires that the instructor write (or select) material that is appropriate for the range of learners and for the instructor's course objectives and then test it (or get other instructors to test it) in a large number of classes. My friends who were Keller-plan enthusiasts ten years ago abandoned the plan because they found that individualized instruction takes too much of their time and effort, even when excellent commercially prepared materials are available. Training student proctors (although a personally satisfying experience) constitutes a teaching overload and a drain on their time and energy. My friends also complain that at least 25 percent of the students in each class they taught were not able to handle the self-paced aspect of the course.

I have, however, observed successful mastery learning courses. They are characterized by well-prepared, interesting materials, including both concrete activities and encompassing a variety of formats—that is, readable written exercises at an appropriate level of readability, audiotapes, and visual materials such as television tapes or filmstrips. However, the most important factor is the instructor. Successful programs have dedicated, skilled, dynamic instructors who can give students the emotional support they need as they work through the program, can explain how the concepts they are learning relate to their other course interests, and are efficient managers. Not all teachers have these qualities.

Successful programs also use student tutors or paraprofessional aides who are trained and guided by the instructor. Student tutors or aides can provide the flexible support students need and help them discover alternative ways of learning the material or solving problems. In other words, they can respond to different learning styles more quickly and efficiently than mechanical devices can.

Students complain that courses based solely on educational technology are dull. Technological programs do not work well as complete courses because many students do not complete "do-it-yourself, by-yourself" courses. Self-paced instruction, with its goal of mastery learning, is most effective when it is used as an adjunct to other teaching methods, when there are good instructors and sensitive and competent aides, and when the program is truly individualized—that is, when not all students have to complete all parts.

Peer Learning. Peer learning is the most popular technique for aiding the underprepared student in both skills and subject-matter areas. Sought most often from the array of services provided by learning centers and other support agencies, and rated most helpful by academically weak students, peer learning also includes peer tutoring (and student proctoring, as in personalized self-instruction courses), peer teaching, dyads and self-contained study groups in which students study regularly together, and classroom grouping procedures, such as the parceled-classroom and group-inquiry methods.

In every skills area, peer-learning methods have been reported as successful, though group learning is still frowned upon by the conservative professoriate.

Not only do good peer-tutoring programs improve the achievement of the tutees, but the student tutors improve their understanding and grades. Tutoring-for-credit courses in which tutors are trained in study skills, counseling, and teaching techniques provide an inexpensive way to help students. Studies and reports suggest that students are more comfortable with, and willing to meet with, peer tutors than they are with graduate assistants or instructors. Younger peer tutors can compensate with enthusiasm and patience for what they lack in experience. Research suggests that peer tutoring is most effective when structured materials are available for the tutors to use with students and when tutors are trained and supported as they work with students.

There are caveats to peer-tutoring programs as well as peer-learning approaches. Peer tutors need strong support and the opportunity to talk their problems over with a trainer. Teaching is hard work, and tutoring a student with learning difficulties can be frustrating and discouraging. It takes patience, fortitude, and ingenuity. So tutors themselves need encouragement if they are to be effective with their tutees.

Careful screening and selection of peer tutors is a necessary part of a successful program. The fact that a person has struggled from the ghetto to graduate school does not guarantee that he will be a good tutor.

Using peer-learning methods effectively in a classroom or group situation also requires special skills of the instructor or group leader. Not all the personal characteristics that good group leaders have are teachable, but if an instructor is interested in learning how to work with groups, his skills can be improved.

What Are the Trends?

Since today's trends suggest tomorrow's conventions, a glimpse at present trends may help us understand what lies ahead. Professors at many institutions (including our most prestigious universities) are rediscovering the undergraduate and his problems. Perhaps the reduction of graduate programs in many fields gives the faculty time and opportunity to turn its attention to beginning college students. As a result, selective institutions are reaffirming standards and reintroducing required courses dropped during the permissive 1960s. For example, foreign-language courses are currently reappearing as freshman requirements in liberal arts colleges. Tests that require sophomores and graduating seniors to demonstrate their proficiency in reading, writing, and mathematics are mandated by prestigious colleges that are not presently concerned about declining admissions. Other colleges, which a few years ago admitted anyone, regardless of background, without testing, are now requiring that entering freshmen take tests, hoping that proper placement will help them retain more students.

Universities are reviving articulation programs with high schools in an effort to improve college preparatory courses and ensure better skills preparation of future college students. These programs too were casualties of the 1960s.

Colleges throughout the country are devoting more of their resources and staff time to basic skills courses. There have been significant changes in this area during the past five years. For example, many more full-time faculty members are teaching composition courses—an increase of 39 percent since 1972—and the same pattern holds true for mathematics and reading courses. Higher-education institutions are offering credit for basic skills courses in greater numbers than ever before—even though the credits students earn may not count toward graduation. Credits are offered more as a sop to students (in an effort to encourage them to work harder) than as evidence of greater academic recognition of the value of skills courses.

Along with the increase in basic skills courses, academic support services for students have expanded, especially learning-assistance centers. The recent growth has been greatest in four-year colleges, particularly in private colleges that rarely offered such services before. This growth has been reflected in the fact that large numbers of people are employed in college remedial work today, and job opportunities are good. There are signs that college learning specialists/remedial instructors are beginning to view themselves as professionals in their special functions (rather than as English teachers or mathematicians or general educators). A number of journals devoted to improving college remedial/developmental skills programs have appeared, and professional organizations are being established. However, graduate schools have done very little in developing courses and programs to train college skills specialists.

The role of members of the learning-center staff and their impact on other facets of the academic community seem to be gradually increasing. The input of learning-skills specialists has been ignored in decisions about students, but there are signs that this is beginning to change. Academic departments and individual faculty members are beginning to request that skills experts help them in developing new courses to meet the needs of under-prepared students.

So some efforts are being made to revise courses and cur-riculums to make them more appropriate for college students with limited skills. More needs to be done in this area if students are to be taught effectively. It is important that course revisers avoid the mistakes made by college remedial teachers in the past. That is, the new courses should not be watered-down versions of traditional college courses; rather, they should be shifted to a lower gear. This latter metaphor implies that students who have attained speed in a lower gear can shift to a higher gear (that is, an advanced course), whereas those who consume a watered-down course cannot ad-vance to more-sophisticated courses.

Another trend that reflects progress in teaching under-prepared students is the publication of new textbooks and other materials that are readable and interesting (and even sometimes amusing) but effectively present in a challenging way information and ideas that are academically sound—for example, cartoon presentations of calculus concepts and humorous yet rigorous grammar handbooks.

There are also signs that professors are beginning to accept their new roles and their changing students. Some of the old myths and stereotypes are beginning to break down. However, I doubt that most professors will agree with Bruffee (1978), who writes eloquently of the profound scholarly opportunity that teaching underprepared students provides.

What Needs to Be Done?

Most of the government funding available to higher-education institutions to enable them to accept underprepared students has been directed toward establishing programs that provide academic support services to students. Very little money has been allocated for developing pre-service or in-service training programs for staff members, conducting basic or applied research, or conducting evaluation studies. These, then, represent the greatest needs in the field.

Graduate programs to train college learning-skills specialists, administrators, and remedial instructors are sorely needed. Few universities offer courses, and even fewer offer programs leading to degrees, for those who plan to teach college reading, writing, basic mathematics, or basic science courses. Because most colleges offer basic skills courses, learning-center services, or both, there are many job opportunities for college skills specialists, but there is only a very small pool of trained, qualified, and experienced people to fill these jobs. Without special incentives, including outside funding, graduate schools of education are not likely to start new programs for college skills teachers.

More and better in-service training programs to help those who are presently employed in college skills programs improve their work are also needed. Regional conferences or special institutes are occasionally offered, but these do not begin to serve the needs of the large number of people in this field. Job turnover tends to be high, and as new people enter college skills work from more traditional teaching positions, they create a continuing need for professional training programs.

Research is needed to find the most effective ways to implement academic support programs within different types of institutions. For example, placing learning-skills specialists in academic departments, where they serve as resource persons for other faculty members, seems an excellent way to help the faculty increase its repertory of teaching skills and thus improve its work with underprepared students. Skills specialists can also help the faculty plan more effective courses. In addition, learning-skills specialists are a valuable source of information about students' learning for those who make decisions about academic policies and those who plan curriculums. Since learning-skills specialists are rarely consulted about such decisions, they represent a neglected resource. Investigations of how learning-skills specialists' talents and information might be effectively used in academic decisions and what kinds of decision models might be tried could yield valuable information for the selection and training of skills-staff members.

There is a great need for more basic research to illuminate the processes involved in teaching basic skills in college and the nature of mature learning and thinking. The research funded by the National Institute for Education has been largely limited to elementary school learning. Studies on the basic reading processes of the academically underprepared adult student and the strategies that can be used to help him are rarely done. Nor is there much information on how skills development can enhance reasoning skills.

I hope that in our present desperation to find ways of meeting the needs of all students, we will not forget that a college education should involve more than an accretion of facts and skills force-fed to students in small amounts. A college education is not complete unless students are exposed to great minds and great ideas and have opportunities to test their thoughts in dialogues with those more learned than themselves so that their views can be questioned and expanded. Passively watching John Kenneth Galbraith or Kenneth Clark on television in living color does not fulfill this need unless students have a chance to talk with mentors about the ideas they have heard. There are great minds in every field—auto mechanics as well as physics, cosmetology as well as philosophy.

Last of all, in our efforts to improve instruction and reduce some of the many learning problems that afflict students, we should not forget what I label as Snow's law (1976): "No matter how you try to make an instructional treatment better for someone, you will make it worse for someone else."

Appendix A

Frequently Used Tests

Screening Tests

Wide Range Achievement Test (WRAT). Jastak Assessment Systems, 1526 Gilpin Ave., Wilmington, Del. 19806. Reading (a one-minute test administered individually in which the student reads orally from a word list of increasing difficulty), spelling, arithmetic computation. Two levels: age 5–11; age 12–adult.

Carver R. Reading Progress Scale. Revrac Publications, 10 West Bridlespur Dr., Kansas City, Mo. 64114. A quick eight-minute test for grades 3–16.

Longer Placement Batteries

Adult Basic Education Student Survey. Follett Educational Corp., Chicago, Ill. Reading comprehension, word recognition, arithmetic computation, arithmetic problems.

Adult Basic Learning Examination. Harcourt Brace Jovanovich, Inc. Level 1 (ABLE 1), grades 1–4, reading, vocabulary, spelling,

arithmetic problems; level 2 (ABLE 2), grades 5–8; level 3
(ABLE 3) for adults reading between grades 9 and 12.

Sequential Tests of Educational Progress (STEP). Cooperative
Tests and Services, Educational Testing Service, Princeton, N.J.
Reading, English expression, basic mathematics concepts, science, social studies, grades 13–14.

McGraw-Hill Basic Skills System. California Test Bureau/
McGraw-Hill, Monterey, Calif. Separate tests in reading, study
skills (including use of library), and mathematics, grades 11
through college. Reading subscores include recreational-reading
rate, study-reading rate, flexibility, retention, skimming and
scanning, paragraph comprehension.

Descriptive Tests of Language Skills. The College Entrance
Examination Board, Princeton, N.J. Reading (understanding
main ideas, understanding direct statements, drawing inferences), sentence structure (using complete sentences, using
coordination and subordination, placing modifiers), logical relations (categorizing ideas, using appropriate connectives, making
analogies, recognizing principles of organization), usage (pronouns, modifiers, diction, idioms, verbs), vocabulary. (These are
new tests and norms are being developed.)

Other Reading Tests

Nelson-Denny Reading Test. Houghton Mifflin Co., New York.
Three scores—vocabulary, comprehension, reading rate.

Davis Reading Test. Psychological Corporation, New York. Two
scores—level and rate of comprehension. Series 1, grades
11–13; Series 2, grades 8–11.

California Phonics Survey. California Test Bureau/McGraw-Hill,
Monterey, Calif. A group test to measure phonics adequacy,
grades 7–12 and college (tapes).

Maintaining Reading Efficiency Tests. Developmental Reading Distributors, 1944 Sheridan Ave., Laramie, Wyo. 82070. Three
scores—reading rate, comprehension, efficiency. Five tests—
history of Brazil, Japan, India, New Zealand, and Switzerland.

RBH Scientific Reading Test. Richardson, Bellows, Henry and Co.,
1140 Connecticut Ave., N.W., Washington, D.C. 20036. Measures ability to read and comprehend technical information that

might appear in journals, project proposals, or research, college-adult.

Iowa Silent Reading Tests: 1973 Edition. Harcourt Brace Jovanovich, 757 Third Ave., New York, N.Y. 10017. Level 2, four scores: vocabulary, reading comprehension, directed reading, reading efficiency, grades 9–14. Level 3, three scores: vocabulary, reading comprehension, reading efficiency, grades 11–16.

Diagnostic Reading Tests: Upper Level (Grades 7–College Freshman Year). Committee on Diagnostic Reading Tests, Inc., Mountain Home, North Carolina 28758. Five parts with scores on rate of reading, comprehension (both silent and auditory), vocabulary (in English, mathematics, science, and social studies), four rates of reading, and work-attack skills, grades 7–13.

Reading Versatility Test (Advanced). Educational Developmental Laboratories, Inc., 284 Pulaski Road, Huntington, N.Y. 11743. Scores on reading flexibility, rate, and comprehension on fiction and nonfiction, skimming and scanning, grades 12–16 and adults.

General

Comparative Guidance and Placement Test. Educational Testing Service, Princeton, N.J. Self-scoring.

Diagnostic Tests

Stanford Diagnostic Reading Test. Harcourt Brace Jovanovich, 757 Third Ave., New York, N.Y. 10017. Comprehension, word meaning, word parts, phonetic analysis, structural analysis, rate, Level III, grades 9–13.

Stanford Diagnostic Mathematics Test. Harcourt Brace Jovanovich, 757 Third Ave., New York, N.Y. 10017. Number system and numeration, computation, applications, grades 7.5–13.

Dialect Interference in Writing

The Relevance of Patterns. Westinghouse Learning Corporation, Self-scoring.

Reading and Study Habits and Attitudes

The Reader's Inventory. Educational Developmental Laboratory/

McGraw-Hill, New York. Attitudes toward reading, interests, habits, educational and vocational background, high school and college.

Brown-Holtzman Survey of Study Habits and Attitudes. Psychological Corporation, New York. Scores: delay avoidance, work methods, study habits, teacher approval, education acceptance, study attitudes, study orientation, grades 7–16.

SR/SE. Science Research Associates. Surveys study habits and attitudes, high school and college.

Self-Concept

Tennessee Self-Concept Scale. Counselor Recordings and Tests, Nashville, Tenn.

Anxiety

Suinn, R.M. "The S.T.A.B.S.: A Measure of Test Anxiety for Behavioral Therapy—Normative Data." *Behavior Research and Therapy,* 1969, *7,* 335–339.

Spielberger, C. D., and others. *The State-Trait Anxiety Inventory.* Palo Alto, Calif.: Consulting Psychologists Press, 1970.

Learning Styles

Canfield Learning Styles Inventory. Humanics Media, Liberty Drawer 7970, Ann Arbor, Mich. 48107.

I-S Scale (Impulsivity-Stability). In D. E. P. Smith (Ed.), *Learning to Learn.* New York: Harcourt Brace Jovanovich, 1961.

Critical Thinking

Watson-Glaser Critical Thinking Test Appraisal. Harcourt Brace Jovanovich, 757 Third Ave., New York, N.Y. 10017. Ability and logic in defining a problem, selecting information for solution, recognizing stated and unstated hypotheses, and drawing valid conclusions.

Underachievement Scales

McQuary-Truax Underachievement Scale. In J. P. McQuary and W. E. Truax, "An Underachievement Scale." *Journal of Educational Research,* 1955, *48,* 393–399. There is an abbreviated eleven-item version in Felton, G.S. "A Brief Scale for Assessing Affective Correlates of Academic Low Achievement." *College*

Student Journal, 1973, *7*, 59–63 and also in the Appendix of Felton, G. S., and Biggs, B. E., *Up from Underachievement*. Springfield, Ill.: Thomas, 1977.

Self-Assessment Instruments

Self-Assessment and Course Selection Inventory. Gwen H. Rippey, Austin Community College, Rio Grande Campus, Austin, Texas. A rating scale for students to self-rate their likes, dislikes, abilities, and high school grades in reading, writing, and mathematics. Scores are weighted and converted into probabilities of succeeding in freshman courses.

Sources for Test Reviews and other Tests:

Buros, O. K. (Ed.). *The Seventh Mental Measurements Yearbook*. Highland Park, N.J.: Gryphon Press, 1972.

Buros, O. K. (Ed.). *Tests in Print II*. Highland Park, N.J.: Gryphon Press, 1974.

Buros, O. K. (Ed.). *Reading Tests and Reviews II*. Highland Park, N.J.: Gryphon Press, 1975.

Gyrafas, E. (Ed.). *Reading Tests: Grades 7–16 and Adults, ETS Test Collection*. Princeton, N.J.: Educational Testing Service, 1975. (An annotated bibliography.)

Appendix B

Job Classifications for Learning Skills Counselors

Learning-skills counselors offer learning-skills assistance to students to enable them to become independent, self-confident, and efficient learners and perform other related duties as required.

Incumbents in this series have the responsibility for aiding students in the development and maintenance of such varied learning skills as reading, writing, study, and test-taking techniques. Incumbents in these positions should possess a broad knowledge of what constitutes competent and creative skill usage at various academic levels and must be proficient at guiding students of di-

Note: This material adapted from the *Staff Personnel Manual*, Univeristy of California, August 1976.

verse educational backgrounds to levels of skill development consistent with university-level standards of satisfactory performance.

Incumbents typically interview individual students, diagnose their respective learning problems, devise methods to solve those problems, and aid students during the process of solution; plan and conduct learning-skills group workshops; develop, test, and evaluate new materials, approaches, and programs; identify research problems and/or develop research proposals of a programmatic, evaluative, or institutional nature; maintain liaison with other campus units and academic departments; develop, plan, and/or conduct appropriate outreach activities; and may participate in the selection and training of learning-skills assistants.

Positions in this series are distinguished from positions in the counseling services series in that they do not normally offer vocational and psychological consultation. They are distinguished from positions in the advising services series in that the primary responsibility of learning-skills counselors is to assist students in the development and maintenance of a variety of learning skills.

Learning Skills Counselor Series

The distinction between the four levels of the Learning-skills-counselor series are based on the scope and complexity of learning-skills functions and the degree of supervision exercised.

Principal Learning-Skills Counselor. Under general direction incumbents are assigned responsibility for developing and directing programs and activities in the area of student learning-skills assistance which are campuswide in scope and impact. Incumbents typically establish administrative and professional policies, procedures, and standards for a learning-skills-assistance unit; interview and select prospective employees; assign and coordinate staff workloads; supervise and evaluate the performance of lower-level learning-skills counselors and/or learning-skills assistants; coordinate in-service professional staff training programs; and are assigned responsibility for the development and administration of the department's annual budget.

Incumbents may develop and evaluate new materials, approaches, and programs; may identify research problems and develop research proposals; and may establish and maintain appropriate liaison with other departments and outreach activities.

Senior Learning-Skills Counselor. Under direction incumbents assist in the development and direction of programs and activities in the area of student learning-skills assistance which are campuswide in scope and impact. Incumbents may act as principal assistants to higher-level learning-skills counselors typically with limited authority to develop and direct a campuswide program and in addition may provide individual and/or group assistance to undergraduate and graduate students with difficult learning problems. Incumbents typically assist in the development of new materials and programs; design and conduct appropriate liaison and outreach activities; may be assigned continuing responsibility for coordinating programs; and may select, train, and supervise lower-level learning-skills counselors and/or learning-skills assistants.

Learning-Skills Counselor. Under general supervision incumbents perform difficult professional work in providing individual and/or group assistance to undergraduate and graduate students with learning problems. Incumbents typically conduct appropriate liaison and outreach activities; may assist in the development of new materials and programs; and may assist in the training of lower-level learning-skills counselors and/or learning-skills assistants. Incumbents may in addition perform the range of duties outlined in the [second and third preceding paragraphs].

Assistant Learning-Skills Counselor. Under supervision incumbents provide individual and/or group assistance to undergraduate students within limited areas of learning problems. Incumbents perform the majority of duties described in the [second and third preceding paragraphs] typically within established procedural guidelines. This is the entry level in the professional series; however, positions may be assigned to this level on a continuing basis.

Minimum Qualifications

Principal Learning-Skills Counselor. Graduation from college with major work in a related field and six years of related experience in a college-level student support service, preferably in a learning-skills service, or an equivalent combination of education and experience; and knowledges and abilities essential to the successful performance of the duties assigned to the position.

Senior Learning-Skills Counselor. Graduation from college with major work in a related field and four years of related experience in a college-level student support service, preferably in a learning-skills service, or an equivalent combination of education and experience; and knowledges and abilities essential to the successful performance of the duties assigned to the position.

Learning-Skills Counselor. Graduation from college with major work in a related field and two years of related experience in a college-level student support service, preferably in a learning-skills service, or an equivalent combination of education and experience; and knowledges and abilities essential to the successful performance of the duties assigned to the position.

Assistant Learning-Skills Counselor. Graduation from college with major work in a related field or an equivalent combination of education and experience; and knowledges and abilities essential to the successful performance of the duties assigned to the position.

Note: A master's degree in a related field may be substituted for one year of the required experience.

Position	Monthly Salary Ranges, 1977–78
Principal Learning-Skills Counselor	$1,607–1,938
Senior Learning-Skills Counselor	1,336–1,607
Learning-Skills Counselor	1,111–1,336
Assistant Learning-Skills Counselor	969–1,161

Appendix C

Difficult Tutoring Situations

The interpersonal dimension of the tutoring process is as important as the tutor's subject competence. And while *most* tutorial sessions offer no significant interpersonal problems, the difficult, ineffective encounter is always possible. The following discussions might be of help if such an encounter should occur.

Dysfunctional Tutee Styles

The majority of contacts between a tutor and a tutee go rather smoothly—both parties honestly and effectively engaging in the learning process. However, there are some tutorial encounters that do not go smoothly because of a disruptive affect or attitude presented by the tutee. Indeed, the student may even assume an

Note: The material reprinted by permission of Mike Rose (1976), tutor coordinator, University of California, Los Angeles.

entire "style" in relating to the tutor. The following taxonomy offers seven such disruptive styles, common identifying characteristics, and suggested approaches to aid in establishing an effective learning relationship.

Two cautions:

1. Do not see these as mutually exclusive or as rigid postures evident from the first day. Under the various pressures of the quarter, a previously efficient student may drift into or assume one or more of these styles. The suggested approaches, however, would remain the same, with the additional suggestion of appealing to history—for example, "Well, three weeks ago, this was going fairly smoothly. Let's figure out when it was that things got confusing."

2. Though much of what a tutor does involves academic "counseling" (for example, tips on classes, study suggestions, warnings about specific professors), a tutor *should not* slip into the role of psychological counselor. With this in mind, the following taxonomy is to be used to *establish an effective learning relationship,* a relationship that allows a tutee to grow intellectually and allows a tutor to avoid frustration and grow as a learning facilitator. The tutor would be extremely cautious about probing into any issues that seem to be highly emotionally charged, deeply defended, or significantly volatile. Doing this can either trigger disruptive emotional material or foster an inappropriate dependency, or both. If you have reason to suspect that your tutee is experiencing emotional difficulties, please consult with the tutorial coordinator and the tutee's AAP counselor.

Style	*Characterized by*	*Approach*
1. Blocking	• low frustration tolerance • immobilization/hopelessness • freezing up/blocking • "It's beyond me" • "I'll never get it" • "I'm stuck"	• determine what the tutee *does* know and discuss that—show him that he has some foundation • begin from what he knows and build, in simple steps, toward increasingly complex material • offer continual support • reinforce success consistently

Style	Characterized by	Approach
2. Confusion (a variation of blocking)	• bafflement/disorientation/disorganization • helpless feeling about the class • "I just don't know what to do" • "I don't know what the prof wants" • "I studied for the test and got a D" • "I'm not sure where we're going"	• utilize the above four approaches • give *structure* and *order* to the tutee's tutorial sessions, to his notes, to papers
3. Miracle Seeking	• global interest or concern but with little specificity • enthusiasm about being with tutor, but fairly passive in actual tutoring process • high (often inappropriate) level of expectation • evasion or inability to concentrate on concrete tasks	• downplay your role (for example, "Look, I've simply had more exposure to this stuff, that's all") • *focus* again and again to specific task • involve student continually with questions, problems • explain significance of *active* participation in learning process
4. Overenthusiasm (somewhat a variation of Miracle Seeking)	• high expectations/demands of self • talk of limited time, long-range goals versus immediate tasks • global interest/enthusiasm • often found with older students (for example, "Look I'm thirty years old; I don't have the time these kids have")	• explain *counterproductive* nature of this eagerness • be understanding, yet assure the student that he has time • utilize numbers 2, 3, and 4 under Miracle Seeking as listed above
5. Resisting	• variations of sullenness/hostility/passivity/boredom • disinterest in class/work/tutor *or* • defensive posture to-	• allow student to ventilate • spend first session—possibly even second—on building relationship

Style	*Characterized by*	*Approach*
	ward class/work/tutor • easily triggered anger	• be pragmatic, yet understanding (for example, "Look, I know this class is a bore, but you need it to graduate—let's make the best of it") • as opposed to 1 under Miracle Seeking, establish your credibility/indicate past successes in similar situations • if it comes up, assure student that his complaints about a class are confidential
6. Passivity (often a variant of Resisting)	• noninvolvement/inattention/low affect • boredom • little discussion initiated/few questions	• empathize (for example, "You're not crazy about asking a lot of questions in class, are you?" or "It's pretty much of a drag to sit here, isn't it?") • attempt to build a relationship and mobilize the student • utilize as many mobilizing techniques as possible—questions, problems, minitasks to be accomplished by next session (even checking a book out of the library) • reinforce all activities and successes
7. Evasion	• manipulation • verbal ability/glibness versus focused writing or problem-solving skills • global/nonspecific praise of tutor's skill, course content, and so on.	• as with 2 under Miracle Seeking, downplay your role • *focus* the student on specific tasks; *involve* him continually with questions, problems

Style	Characterized by	Approach
		• if evasion continues, you should ask, in a nonthreatening way, why the student has come for tutoring and what he expects from you (for example, "You know, we've met several times already, but we haven't gotten much done—what do you think we should plan for future sessions?" *or* "My biggest concern is your success in this class; how, specifically, can I help you with that?")

Difficulties with an Older Student

Some tutoring considerations derived from a case study: Susan Williams is thirty-seven years old. Except for a few scattered adult school or junior college classes, she hasn't been in school for over fifteen years. Two years ago she divorced her husband and, as part of her movement toward autonomy, began a curriculum at a community college; now she is in her second quarter at UCLA: a junior sociology major. Her tutor is Betty, a twenty-one-year-old senior who is bright, enthusiastic, and very friendly. In almost a year of tutoring, Betty has had nothing but positive experiences.

After four sessions with Susan, however, Betty reported that she was unhappy about her work with this student; she wasn't sure about the roots of her disappointment, but she did say: "We get off the track; there's some material that doesn't get covered." Several consultations later, the following picture emerged:

Susan was:	*Betty would:*
(1) given to mood swings— one session she would appear	Go with the mood. She had good sessions when Susan was

Susan was:	*Betty would:*
collected and fairly calm, another session she would be confused, pushy, irritated, and irritating.	composed, but when Susan was scattered and aggressive, the sessions would quickly lose direction. Betty felt "time was wasted."
(2) given to talking—in her anxious times more than others—about tangential, even unrelated, topics. Often these topics were related to life experiences that her years had afforded her.	Betty, having learned that a "good teacher" should give a student "freedom to be and explore," was reluctant to pull Susan back to the specific subject. Betty also "felt my youth" here versus the "experience" of Susan.
(3) at times extremely friendly, almost motherly. (She even called Betty several times "just to talk.") This would sharply contrast with the pushy, abrasive side of her personality.	feel quite good about the warmth and feel hurt by the abrasiveness.
(4) given to requesting a change in the topic Betty had planned to discuss in a session. Something else, in Susan's eyes, seemed to be more important or, at least, more interesting.	feel frustrated ("wasting time") about the request, but did want to keep Susan interested in the material, and, also, accepted the idea that learning should be "student centered."

By the fifth week, Betty was angry, frustrated, and felt manipulated. To make matters worse, Susan got a D on the midterm. Going back to the above (admittedly simplified) representation of their relationship, the causes of ill feelings and poor grades are obvious:

• Susan was anxious and unsure at UCLA and a bit troubled, perhaps, in other areas of her life. She would bring *both* her needing and her abrasive side to the sessions.

- Furthermore, she not only felt insecure about the material but probably felt a loss of esteem since the "expert" was young enough to be her daughter.
- Finally, she was a classic avoider and manipulator—dodging the challenge of the material by raising more secure interests from her own life and defending against the humiliation of having a young tutor by making a little girl of Betty.

Simply stated, Susan was a troublesome tutee even for the experienced Betty; Betty obviously needed some advice. After the consultations, Betty was able to conduct effective sessions and feel rewarded. The best news, however, was that Susan got a B on the final exam.

What happened?

What Betty came to understand was:

That tutoring is not the same as a peer relationship (though many new tutors find this hard to admit). Therefore, though in many areas of life experience Susan *was* more knowledgeable than Betty, when it came to academic sociology Betty *did* know what was best and, therefore, should guide the direction of the sessions. (The same point could be made here substituting a father, a veteran, an ex-convict, an athlete, and so on, in place of Susan.)

That a helping relationship like tutoring exposes one to the disparate but strangely connected possibilities of dependency or inappropriate hostility. If you (like Betty) feel that a student is getting a little too needy or, on the other hand, is treating you harshly, you should consult with your supervising tutor or the center coordinator to get another perspective on the situation. Are you inviting dependency? (I suspect, for example, that Betty occasionally liked being Susan's "daughter.") Do you know how to gently but firmly put limits on your time and energy? (It's surprising how often we will *not* say no when we really should—dependency results on one end and anger results on ours.) Conversely, are *you* too harsh because a student reminds you of someone else or "is not your kind of person?"

That anxiety can express itself through a variety of behaviors, not just "the jitters." Confusion, digressing, abrasiveness can all indicate that a student hasn't prepared, doesn't understand the material, is apprehensive about an exam, etc. If you suspect that this is the case, gently raise the possibility: for example—"I wonder if that test next week has got you jumpy." "Maybe not getting that material read last night has thrown you today." Once the basis of the anxiety is uncovered and briefly discussed, you can get down to some productive work.

That very valuable processes like student-centered learning, inquiry learning, "education for relevance," etc., should not be confused with the tangential, avoidance-laden reminiscences and curiosities of a student like Susan. This is definitely not to say that Susan couldn't profit from relevant discovery and self-directed inquiry in an unlimited variety of educational situations. But in the encounters with Betty, the digressions *always* seemed to occur when Susan was confused about specific material; furthermore, they occurred continually. This should be sufficient indication that the student is avoiding, and therefore, the tutor should gently but assertively refocus the discussion, consistently backtracking to known material to engender security, then moving progressively ahead into the troublesome areas. Yes, the student might get angry, but face the anger and be honest. Say: "This is important material that I'm sure will appear on a test. I realize it's difficult, but if we take it slowly, we can master it. Understand, I'm going to keep us on this stuff until you get it. And you *can* get it."

Admittedly, the interaction between Susan and Betty was not representative of most tutorial encounters. Yet our examination brought into focus some considerations that are critical in any tutoring contact, issues of role—definition, dependence, guidance, and assertiveness. And these issues, as you saw, are as important as one's knowledge of the material being tutored.

The Student Who Glides into Failure

Some implications from a pilot study (with thanks to Phil Volland for doing the research described [next]): We are all familiar with the student who is anxious, irritable, and on edge because he is doing poorly in school. A lot more puzzling, however, is the student who seems calm, in control, even confident and yet ends up on probation. In some cases, he may flunk out of the university. This kind of student is especially problematic for the tutor who must monitor progress and who must often do so through the verbal reports of the tutee.

Recent preliminary research conducted by the AAP tutorial center adds another dimension to this puzzle. Brief reports received through a series of telephone interviews indicate that students with a GPA below 2.3 often explain away their need of tutorial support with the same reasons offered by students with GPAs of 3.5 and above. To put it simply, many students with low GPAs say that tutorial support "seems unnecessary," "can't be fit into a busy schedule," "isn't needed yet," etc. These comments are not unlike those offered by high achievers and if taken at face value can be enough to mislead or at least confuse a tutor. . . . Many new tutors often will agree to skip an appointment, abbreviate a session, or skim material because of the apparent self-confidence of a tutee. Inevitably, however, harsh reality comes crashing down in the form of a D or an F on a quiz, test, or paper. Yet it is still not uncommon for this type of student to quickly regain composure, after the initial shock, and continue to "assure" himself and the tutor.

What's Going On Here? Well, one possibility is that the student simply has a very poor ability to assess his own skills and the requirements of the university. Another, perhaps more likely, explanation is that the student is quite aware, on some level, that he is in serious difficulty. . . . His entire perception of his intelligence might be very bleak. Underneath the patina of assurance and self-reliance (superficially like that of the successful student) might well be a kind of despair. His defense, to self and others, becomes a variation of denial, a whistling by the academic graveyard.

What to do? Whether we're dealing here with poor self-assessment or with elaborate defensiveness, it's not a tutor's job to probe psychologically. The roots of inadequate self-assessment might go quite deep, and as for defenses, it takes a great deal of skill and time to alter them. However, a combination of reality, focusing, and assertiveness could be of great—and unthreatening—assistance:

1. First of all, you should never take a student's word on

progress for more than several sessions. Quiz informally, ask to see exam results, confer with TAs or instructors.

2. If your evidence indicates that the student is doing poorly but he denies it in some way, gently but firmly raise the facts to him. For example: "Well, this D doesn't seem to go along with what you're telling me. How would you explain it?" "You know, I've tutored a lot of people in French, and the ones who are where you're at now usually don't do well on the midterm. What can we do?" "Gee, you're pretty confident, yet you've got all this to read and the exam is only three days away. How are you going to swing it?"

3. Raise what may well be the misconception at the base of the student's denial, but do it cautiously and indirectly. For example, "You know, it's clear to me that you're good at working equations, but word problems seem to throw you." "I've worked with lots of people who think they're just terrible at understanding literature, yet usually it's just a few authors that give them trouble." "It amazes me how folks seem to think that because they can't read music, they'll have an impossible time with ethnomusicology."

What these kinds of questions hopefully tap safely into is the student's global attitude toward his own intelligence. Rather than being able to focus on single difficulties, many students quickly generalize about their overall abilities. (That is: "I'm not just unskilled in mathematics; I'm unskilled period.") Sometimes this is deeply rooted. *Focus on specifics; guide the student into seeing what he does and doesn't know.* This kind of reality testing might be the first step in his moving away from discouragement and toward a realistic understanding of his strengths and weaknesses.

4. Though I've stressed being gentle when dealing with the psychological side of all this, the tutor should be fairly assertive when it comes to scheduling tasks, receiving assignments, etc. *Don't get caught up in the student's cavalier front.* Set firm schedules; keep focused on tasks; show the student how to *study ahead*; review material *with* him. You need to become very directive, even to the point of sitting alongside him and guiding his study. For example, "I know this is a drag, but I want us to work one more hour. It's no fun, but it's absolutely necessary if you're going to make it through this course."

Babysitting? Yes, to a degree. But the hope is that all the avoidance and denial is rooted in insecurity and that insecurity can be slowly remedied through mastery. As the student begins to see that he can understand material, he should become at least a little more curious and self-directing. Then you can begin to slowly decrease the intensity of your guidance. A truer, more lasting assurance will have been generated.

Appendix D

===

Sources of Information for Developmental Skills Specialists

===

Journals of General Interest

Journal of Personalized Instruction

A quarterly featuring research reports, articles, and book reviews in the field of individualized instruction. Address: 29 Loyola Hall, Georgetown University, Washington, D.C. 20057.

Community College Frontiers

Articles of special concern to community college instructors and developmental teachers. Editor: Richard Johnston, Sangamon State University, Springfield, Ill. 62708.

Journal of Developmental Education

A new quarterly edited by Milton G. Spann, Center for Developmental Education, Appalachian State University, Boone, N.C. 28608.

Journal of the Society of Ethnic and Special Studies

An annual published in January. The first issue, January 1977, concerned the problems of minorities in the sciences and contained some excellent surveys, program descriptions, and strategies for recruiting and teaching misprepared students in engineering and other science fields.

WCRA Insights

An occasional journal to be published by the Western College Reading Association. The first issue focused on the topic "What Constitutes College-Level Learning?" Editor: Randy Silverston, Center for Skills and Assessment, California State University at Dominguez Hills, Carson, Calif. 90747.

Change Magazine

Publishes general articles on higher education and occasionally (three or four times a year) produces a separate issue, *Report on Teaching*, on new instructional processes. So far, innovations in twelve disciplines have been covered. Address: NBW Tower, New Rochelle, New York, 10801.

Newsletters

Writing Lab. Newsletter

Editor: Muriel Harris. Address: Department of English, Purdue University, West Lafayette, Ind. 47907. This publication contains current information on teaching strategies and other topics of interest to those interested in improving student writing.

Networks

Editor: Virgil Logan. Address: Gould Memorial Library, Bronx Community College, 181st St. and University Ave., Bronx, N.Y. 10453. This is a FIPSE-funded project with the goal of stimulating the development of effective programs for underprepared college students through exchange of information, a national conference, and the development of regional workshops.

National Association for Remedial/Developmental Studies in Post-Secondary Education Newsletter
        Address: Chicago State University, Room E-210, Ninety-fifth St. at King Drive, Chicago, Ill. 60628.

Tutor Talk
        A monthly newsletter with tips about tutoring, published by the National Association of Tutorial Services, Post Office Box 160, Forestville, Calif. 95436. (Formerly called *About Tutoring*.)

Yearbooks and Conference Proceedings

College Reading Association. William Gage, Rochester Institute of Technology, One Lomb Memorial Drive, Rochester, N.Y. 14623.

National Reading Conference. Gordon Gray, 217 Godfrey, Clemson University, Clemson, S.C. 29631.

Western College Reading Association. Seymour Prog, Rio Hondo College, Whittier, Calif. 90608.

Proceedings of the Final Conference of National Project II and the *Final Report of National Project II (Alternatives to the Revolving Door)*. Fran Resto, Networks, Gould Memorial Library, Bronx Community College, 181st Street and University Ave., Bronx, N.Y. 10453.

Yearbook of the North Central Reading Association. Published biannually. Dr. David Wark, Student Counseling Center, University of Minnesota, 190 Coffrey Hall, St. Paul, Minn. 55108.

Reading

Journal of Reading
        Monthly journal of the International Reading Association. Articles on high school and college reading practices, programs, and issues. Address: 800 Barksdale Road, Newark, Del. 19711.

Reading World
        A quarterly journal of general interest to college/adult reading specialists, published by the College Reading Association. For

information, address William Gage, Rochester Institute of Technology, One Lomb Memorial Drive, Rochester, N.Y. 14623.

Reading Improvement
A quarterly journal devoted to the teaching of reading. Short articles for the classroom teacher in high school or college reading. Address: Project Innovation, Chula Vista, Calif. 92010.

Writing

Journal of Basic Writing
A new journal with articles concerning problems and techniques for teaching college remedial writing to adult nonwriters and those for whom English is a second language. Published by the Department of English, City College of New York, 138th St. and Convent Ave., New York, N.Y. 10031. Editor: Sally Heaphy.

College English and *College Composition and Communication*
The National Council of Teachers of English publishes these journals plus a number of monographs of interest to college developmental writing specialists. Address: 1111 Kenyon Road, Urbana, Ill. 61801.

Counseling

Journal of College Student Personnel
The American Personnel and Guidance Association/ American College Personnel Association has a task force on learning centers. Address: American Personnel and Guidance Association, 1607 New Hampshire Ave., N.W., Washington, D.C. 20009.

Learning Disabilities

Academic Therapy Quarterly
Published by the DeWitt Reading Clinic, 1543 Fifth Ave., San Rafael, Calif. 94901.

English as a Second Language

The Center for Applied Linguistics, 1611 Kent St., Arlington, Va. 22209, publishes a *Selected List of Materials for Teachers of English as a Second Language* and the *Linguistic Reporter: A Newsletter in Applied Linguistics.*

Appendix E

=====================================

Points of
Interference
in Learning English
as a Second Language

=====================================

Tone

Spanish: In both English and Spanish there are four tone levels, but Spanish speakers use only the three lower-pitch tones, except when they express extreme anger or alarm. Then the fourth, upper-pitch tone is used.

Note: This material is adapted from California State Board of Education (1973), Johnson (1975), Labov (1972), Tucker (1969).

Stress

Spanish: Most Spanish words are stressed on the last or next-to-last syllable; most English words are stressed on the first or second syllable. In English a word may have two or three stresses; Spanish generally uses only one stress except for a few adverbs.

Pronunciation

Asian Languages: Chinese use a tone system for distinguishing word meanings. Words having the same pronunciation may have four or more different tones to represent different meanings. These meanings would be represented by four written forms.

Black Dialect: In words where /r/ and /l/ appear in medial or final position, dialect speakers often drop these sounds.

Dialect speakers often change the pronunciation of English words with a medial or final *th,* saying "wit" or "wif" for "with" and "muver" for "mother."

Vowels

Spanish: Spanish does not have short vowel sounds for *a, i, o,* and *u,* as English does, although there are five vowel sounds in Spanish with corresponding sounds in English: *a* as in *father, e* as in *step, i* as in *machine, o* as in *over,* and *u* as in *ooze.*

Consonants

Spanish: Consonant sounds *v, b, d, t, g, h, j, l, r, w, v,* and *z* are not the same in Spanish as in English, and students must be taught the point of articulation to produce these sounds in order to become aware of the differences.

Asian Languages: The schwa sound that is used in English does not exist in Chinese, Japanese, or Korean. Chinese speakers usually cannot distinguish the English sounds /v/ and /b/ or /l/ and /r/.

Cantonese speakers use /l/ and /n/ interchangeably.

Consonant Clusters

Spanish: Spanish words never begin with the following consonant clusters: *sp*eak, *st*ay, *sc*are, *sc*hool, *st*reet, *sp*ring, *scr*atch, *sph*ere, *sl*ow, *sm*all, *sv*elte. Spanish speakers will add an initial vowel when pronouncing such words: *e*street, *e*speak. Spanish speakers often have problems with the 371 consonant-cluster endings used in English.

Spanish speakers are often confused by the use of English *s* endings to indicate a plural noun but a singular verb.

There is a strong carryover from the Spanish /ch/ to the English /sh/, and the student may say "share" for "chair" and "shoes" for "choose."

The /b/ and /v/ sounds in Spanish are exactly alike phonetically in that each has two sounds. Which sound is used is determined by the surrounding sounds.

Asian Languages: Cantonese has no consonant clusters, and as a result Cantonese speakers usually hear and pronounce just one of the sounds in an English cluster. Since there are so many consonant clusters in English, this creates severe problems. Many English clusters are formed or augmented by important syntactical elements, as in the expression *What's this?* The addition of /'s/ forms a cluster that gives an important clue to the meaning of the sentence, but the Cantonese student can neither hear nor say it.

Explicit plural markers are not used in Chinese or Japanese. The spoken language does not contain the sibilant /s/ sound. Plurals are formed by placing auxiliaries before the noun. An example (translated literally into English) is *"three* boy."

Black Dialect: When two or more consonant sounds appear at the end of words, they tend to be reduced by dialect speakers: /tes/ for "test" and /des/ for "desk." This reduction in consonant clusters affects words ending in /s/, third-person singular forms, and possessives.

Word Endings

Spanish: Spanish words can end in any of the five vowels (*a, e, i, o,* or *u*) or any of the following consonants: /l/, /d/, /r/, /z/, /j/, /y/, /n/, or /s/. Spanish speakers often have difficulty with words ending in /m/, /p/, /k/, /c/, /b/, /d/, /f/, /g/, /l/, /y/, /v/, and /x/ (when voiced as /z/.)

Asian Languages: Chinese, Japanese, and Korean speakers tend to drop, glottalize, or add a vowel to the English word endings /t/, /d/, /s/, /l/, /p/, /b/, /k/, /f/, /g/, /r/, and /v/. For instance, they may pronounce "college" as "collegi" and "church" as "churchi."

Grammar

Verbs

Spanish: Spanish speakers often have problems distinguishing between the uses of the simple past ("he worked") and present perfect ("he has worked") because the rules for their use are different in Spanish. Spanish speakers are also confused by the double meaning of the *-ed* ending, which is in part comparable to the Spanish *-ado,* which signifies the past participle, and in part comparable to the endings for the simple past.

Asian Languages: The Chinese verb has only one form and is not conjugated to indicate tense. Tenses are formed by placing auxiliaries before or after the stable verb form.

Black Dialect: The use of the verb *to be* is different in black dialect. Often it will be absent in situations in which a contraction is used in standard English, especially in the present tense. For example, dialect speakers say "I here" and "We going."

Dialect speakers drop the *-ed* endings on the past tense in both speech and writing.

Negative

Black Dialect: The use of more than one negative form is acceptable in black dialect sentences like "I don't take no stuff from nobody."

Word Order

Spanish: Spanish speakers need to cultivate the idea that English relies heavily on word order to indicate grammatical relations where Spanish relies on morphological change. Word order is sometimes flexible in Spanish, but never in English. This difference leads to confusion when Spanish speakers translate direct and indirect questions literally. For example, the question "What are you doing?" may be stated in Spanish as "I do not know what you are doing." The distinction in Spanish lies in the form of "what"—/que/versus /lo que/, in this example, rather than word order.

In Spanish the adjective usually follows the noun and must agree with it in gender and number. In English the adjective usually precedes the noun.

In Spanish the adverb usually follows the verb, rather than following the direct object—for example, *Yo vi inmediatamente . . .* ("I immediately saw . . .").

Asian Languages: Chinese do not manipulate word order to change meaning. For example, it is impossible in Chinese to reposition *is* to convert a statement to a question, as in "He is a teacher" and "Is he a teacher?"

Articles

Spanish: In Spanish, articles are placed in some positions where English does not require them—for example, *Veo al doctor Brown* ("I see *the* Doctor Brown").

Asian Languages: The article *a* is used in Chinese for a very specific reason, as a unit of measure rather than a general article as in English. Korean and Japanese use only function words or function particles that follow content words, unlike English, which uses a combination of function words (articles and auxiliary verbs) as well as word endings to show grammatical distinctions.

Comparative and Superlative

Spanish: Spanish speakers tend to express comparative and superlative by using *more* and *most* where English uses *-er* and *-est;*

thus expressions like "He is more big" or "He is the most tall student" reflect Spanish structure.

Pronouns

Asian Languages: In both Mandarin and Cantonese, a single sound represents the pronouns *he* and *she*; however, the written forms for these and the other third-person singular forms are very distinct. Often Chinese students use the spoken "he" for both "he" and "she."

It-There

Spanish: In Spanish one word (*es*) is used for *it is, there is,* and *there are.*

Asian Languages: Words like *there* and *it* in expressions like "It is cold" and "There are many clouds" do not exist.

Black Dialect: Dialect speakers use *it* for *there.* For example, instead of "There's a rug on the floor," they say, "It's a rug on the floor."

Spelling

Spanish: Although both Spanish and English have words of Latin origin, Spanish spelling does not use the following doubled or combined consonants: /bb/, /dd/, /ff/, /gg/, /mm/, /pp/, /ss/, /th/, /zz/, /gh/, /ph/, or /hn/. As a result, English spelling patterns using these forms are confusing for the Spanish speaker.

There are similar words in Spanish and English which create false analogies and confusion. For example, *lectura* means "reading," while the Spanish equivalent of *lecture* is *conferencia*.

Asian Languages: Dictionary skills must be taught Asian students, for the Chinese dictionary does not list words in alphabetical order, but by the traditional word-radical groups and the number of strokes each character has. Both Japanese and Korean share the Chinese ideographic writing system, but Japanese uses a supplementary syllabic system and Korean uses a supplementary alphabetic system.

Black Dialect: Dialect speakers have difficulty spelling word endings and vowel sounds in syllables they do not pronounce or hear.

Dialect speakers attach meanings to words that are different from the meanings in standard English and are based on different experiences. For example, the words *bad* and *poor* may be used to mean "good."

Appendix F

How to Study Chemistry

An Overall Study Strategy

For an introductory science course such as Chemistry 1A, lectures usually provide the best guide to the study of the subject. The instructor presents and explains important material in lectures. Examinations are based primarily on lecture material. The text is often used only to explain more fully material covered in lectures and as a source for homework problems.

For these reasons, this study guide focuses on taking good

Note: This material abridged and adapted from Colin Watanabe and Friedel Gordon, *How to Study Chemistry,* rev. ed. (Berkeley: Student Learning Center, University of California, 1977). Copies of the complete booklet, which includes "Are You Prepared for Chemistry 1A? A Diagnostic Quiz," are available at cost from Colin Watanabe, Science Coordinator, Student Learning Center, University of California, Berkeley, Calif. 94720.

lecture notes and suggests the following strategy: (1) Prepare yourself *before* each lecture by reading relevant portions of your text;
(2) do your best to take complete, accurate, and organized notes;
(3) review your notes as soon as possible after each lecture; and
(4) use your text to clarify and complete your notes.

For maximum effectiveness, you should preread and review
within twenty-four hours of the lecture. If you decide to use this
strategy, you will find yourself studying regularly, reading and/or
reviewing a little each night. Many surveys have shown that regular
study produces best results—both in understanding and in grades.

You can also integrate homework, lab work, and additional
in-depth reading into this regular cycle of prereading, notetaking,
and review. In addition to the regular review of your lecture notes,
you may find that a weekly or biweekly review will help you gain a
clearer picture of the entire course and will help you prepare for
quizzes and exams. Frequent review results in better retention than
does a single, intensive review.

Whether you use the suggested strategy or decide to devise
one of your own, you should keep in mind the advice given by last
year's chemistry students: Don't get behind; keep up with the reading assignments; don't miss any lectures; do all assigned problems;
use your TA (or someone else's); get help quickly if you find yourself in trouble.

Lectures and Notetaking

A. *Preread the assigned reading before class.* At this point, don't try to
   understand everything; just get a general idea of what the lecture will cover and become familiar with new terms. Look at
   chapter headings, subtitles, and *diagrams* and their *captions,* and
   scan the text briefly. This procedure does not take very long,
   but it will be of great help in following the lecture.
B. *Come early to the lectures and leave late.* Often instructors give
   helpful hints in the first and last minutes of their lectures—just
   when most people aren't listening. Frequently they give an outline of the lecture, or they at least *imply* their organization in the
   beginning, for example: "Today we will get into 'Metal Ions,'
   but before we start with the topic we'll talk a little about. . . ."

Your notes and, what's more important, your understanding will be clearer if you are able to fit the pieces together by paying attention to such verbal outlines.

C. *Take good notes.* The harder you work during one hour of lecture, the less studying you will have to do at home. Your notes should be complete, though not to the point of looking like a transcript; little words, repetitions, and digressions can and should be eliminated. Some students feel that all they have to write down is the information on the blackboard; but what is on the board is frequently not sufficient for understanding. It is very important to listen carefully to the verbal elaborations and to take notes on them.

Following are some specific suggestions for notetaking.

- Write on one side of the page only, leaving the back of each sheet empty. Use the empty side to rewrite messy or unclear sections, to add information when studying the book at home, or to write down related material from the discussion group. This way you can create one convenient source for study and review.

- Use *abbreviations* to cut down on writing time. Apply symbols like → (leads to); ↑ (increase); ↓ (decrease) in regular sentences as well as in formulas.

- *Identify unclear areas.* If you miss part of a section or don't understand what's being presented in a part of the lecture, write down as much as you *can* catch, especially key words; skip several lines in your notes; make a big question mark in the margin of your notes. Later you will be aware that there is something you must clear up and complete.

- *Indicate experiments and demonstrations in your notes.* Watch carefully and listen for an explanation of the concept being exemplified.

- *Look and listen for relationships.* Each lecture will have a main topic (for example, "Metal Ions") and about three to six subtopics. If these topics are stated by the professor in the form of an outline, very good; but if they are not stated directly, they are nevertheless implied, and you should try to discover them when studying your notes at home. Make it a habit to think about and write down a brief outline for each lecture, and you will gain a much better sense of how the whole course hangs together, how the details fit into the total framework, and what the relationships are between the different parts. This is also one of the best techniques to *improve memory*, because things are remembered better when they are seen in relationship.

- *Look for categories of information.* A student might have a list of facts in her notes without knowing what they belong to. This happens a lot when students just copy what is on the board. Example:

  1. Methyl alcohol CH_3OH
  2. Hardening fats, margarine, and so on.
  3. NH_3—ammonia
  4. Filling ballons

Without a categorizing label these facts are almost meaningless. In this case, the title would be "Uses of Hydrogen."

- *Add explanations and labels to diagrams, charts, and formulas.* Beware of simply copying what is on the board and spending too much time on the artwork. Diagrams and pictures can often be found in your text; so sketch them quickly and concentrate on the lecturer's comments.

  Comments and labels will (1) provide connections to preceding and subsequent material and (2) provide more complete notes, which will facilitate review.

D. *Review your notes as soon as possible after class.* Many studies have shown that long-term memory increases dramatically if this is done. If you review your notes, even just briefly, on the day of the lecture, it will save you a great deal of study time.

Some students have found it helpful to stay right in their seats after class and immediately go over their notes. Or, while walking to the next lecture, try repeating in your mind what you have just heard, asking yourself questions: What was covered today? What was it all supposed to mean? What were the topics? What did I not understand?

That same night, study your notes carefully and use your text to clarify confusing points.

Reading the Text

A. *Read selectively.* Not all parts of the text should be studied with equal care. Reading assignments are often vague (for example, "Read chapters 9 and 10 this week"), and you must decide for yourself how to organize your reading. Here are three tools to guide you:

1. Use your lecture notes and assigned problems to determine reading priorities, that is, important points (topics extensively covered in lecture on which problems have been assigned), digressions (examples or special cases of important points), and background information (topics not emphasized in lecture).

2. Preread before studying a section in detail. Quickly scan the text to get an overview of the material and how it is organized. Look at the table of contents; titles and subtitles; diagrams, illustrations, and their captions; and introductions and summaries. Prereading is very effective in improving concentration, comprehension, and long-term memory.

3. Use problems to guide you to important material. Before reading your text, look at the example problems and the problems listed at the end of the section or chapter. Note the variables (for example, temperature, pressure, concentration, volume) which appear in the problems. Look for definitions and concepts involving these variables when reading the text.

B. *Read actively—ask questions.*

1. Before reading a section or chapter, formulate questions by extracting questions implied in the problems and turning titles and headings into questions. Title: "Some Chemical Systems at Equilibrium." A student's questions: "What is a chemical system?" "What conditions define equilibrium?" "Why is 'equilibrium' important?" Look for answers to your questions as you read.

2. During the actual reading, continue to question. You needn't question so much the detail as the organization and the importance of what you are reading. Ask: "Why was this section placed here?" or "Can I skip this section?" or "How does this new concept relate to previous concepts?"

C. *Find connections and relationships in the material.* In order to understand and better remember the overwhelming quantity of information contained in your notes and text, you will need to construct an organizing framework:

- Bring together all material on each topic. Create a single study source by integrating your lecture and lab notes with textbook material.
- Outline the reading assignment. Make a list of section titles. A pattern should emerge. This is especially important if the lecture and text follow different organizational schemes.
- Use introductions and summaries in your text and lab manual to gain an overview of a topic.
- Create your own summaries of the assigned reading. Try to condense each chapter into a single page of notes.

D. *Underline and mark the text with care.* Your goal in marking should be to create a visual summary which will be meaningful when reviewing the text days or weeks later. Here are some general guidelines. (1) Read a paragraph or section *before* underlining. Then go back and mark selectively. (An effective form of instant review.) (2) Use your hi-liter sparingly; avoid indiscriminate underlining. Circle or underline key words or the topic of a paragraph. Underline summarizing sentences. (3) Write comments in the margin which will reorganize the text to meet your needs.

E. *Use the index.* The index can transform your text into a private instructor ready to answer your questions, clarify your notes, point out relationships. For example, a student might find in his lecture notes a complicated diagram, copied from the board without clarifying labels, and remember only that the instructor mentioned "hydrogen atom." Looking in the index under this heading, he is referred to "H atom," where he sees the following:

> H atom
> boundary conditions, 487
> energy level diagram, 488
> energy levels of, 472, 484, 487
> line spectrum of, 469, 472
> orbitals, 483, 487 . . .

He is not sure where to look next, but he does notice that most of the entries cluster around page 480. He turns to this page and begins to scan nearby pages. On page 488, he sees something resembling the diagram in his notes.

Another index may organize the same topic differently:

> Atomic structure
> Bohr model, 470
> hydrogen atom, 476–487 . . .

Try looking under each word, for example, *hydrogen* and *atom*.

If you cannot find your subject, think of a larger category that may include your subject as a subcategory.

Notice the other entries under your subject. You may find additional information and begin to see relationships more clearly.

Problem Solving

Chemistry is a problem-oriented course. In studying chemistry, you should keep in mind that your knowledge will eventually be used to solve problems. You may understand chemical concepts, definitions, formulas, and so on, but this knowledge will be of little value unless you can use it to solve problems. You should organize your studying accordingly:

- *Study the example problems.* Even though you may understand the concepts, working through an example problem will often disclose mathematical techniques, "tricks," or shortcuts you need to know in order to apply your conceptual understanding.
- *Do all assigned problems,* even if they are not to be turned in. Many instructors give similar (sometimes identical!) problems on their exams.
- *Practice problem solving.* One of the best ways to prepare for an exam is to practice solving the kinds of problems you think will be covered. Look at assigned problems for clues. The more practice you have in problem solving, the less likely you are to make those obvious mistakes that cost valuable points.

A. *Understanding the problem.* Most problems, both on homework and exams, are "word" problems. You will almost never be asked just to solve an equation; instead you must sort through a lot of words to get the information needed to set up an equation. *The most important step in solving any problem is to establish clearly WHAT IS GIVEN and WHAT IS WANTED.* Here are some techniques helpful in sorting out the information given in word problems:

1. *Find out what is WANTED.* Set it off clearly from everything else in the problem by circling, underlining, etc. Reread what you have marked, and don't jump to conclusions because your problem is similar to another problem you remember. Take time to make sure you understand what you are to do. There are few things more frustrating than getting the right answer to the wrong problem.

2. *Examine the data you have been GIVEN.* Set off the important information by underlining or some other means (but use a different mark to distinguish the GIVEN from the WANTED). On long word problems especially, some students find it helpful to summarize both the GIVEN and the WANTED before starting to solve the problem.

- *Too little information.* Some problems will omit "obvious" information (such as the value of the gas constant R or relevant thermodynamic data). You are expected either to know or to be able to look up such data. On tests many instructors will give you this information on the first sheet of the exam; in textbook problems such information is usually tabulated in the text or is given in an appendix at the back of the book.
- *Too much information.* In multipart problems, you must select from all of the given data that which is needed to solve each part of the problem.

B. *Doing it.* Although you may clearly understand what is wanted and what is given, the connection between the two may not be clear. Here are some ways to clarify the connection:

- Draw a picture or a diagram.
- Summarize a chemical process by writing a reaction.
- Analyze definitions. Important relationships are sometimes hidden in definitions: Density is defined as the ratio of mass

to volume. Pressure is defined as force per area. Molarity is defined as moles of solute per liter of solution.

- Look for similar example problems in the text.
- Set subgoals. Ask yourself, "What do I need to know to be able to solve the problem?" Set as your subgoal the task of finding any missing pieces of information.
- Use your imagination. Pretend you are looking into a very powerful microscope and can actually see atoms and molecules. How do they interact with one another?
- Reread the problem for word clues. Important information is often given in short phrases which are easily overlooked: "at constant pressure," "for an ideal gas," "for complete combustion," "in an acidic solution."
- Brainstorm. Write down everything you know about the kind of situation described in your problem. Assemble all your fragments of knowledge and see whether you can piece together a way to solve your problem.

C. *Checking your answers.*

- Is there a type of mistake you tend to make? Do you often make errors when working with scientific notation or when dividing fractions? Recheck these steps.
- Question your calculator. It will always give an answer, but only you can tell whether it is the *right* answer.
- Always ask yourself whether your answer makes sense: If you were asked to calculate the molecular weight of compound X, your calculated weight cannot be less than 1 gm/mole. (No element or compound is lighter than hydrogen.) If you were asked to calculate the pH of a 0.1 M aqueous solution of a weak acid using its dissociation constant, your calculated pH cannot be greater than 7. (The solution cannot be basic.)
- Use units to check your answer: Given 3 liters of 0.5 M NaOH, how many moles of NaOH do you have? Your answer should be in *moles*.

Exams

Some chemistry instructors prefer frequent short quizzes, others give only a midterm and a final. Quizzes require keeping up with course work because some instructors will announce a quiz only a few days before it is to be given, leaving you little time to prepare. Midterms and finals, on the other hand, require carefully planned selective review.

A. *Preparing for an Exam.*

    1. *Predicting the exam.* Find out as much as you can about format and content of the impending exam. Ask fellow students, your TA, the professor, and try to obtain copies of old exams from the library or other souces.

    Preliminaries. When and where will the exam be given? (Exams are sometimes not given in the regular classroom.) What is the grading policy? (Is partial credit given? Will you be penalized for guessing?) Will the exam be open- or closed-book? Can you use your calculator? Should you bring a bluebook?

    Format: Will the exam contain problems requiring calculation, short-answer questions, multiple-choice questions, essay questions? How many of each type; how will the points be distributed?

    Content.

- Will the exam be cumulative (that is, will it cover all material to date), or will it cover only material introduced since the last exam? Will lab material be included?
- Listen carefully. Has the instructor raised questions and problems in recent lectures without giving answers? Has he mentioned topics covered in earlier lectures? Has he suggested that the class "think about" certain concepts?
- Make a list of assigned readings. Include not only page numbers but also chapter titles and/or section headings. Note sections and chapters *not* to be covered by the exam.
- Make a list of assigned problems, noting what you were given and what you were asked to find.
- Look at your lecture notes, your list of assigned readings, your list of assigned problems. Which topics seem to have received the most emphasis? What kinds of questions have you been asked about these topics; what kinds of questions would you ask if you were trying to design an exam to cover these topics?

2. *Scheduling your time.* Make a long-range schedule. This should be done about three weeks prior to the exam. Note all commitments (deadlines for papers, exams in other classes, etc.) to get an overview of what you must do and how much time you can allot to each demand. Many students make such a schedule for the entire quarter.

Make a detailed schedule. Some students set deadlines by which they will have covered a certain portion of the material. Others schedule study time each day and use the time flexibly. Some combine both methods. Choose whichever method seems to work for you.

Reassess your progress every few days. Are you falling behind? Can you take time from other activites; can you make your review more selective? Beware of cutting down on sleep—this usually reduces efficiency.

3. *Setting priorities.* Apply this rule: If you can't study everything, or if you must cram, concentrate on a few topics and review them thoroughly. Understand basic information first. The most difficult topics are not always the most important. In introductory courses, difficult material is sometimes presented to preview more advanced classes. You will often not be responsible for such material.

4. *Taking a practice test.* This is an important strategy suggested by many learning specialists to counteract test anxiety. You can "desensitize" yourself by simulating an actual test situation and applying your knowledge under realistic conditions. The method:

- Make a list of problems and questions, using old exam questions, homework problems, and your own questions.
- Set a time limit, one which will force you to work at top efficiency.
- Work without interruption; try to finish your "exam." Stop when time has expired.
- Evaluate your performance, give yourself a "grade." Determine your strengths and weaknesses. Decide where you need more review.

B. *Test-taking strategies.*

1. *Assessing the quiz or exam.* Before starting to write, glance over the whole exam quickly, assessing questions as to their level of difficulty and point value.

Get a sense of how much time to spend on each question.

Begin to work on those questions with which you are most comfortable and/or those worth the most points. In general, in problem-solving exams, as in essay exams, it is better to do the easiest questions first. In multiple-choice exams, on the other hand, it is probably better to work through from beginning to end (again, however, skipping very difficult questions). Never leave a question completely blank. Write down everything that seems to apply—you may receive partial credit.

2. *Analyzing the question.* Read each question carefully.

Underline or circle key words (see "Problem Solving").

Jot comments and ideas in the margin as you think about the question.

Ask yourself: What is this question asking? How is it related to what I've been studying? Have I seen a similar question?

Clarify confusing questions. Add comments, clarifying remarks.

3. *Writing down the answer.* Show all work clearly. You may lose points for incomplete or messy answers.

Write in pencil—not ink—so you can erase.

If you write on the back of a page, make a note so that the reader will not overlook it.

Evaluate your answer. Does it make sense? See "Problem Solving" for techniques.

Laboratory

Your lab work will account for about 30 percent of your total grade. In addition, many exams and quizzes will contain questions pertaining to laboratory material.

- *Be prepared.* You should read the current experiment twice *before* coming to lab. On the first reading, read the introduction and skim the text to get a general picture of the experiment (that is, procedures, amount of time required, objectives) and its relationship to previous experiments and/or the lecture. Look at the problems and questions for clues to procedures and concepts. Go through the procedure in detail during the second reading. Some students write outlines or draw detailed flow charts complete with pictures of test tubes, beakers, and so on, labeled with experimental conditions such as temperature, molarity, volume, weight.

- *Get help before you make a mistake.* Ask your TA about confusing points before you proceed. Rely on the advice of your TA rather than that of fellow students, who may also be confused.

- *Analyze your data as soon as possible after completing an experiment.* If you complete your lab work early, you may want to stay and analyze your data. This will give you a chance to confer with other students or your TA if you have difficulty with calculations or the interpretation of your data.

- *Notebook policy varies from TA to TA.* Listen carefully to your TA's instructions. Ask questions if you are not sure about notebook policy. Here are some commonly followed notebook policies:

    Use a bound notebook with numbered pages (not a spiral-bound notebook).

    Save the first few pages for a table of contents.

    Record all observations and primary data (temperature, weights, volumes, the date, and so on), *directly* into your notebook. Do not record data on scratch paper for later transfer to your notebook.

    Do not remove pages from your notebook.

    Draw a line through incorrect data; do not erase or obliterate.

    Show all calculations; do not give just the answer.

    Write answers to all questions and problems.

Appendix G

How to Study
Physics

College-level physics is generally viewed by students as one of their more difficult courses. There is a tendency for physics students to be overwhelmed by the many new terms and equations that they encounter. Moreover, many students have not had extensive experience with problem-solving courses and tend to get lost when trying to apply information from the text and lectures to an actual physics problem.

Difficulties often arise when students "think small" and get overly involved in memorization of specific details without understanding the underlying principles or without perceiving how to apply specific knowledge to the problems.

Note: This material abridged from David R. Hubin and Charles Riddell, "How to Study Physics" (Irvine: Learning Skills Center, University of California, 1977).

Getting an Overview

It is of utmost importance to recognize that physics is a *problem-solving discipline.* A physics instructor will be stressing major themes and principles; his goal is that you will be able to *understand and solve problems.* Your approach to the study of physics, during the time spent in lecture, reading the text, or reviewing for exams, should focus on the fact that in a physics course, you are expected to solve problems.

An overview of your course can help you organize your efforts and increase your efficiency. Understanding and retention of specific data or formulas are enhanced when a person perceives underlying principles or connecting themes. Furthermore, in some instances it is inevitable that you will forget a formula, and an understanding of the underlying principle will sometimes allow you to generate the formula for yourself.

There are several steps to getting an overview of the material in a physics course. These steps should be taken early in the term so that all subsequent material can be integrated into your overview.

1. *Examine carefully the information given in the course syllabus* or reading list. Look for underlying themes or a pattern on which the course is developed.
2. *Preview the textbook:* Read the introduction, the table of contents, the "notes to the student," and the preface. Check the syllabus to see what chapters are assigned. Are they assigned in the same order as in the table of contents? If not, can you see a reason for your professor's decision to alter the order of presentation?
3. As you preview the course, *look for important themes and principles.* Glance at some of the problems. How are important themes illustrated in these problems?

Effective Participation in a Physics Lecture

In most introductory science courses, the lecture gives the best indication of the emphasis of the course. *It is important that you be well prepared for lecture* in order to fully utilize its potential for integrating the course material. [Much of Hubin and Riddell's advice on prereading the textbook and taking lecture notes resembles that in *How to Study Chemistry* (Appendix F) and so is not reproduced here. Hubin and Riddell make the following additional points.]

1. [When prereading the textbook] make notes of new words, new units of measure, statements of general laws, etc. Do not try to underline, since you do not yet know what will be emphasized by the instructor.
2. Another good preparation for lecture is to spend any time available right before the beginning of class to *check over your notes from the last lecture*. This will prepare you to listen to the new physics lecture as part of an integrated course and will help you to see the broad development of themes.
3. If you are prepared for class, have previewed your text, and are attentive, you should not be embarrassed to *ask your instructor questions*. Many instructors depend on feedback from students to help them set a proper pace for the lecture.
4. Immediately after lecture, or as soon as possible, *review and edit your notes*. You need not rewrite your notes: Rather, you should look for important ideas and summarize these in the margin. It is also important that you use this time to look for relationships among major topics covered by the instructor. (As you review your notes, questions may come to mind. In the notetaking format you choose, leave space for the recording of these questions.)

Reading Your Physics Text

Reading the text and solving homework problems can be viewed as a cycle: (1) raising questions and (2) finding answers that lead back to "(1)"—more questions. An entire chapter will often be devoted to the consequences of a single basic principle. You should seek out these basic principles. These so-called "laws of nature" give order to the physicist's view of the universe. Moreover, nearly all the problems that you will be faced with in a physics course can be analyzed by means of one or more of these laws.

When looking for relationships among topics, you may note that in many instances a specific problem is analyzed in great detail, then the setting of the problem is generalized into more abstract results. When such generalizations are made, you should refer back to the specific case that was previously cited and make sure that you understand how the general theory applies to the specific problem. Then, see if you can think of other problems to which that general principle would apply.

Here are some suggestions to help you get more out of your physics reading:

1. Make use of the *preview* that you did prior to the lecture. Again, quickly look at the major points of the chapter. Think back to the points stressed in lecture.
2. *Read the homework problems first,* if you have them. Critically assess what principles seem to be most significant in the assigned chapter. Based upon your brief review of the lecture and your examination of the assigned problems, try to generate questions that you want to answer.
3. *Read actively with questions in mind.* A passive approach to reading physics is wasting your time. If you find that you are not "reading actively," once again take a look at the problems and the lecture notes. *Read to learn, not to cover material.*
4. *Stop periodically and pointedly recall the material* that you have read. Often repeating material aloud will successfully demand use of your "recalling" and "retention" processes.
5. During your reading you will notice sections that apply directly to assigned problems. After you have read a section, stop and *analyze its application to a homework problem.*

The interplay of reading and problem solving can help you gain insights that are not possible by careful reading alone. When you read passively, you simply follow the chain of thought presented by the text. Your mind is not exploring the possibilities of what is being said. By actively combining the questioning inherent in problem solving with your reading, you can enhance both your concentration while reading and your ability to recall and apply material.

Problem Solving in Physics

Two things are important to remember in solving physics problems. First, a physicist seeks those problems which can be modeled or represented pictorially or schematically. This means that *almost any problem you encounter in a physics course can be described with a drawing.* Moreover, such a drawing usually contains or suggests the solution to the problem. Second, *a physicist seeks to find unifying principles* which can be expressed mathematically and applied to the broad classes of physical situations. While your physics textbook contains many specific formulas, the broader "laws of nature" must be understood in order to grasp the general overview of physics. This broad conceptualizing is vital if you are to solve those problems which embody several different principles. Virtually all specific formulas in physics are combinations of "the basic laws."

The following is a general outline of how to approach a physics problem:

1. *Read the problem* and make sure that you understand all the terminology used. Look up the meanings of any terms that you do not know.
2. *Make a drawing of the problem.* In your drawing, you should identify the quantity you are seeking; identify the given values of the parameters (variables) on which the solution depends; identify unknown parameters which must be calculated from other information in order to find the solution; and make sure that all quantities in the problem are expressed in [consistent units of measure].
3. *Establish which general principle relates the given parameters to the quantity you are seeking.* Usually your picture will suggest the correct formulas. However, at times, further information will have to be generated before the proper formulas can be chosen. This is especially true of problems in which the solution you seek must be calculated indirectly from the given information.
4. *Calculate the solution* (a) by calculating the values of any parameters which were obtained from the given information (if any such parameters were necessary), then (b) by putting the values

of all the parameters, both given and calculated, into the main question.

5. *Criticize your solution to see if it makes sense.* Compare your solution to any available examples. Many times an error in a calculation will result in a solution that will be obviously wrong. Check the units of your solution to be sure that they are appropriate. *Examining your solutions will develop your intuition about the correctness of solutions—an intuition immensely valuable to use with problems that you will later encounter on an exam.*

When you have completed a problem, you should be able (at some later time) to read the solution and understand it without referring to the text. This means that you should include necessary notation as to which principle you have applied. If, when you read a solution, you come to a step that you do not understand, then you have either omitted a step that is necessary to the logical development of the solution, or you need to write notes in your solution to remind you of the reasons for each step.

While it may take more time to write careful and complete solutions to homework problems, you will find that this will be "paid back" by the help in problem solving, as you are prevented from overlooking essential information; it will also provide excellent review material for exam preparation.

Effective Test Preparation

If you have followed an active approach to study similar to the one suggested in this handout, your preparation for exams will not be overly difficult. Let us repeat that *physics courses, and therefore physics exams, involve problem solving.* Therefore your approach to studying for exams should stress problem solving.

Here are some principles:

1. In the week prior to the exam, completing steps a, b, and c below should give you a reasonably good idea of what has been stressed and on what you can expect to be tested. (a) Quickly review your notes and recheck the syllabus. (Your goal at this point is to ascertain what has been emphasized.) (b) Reread

A Weekly Flow Chart for Studying Physics

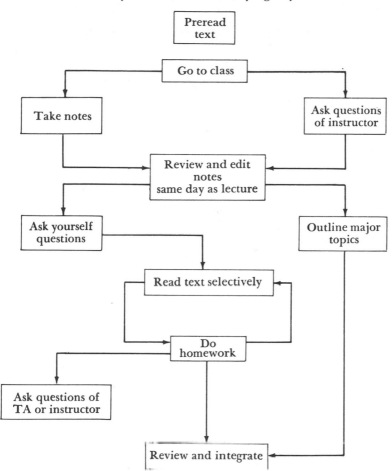

quickly your solutions to the homework problems. (Remember that these solutions, if complete, will note underlying principles of laws.) (c) Quickly review the assigned chapters. (Once again, your purpose in this early stage of exam preparation is to ascertain what topics or principles have been emphasized.)

2. From this rapid overview, generate a list of themes, principles, and types of problems that you expect to be covered.

3. *Review Actively.* Don't mistake recognition of a principle when you see it for actual knowledge that will be available for recall in

a test situation. *Try to look at all the possible ways that a principle can be applied.* For example: If velocity and acceleration principles have been stressed, look over *all* your homework problems to see if they, in any way, illustrate these principles. Then, if you also can anticipate an emphasis on friction and inertia, once again review *all* your homework problems, checking to see if they illustrate, in any way, those principles.

Effective examination preparation involves your developing an interaction between homework problems, the lecture, and the text. If you review actively and "self-test," including creating on your own problems which involve a combination of principles, you are not likely to look back on an exam and say, "I knew how to do friction problems, it's just that they were asked in a weird way, so I didn't recognize them."

Appendix H

Research and
Program Evaluation

Introduction

Over the past ten years the profession of program evaluation has emerged out of the various social science disciplines. While there have been some differences of opinion, there is an increasing consensus that while program evaluation may use the methodology of the social sciences, it is not confined to this methodology.

Program evaluation in some form is inevitable. There is no chance that a program will be developed and put into place without its founders, funders, directors, and participants having opinions

Note: This material abridged from Samuel Ball, "Research and Program Evaluation: Some Principles, Precepts, and Practices" in *The Final Report of National Project II, Alternatives to the Revolving Door.* New York: Bronx Community College, n.d.).

443

and feelings about it. The only question is whether these opinions and feelings are based upon systematically gathered data and are consciously arrived at using some planned process or whether they are simply ad hoc and unconsciously developed.

In a survey of practices in program evaluation, Ball and Anderson (1975) examined some 200 educational programs divided equally among the Department of Defense, other federal government departments and agencies, private industrial and commercial enterprises, and junior and community colleges. They found that most of the Department of Defense, other federal government programs, and private sector industrial and commercial enterprises were receiving some form of program evaluation. Most of these evaluations involved questionnaires of teachers and students to obtain evidence on their perceptions of the program. However, it was very clear that the traditional formal educational institutions—the colleges—rarely indulge in program evaluation in any formal sense of that term. It seems that once a program is installed at the college level, it becomes sufficient unto itself, or "functionally autonomous"; and it is unlikely that any formal effort will occur to gather evidence concerning the need for program modification or continuation.

We wish to emphasize that the major function of program evaluation is to provide information for decision makers. Evaluation assumes current or past program development; it offers to extend our knowledge about specific program practices; it provides immediate payoff without necessarily providing generalizable knowledge; but, above all, it is decision-oriented.

Because it is decision-oriented (in contrast to the knowledge-orientation of "pure" or "abstract" or "basic" research), certain additional criteria of quality become important. Timeliness of the results of program evaluation is important. If the results are to feed into decision making, they must be made available before the decision is made—and *when* a decision is to be made is usually a political or economic matter not bound to scientific niceties.

Relevance is a second additional criterion. The results must be relevant to the decisions to be made. The evaluator, unlike the pure researcher, cannot define the problem without regard for the audience for the results. If the decision maker, on hearing the results of the evaluation, yawns and mutters, "So what!", then the evaluation, which may be scientifically rigorous and technically sophisticated, is without value.

Comprehensibility is a third, related criterion of successful program evaluation. There are multiple audiences[1] for program evaluation, and at least the major audiences need to be provided with a reporting of procedures and results in a form each finds comprehensible. Usability is jeopardized if comprehensibility is absent.

Thus, program evaluation provides evidence in usable forms to a variety of decision makers; and a wide variety of techniques for gathering the evidence [are] used. In the following sections of this essay, these points will be elaborated upon. Two areas will receive special attention—the kinds of evidence, and the kinds of decisions to be made on the basis of that evidence.

Evidence (Hard vs. Soft)

In general, hard evaluation is regarded as rigorous by its friends and trivial by its enemies.[2] Soft evaluation is regarded as sensitive by its friends and unscientific by its enemies. A few brave people obliquely challenge these assertions, saying that there is no such thing as hard or soft evaluation—only hard or soft evaluators. Like most shibboleths (pet phrases that help distinguish adherents of different parties or sects from one another),[3] the terms *hard* and *soft* have often been applied thoughtlessly. In common parlance, a hard evaluation usually involves (1) a research design capable of discerning causal relationships; (2) the collection of data that are

[1] There are many groups who may want to make decisions concerning a program. These audiences include, but are not limited to, government funding agencies, the program's director and developer, clients and potential clients of the program, and the community that provides the program's context.

[2] This section is based on an article: Ball, S., "Hard and Soft—Shibboleths in Evaluation," in Anderson, S. B., Ball, S., and Murphy, R. T., and Associates, *Encyclopedia of Educational Evaluation: Concepts and Techniques for Evaluating Education and Training Programs.* (San Francisco: Jossey-Bass, 1975).

[3] Scott wrote that knaves and fools invent catchwords and shibboleths to keep honest people from coming to a just understanding.

objective, reliable, and valid; (3) the analysis of these data by sophisticated statistical techniques. A soft evaluation usually involves (1) a research design that, at most, can point to correlationships; (2) data that are subjective and judgmental; (3) an absence of sophisticated statistical analysis of the data. (Many evaluations based on the case-study method exemplify soft evaluation, as do many of the efforts carried out as part of an accreditation process.)

James C. Stone (University of California, Berkeley) in a personal communication has used the term *phenomenological evaluation* to label one kind of soft evaluation. Here the personal viewpoints, reactions, and experiences of participants are collected, and the interaction between and among them is documented; the process may involve logs, diaries, informal feedback, self-reports, and observations. The evaluator becomes a participant-observer in phenomenological evaluation, identifying with the participant and systematically recording his or her own reactions as well as those of the participants.

The degree of difference between hard and soft evaluation is shown in Figure 1, a simple scheme based on some of the major components involved. The hardest kind of evaluation (the front lower-left-hand cube) is a sophisticated statistical analysis of objective data obtained from a true experimental design. The softest kind of evaluation (the back upper-right-hand cube) is an unsophisticated statistical analysis of subjective data obtained from a nonexperimental evaluation design. In practice, evaluations may include a number of these "cubes"; and on the basis of the "cube," with the appropriate reasoning, a piece of evidence is established. Since evaluators will usually want to present a variety of evidence, evaluation might include both objective and subjective data; and some of these data may be presented at the descriptive level, while others may be subjected to a more sophisticated level of statistical analysis (for example, multivariate analysis).

Extremists in the hard-evaluation camp view soft evaluation as indicative of soft headedness and insufficient training on the part of the evaluator. They further agree that the results of a soft evaluation are not open to replication and that subjectivity is so rampant that it is impossible to tell what are legitimate conclusions and what are the formal statements of prejudgments or chance

Figure 1. Components Involved in Hard and Soft Evaluations

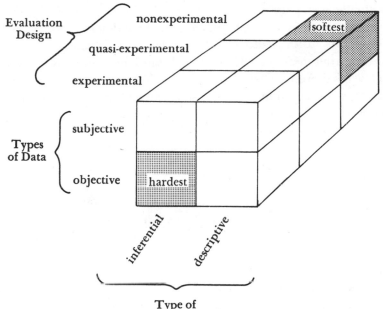

occurrences. Extremists in the soft-evaluation camp look with similar disfavor on hard evaluation. They claim that hard evaluations miss the essence of a program's impact; ignore the variables that currently available objective measures cannot assess adequately; and are mechanistic, basing conclusions on statistical tests of relatively trivial data rather than on intelligent judgments.

A major issue in all of this is the kind of evidence an evaluator finds acceptable. Which is a more acceptable kind of evidence: a statistically significant higher mean gain by an experimental group (compared with a control group) on a standardized achievement test, or a consistent report by the experimental students that they feel they are learning more? If there is no statistically significant difference between the achievement of students taught by Method A as compared with Method D, but teachers prefer to teach by Method A, which piece of evidence (which "cube") should an evaluator prefer?

The word *acceptable* implies that there is some purpose for the evaluation. Thus, the kind of evidence that an evaluator finds acceptable is in part dependent on what he wants to find out. (The term *evidence* is used here to include the data, design, and analysis.) If he wants to find out which method has the greatest impact on student attainment, he will not be substantially helped by evidence on teachers' preferences; if he wants to find out whether the school system is successful in retaining staff, he will not regard students' scores as useful evidence. In short, the evidence—whether based on objective or subjective data, whether collected within an experimental, quasi-experimental, or nonexperimental design, whether statistically analyzed or not—should be appropriate to the question being asked.

Furthermore, as evaluators we should obtain the best evidence that it is feasible to obtain. Considerations here include practicality and cost. Thus, it may not be practical to assign subjects randomly to treatments and construct a true experiment. Computer technology in a school system may not be capable of handling an analysis of covariance. The cost of obtaining objective observational data may be too great for the evaluation budget. Demanding a particular kind of evidence that cannot be obtained is tantamount to saying that no evidence will be presented. Usually, it is better to have tried and gotten some evidence than never to have tried at all.

Finally, the questions about the technical quality of the data cannot be ignored; that is, whether the data are objective or subjective, they still have to meet reasonable criteria of reliability and validity. One must also demand that the design and analysis be properly carried out. An unreliable judgment in a case study is as bad as an inappropriate error term in an analysis of variance.

In general, the hard-versus-soft argument would suggest that objective measures are probably more reliable than subjective measures but that subjective measures may be more valid than objective measures. But this kind of argument can too easily be misinterpreted. Both objective and subjective measures must have sufficient reliability in an evaluation to ensure the possibility of obtaining reliable assessments across groups. If we are assessing a relatively stable characteristic (students' achievement in mathematics, adults' skill in typing), an unreliable measure, no matter how

"sensitive," cannot be valid. The presence of either validity or reliability cannot make up for the absence of the other. It is incumbent
on both the soft and hard evaluators to indicate how reliable and
valid their data are.

In short, it is imprudent to prejudge and stereotype "hard"
and "soft" evaluation. These are extreme forms of a continuum
that enmeshes design, data, and analysis. There are good hard and
good soft evaluations (appropriate to the questions raised, feasible,
and technically sound). And, just as clearly, there are bad hard and
bad soft evaluations. But most comprehensive evaluations, of
necessity, include both hard and soft components; and both are
almost bound to find their critics as well as their praisers.

Decisions and Evaluations

Evaluations are undertaken for a great many reasons or
purposes. These reasons or purposes mandate areas of involvement for the evaluator attempting to provide relevant information
for decision makers. We have distinguished six major purposes or
areas of involvement, and each of these six has been broken down
into a number of components, as shown in Table 1.[4] Table 1 also
includes a matching of evaluation purposes-components to likely
general methods of investigation. Let us examine each of the six
major evaluation purposes in turn.

I. *To contribute to decisions about program installation.* Historically the evaluation process has been thought of as beginning *after*
the decision to implement an education/training program. However, a number of the skills and techniques usually associated with
evaluation of existing or planned programs are applicable to what
has been called "front-end analysis." Assessment of the frequency
and/or intensity of needs for a program, evaluation of the initial
conception, and estimates of costs, operational feasibility, and demand and support are all important precursors to decisions about

[4]The content of this list of evaluation purposes benefited from
Scriven's (1974) "Product Check List." It should be noted, however, that
Scriven's list is designed to be used primarily for appraising completed
educational products or evaluation proposals, while Table 1 is intended as
an aid to overall evaluation planning.

Table 1. Purposes and General Methods of Program Evaluation

Likely investigation method	Experimental Study	Quasi-Experimental Study	Correlational Status Study	Survey	Personnel or Student Assessment	Systematic "Expert" Judgments	Clinical or Case Study	Informal Observation and/or Testimony
I. To contribute to decisions about program installation								
A. Need								
1. Frequency								
a. Student				X	X	X		
b. Society				X		X		X
c. Other (for example, industrial, professional, governmental)								
2. Intensity								
a. Student				X	X	X		X
b. Society				X	X	X	X	X
c. Other				X		X	X	X
B. Program conception								
1. Appropriateness						X		
2. Quality						X		
3. Priority in the face of competing needs						X		
C. Estimated cost								
1. Absolute cost				X		X		

X Likely investigation method

2. Cost in relation to alternative strategies oriented toward same need

D. Operational feasibility
   1. Staff
   2. Materials
   3. Facilities
   4. Schedule

E. Projection of demand and support
   1. Popular
   2. Political/financial
   3. Professional

II. To contribute to decisions about program continuation, expansion, and/or "accreditation"

A. Continuing need
   1. Frequency
     a. Student
     b. Society
     c. Other
   2. Intensity
     a. Student
     b. Society
     c. Other

B. Global effectiveness in meeting need
   1. Short-term
   2. Long-term

C. Minimal negative side effects

D. Important positive side effects

Item	1	2	3	4	5	6
2. Cost in relation to alternative strategies oriented toward same need	X			X		
D. Operational feasibility						
1. Staff	X	X	X	X		X
2. Materials	X		X	X		X
3. Facilities	X	X	X	X		X
4. Schedule			X	X		
E. Projection of demand and support						
1. Popular	X		X	X		X
2. Political/financial	X		X	X		X
3. Professional	X		X	X		X
II. heading						
A. Continuing need						
1. Frequency						
a. Student	X	X	X		X	
b. Society	X	X	X		X	
c. Other	X	X	X			
2. Intensity						
a. Student	X	X	X	X	X	
b. Society	X	X	X	X	X	
c. Other	X	X	X	X		
B. Global effectiveness in meeting need						
1. Short-term	X	X				
2. Long-term	X	X				
C. Minimal negative side effects	X	X		X		
D. Important positive side effects	X	X		X		

Table 1. Purposes and General Methods of Program Evaluation (Continued)

	Experimental Study	Quasi-Experimental Study	Correlational Status Study	Survey	Personnel or Student Assessment	Systematic "Expert" Judgments	Clinical or Case Study	Informal Observation and/or Testimony
E. Cost								
1. Absolute cost				X				
2. Cost in relation to alternative strategies oriented toward same need				X				
3. Cost in relation to benefits			X					
F. Demand and support								
1. Popular				X				X
2. Political/financial				X		X		X
3. Professional				X		X		X
III. To contribute to decisions about program modification								
A. Program objectives								
1. Validity and utility (in meeting needs)						X		
2. Popular acceptance				X				X
3. Professional acceptance				X		X		X
4. Student acceptance				X				X
5. Instructor acceptance				X		X		X

B. Curriculum content						
1. Relevance to program objectives				X		
2. Coverage of objectives				X		
3. Technical accuracy				X		
4. Degree of structure				X		
5. Relevance to backgrounds of students			X	X		
6. Effectiveness of components	X	X				
7. Sequencing of components	X	X		X		
8. Difficulty			X	X		
9. Popular acceptance			X			X
10. Professional acceptance			X	X		X
11. Student acceptance			X			X
12. Instructor acceptance			X	X		X
C. Instructional methodology						
1. Degree of student autonomy				X		
2. Effectiveness of presentation methods	X	X				
3. Pacing and length	X	X		X		
4. Reinforcement system	X	X				
5. Student acceptance			X			X
6. Instructor acceptance			X	X		X
D. Program context						
1. Administrative structure, auspices				X		X
2. Program administration procedures				X		X
3. Staff roles and relationships			X	X	X	X
4. Public relations efforts			X	X		X
5. Physical facilities and plant				X		X
6. Fiscal sources and stability				X		
7. Fiscal administration procedures				X		

Table 1. Purposes and General Methods of Program Evaluation (Continued)

	Experimental Study	Quasi-Experimental Study	Correlational Study	Status Study	Survey	Personnel or Student Assessment	Systematic "Expert" Judgments	Clinical or Case Study	Informal Observation and/or Testimony
E. Personnel policies and practices									
1. Students									
a. Recruitment	X		X	X	X	X	X		
b. Selection and placement			X	X	X	X	X		
c. Evaluation	X		X	X	X				
d. Discipline			X	X	X	X	X	X	X
e. Retention			X			X		X	X
2. Instructors									
a. Selection and placement		X	X	X	X	X			
b. In-service training		X	X	X	X		X		
c. Evaluation for promotion, guidance, retention, etc.			X		X				
3. Administrators									
a. Selection			X	X		X	X		
b. Evaluation for promotion, retention, etc.			X	X			X		
IV. To obtain evidence favoring program to rally support									
A. Popular	X	X	X	X	X	X	X		
B. Political/financial	X	X	X	X	X	X	X		X

C. Professional	X	X			X		X
V. To obtain evidence against program to rally opposition							
A. Popular	X	X	X	X	X		X
B. Political/financial	X	X	X	X	X		
C. Professional	X	X			X		
VI. To contribute to the understanding of basic processes							
A. Educational	X	X	X				
B. Psychological	X	X	X		X	X	
C. Social	X	X	X		X	X	
D. Economic	X	X	X				
E. Evaluation (Methodology)	X	X	X	X	X		X

whether to implement a program and about the size and scope of the installation.

II. *To contribute to decisions about program continuation, expansion (or contraction), and/or "accreditation."* This purpose is the one usually served by what is popularly called "summative evaluation"; however, more is included here than is sometimes intended by that term. For example, investigations under Purpose II may involve some of the same components as investigations under Purpose I; after a program is in operation, it is important to monitor the continuing needs for the program (some of them *may* change or even go away) and to assess actual costs and demand/support. Results of these investigations need to be considered along with results of impact studies (focusing on both intended and unintended outcomes) in making decisions about program continuation, expansion, or "accreditation."

III. *To contribute to decisions about program modification.* This purpose corresponds to the one usually ascribed to formative evaluation, although information about program components can also be obtained after a program is in full operation and in the context of a global appraisal of its effectiveness. Of course, if a program is cast in an unchangeable mold, the evaluator is wasting his time seeking information to help make it better. A major distinction between evaluation efforts devoted to Purpose III, as opposed to Purpose II, is in the emphasis on describing program processes in contrast to program products. As Table 1 indicates, the evaluator may seek information to guide program improvement in a broad range of areas, including program objectives (for example, validity and utility in meeting needs, popular acceptance), curriculum content (for example, relevance to objectives, technical accuracy), instructional methodology (for example, degree of student autonomy, pacing), program context (for example, administrative structure, staff roles), and personnel policies and practices (for example, student recruitment, instructor selection).

IV. and V. *To obtain evidence favoring a program to rally support* or *To obtain evidence against a program to rally opposition.* These two purposes are presented in recognition of the realities of program evaluation. Many evaluators shun evaluations with these purposes; many people who "commission" evaluations are unwilling to admit to their real motives. But there are indeed occasions when decision makers must rally support for a program in order to sustain it, or opposition to it in order to "kill it" so that funds can be diverted to other things. And there may be occasions when decision makers are willing to entertain both negative and positive evidence about the effectiveness of a program. The adversary model of evaluation integrates this purpose with the full thrust of the evaluation effort. In any case, it is better if the evaluator's client faces up to the real reasons for the evaluation and does not keep them hidden from the evaluator. The evaluator's responsibilities, in turn, include defining clearly the nature of the evidence being presented, indicating its lack of representativeness if that is indeed the case, and ensuring the validity of the evidence even if it is only a partial picture of the total state of affairs.

VI. *To contribute to the understanding of basic processes.* Pursuing the purposes of a decision-oriented evaluation does not preclude investigating, within the context of the same study, basic processes in at least one of the disciplines listed under Purpose VI, Table 1. However, evaluators cannot afford to lose sight of the fact that the program must be the central focus. A search for understanding of basic processes can be a means to sharpen the focus of the investigation.

Some Concluding Comments

Program evaluation is a young, multidisciplined, and, some might add, ill-disciplined profession. We have argued here that it is an important profession because it attempts to ensure that decision makers are provided the kinds of evidence necessary for wise decisions. It does not ensure that wise decisions are made, but it certainly is an important facilitator. Flying blind is not a recommended practice in aeronautics, even though it has been a typical practice in educational program development.

References

Abramowitz, S. I., and others. "Usefulness of In-Service Training Workshops for Counselors." *American Psychologist,* 1974, *29,* 850–854.

Adams, J. L. *Conceptual Development.* San Francisco: W. H. Freeman, 1974.

Adams, N. E., and Stevenson, B. J. "A Systems Approach to Planning, Implementing, and Evaluating Peer Counseling Programs." In R. Sugimoto (Ed.), *The Spirit of '76: Revolutionizing College Learning Skills.* Proceedings of 9th annual conference of Western College Reading Association, 1976.

Adams, W. R. *How to Read the Sciences.* Glenview, Ill.: Scott, Foresman, 1970.

Adler, M. J. *How to Read a Book.* New York: Simon & Schuster, 1940.

Admissions Testing Program of the College Entrance Examination Board. *National Report—College Bound Seniors, 1975–6.* Princeton, N.J.: College Entrance Examination Board, 1976.

Advancement. "Mentor Program Begins 2nd Year." Academic Advancement Program Quarterly Newsletter, University of California at Los Angeles, Spring 1976, *2,* 2.

Ahrendt, K. "The Training and Use of Paraprofessionals in the College Reading Program." In F. L. Christ (Ed.), *Interdisciplinary Aspects of Reading Instruction.* Proceedings of 4th annual conference of Western College Reading Association. 1971.

Ahrendt, K. *Community College Reading Programs.* Newark, Del.: International Reading Association, 1975.

Allen V. L. (Ed.). *Children as Teachers: Theory and Research on Tutoring.* New York: Academic Press, 1976.

Alpert, R., and Haber, R. N. "Anxiety in Academic Achievement Situations." *Journal of Abnormal and Social Psychology,* 1960, *61,* 207–215.

"Alternatives to the Revolving Door" *Newsletter #1.* New York: Bronx Community College, 1976a.

"Alternatives to the Revolving Door" *Newsletter #2.* New York: Bronx Community College, 1976b.

Amann, C. A. "Teacher Spare Us the Unneeded Book." *Chronicle of Higher Education,* August 1, 1977, p. 32.

Ambrosino, R. J., and others. "Reading: A Potential Source of Academic Difficulty in Medical School." *Journal of Reading Behavior,* 1974, *6,* 367–373.

American College Testing Program. *Promoting Student Learning in College by Adapting to Individual Differences in Educational Cognitive Style.* Final Evaluation Report. Iowa City: American College Testing Program, 1977.

American Council of Education. "Freshmen: On Making the Inflated Grade." *Science News,* 1978, *113* (4), 54.

Anastasio, E. J. *Evaluation of PLATO and TICCIT CAI Systems: A Preliminary Plan.* Princeton, N.J.: Educational Testing Service, 1972.

Anderson, S. B., and Ball, S. *The Profession and Practice of Program Evaluation.* San Francisco: Jossey-Bass, 1978.

Anderson, W. W. "Evaluation of College Reading and Study Skills Programs, Problems, and Approaches." *Reading World,* 1975, *14,* 191–197.

Anonymous. "Reading Readability Formulae." *Teaching of Psychology,* 1977, *4,* 49–51.

Appleton, W. S. "Concentration: The Phenomenon and Its Disruption." *Archives of General Psychiatry*, 1967, *16*, 373–381.

Ardinger, B. "A Writing Program That Sticks to the Basics: Grammar, Rhetoric, and Logic." *Chronicle of Higher Education*, November 29, 1976, p. 17.

Astin, A. W. *Preventing Students from Dropping Out*. San Francisco: Jossey-Bass, 1975.

Astin, A. W. *Four Critical Years: Effects of College on Beliefs, Attitudes, and Knowledge*. San Francisco: Jossey-Bass, 1977.

Aukerman, R. C. "Viewpoints of the College Reading from the Administrative Point of View." In J. A. Figurel (Ed.), *Improvement of Reading Through Classroom Practice*. Proceedings of conference of International Reading Association. Newark, Del.: International Reading Association, 1964.

Ausubel, D. P. "The Use of Advance Organizers in the Learning and Retention of Meaningful Verbal Material." *Journal of Educational Psychology*, 1960, *51*, 267–274.

Ausubel, D. P. *The Psychology of Meaningful Verbal Learning*. New York: Grune and Stratton, 1963.

Ausubel, D. P. "The Facilitation of Meaningful Verbal Learning in the Classroom." *Educational Psychologist*, 1977, *12*, 162–178.

Avis, J. P., and Stewart, L. H. "College Counseling: Intentions and Change." *Counseling Psychologist*, 1976, *6*, 74–77.

Baird, L. L. "Teaching Styles: An Exploratory Study of Dimensions and Effects." *Journal of Educational Psychology*, 1973, *64* (1), 15–21.

Baker, S. R., and Talley, L. H. "The Relationship of Visualization Skills to Achievement in Freshman Chemistry." *Journal of Chemical Education*, 1972, *49*, 445.

Ball, S. "Research and Program Evaluation: Some Principles, Precepts, and Practices." In *The Final Report of National Project II, Alternatives to the Revolving Door*, New York: Bronx Community College, n.d.

Ball, S., and Anderson, S. B. *Practices in Program Evaluation: A Survey and Some Case Studies*. Princeton, N.J.: Educational Testing Service, 1975.

Bandt, P. L., and others. *A Time to Learn: A Guide to Academic and Personal Effectiveness*. New York: Holt, Rinehart and Winston, 1974.

Barron, R. F., and Stone, V. F. "The Effects of Student Constructed Graphic Post-organizers upon the Learning of Vocabulary Relationships in Tenth Grade Biology." Paper read at the National Reading Conference, Houston, Texas, 1973.

Baum, P., and Scheuer, E. M. *Statistics Made Relevant: Casebook of Real Life Examples.* New York: Wiley, 1976.

Beaman, A. L., and others. "Effects of Voluntary and Semivoluntary Peer Monitoring Programs on Academic Performance." *Journal of Educational Psychology*, 1977, *69*, 109–115.

Beatty, W. H. (Ed.). *Improving Educational Assessment and an Inventory of Measures of Affective Behavior.* Washington, D.C.: Association for Supervision and Curriculum Development, National Education Association, 1971.

Beery, R. G. "Fear of Failure in the Student Experience." *Personnel and Guidance Journal*, 1975, *54*, 191–202.

Beitler, L., and Martin, I. "Tutorial Assistance in College Programs." in P. L. Nacke (Ed.) *Programs and Practices for College Reading.* 22nd Yearbook of the National Reading Conference. Vol. 2. Boone, N.C.: National Reading Conference, 1973.

Benet, J. "Building Foundations." *Change Report on Teaching #1*, March 1976, pp. 10–13.

Berger, A., and Peebles, J. D. *Rates of Comprehension: An Annotated Bibliography.* Newark, Del.: International Reading Association, 1976.

Berger, N. S., and Perfetti, C. A. "Reading Skills and Memory for Spoken and Written Discourse." *Journal of Reading Behavior*, 1977, *9*, 7–16.

Bernstein, D. A., and Borkovec, T. D. *Progressive Relaxation Training.* Champaign, Ill.: Research Press, 1973.

Bernstein, H. R. *Manual for Teaching.* Ithaca, N.Y.: Center for Improvement of Undergraduate Education, Cornell University, 1976.

Bernstein, T. M. *Miss Thistlebottom's Hobgoblins: The Careful Writer's Guide to the Taboos, Bugbears, and Outmoded Rules of English Usage.* New York: Farrar, Strauss, & Giroux, 1971.

Berte, N. R. (Ed.). *New Directions for Higher Education: Individualizing Education by Learning Contracts*, no. 10. San Francisco: Jossey-Bass, 1975.

Bird, C. *The Case Against College.* New York: McKay, 1975.

Black, R. *Dear Arby: A T.E.S.L. Guide—How Do I Teach English as a Second Spoken Language?* Calif.: Central Orange County Literacy Council, 1975.

Blake, K. A. *College Reading Skills.* Englewood Cliffs, N.J.: Prentice-Hall, 1977.

Blake, W. S. "Do Probationary College Freshmen Benefit from Compulsory Study Skills and Reading Training?" *Journal of Experimental Education,* 1956, *25,* 91–93.

Blanton, W. E., and Bullock, T. "Cognitive Style and Reading Behavior." *Reading World,* 1973, *12,* 276–287.

Bliesmer, E. P. "Materials for the More Retarded College Reader." In O. S. Causey (Ed.), *Techniques and Procedures in College and Adult Reading Programs.* Sixth Yearbook of the Southwestern Reading Conference. Fort Worth: Texas Christian University Press, 1957.

Bloom, B. S. *Human Characteristics and School Learning.* New York: McGraw-Hill, 1976.

Bloom, B. S., and Broder, L. *Problem-Solving Processes of College Students.* Chicago: University of Chicago Press, 1950.

Bloom, B. S., and others. *Handbook on Formative and Summative Evaluation of Student Learning.* New York: McGraw-Hill, 1971.

Bloom, S. *Peer and Cross-Age Tutoring in the Schools: An Individualized Supplement to Group Instruction.* Chicago: District 10, Chicago Board of Education, n.d.

Boatner, M. T. *A Dictionary of Idioms for the Deaf.* West Hartford, Conn.: American School for the Deaf, 1966.

Bogaard, B. R. *College of Dupage Developmental Learning Laboratory Report, 1969–1974.* Dupage, Ill.: Developmental Learning Laboratory, College of Dupage, 1974.

Bogaard, B. R., and others. "Human Options for Human Beings." In G. Kersteins (Ed.), *Technological Alternatives in Learning.* Proceedings of 6th annual conference of Western College Reading Association. 1973.

Bormuth, J. R. "Cloze Tests as Measures of Readability and Comprehension Ability." Unpublished doctoral dissertation, Indiana University, 1962.

Bossone, R. M., and Troyka, L. Q. *A Strategy for Coping with High School and College Remedial English Problems.* New York: Center for Advanced Study in Education, Graduate School, City University of New York, 1976.

Bossone, R. M., and Weiner, M. *Three Modes of Teaching Remedial English: A Comparative Analysis*. New York: Baruch College and the Graduate School of the City University of New York, 1973.

Bossone, R. M., and Weiner, M. *City University English Teachers: A Self-Report Regarding Remedial Teaching*. New York: Center for Advanced Study in Education, Graduate School, City University of New York, 1975.

Brandt, W. H. *The Student's Guide to Optical Microscopes*. Los Altos, Calif.: William Kaufman, 1976.

Branson, H. R. "Blacks and Science." *Journal of the Society of Ethnic and Special Studies*, 1977, *1*, 15–21.

Breed, A. E., and others. *Through the Molecular Maze: A Helpful Guide to Chemistry for Life Science Students*. Los Altos, Calif.: William Kaufman, 1976.

Brooks, L. "Supermoms Shift Gears: Re-entry Women." *Counseling Psychologist*, 1976, *6*, 33–37.

Brooks, P. "Mimesis: Grammar and the Echoing Voice." *College English*, 1973, *35*, 161–169.

Brooks, P. "When the Bilingual Student Goes to College." Unpublished paper, Subject A Department, University of California, Berkeley, 1978.

Brown, G. M., and Hulbert, M. J. *Letters, Sounds, and Words*. Dubuque, Iowa: Kendall/Hunt, 1976.

Brown, J., and Associates. *Free Writing: A Group Approach*. Rochelle Park, N.J.: Hayden, 1977.

Brown, S. K. "Experiencing a Tutor Training Workshop." In R. Sugimoto (Ed.), *The Spirit of '76: Revolutionizing College Learning Skills*. Proceedings of 9th annual conference of Western College Reading Association. 1976.

Brown, W. H., and Holtzman, W. H. *Survey of Study Habits and Attitudes*. New York: Psychological Corporation, 1966.

Brubacher, J. S., and Willis, R. *Higher Education in Transition: A History of American Colleges and Universities 1636–1976*. (3rd ed.) New York: Harper & Row, 1976.

Bruffee, K. A. "Collaborative Learning: Some Practical Models." *College English*, 1973, *34*, 634–643.

Bruffee, K. A. "A New Intellectual Frontier: Basic Studies Offers an Enormous Scholarly Opportunity." *Chronicle of Higher Education*, February 27, 1978, p. 40.

Bruner, J. S., and others. *A Study of Thinking*. New York: Wiley, 1956.

Budzynski, T. H. *Relaxation Training Program*. New York: Bio-Monitoring Applications, 1976.

Burgess, B. A., and others. "Effect on Academic Achievement of a Voluntary Reading Program." *Journal of Reading*, 1976, *19*, 644–646.

Burkheimer, G., and others. *A Census of Special Support Programs for Disadvantaged Students in American Institutions of Higher Education, 1971–2*. Princeton, N.J.: Educational Testing Service, 1973. (ERIC Document Reproduction Service No. ED 112 791)

Buros, O. K. (Ed.). *Reading Tests and Reviews II*. Highland Park, N.J.: Gryphon Press, 1975.

Buzan, T. *Use Your Head*. London, England: British Broadcasting Co., 1974.

Buzan, T. *Use Both Sides of Your Brain*. New York: Dutton, 1976.

Bye, M. P. *Reading in Mathematics and Cognitive Development*. 1975, (ERIC Document Reproduction Service No. ED 124 926)

California State Board of Education. *State Framework in Reading*. Sacramento: California State Board of Education, 1973.

Call, R. J., and Wiggins, N. A. "Reading and Mathematics." *Mathematics Teacher*, 1966, *59*, 49–57.

Campbell, D. T., and Stanley, J. C. *Experimental and Quasi-Experimental Designs for Research on Teaching*. Chicago: Rand McNally, 1963.

Canfield, A. *The Learning Styles Inventory*. Ann Arbor, Mich.: Humanics Press, 1976.

Carkeet, D. "How Critics Write and How Students Write." *College English*, 1976, *37*, 599–604.

Carlson, J. C., and Minke, K. "The Effect of Student Tutors on Learning by Unit Mastery Instructional Methods." *Psychological Record*, 1974, 533–543.

Carman, R. A. "A Long Term Study of the Effects of Tutoring in Developmental Mathematics." Santa Barbara, Calif.: Santa Barbara Community College, 1975. (ERIC Document Reproduction Service No. ED 112 983 [764])

Carman, R. A., and Adams, W. R. *Study Skills: A Student's Guide for Survival.* New York: Wiley, 1972.

Carrier, N. A. "The Relationship of Certain Personality Measures to Examination Performance Under Stress." *Journal of Educational Psychology,* 1957, *48,* 510–520.

Carver, R. P. *Sense and Nonsense in Speed Reading.* Silver Spring, Md.: Revrac Publications, 1971.

Case, K. E., and Vardaman, G. T. *Mature Reading and Thinking.* Denver: Communication Foundation, 1959.

Castro, B. "Report from a Ghetto College." *Harvard Educational Review,* 1974, *44,* 270–294.

Causey, O. S. "A Report on College Reading Programs in the Nation." In O. S. Causey (Ed.), *Evaluating College Reading Programs.* 4th Yearbook of the Southwest Reading Conference for Colleges and Universities. Fort Worth: Texas Christian University Press, 1955.

Center, S. *The Art of Book Reading.* New York: Scribner's, 1952.

Chaplin, M. T. "Practical Applications of Piagetian Theory to College Reading Instruction." 1976. (ERIC Document Reproduction Service No. CS 002 810, ED)

Chiapetta, E. L. "A Review of Piagetian Studies Relevant to Science Instruction at the Secondary and College Level." *Science Education,* 1976, *60,* 253–261.

Chickering, A. W. *Education and Identity.* San Francisco: Jossey-Bass, 1969.

Chickering, A. W. "The Double Bind of Field Dependence/ Independence in Program Alternatives for Educational Development." In S. Messick and Associates, *Individuality in Learning: Implications of Cognitive Styles and Creativity for Human Development.* San Francisco: Jossey-Bass, 1976.

Christ, F. L. "The SR/SE Laboratory: A Systems Approach to Reading/Study Skills Counseling." In G. B. Schick and M. M. May (Eds.), *The Psychology of Reading Behavior.* 18th Yearbook of the National Reading Conference. Milwaukee: National Reading Conference, 1969.

Christ, F. L. "Systems for Learning Assistance: Learners, Learning Facilitators, and Learning Centers." In F. L. Christ (Ed.), *Interdisciplinary Aspects of Reading Instruction.* Proceedings of 4th annual conference of Western College Reading Association. 1971.

Christ, F. L. "Learning Assistance Support Systems at California State University, Long Beach." *Journal of Media and Technology,* 1973, *18,* 19–20.

Christ, F. L. "Management of a Learning Assistance Sector." In G. Enright (Ed.), *Personalizing Learning Systems: Ecologies and Strategies.* Proceedings of 10th annual conference of Western College Reading Association. 1977.

Christ, F. L., and Adams, R. *You Can Learn to Learn.* Englewood Cliffs, N.J.: Prentice-Hall, 1978.

Clark, D. R. *The Law School Admission Test Workshops.* College Park: Reading and Study Skills Laboratory, University of Maryland, 1977.

Cline, R. K. J. "Those Who Don't Read Have No Advantage over Those Who Can't." *Arizona English Bulletin,* 1972, *14,* 111–115.

Clouser, J. L. *Keller Plan for Self-Paced Study Using Masterson and Slowinski's Chemical Principles.* Philadelphia: Saunders, 1977.

Cloward, R. D. *Studies in Tutoring.* New York: Social Work Research Center, Columbia University, 1966.

"Code of Ethics." *Tutor Talk,* 1977, *1,* 15.

Coleman, E. B., and Miller, G. R. "A Measure of Information Gained During Prose Learning." *Reading Research Quarterly,* 1968, *3,* 369–386.

College Entrance Examination Board. *Effects of Coaching on Scholastic Aptitude Scores.* Princeton, N.J.: College Entrance Examination Board, 1968.

Commission on Mathematics. *Program for College Preparatory Mathematics.* New York: College Entrance Examination Board, 1959.

Committee of Standards and Testing of CAWS (City University of New York's Association of Writing Supervisors). "The CAWS Statement on the College Board's Test of Standard Written English." *College Composition and Communication,* 1976, *27,* 287–289.

Committee on Learning Skills Centers. *Learning Skills Centers: A CCCC Report.* Urbana, Ill.: ERIC Clearinghouse on Reading and Communication Skills and Conference on College Composition and Communication, 1976.

Comptroller General of the United States. *Problems of the Upward Bound Program in Preparing Disadvantaged Students for a Postsecon-*

dary Education: A Report to the Congress. Washington, D.C.: Comptroller General of the United States, n.d. (ERIC Document Reproduction Service No. EDO 90349 UD014170)

Conference Board of the Mathematical Sciences National Advisory Committee on Mathematical Education. *Overview and Analysis of School Mathematics—Grades K–12.* Washington, D.C.: Conference Board of the Mathematical Sciences, 1975.

Connelly, P. J., and Irving, D. C. "Composition in the Liberal Arts: A Shared Responsibility." *College English,* 1976, *37,* 668–670.

Cook, W. D. *Adult Literacy in the United States.* Newark, Del.: International Reading Association, 1977.

Cooke, W. B. *Resources for Student Learning Research Report: 1977.* National Project II: Alternatives to the Revolving Door. Whiteville, N.C.: Southeastern Community College, 1977.

Cottle, T. J. *College: Reward and Betrayal.* Chicago: University of Chicago Press, 1977.

Coulton, J. "Automation, Electronic Computers, and Education." *Phi Delta Kappan,* 1966, *47,* 340–344.

Cox, G. L. "Different Effects of Instructional Strategies on Reading Rate Flexibility and Comprehension." Paper read at meeting of American Psychological Association, San Francisco, August 27, 1977.

Crafts, G., and Gibson, A. "College Reading Specialists: Are They Being Short-changed by Graduate Schools?" In R. Sugimoto (Ed.), *College Learning Skills: Today and Tomorrowland.* Proceedings of 8th annual conference of Western College Reading Association, 1975.

Cranney, A. G., and others. "Initiating a Program for Training Junior College Reading Teachers." In P. L. Nacke (Ed.), *Programs and Practices for College Reading.* Twenty-second Yearbook of the National Reading Conference. Vol. 2. Boone, N.C.: National Reading Conference, 1973.

Crews, F. *The Random House Handbook.* (2nd ed.) New York: Random House, 1977.

Croll, W., and Moskaluk, S. "Should Flesch Counts Count?" *Teaching of Psychology,* 1977, *4,* 48–49.

Cross, K. P. *Beyond the Open Door: New Students to Higher Education.* San Francisco: Jossey-Bass, 1971.

Cross, K. P. *Accent on Learning: Improving Instruction and Reshaping the Curriculum.* San Francisco: Jossey-Bass, 1976.

Cross, K. P. "Responding to New Learning Needs." In *Entering Freshmen: Their Specific Education—Proceedings of A Joint Conference, December 3–5, 1976.* Berkeley: University of California and California State Universities and Colleges, 1977.

Cummings, J. "Return to Howard: The Turbulent 60s Seem Long Ago." *New York Times,* November 16, 1975, p. 14.

Dale, E., and Chall, J. S. "A Formula for Predicting Readability." *Educational Research Bulletin,* 1948, *27,* 11–20; 28.

Daly, J. A., and Miller, M. D. "The Empirical Development of an Instrument to Measure Writing Apprehension." *Research in the Teaching of English,* 1975, *9,* 242–249.

Davidson, S. "4T's: Teacher/you, Text, Talk, and Test—A Systematic Approach to Learning Success." Unpublished paper, Learning Assistance Center, California Polytechnic University, San Luis Obispo, 1977.

Davis, J., and others. *The Impact of Special Services Programs in Higher Education for "Disadvantaged" Students.* Princeton, N.J.: Educational Testing Service, 1975. (ERIC Document Reproduction Service No. ED 112 790)

Deegan, A. X., and Fritz, R. J. *MBO Goes to College.* Boulder: Center for Management and Technical Programs, University of Colorado, 1975.

Denny, R. T. "An Analysis of the Relationship Between Certain Mathematical Skills and Chemistry Achievement." Unpublished doctoral dissertation, University of Pennsylvania, 1970.

Devirian, M. C. "Data Collection: A Cybernetic Aspect of a Learning Assistance Center." In G. Kersteins (Ed.), *Technological Alternatives in Learning.* Proceedings of 6th annual conference of Western College Reading Association, 1973.

Devirian, M. C., and others. "A Survey of Learning Program Centers in U.S. Institutions of Higher Learning." In R. Sugimoto (Ed.), *College Learning Skills: Today and Tomorrowland.* Proceedings of 8th annual conference of Western College Reading Association. 1975.

Diamond, L. D. "The Influence of an Integrated Coordinated Reading Program on Skills Development of Underprepared

College Students." Paper presented at 21st annual convention of International Reading Association, Anaheim, Calif., May 1976.

Diederich, P. B. *Measuring Growth in English.* Urbana, Ill.: National Council of Teachers of English, 1974.

Donovan, R. A. *National Project II: Alternatives to the Revolving Door.* New York: Bronx Community College, 1975.

Donovan, R. A. "The Southwest Institution of National Project II." *Alternatives to the Revolving Door Newsletter #2,* July 1976, pp. 1–6.

Douglas, J. "The Librarian-Tutor in an Innovative College Experiment." *Learning Today,* Fall 1971, *4,* 44–53.

Driskell, J. *A Guide to Tutoring.* Moscow: University of Idaho Press, 1977.

Drucker, R. P. "Report on the Peer-Tutoring Program for Women and Minority Freshmen in the Sciences and Mathematics." Berkeley: Student Learning Center, University of California, 1976.

Dueker, J. S. *Writing Better Bluebooks: Techniques for Taking Essay Exams.* Belmont, Calif.: Fearon, 1967.

Duffin, B., and others. *A Study of Writing Problems in a Remedial Writing Program for EOP Students.* Davis: Department of English, University of California, 1977.

Dugger, R. "Cooperative Learning in a Writing Community." *Change Report on Teaching #2,* July 1976, pp. 30–33.

Dupuis, M. M., and Askov, E. N. *An Annotated Bibliography of Adult Basic Education Instructional Materials.* State College: Content Area Reading Project, Pennsylvania State University, n.d.

Eanet, M. G., and Manzo, A. V. "REAP: A Strategy for Improving Reading/Writing/Study Skills." *Journal of Reading,* 1976, *20,* 647–652.

Earle, R. A. *Teaching Reading and Mathematics.* Newark, Del.: International Reading Association, 1976.

Edmonds, M. K. "Reading/Writing: Learning and Teaching of Literary Skills." Unpublished doctoral dissertation, University of Michigan, 1976.

Educational Testing Service. *Multiple-Choice Questions: A Closer Look.* Princeton, N.J.: Educational Testing Service, 1963.

Elbow, P. *Writing Without Teachers.* New York: Oxford University Press, 1973.

Ellis, A. *Humanistic Psychotherapy: The Rational Emotive Approach.* New York: Julian Press and McGraw-Hill Paperbacks, 1973.

Ellis, A. "Rational-Emotive Therapy: Research Data That Supports the Clinical and Personality Hypotheses of RET and Other Modes of Cognitive-Behavior Therapy." *Counseling Psychologist,* 1977, *7,* 2–42.

Ellson, D. G., and others. "A Field Test of Programed and Directed Tutoring." *Reading Research Quarterly,* 1968, *3,* 307–336.

Enright, G. "College Learning Skills: Frontierland Origins of the Learning Assistance Center." In R. Sugimoto (Ed.), *College Learning Skills: Today and Tomorrowland.* Proceedings of 8th annual conference of Western College Reading Association. Long Beach, Calif.: Western College Reading Association, 1975.

Enright, G. "The Study Table and Panic Clinic." In R. Sugimoto (Ed.), *The Spirit of '76: Revolutionizing College Learning Skills.* Proceedings of 9th annual conference of Western College Reading Association. 1976.

Entwisle, G., and Entwisle, D. R. "Study Skills Courses in Medical Schools?" *Journal of Medical Education,* 1960, *35,* 843–848.

Eraut, M. "The Development of Instructional Systems with Variable Input." Paper read at meeting of National Society for Programmed Instruction, Boston, April 1967.

Ernest, J. *Mathematics and Sex.* Preprint. Department of Mathematics, University of California at Santa Barbara, 1976.

Even, A. "Patterns of Academic Achievement in Grade 12 Chemistry and Their Relationship to Personal, Attitudinal, and Environmental Factors." Paper read at annual meeting of American Educational Research Association, Los Angeles, February 6, 1969.

Fairbanks, M. M. "The Effect of College Reading Programs on Academic Achievement." In P. L. Nacke (Ed.), *Interaction: Research and Practice for College-Adult Reading.* 23rd Yearbook of the National Reading Conference. Clemson, S.C.: National Reading Conference, 1974.

Fairbanks, M.M., and Snozek, D. A. "Checklist of Current Practices in Reading and Study Skills Programs for College Students." Paper read at 17th annual meeting of College Reading Association, Silver Spring, Md., November 1973. (ERIC Document ReproductionService No. ED 088 020)

Farr, J. N., and others. "Simplification of Flesch Reading Ease Formula." *Journal of Applied Psychology*, 1951, *35*, 333–337.

Feldstein, J. H. "Reading Ease and Human Interest Scores of Thirty-two Recent Child and Developmental Psychology Tests." *Teaching of Psychology*, 1977, *4*, 43–44.

Felton, G. S., and Biggs, B. E. *Up from Underachievement*. Springfield, Ill.: Thomas, 1977.

Ferguson, D. "A Structure for Unstructured Lectures." *American Mathematics Monthly*, 1974, *81*, 512–514.

Ferguson, J. "Teaching the Reading of Biology." In H.A. Robinson and E. L. Thomas (Eds.), *Fusing Reading Skills and Content*. Newark, Del.: International Reading Association, 1969.

Ferrin, R. I. *Developmental Programs in Midwestern Community Colleges*. Higher Education Surveys Report No. 4. Princeton, N.J.: College Entrance Examination Board, 1971.

Fisher, J. *Reading to Understand Sciences: A Program for Self-Instruction*. New York: McGraw-Hill, 1970.

Fitts, F. "Guide to Berkeley Calculus and Pre-calculus Courses." Berkeley: Department of Mathematics, University of California, 1976.

Fitts, W. H. *Tennessee Self-Concept Scale*. Nashville, Tenn.: Counselor Recordings and Tests, 1965.

Flanagan, J. C. "The Critical Incident Technique." *Psychological Bulletin*, 1954, *51*, 327–358.

Flesch, R. *Marks of Readable Style: A Study in Adult Education*. New York: Bureau of Publications, Teachers College, Columbia University, 1943.

Flesch, R. "A New Readability Yardstick." *Journal of Applied Psychology*, 1948, *32*, 221–223.

Flesch, R. *How to Test Readability*. New York: Harper & Row, 1951.

Flesch, R. *A New Way to Better English*. Garden City, N.Y.: Dolphin, 1958.

Footlick, J. K. "Self-Paced Calculus Grows Up." *Change Report on Teaching #3*, January 1977, pp. 36–39.

Fox, R. P. (Ed.). *Essays on English as a Second Language and Second Dialect*. Urbana, Ill.: National Council of Teachers of English #12275, 1973.

Foxe, E. K. "An Experimental Investigation of the Effectiveness of a Brief Study Skills Program for Freshmen College Chemistry

Students." Unpublished doctoral dissertation, University of Maryland, 1966.

Frank, A. C., and Kirk, B. "Differences in Outcomes for Users and Non-users of a University Counseling and Psychiatric Service: A Five-Year Accountability Study." Berkeley: Counseling Center, University of California, 1974.

Fraser, S. C., and others. "Two, Three, or Four Heads Are Better than One: Modifications of College Performance by Peer Monitoring." *Journal of Educational Psychology,* 1977, *69,* 101–108.

Fry, E. "A Readability Formula That Saves Time." *Journal of Reading,* 1968, *11,* 513–516; 575–578.

Fry, E. *The Emergency Reading Teacher's Manual.* Highland Park, N.J.: Dreier Educational Systems, 1969.

Fry, E. *Reading Instruction for Classroom and Clinic.* New York: McGraw-Hill, 1972.

Fry, E. "Fry's Readability Graph: Clarification, Validity, and Extension to Level 17." *Journal of Reading,* 1977, *21,* 242–252.

Fuller, R. B. *Education Automation—Freeing the Scholar to Return to His Studies.* Carbondale: Southern Illinois University Press, 1962.

Gaonker, G. H., and others. "Quasi-Modular Approach in Mathematics for the Disadvantaged." *American Mathematical Monthly,* 1977, *84,* 211–216.

Gartner, A., and others. *Children Teach Children: Learning by Teaching.* New York: Harper & Row, 1971.

Gaudry, E., and Spielberger, C. D. "Anxiety and Intelligence in Paired Associate Learning." *Journal of Educational Psychology,* 1970, *61,* 386–391.

Geerlofs, M. W., and Kling, M. "Current Practices in College and Adult Developmental Reading Programs." *Journal of Reading,* 1968, *11,* 517–520; 569–575.

Gibbons, J. F., and others. "Tutored Videotape Instruction: A New Use of Electronics in Education." *Science,* 1977, *195,* 1139–1146.

Gibbs, G., and Northedge, A. "Learning to Study: A Student Centered Approach." London, England: Tuition and Counselling Research Group, Open University, 1976.

Gilbert, D. W. *Study in Depth.* Englewood Cliffs, N.J.: Prentice-Hall, 1966.

Gilbreath, S. H. "Appropriate and Inappropriate Counseling with Academic Underachievers." *Journal of Counseling Psychology,* 1968, *15,* 506–511.

Gillen, B. "Readability and Human Interest Scores of Thirty-four Current Introductory Psychology Texts." *American Psychologist,* 1973, *28,* 1010–1011.

Gillen, B. "Readability and Human Interest Scores of Thirty-two Introductory Psychology Texts: Update and Clarification." *Teaching of Psychology,* 1975, *2,* 175–176.

Gillen, B., and others. "Reading Ease and Human Interest Scores: A Comparison of Flesch Scores with Subjective Ratings." *Teaching of Psychology,* 1977, *4,* 39–41.

Gladstein, G. A. *Individualized Study: A New Approach to Succeeding in College.* Chicago: Rand McNally, 1967.

Glass, M. L. "A Look at the Bay Area Writing Project." *California English,* 1975, *11,* 16.

Glasser, W. *Reality Therapy: A New Approach to Psychiatry.* New York: Harper & Row, 1965.

Glock, M. D., and others. *Probe: College Developmental Reading.* Columbus, Ohio: Merrill, 1975.

Godshalk, F. I., and others. *The Measurement of Writing Ability.* Princeton, N.J.: College Entrance Examination Board, 1966.

Goldfried, M., and Goldfried, A. "Cognitive Change Methods." In F. Kanfer and A. Goldstein (Eds.), *Helping People Change: A Textbook of Methods.* Elmsford, N.Y.: Pergamon Press, 1975.

Goldschmid, B., and Goldschmid, M. L. "Enabling Students to Learn and Participate Effectively in Higher Education." *Journal of Personalized Instruction,* 1976a, *1,* 70–75.

Goldschmid, B., and Goldschmid, M. L. "Peer Tutoring in Higher Education: A Review." *Higher Education,* 1976b, *4,* 9–33.

Gordon, E. W. "Programs and Practices for Minority Group Youth in Higher Education." In L. C. Solomon and P. J. Taubman (Eds.), *Does College Matter? Some Evidence of the Impact of Higher Education.* New York: Academic Press, 1973.

Gordon, E. W. *Opportunity Programs for the Disadvantaged in Higher Education.* ERIC/Higher Education Research Report No. 6. Washington, D.C.: ERIC Clearinghouse on Higher Education, George Washington University, 1975.

Gourdine, E. B. (Ed.) *The Emerging Role of Learning Centers in the University of California: Report of a Statewide Conference of Learning Center Directors of University of California Campuses, January 30, 1976.* Davis: Learning Assistance Center, University of California, 1976a.

Gourdine, E. B. "Training Paraprofessionals to Deliver Test-Anxiety Desensitization." In R. Sugimoto (Ed.), *The Spirit of '76: Revolutionizing College Learning Skills.* Proceedings of 9th annual conference of Western College Reading Association. 1976b.

Grant, G., and Riesman, D. *The Perpetual Dream: Reform and Experiment in the American College.* Chicago, University of Chicago Press, 1978.

Gray, J., and Myers, M. "The Bay Area Writing Project." *Phi Delta Kappan,* 1978, *59,* 410–413.

Gray, W. S., and Leary, B. *What Makes a Book Readable.* Chicago: University of Chicago Press, 1935.

Grob, J. A. "Reading Rate and Study-Time Demands on Secondary ·Students." *Journal of Reading,* 1970, *13,* 285–288; 316.

Grobman, A. B. "Shortchanging the Disadvantaged Student." *Science,* 1972, *177,* 1.

Gross, T. L. "How to Kill a College: The Private Papers of a Campus Dean." *Saturday Review,* February 4, 1978, pp. 12–20.

The Group for Human Development in Higher Education. *Faculty Development in a Time of Retrenchment.* New Rochelle, N.Y.: Group for Human Development in Higher Education and *Change* Magazine, 1974.

Groveman, A. M., and others. *Literature Review, Treatment Manuals, and Bibliography for Study Skills Counseling and Behavioral Self-Control Approaches to Improving Study Behavior.* Journal Supplement Abstract Series. Washington, D.C.: American Psychological Association, 1975.

Gunning, R. *The Technique of Clear Writing.* New York: McGraw-Hill 1952.

Guralnick, E. S., and Levitt, P. M. "Improving Student Writing: A Case History." *College English,* 1977, *38,* 506–511.

Gyrafas, E. (Ed.). *Reading Tests: Grades 7 to 16 and Adults.* Princeton, N.J.: Educational Testing Service, 1975.

Haase, A. M. B., and others. "Evaluating the College Reading Program: A Management Audit." In P. D. Pearson and J. Hansen (Eds.), *Reading: Theory, Research, and Practice.* 26th Yearbook of the National Reading Conference. 1977.

Haburton, E. "Impact of an Experimental Reading-Study Skills Course on High-Risk Student Success in a Community College." In P. D. Pearson and J. Hansen (Eds.), *Reading: Theory, Research, and Practice.* 26th Yearbook of the National Reading Conference. 1977.

Haight, G. P. "Balancing Chemistry's Priorities." *Change Report on Teaching #1,* March 1976, pp. 4–5.

Hall, C. "Interfacing Tutoring and Reading Programs: Training Tutors to Do My Job." Austin: Reading and Study Skills Laboratory, University of Texas, 1975. (ERIC Document Reproduction Service No. ED 112 366)

Hall, E. T. "Teaching Students in Africa to Write Better English than Americans of the Same Age." *Yale Review,* 1977, *67,* 23–25.

Hanau, L. *The Study Game: How to Play and Win with "Statement-Pie."* New York: Barnes & Noble, 1972.

Hanf, M. B. "Mapping: A Technique for Translating Reading into Thinking." *Journal of Reading,* 1971, *14,* 225–230; 270.

Hanks, K., and others. *Design Yourself!* Los Altos, Calif.: William Kaufman, 1977.

Hansen, D. "TICCIT: Computer-Assisted Instruction in Critical Reading." Paper read at the National Reading Conference, Atlanta, December 1976.

Hansen, D. M. "A Discourse Structure Analysis of the Comprehension of Rapid Readers." In P. D. Pearson and J. Hansen (Eds.), *Reading: Theory, Research, and Programs.* 26th Yearbook of the National Reading Conference. Clemson, S.C.: National Reading Conference, 1977.

Harris, D. P. *Reading Improvement Exercises for Students of English as a Second Language.* Englewood Cliffs, N.J.: Prentice-Hall, 1966.

Harris, M. B., and Liquori, R. A. "Some Effects of a Personalized System of Instruction in Teaching College Mathematics." *Journal of Educational Research,* 1974, *68,* 63–66.

Harrison, G. V. "Tutoring: A Remedy Reconsidered." *Improving Human Performance: A Research Quarterly,* 1972a, *1,* 1–5.

Harrison, G. V. "Use of a Structured Tutorial Reading Program in

Teaching Nonreading Second Graders in Title I Schools to Read." Paper read at annual meeting of American Educational Research Association, Chicago, February 1972b.

Hartkopf, R. *Math Without Tears.* Buchanan, N.Y.: Emerson Books, 1976.

Hawkins, T. *Benjamin: Reading and Beyond.* Columbus, Ohio: Merrill, 1972.

Hawkins, T. *Group-Inquiry Techniques for Teaching Writing.* Theory and Research into Practice Series. Urbana, Ill.: ERIC Clearinghouse in Reading and Communication Skills and National Council of Teachers of English, 1976. (ERIC Document Reproduction Service No. 18976J)

Hawkins, T. "Training Peer Writing Tutors." Paper read at annual convention of National Council of Teachers of English. New York City, November 25, 1977.

Heard, P. "College Learning Specialists: A Profession Coming of Age." In R. Sugimoto (Ed.), *The Spirit of '76: Revolutionizing College Learning Skills.* Proceedings of 9th annual conference of Western College Reading Association. 1976.

Heaton, C. P. (Ed.). *Management by Objectives in Higher Education: Theory, Cases, and Implementation.* Research Triangle Park, N.C.: National Laboratory for Higher Education Publications, 1977.

Hebb, D. O., and Bindra, D. "Scientific Writing and the General Problem of Communication." *American Psychologist,* 1952, 7, 569–573.

Hedges, L. V. *Teacher Education Program 196.* OASIS Report No. 1. San Diego: Office of Academic Support and Instructional Services, University of California, 1975.

Hedges, L. V., and Majer, K. *A Longitudinal Comparative Study of a Process Oriented Tutorial Program.* OASIS Research Report No. 5. San Diego: Office of Academic Support and Instructional Services, University of California, 1976.

Hedges, L. V., and others. *The Effects of Peer Tutoring on Medical Admissions Test Scores.* OASIS Report No. 6. San Diego: Office of Academic Support and Instructional Services, University of California, 1976.

"Help for the Brightest." *Time,* February 2, 1976, p. 44.

Henderson, L. A. "Training Educators to Use Cognitive Style

Maps." Paper read at convention of American Psychological Association, Washington, D.C., September 1976.

Henkin, L. A. "Skills and Skills." In *Conference on Basic Mathematical Skills and Learning, 1,* National Institute of Education. Washington, D.C.: U.S. Government Printing Office, 1975.

Herber, H. L. *Teaching Reading in Content Areas.* Englewood Cliffs, N.J.: Prentice-Hall, 1978.

Herlin, W. A. "A Required Critical Reading Evaluation: Content, Rationale, and Results." Paper read at annual meeting of National Reading Conference, Atlanta, December 1976.

Hertz, S. M., and others. "College Credit for Reading Courses? Yes!" *Journal of Reading,* 1977, *20,* 688–692.

Heys, F. "Theme-a-Week Assumption: Report of an Experiment." *Journal of English,* 1963, *24,* 320–322.

Hill, J. E. *The Educational Sciences.* Oakland, Mich.: Oakland Community College, n.d.

Hill, W. F. *Learning Through Discussion: Guide for Leaders and Members of Discussion Groups.* Beverly Hills, Calif.: Sage, 1975.

Hodgkinson, H. L. "How Deans of Students Are Seen by Others — and Why." *National Association of Student Personnel Administrators' Journal,* 1970, *8,* 49–54.

Hodgkinson, H. L., and others. "Current Evaluation Practices in 'Innovative' Colleges and Universities." Draft. Berkeley: Center for Research and Development in Higher Education, University of California, n.d.

Hofmann, R. J., and Vyhonsky, R. J. "Readability and Human Interest Scores of Recently Published Introductory Educational Psychology Texts." *American Psychologist,* 1975, *30,* 790–792.

Holt, J. *How Children Fail.* New York: Dell, 1964.

Hoover, R. M. "Experiments in Peer Teaching." *College Composition and Communication,* 1972, *23,* 421–423.

Horner, D. R. "Nonlab, Nonprogrammed, and Nonlecture: Any Chance?" *Two Year College Mathematics Journal,* 1974, *5,* 39–44.

Houston, R. D. "A Learning Center Approach to ESL." In R. Sugimoto (Ed.), *The Spirit of '76: Revolutionizing College Learning Skills.* Proceedings of 9th annual conference of Western College Reading Association. 1976.

Hubin, D. R. "Subject Area Tutoring: A Wild Card in the Learning Center." In R. Sugimoto (Ed.), *The Spirit of '76: Revolutionizing College Learning Skills.* Proceedings of 9th annual conference of Western College Reading Association, 1976.

Hubin, D. R., and Riddell, C. "How to Study Physics." Unpublished paper, Learning Skills Center, University of California at Irvine, 1977.

Hurst, B. "Current Status of Blacks in Engineering, Architecture, and Science Professions." *Journal of the Society of Ethnic and Special Studies,* 1977, *1,* 3–6.

Huslin, R. A. "What's Happening in College and University Developmental Reading Programs? Report on a Survey." *Reading World,* 1975, *14,* 202–214.

Huxley, A. "Education on the Nonverbal Level." *Daedalus,* 1962, *91,* 279–294.

Ivey, A. E., and Authier, J. *Microcounseling: Innovations in Interviewing, Counseling, Psychotherapy, and Psychoeducation.* Springfield, Ill.: Thomas, 1978.

Ivey, A. E., and Gluckstern, N. B. *Basic Attending Skills: An Introduction to Microcounseling and Helping.* North Amherst, Mass.: Microtraining Associates, 1974.

Jackson, B., and Van Zoost, B. "Self-Regulated Teaching of Others as a Means of Improving Study Habits." *Journal of Counseling Psychology,* 1974, *21,* 489–493.

Jackson, P. W. *The Teacher and the Machine.* Horace Mann Lecture. Pittsburgh: University of Pittsburgh Press, 1968.

Jacobs, J. E. "Focus: Women and Mathematics—Must They Be at Odds?" *Pi Lambda Theta Newsletter,* September-October 1977, p. 10.

Jacobson, E. *Progressive Relaxation.* Chicago: University of Chicago Press, 1938.

Jason, E., and others. "Introduction to an Acceleration Program in Science and Technology for the Disadvantaged." *Journal of the Society of Ethnic and Special Studies,* 1977, *1,* 36–39.

Jenkins, E. "The Potential of PLATO." *Change Report on Teaching #1,* March 1976, pp. 6–9.

Joffe, I. L. *Opportunities for Skillful Reading.* Series of ten workbooks. Belmont, Calif.: Wadsworth, 1970–1971.

Johnson, K. R. "Black Dialect Shift in Oral Reading." *Journal of Reading*, 1975, *18*, 535–540.

Johnson, K. R. "Proctor Training for Natural Control." *Journal of Personalized Instruction*, 1977, 2, 230–237.

Johnson-Davidson, S., and McCarty, C. "Academic Improvement Groups: An Innovative Way to Help Students Build Better Study Habits." In G. Enright (Ed.), *Personalizing Learning Systems: Ecologies and Strategies*. Proceedings of 10th annual conference of Western College Reading Association, 1977.

Jolly, C., and Jolly, R. *When You Teach English as a Second Language*. Brooklyn, New York: Book-Lab, 1974.

Jones, E. "Selection and Motivation of Students." In O. S. Causey (Ed.), *Starting and Improving College Reading Programs*. 8th Yearbook of the National Reading Conference. Fort Worth: Texas Christian University Press, 1959.

Kagan, N. *Interpersonal Process Recall. Unit #1: Elements of Facilitating Communication*. Mason, Mich.: Mason Media, 1973.

Kagan, N. "Influencing Human Interaction: Eleven Years of IPR." Unpublished paper, Michigan State University, n.d.

Kahn, G. B. "The Effects of Two Behavioral Treatments upon Reading Achievement and Test Anxiety." Paper read at the National Reading Conference, Atlanta, December 1976.

Kai, F. S., and Kersteins, E. J. *Study-Reading for College Courses*. New York: MacMillan, 1968.

Karlin, R. *Teaching Reading in High School: Improving Reading in Content Areas*. (3rd ed.) Indianapolis, Ind.: Bobbs-Merrill, 1977.

Karliner, A. *Report on the Problems of Subject A/Composition Program*. San Diego: University of California, 1974.

Karwin, T. J. *Flying a Learning Center: Design and Costs of an Off-Campus Space for Learning*. Berkeley, Calif.: Carnegie Commission on Higher Education, 1973.

Kaufman, H., and Botwinick, R. *Student Graduation at the City University of New York: Fall 1970—Spring 1974*. New York: Office of Program and Policy Research, City University of New York, 1975.

Keetz, M. "An Experimental Investigation of the Effectiveness of a College Reading and Study Skills Course for Freshman Students Enrolled in Scientific Course of Study." Paper read at convention of International Reading Association, Anaheim, Calif., May 1970.

Kenny, J. A., and Herzing, H. "Games Professors Play." *Journal of Higher Education,* 1969, *40,* 624–635.

Kershner, A. M. "Speed of Reading in an Adult Population Under Differential Conditions." *Journal of Applied Psychology,* 1964, *48,* 25–28.

Kersteins, G. *Junior-Community College Reading/Study Skills.* Newark, Del.: International Reading Association, 1971.

Kincaid, J. P., and Gamble, L. G. "Ease of Comprehension of Standard and Readable Automobile Insurance Policies as a Function of Reading Ability." *Journal of Reading Behavior,* 1977, *9,* 85–87.

King, F. J., and others. "An Investigation of the Causal Influence of Trait and State Anxiety on Academic Achievement." *Journal of Educational Psychology,* 1976, *68,* 330–334.

Kingston, A. J. "Problems of Initiating a New College Reading Program." In O. S. Causey (Ed.), *Starting and Improving College Reading Programs.* 8th Yearbook of the National Reading Conference. Forth Worth: Texas Christian University Press, 1959.

Kirk, B. A. "Test Versus Academic Performance in Malfunctioning Students." In M. Kornrich (Ed.), *Underachievement.* Springfield, Ill.: Thomas, 1965.

Kirk, B. A. "The Relationship of College Reading Programs to Educational Counseling." In G. B. Schick and M. M. May (Eds.), *The Psychology of Reading Behavior.* 18th Yearbook of the National Reading Conference. Milwaukee: National Reading Conference, 1969.

Kitzhaber, A. R. *Themes, Theories, and Therapy: The Teaching of Writing in College.* New York: McGraw-Hill, 1963.

Klein, M. H. *Dynamics of Comprehension: How to Learn from a College Textbook.* New York: New Century/Meredith, 1970.

Klingelhofer, E. L., and Hollander, L. *Educational Characteristics and Needs of New Students: A Review of the Literature.* Berkeley: Center for Research and Development in Higher Education, University of California, 1973.

Koberg, D., and Bagnall, J. *The Universal Traveler: A Soft-Systems Guide to Creativity, Problem-Solving, and the Process of Reaching Goals.* Los Altos, Calif.: William Kaufman, 1976.

Kogelman, S., and Warren, J. *Mind over Math.* New York: Dial, 1978.

Kolata, G. B. "Communicating Mathematics: Is It Possible?" *Science,* 1968, *187,* 732.

Kolata, G. B. "Aftermath of the New Math: Its Originators Defend It." *Science,* 1977, *195,* 854–857.

Kornrich, M. (Ed.). *Underachievement.* Springfield, Ill.: Thomas, 1965.

Kotnik, L. J. "Teaching Science to the Disadvantaged Student in an Urban Community College." *Chemistry in the Two-Year College,* 1972, *1,* 43.

Kotnik, L. J. *Introduction to Chemistry.* Dubuque, Iowa: Kendall/Hunt, 1975.

Kozma, R. B., and others. *Guide for PSI Proctors.* Washington, D.C.: Center for Personalized Instruction, 1976.

Kramer, R., and others. *Characteristics of Enrollees and Non-enrollees Among Freshmen, 1972.* New York: Office of Program and Policy Research, City University of New York, 1974.

Kulik, J. A., and Kulik, C. L. "The Keller Plan in Science Teaching." *Science,* 1974, *183,* 379–383.

Labov, W. "Academic Ignorance and Black Intelligence." *Atlantic,* June 1972, pp. 59–67.

Lamberg, W. J. "Major Problems in Doing Academic Writing." *College Composition and Communication,* 1975, *26,* 26–29.

Lange, R. "Flipping the Coin: From Test Anxiety to Test Wiseness." *Journal of Reading,* 1978, *22,* 274–277.

Larkin, J. H., and Reif, F. "Analysis and Teaching of a General Skill for Studying Scientific Text." *Journal of Educational Psychology,* 1976, *68,* 131–140.

Lay, N. D. S. "Chinese Language Interference in Written English." *Journal of Basic Writing,* 1975, *1,* 50–61.

Lazar, R., and others. "Tutorial Training for PSI Proctors in the Large-Enrollment Course." *Journal of Personalized Instruction,* 1977, *2,* 226–229.

"Learning to Live with Criticism." *Harper's,* 1975, *251* (1505), 8.

Lees, F. "Mathematics and Reading." *Journal of Reading,* 1976, *19,* 621–626.

Lesser, G. S. "Cultural Differences in Learning and Thinking

Styles." In S. Messick and Associates, *Individuality in Learning: Implications of Cognitive Styles and Creativity for Human Development*. San Francisco: Jossey-Bass, 1976.

Liebert, R., and Morris, L. "Cognitive and Emotional Components of Text Anxiety: A Distinction and Some Initial Data." *Psychological Reports*, 1976, *20*, 975–978.

Lloyd-Jones, R. "Is There a Crisis in Writing Skills?" *Today's Education*, 1976, *65*, 69–70.

Lombardi, J. "The Open-Door College: A Commitment to Change." In B. L. Johnson (Ed.), *System Approaches to Curriculum and Instruction in the Open-Door College*. Los Angeles: Junior College Leadership Program, School of Education, University of California, 1967.

Longstreth, L. E., and Jones, D. "Some Longitudinal Data on Grading Practices at One University." *Teaching of Psychology*, 1976, *3*, 78–81.

Lorge, I. *The Lorge Formula for Estimating Difficulty of Reading Material*. New York: Teachers College Press, Columbia University, 1959.

Lowery, L. P. "Learning About Learning: Propositional Abilities." Unpublished paper, School of Education, University of California at Berkeley, 1974.

Lyons, G. "The Higher Illiteracy." *Harper's*, September 1976, pp. 33–40.

McCallum, G. P. Idiom Drills. New York: Crowell, 1970.

McClintock, E., and Sonquist, J. A. "Cooperative Task-Oriented Groups in a College Classroom: A Field Application." *Journal of Educational Psychology*, 1976, *68*, 588–596.

McHargue, M. *Learning Assistance Center, Autumn 1975*. Stanford, Calif.: Learning Assistance Center, Stanford University, 1975.

McKeachie, W. J. *A Guidebook for the Beginning College Teacher*. Lexington, Mass.: Heath, 1969.

McKeachie, W. J. "Psychology in America's Bicentennial Year." *American Psychologist*, 1976, *31*, 834–842.

McLaughlin, G. H. "Reading at Impossible Speeds." *Journal of Reading*, 1969a, *12*, 449–454; 502–510.

McLaughlin, G. H. "SMOG Grading: A New Readability Formula." *Journal of Reading*, 1969b, *12*, 639–646.

McWhorter, K. T., and Levy, J. "The Influence of a Tutorial Program upon Tutors." *Journal of Reading*, 1971, *14*, 221–224.

McWilliams, K. L. "The History, Development, and Application of the Audio-Tutorial Delivery System in Mathematics, Science, and Engineering." In G. Enright (Ed.), *Personalizing Learning Systems: Ecologies and Strategies*. Proceedings of 10th annual conference of Western College Reading Association. 1977.

Maeroff, G. I. "Rise in Need for Remedial Math and Writing Courses Is Taxing Colleges." *New York Times*, March 7, 1976, p. 14.

Majer, K. *Minority Underrepresentation in Natural Science Graduate Programs*. OASIS Report. San Diego: Office of Academic Support and Instructional Services, University of California, 1975.

Mandler, G., and Sarason, S. "A Study of Anxiety and Learning." *Journal of Abnormal and Social Psychology*, 1952, *47*, 228–229.

Mann, R. D., and others. *The College Classroom: Conflict, Change, and Learning*. New York: Wiley 1970.

Marron, J. F. *Special Test Preparation: Its Effect on College Board Scores and the Relationship of Effected Scores on Subsequent College Performance*. New York: Office of the Director of Admissions and Registrar, U.S. Military Academy, West Point, 1965.

Martens, K. A. *A Program for Correct Terms for Cognitive Style Maps*. Albany, N.Y.: Two-Year College Student Development Center, 1973.

Martin, D. C., and others. *The Learning Center: A Comprehensive Model for Colleges and Universities*. Grand Rapids, Mich.: Aquinas College, 1977.

Marzolf, S. S. "Fear and Low Productivity Among Superior Students: The Interaction of School Experiences and the Self-Concept." *Journal of Higher Education*, 1962, *33*, 265–269.

Maslach, C. "Burned-Out." *Human Behavior*, September 1976, pp. 16–22.

Maxwell, M. J. "An Individualized College Learning Laboratory." *Reading Improvement*, 1966a, *4*, 5–6.

Maxwell, M. J. "Training College Reading Specialists." *Journal of Reading*, 1966b, *9*, 147–155.

Maxwell, M. J. "Integrating the College Reading Program with Science and Mathematics." In J. A. Figurel (Ed.), *Vistas in Reading*.

Part 1. Proceedings of 11th annual conference of International Reading Association. Newark, Del.: International Reading Association, 1967.

Maxwell, M. J. "Ethics Revisited: The Current Dilemma Facing the College-Adult Reading Specialist." In G. B. Schick and M. M. May (Eds.), *Multi-disciplinary Aspects of College-Adult Reading.* 17th Yearbook of the National Reading Conference. Milwaukee: National Reading Conference, 1968a.

Maxwell, M. J. "Reading in the Content Areas." *Reading Improvement, 5,* 1968b, 21–22.

Maxwell, M. J. *Skimming and Scanning Improvement.* New York: McGraw-Hill, 1968c.

Maxwell, M. J. "Ethical Problems Confronting the College-Adult Reading Specialist." In D. Wark (Ed.), *College and Adult Reading.* 5th Yearbook of the North Central Reading Association. Minneapolis: North Central Reading Association, 1969.

Maxwell, M. J. "Evaluating College Reading and Study Skills Programs." *Journal of Reading,* 1971a, *14,* 214–221.

Maxwell, M. J. "The Role of Attitudes and Emotions in Changing Reading and Study Skills Behavior of College Sttdents." *Journal of Reading,* 1971b, *14,* 359–364; 420–422.

Maxwell, M. J. "Evaluating an Individualized College Reading Service: Alternative Criteria and Statistical Models to the Test-Retest Paradigm." *Journal of Reading Behavior,* 1972, *4,* 1–8.

Maxwell, M. J. "Learning Style and Other Correlates of Gains in Scanning Speed." *Journal of Reading Behavior,* 1978, *10,* 49–56.

Maxwell, M. J., and Magoon, T. M. "Self-Directed vs. Traditional Study Skills Programs—A Descriptive and Comparative Evaluation." *Journal of College Student Personnel.* 1962, *3,* 385–387.

Maxwell, M. J., and Magoon, T. M. *An Evaluation of Self-Help Reading and Study Skills Programs for Low Achieving College Applicants.* College Park: Counseling Center, University of Maryland, 1963.

Maxwell, M. J., and Zitterkopf, D. "Evaluation of the Writing Workshops Offered PCSS Students During the Summer of 1964." Reading and Study Skills Laboratory Research Report No. 65–01. College Park: Counseling Center, University of Maryland, 1965.

Mayfield, C. K. "Establishing a Reading and Study Skills Course for Law Students." *Journal of Reading,* 1977, *20,* 285–287.

Meichenbaum, D. "Cognitive Modification of Test Anxious Students." *Journal of Consulting and Clinical Psychology,* 1973, *39,* 370–386.

Messick, S., and Associates. *Individuality in Learning: Implications of Cognitive Styles and Creativity for Human Development.* San Francisco: Jossey-Bass, 1976.

Miles, J. *Style and Proportion: The Language of Prose and Poetry.* New York: Little, Brown, 1967.

Miles, J. "What We Already Know About Composition and What We Need to Know." *California English,* 1975, *11,* 14–15.

Miller, L. *Teaching Efficient Reading Skills.* Laramie, Wyo.: Developmental Reading Distributors, 1972.

Millman, J., and Pauk, W. J. *How to Take Tests.* New York: McGraw-Hill, 1969.

Mills, H. *Commanding Sentences.* Glenview, Ill.: Scott, Foresman, 1974.

Mills, H. *Commanding Paragraphs.* Glenview, Ill.: Scott, Foresman, 1976a.

Mills, H. "Language and Composition: Three Mastery Learning Courses in One Classroom." *Journal of Basic Writing,* 1976b, *1,* 44–59.

Mitchell, K. R., and Ng, K. T. "Effects of Group Counseling and Behavior Therapy on the Academic Achievement of Test-Anxious Students." *Journal of Counseling Psychology,* 1972, *19,* 491–497.

Moore, J. C. "Test-Wiseness and Analogy Test Performance." *Measurement and Evaluation in Guidance,* 1971, *3,* 198–202.

Moore, R. H. "The Writing Clinic and the Writing Laboratory." *College English,* 1950, *11,* 388–393.

Moskowitz, D. S. *Introductory College Mathematics and Modular Instruction.* Newton, Mass.: Project CALC, Education Development Center, 1976.

Most, J. M. "A Preliminary Course for Underprepared College Chemistry Students." In *Abstracts of the Pennsylvania State University Priestley Conference.* Chemical Education Division, American Chemical Society, 1974.

Mullins, R. T. "A Description of the Stevens Technical Enrichment Program (STEP)—An Engineering Preparatory and Service Program at a Small Private College." *Journal of the Society of Ethnic and Special Studies,* 1977, *1,* 13–15.

Munday, L. A. *Declining Admission Test Scores.* Iowa City: American College Testing Program, 1976.

Napell, S. "Six Common Non-facilitating Teaching Behaviors." Berkeley: Graduate Assistants Teaching Program, University of California, n.d.

National Assessment of Educational Progress. *Writing Mechanics, 1969–1974: A Capsule Description of Changes in Writing Mechanics.* Writing Report No. 05-W-01. Washington, D.C.: U.S. Government Printing Office, 1975.

National Assessment of Educational Progress. *Reading in America: A Perspective on Two Assessments.* Reading Report 06-R-01 1974–5 Assessment. Washington, D.C.: National Institute for Education, 1976.

New England Association of Academic Support Personnel. *First Conference Report.* Wellesley, Mass.: Wellesley College, 1977.

Newman, L. "The Paraprofessional in the Community College Reading and Study Center." In F. L. Christ (Ed.), *Interdisciplinary Aspects of Reading Instruction.* Proceedings of 4th annual conference of Western College Reading Association. 1971.

Nold, E. W. "Fear and Trembling: The Humanist Approaches the Computer." *College Composition and Communication,* 1975, *26,* 269–273.

Obler, M., and others. "Combining of Traditional Counseling, Instruction, and Mentoring Functions with Academically Deficient College Freshmen." *Journal of Educational Research,* 1977, *5,* 192–197.

Orr, J. V. "A Conceptual Framework for Educational Cognitive Styles." Paper presented at convention of American Psychological Association, Washington, D.C., September 1976.

Osguthorpe, R. T. *General Techniques for Tutoring Deaf Students.* Rochester, N.Y.: National Technical Institute for the Deaf, 1975.

Osguthorpe, R. T. "The Hearing Peer as a Provider of Educational Support to Deaf College Students." Paper presented at annual meeting of American Educational Research Association, San Francisco, April 1976.

Osguthrope, R. T. *The Tutor/Notetaker: A Guide for Providing Academic Support for Deaf Students Through Peer-Tutoring and Notetaking.* Rochester, N.Y.: Division of Integrated Educational Programs, National Technical Institute for the Deaf, n.d.

Osguthorpe, R. T., and others. *The Tutor Notebook: A Guide for Providing Academic Support to College Students Through Peer Tutoring.* Rochester, N.Y.: Division of Integrated Educational Programs, National Technical Institute for the Deaf, n.d.

Ott, C. E. "Peer Tutoring in Second Language Instruction." Paper presented at annual meeting of American Educational Research Association, San Francisco, April 1976.

Otto, W., and Erickson, L. *Inservice Education to Improve Reading Instruction.* Newark, Del.: International Reading Association, 1973.

Ozsogomonyan, A. "Three Cognitive Skills and Their Application to Stoichiometry." Unpublished doctoral dissertation, University of California at Berkeley, 1977.

Pauk, W. *How to Study in College.* (2nd ed.) Boston: Houghton Mifflin, 1974a.

Pauk, W. *Six-Way Paragraphs.* Providence, R.I.: Jamestown, 1974b.

Paulson, C. B., and Bruder, M. N. *Teaching English as a Second Language: Techniques and Procedures.* Cambridge, Mass.: Winthrop, 1976.

Peng, S. S. "Trends in the Entry to Higher Education." *Educational Researcher,* 1977, *6,* 15–19.

Perry, W. G., Jr. "Students' Use and Misuse of Reading Skills: A Report to the Harvard Faculty." *Harvard Educational Review,* 1959, *29,* 193–200.

Perry, W. G., Jr. *Forms of Intellectual and Ethical Development in the College Years: A Scheme.* New York: Holt, Rinehart and Winston, 1968.

Perry, W. G., Jr. "Comments, Appreciative and Cautionary." *Counseling Psychologist,* 1977, *6,* 51–52.

Peterson, G. T. *The Learning Center.* Hamden, Conn.: Shoe String Press, 1975.

Peterson, G. T., and others. *West Valley College Comprehensive Plan for Special Education, 1978–1979.* Saratoga, Calif.: West Valley College, 1978.

Piasco, J., and others. *Review of the Evaluative Literature on Open*

Admissions at CUNY. New York: Office of Program and Policy Research, City University of New York, 1974.

Pitcher, R. W., and Blaushild, B. *Why College Students Fail.* New York: Funk and Wagnalls, 1970.

Popham, W. J. *Educational Evaluation.* Englewood Cliffs, N.J.: Prentice-Hall, 1975.

Postlethwait, S. N. *Biological Sciences Curriculum Study.* Purdue University Mini-course Development Project. Philadelphia: Saunders, 1975.

Prelog, V. "Chirality in Chemistry." *Science,* 1976, *193,* 17–24.

Rauch, S. J. *Handbook for the Volunteer Tutor.* Newark, Del.: International Reading Association, 1969.

Rauch, S. J., and Weinstein, A. B. *Mastering Reading Skills.* New York: American Book Co., 1968.

Raygor, A. L. "Individualizing a College Reading Program." In J. A. Figurel (Ed.), *Reading and Inquiry.* Part 1. Proceedings of International Reading Association. Newark, Del.: International Reading Association, 1965.

Raygor, A. L. *Guide to the McGraw-Hill Basic Skills System.* New York: McGraw-Hill, 1969.

Raygor, A. L., and Vavoulis, A. "Training Reading and Study Skills Specialists at the University of Minnesota." In P. L. Nacke (Ed.), *Programs and Practices for College Reading.* 22nd Yearbook of the National Reading Conference, Vol. 2. Boone, N.C.: National Reading Conference, 1973.

Reed, R. *Peer-Tutoring Programs for the Academically Deficient Student in Higher Education.* Berkeley: Center for Research and Development in Higher Education, University of California, 1974.

Retention Task Force. *Retention of Minority Students in Engineering.* Washington, D.C.: Retention Task Force, Committee on Minorities in Engineering, National Research Council, National Academy of Sciences, 1977.

Richards, I. A. *How to Read a Page.* New York: Norton, 1942.

Rigney, J. W., and Lutz, K. A. "Effect of Graphic Analogies of Concepts in Chemistry on Learning and Attitude." *Journal of Educational Psychology,* 1976, *68,* 305–311.

Ringwald, B. E., and others. "Conflict and Style in the College Classroom." *Psychology Today,* February 1971, *4* (9), 78–79.

Robinson, F. P. *Effective Study.* (4th ed.) New York: Harper & Row, 1970. (Originally published 1946.)

Robinson, H. A. *Teaching Reading and Study Strategies: The Content Areas.* Boston: Allyn & Bacon, 1975.

Robyak, J. E., and Patton, M. J. "The Effectiveness of a Study Skills Course for Students of Different Personality Types." *Journal of Counseling Psychology,* 1977, *24,* 200–207.

Rose, M. *Tutor Training Manual.* Los Angeles: Academic Advancement Program, University of California, 1976.

Rosen, D., and others. *Open Admissions: The Promise and the Lie of Open Access to American Higher Education.* Lincoln: Student Committee of the Study Commission on Undergraduate Education and the Education of Teachers, Nebraska Curriculum Development Center, University of Nebraska, 1973.

Rosen, S., and others. "Peer-Tutoring Outcomes as Influenced by the Equity and Type of Role Assignment." *Journal of Educational Psychology,* 1977, *69,* 244–252.

Ross, S. F. "A Study to Determine the Effect of Peer Tutoring on the Reading Efficiency and Self-Concept of Disadvantaged College Freshmen." 1972. (ERIC Document Reproduction Service No. ED 081 415)

Rossman, J. E., and others. *Open Admissions at City University of New York: An Analysis of the First Year.* Englewood Cliffs, N.J.: Prentice-Hall, 1975.

Roth, R. M., and Meyersburg, A. "The Non-Achievement Syndrome." *Personnel and Guidance Journal,* 1963, *41,* 535–539.

Rothkopf, E. Z. "The Concept of Mathemagenic Activities." *Review of Educational Research,* 1970, *40,* 325–335.

Rotter, J. B. "Generalized Expectancies for Internal Versus External Control of Reinforcement." *Psychological Monographs,* 1966, *80,* 1–28.

Roueche, J. E., and Hurlburt, A. S. "Open Door College: The Problems of the Low Achiever." *Journal of Higher Education,* 1968, *39,* 453–456.

Roueche, J. E., and Kirk, R. W. *Catching Up: Remedial Education.* San Francisco: Jossey-Bass, 1973.

Roueche, J. E., and Pitman, J. C. *A Modest Proposal: Students Can Learn.* San Francisco: Jossey-Bass, 1972.

Roueche, J. E., and Snow, J. J. *Overcoming Learning Problems.* San Francisco: Jossey-Bass, 1977.

Ryan, B. A. *PSI: Keller's Personalized System of Instruction—An Appraisal.* Washington, D.C.: American Psychological Association, 1974.

Sack, A., and Yourman, J. *The Sack-Yourman Developmental Speed Reading Course.* New York: College Skills Center, 1965.

Samson, R. W. *Problem Solving Improvement.* New York: McGraw-Hill, 1970.

Sandberg, K. C. *Writing Laboratories: A New Approach to Teaching.* Tucson: Department of Romance Languages, University of Arizona, 1967. (ERIC Document Reproduction Service No. ED 018 799)

Sandberg, K. C. "Discussion of a General Education Critical Reading Requirement for All Freshmen Students: What, Why, How?" Paper presented at annual meeting of National Reading Conference, Atlanta, December 1976.

Santa Barbara City College. "An Analysis of the Effectiveness of Tutorial Assistance in English 42: Performance and Persistence Among Low Achieving Students." 1970. (ERIC Document Reproduction Service No. ED 042 442) Jc700203.

Santeusanio, R. P. "Do College Reading Programs Serve Their Purpose?" *Reading World,* 1974, *13,* 258–271.

Saretsky, G. "The OEO O.C. Experiment and the John Henry Effect." *Phi Delta Kappan,* 1972, *53,* 579–581.

Scandura, J. M. "Structural Approach to Instructional Problems." *American Psychologist,* 1977, *32,* 33–53.

Schell, L. *A Comprehensive Model of Peer Teaching in a General Public School Context.* Berkeley: Alternatives Through Peer Teaching, Lawrence Hall of Science, University of California, 1976.

Schermerhorn, S. M., and others. "Learning Basic Principles of Probability in School Dyads: A Cross-Age Comparison." *Journal of Educational Psychology,* 1975, *67,* 551–557.

Schey, T., and others. "A Laboratory Computer and Calculus Based Course in Mathematics." *Journal of Mathematics Education and Science Technology,* 1970, *1,* 115–130.

Schick, G., and Schmidt, B. *A Guide to the Teaching of Reading.* Glenview, Ill.: Psychotechnics, 1973.

Schmeiser, C. R., and Stiggins, R. J. "The Goals of Evaluation." Paper presented at convention of American Psychological Association, Washington, D.C., September 1976.

Schmidt, C. L., and others. *Hands on Botany: An Audiotutorial Approach.* New York: Wiley, 1976.

Schnell, T. R. "The Community College Reading Teacher: A Profile." *Journal of Reading,* 1974, *18,* 1–11.

Scriven, M. "Evaluation Perspectives and Procedures." In J. Popham (Ed.), *Evaluation in Education: Current Applications.* Berkeley, Calif.: McCutchan, 1974.

Sells, L. W. "Constraits on Minorities and Women in Higher Education." *Intellectually Talented Youth Bulletin,* July 16, 1976. Baltimore, Md.: Johns Hopkins University.

Shapiro, D. H., Jr., and Zifferblatt, S. M. "Zen Meditation and Behavioral Self-Control." *American Psychologist,* 1976, *31,* 519–531.

Shapiro, L. "Opting for Computer Aids in Calculus." *Change Report on Teaching #3,* January 1977, p. 44.

Shatin, L. "Study Skills in Medical Education: A Report and Analysis." *Journal of Medical Education,* 1967, *42* (9), 833–840.

Shaughnessy, M. P. "Open Admissions and the Disadvantaged Teacher." *College Composition and Communication,* 1973, *24,* 401.

Shaughnessy, M. P. "Diving In: An Introduction to Basic Writing." *College Composition and Communication,* 1976, *27,* 234–239.

Shaughnessy, M. P. *Errors and Expectations: A Guide to the Teacher of Basic Writing.* New York: Oxford University Press, 1977.

Shavelson, R. J. "Some Aspects of the Correspondence Between Content and Cognitive Structure in Physics Instruction." *Journal of Educational Psychology,* 1972, *63,* 225–234.

Shaver, J. P., and Nuhn, D. "Effectiveness of Tutoring Underachievers in Reading and Writing." *Journal of Educational Research,* 1971, *65* (3), 107–112.

Shaw, P. "Reading in College." In N. B. Henry (Ed.), *Development In and Through Reading.* 60th Yearbook of the National Society for the Study of Education, Part 1. Chicago: University of Chicago Press, 1961.

Sheldon, W. "An Evaluation of an Experimental Reading Program for Medical Students." *Journal of Educational Psychology,* 1948, *39,* 298–303.

Shepherd, D. L. "Reading and Science: Problems Peculiar to the Area." In H. A. Robinson and E. L. Thomas (Eds.), *Fusing Reading Skills and Content.* Newark, Del.: International Reading Association, 1969.

Shepherd, J. F. "The Future of Noncredit College Reading Courses." *Journal of Reading,* 1977, *20,* 493–497.

Shreve, B., and others. *The Oasis Peer Tutoring Program: A Model for Academic Support.* San Diego: Office of Academic Support and Instructional Services, University of California, 1976.

Siegel, L., and Siegel, L. C. "Educational Set: A Determinant of Acquisition." *Journal of Educational Psychology,* 1965, *56,* 1–12.

Silver, E. S. (Ed.). *Declining Test Scores: A Conference Report.* Washington, D.C.: National Institute of Education, 1976.

Simmons, E. S. "The Effects of Kinetic Structure on Knowledge About and Performance of a Psychomotor Skill: Teaching Students to Use a Compound Microscope." Unpublished doctoral dissertation, University of Iowa, 1976.

Skinner, B. F. "Teaching Science in High School: What Is Wrong." *Science,* 1968, *159,* 704–710.

Slotnik, H. B. "Toward a Theory of Computer Essay Grading." *Journal of Educational Measurement,* 1972, *9,* 253–263.

Smith, D. E. P. (Ed.). *Learning to Learn.* New York: Harcourt Brace Jovanovich, 1961.

Smith, D. E. P., and others. "Reading Improvement as a Function of Student Personality and Teaching Method." *Journal of Educational Psychology,* 1956, *47,* 47–59.

Smith, G. D., and others. "A National Survey of Learning and Study Skills Programs." In G. B. McNinch and W. B. Miller (Eds.), *Reading Convention and Inquiry.* Twenty-fourth Yearbook of the National Reading Conference. Clemson, S.C.: National Reading Conference, 1975.

Smith, M. "Peer-Tutoring in a Writing Workshop." Unpublished doctoral dissertation, University of Michigan, 1975.

Snow, R. E. "Aptitude-Treatment Interactions and Individualized Alternatives in Education." In S. Messick and Associates, *Individuality in Learning: Implications of Cognitive Styles and Creativity for Human Development.* San Francisco: Jossey-Bass, 1976.

Sollimo, B. "An Audio-tutorial Approach in General Chemistry Using the Popham Paradigm." *Chemistry in the Two-Year College,* American Chemical Society, 1972, *1,* 41.

Sommer, R. "The Social Psychology of Cramming." *Personnel and Guidance Journal,* 1968, *47,* 104–109.

Sowande, B. F. "Modular Reading Program: An Educational Alternative." *Journal of Reading,* 1977, *21,* 135–138.

Sowell, T. "The Plight of Black Students in the United States." *Daedalus,* 1974, *103,* 179–196.

Spache, G. D. "Trends in College Reading." In O. S. Causey (Ed.), *Evaluating College Reading Programs.* 4th Yearbook of the Southwest Reading Conference for Colleges and Universities. Fort Worth: Texas Christian University Press, 1955.

Spache, G. D. "Is This a Breakthrough in Reading?" *Reading Teacher,* 1962, *15,* 258–263.

Spache, G. D., and Berg, P. C. *The Art of Efficient Reading.* (2nd ed.) New York: Macmillan, 1966.

Spache, G. D., and others. "College Reading Programs." *Journal of Developmental Reading,* 1959, *2,* 35–46.

Spargo, E., and Williston, G. R. *Timed Readings.* Providence, R. I.: Jamestown, 1975.

Spielberger, C. D., and others. *Manual for the State-Trait Anxiety Inventory.* Palo Alto, Calif.: Consulting Psychologists Press, 1970.

Spielberger, C. D., and others. "Anxiety, Drive Theory, and Computer Assisted Instruction." In B. A. Maher (Ed.), *Progress in Experimental Personality Research.* Vol. 6. New York: Academic Press, 1972.

Spring, K. S. "How Much Do Community College Students Learn from Their Textbooks?" *Journal of Reading,* 1975, *19,* 131–136.

Stanley, J. C. "Predicting College Success of the Educationally Disadvantaged." *Science,* 1971, *171,* 640–647.

Stasz, C., and Shavelson, R. J. "Field Independence and the Structuring of Knowledge in a Social Studies Minicourse." *Journal of Educational Psychology,* 1976, *68,* 550–558.

Staw, B. M. *Intrinsic and Extrinsic Motivation.* University Programs Moddular Studies. Morristown, N.J.: General Learning Press, 1976.

Stebens, L. D., and Belden, B. R. "Rentention of Gains in Reading after Five Semesters." *Journal of Reading,* 1970, *13,* 339–344.

Stent, A. "Can Math Anxiety Be Conquered?" *Change Report on Teaching #3,* January 1977, pp. 40–43.

Stern, G. G., and others. *Methods in Personality Assessment.* New York: Fress Press, 1956.

Stevens, S. S., and Stone, G. "Psychological Writing, Easy and Hard." *American Psychologist,* 1947, *2,* 230–235.

Stodolsky, S. S., and Lesser, G. "Learning Patterns in the Disadvantaged." *Harvard Educational Review,* 1967, *37,* 546–593.

Strang, R. *Problems in the Improvement of Reading in High School and College.* Ephrata, Pa.: Science Press, 1938.

Stryker, W. "Improving Basic Writing Skills: A Progress Report." *Future Talk: Educating for the '80s.* Long Beach: Office of the Chancellor, California State Universities and Colleges, Spring 1977, 1–5. (A monthly newsletter.)

Sue, D. W., and Frank, A. C. "A Typological Approach to the Psychological Study of Chinese and Japanese American College Males." *Journal of Social Issues,* 1973, *29,* 129–148.

Sue, D. W., and Kirk, B. A. "Psychological Characteristics of Chinese-American Students." *Journal of Counseling Psychology,* 1972, *6,* 471–478.

Suinn, R. M. "The STABS: A Measure of Test Anxiety for Behavioral Therapy—Normative Data." *Behavior Research and Therapy,* 1969, *7,* 335–339.

Sullivan, L. L. *A Guide to Higher Education Learning Centers in the United States and Canada.* Portsmouth, N.H.: Entelek, 1978.

Sullivan, L. W. "Representation of Minorities in Dental and Medical Schools: Comparative Studies." *Journal of the Society of Ethnic and Special Studies.* 1977, *1,* 1–2.

Swalm, J. F., and Cox, G. A. "A Formalized Diagnostic Approach to Study Skills Instruction for Specially Admitted Freshmen." In P. L. Nacke (Ed.), *Programs and Practices for College Reading.* 22nd Yearbook of the National Reading Conference. Boone, N.C.: National Reading Conference, 1973.

Swann, H., and Johnson, J. *Prof. E. McSquared's Original, Fantastic, & Highly Edifying Calculus Primer.* Los Altos, Calif.: William Kaufman, 1976.

Talley, L. H. "The Use of Three-Dimensional Visualization as a

Moderator in the Higher Cognitive Learning of Concepts in College Level Chemistry." *Journal of Research in Science Teaching,* 1973, *10,* 263.

Taylor, S. E. "An Evaluation of Forty-One Trainees Who Had Recently Completed the 'Reading Dynamics' Program." In E. P. Bliesmer and R. C. Staiger (Eds.), *Problems, Programs, and Projects in College-Adult Reading.* 11th Yearbook of the National Reading Conference, 1962.

Taylor, W. "Cloze Procedure, A New Tool for Measuring Readability." *Journalism Quarterly,* 1953, *30,* 414–438.

Taylor, W. W., and Ellison, R. L. "Biographical Predictors of Science Performance." *Science,* 1967, *155,* 1075–1080.

Thelen, J. *Improving Reading in Science.* Newark, Del.: International Reading Association, 1976.

Tobias, S. *Overcoming Math Anxiety,* New York: Norton, 1978.

Tomlinson, B., and others. "A Preliminary Report on a Project Integrating the Teaching of Reading and Studying in Science with Biology 4 ABC." Unpublished paper, University of California, Riverside, 1974.

Tomlinson, B. M., and Green, T. "Integrating Adjunct Reading and Study Skills Classes with the Content Areas." In R. Sugimoto (Ed.), *The Spirit of '76: Revolutionizing College Learning Skills.* Proceedings of 9th annual conference of Western College Reading Association. 1976.

Touchton, J. G., and others. "Career Planning and Decision-Making: A Developmental Approach to the Classroom." *Counseling Psychologist,* 1977, *6,* 42–43.

Townsend, A. "How Can We Help College Students Develop Critical Reading of Textbooks and Resource Materials?" In W. S. Gray and N. Larrick (Eds.), *Better Readers for Our Time.* Proceedings of International Reading Association. New York: Scholastic Magazines, 1956.

Trani, E. P., and others. "College Teaching and the Adult Consumer: Toward a More Sophisticated Student Body." Proceedings of the Institute of Electrical and Electronics Engineering, 1978, *66,* 838–846.

Treisman, P., and Ferguson, D. "Some Observations of Advanced High School Students' Attempts at Reading Calculus Material."

Unpublished paper, Department of Mathematics, University of California at Berkeley, 1977.

Trow, M. "The Undergraduate Dilemma in Large State Universities." *University Quarterly*, 1966, *21*, 17–43.

Tucker, C. A. "The Chinese Immigrant's Language Handicap: Its Extent and Its Effect." *The Florida FL Reporter—A Language Education Journal*, Spring/Summer, 1969, pp. 44–45; 170.

Turner, C. S., and others. "The Effects of a Developmental Program on University Grades." *Journal of Reading*, 1974, *17*, 531–537.

Turner, R. H. *Report to the Academic Senate on Subject A.* Berkeley: Academic Senate, University of California, 1972.

Undergraduate Mathematics and Its Applications Program. *Index and Descriptions of Available Mathematics Modules.* Vol. 1. Newton, Mass.: Education Development Corporation/Undergraduate Mathematics and Its Applications Program, 1977.

Upton, A., and Samson, R. W. *Creative Analysis.* New York: Dutton, 1961.

U.S. Office of Education. *Tutor-Trainer's Resource Handbook: Part A, Reading Directors' Organizational Guidelines; Part B, Tutor Trainers' Guidelines; and Part C, Teacher Orientation Guidelines.* Washington, D.C.: U.S. Office of Education, 1974. (ERIC Document Reproduction Service No. ED 109 645)

Vavoulis, A., and Raygor, A. L. "The Training of College Reading and Study Skills Specialists: A Survey of Expert Opinion." In P. L. Nacke (Ed.), *Programs and Practices for College Reading.* Vol. 22. 22nd Yearbook of the National Reading Conference. Boone, N.C.: National Reading Conference, 1973.

Very, P. S. "Differential Factor Structures in Mathematical Ability." *Genetic Psychology Monographs*, 1967, *75*, 169–207.

Voeks, V. *On Becoming an Educated Person*, (3rd ed.) Philadelphia: Saunders, 1970.

Wagner, G. "On Remediation." *College English*, 1976, *38*, 153–158.

Waller, M. I., and others. "A Measure of Student Attitudes Toward Reading and Self as a Reader: A Summary Report." *Journal of Reading Behavior*, 1977, *9*, 123–128.

Walter, R. E. (Ed.). *Chemical Education for Underprepared Students.* Champaign, Ill.: Stipes Publishing Co., 1971.

Walter, T., and Siebert, A. *How to Be a Better Student and Still Have Time for Your Friends*. New York: Holt, Rinehart and Winston, 1976.

Wark, D. M. "Application of Operant Conditioning in a College Reading Center." In G. B. Schick and M. M. May (Eds.), *Junior College and Adult Reading Programs: Expanding Fields*. 16th Yearbook of the National Reading Conference. Milwaukee: National Reading Conference, 1967.

Wark, D. M., and Johnson, S. "Test Panic, Daydreaming, and Procrastination." Paper read at 12th annual conference of North Central Reading Association, Flint, Mich., October 31, 1969.

Warnath, C. F. *New Myths and Old Realities: College Counseling in Transition*. San Francisco: Jossey-Bass, 1971.

Watanabe, C. "1971 Asian Studies Report on Composition and Reading Problems Among Asian Students." *Journal of Educational Change*, 1972, *4*, 1;3.

Watanabe, C. "Self-Expression and the Asian-American Experience." *Personnel and Guidance Journal*, 1973, *51*, 390-396.

Watanabe, C., and Gordon, F., *How to Study Chemistry*. Berkeley: Student Learning Center, University of California, 1977.

Watanabe, C., and Maxwell, M. J. "Patterns of EOP Students' Use of the Student Learning Center's Chemistry Tutoring Program and Final Grades in Freshman Chemistry." Berkeley: Student Learning Center, University of California, 1975.

Weaver, W. *Lady Luck: The Theory of Probability*. New York: Doubleday Anchor Books, 1963.

Webb, E. J., and others. *Unobtrusive Measures: Nonreactive Research in the Social Sciences*. Chicago: Rand McNally, 1966.

Weigand, G. R. J. "Motivational Factors Associated with Success and Failure of a Group of Probational Students." Unpublished doctoral dissertation, University of Maryland, 1949.

Weigand, G. R. J., and Blake, W. S. *College Orientation*. Englewood Cliffs, N.J.: Prentice-Hall, 1955.

Weinstein, P., and Gipple, C. "The Relationship of Study Skills to Achievement in the First Two Years of Medical School." *Journal of Medical Education*, 1974, *49* (9) 902–905.

Whimbey, A. E. "Better than Binet." *Saturday Review/World*, June, 1974, pp. 50–53.

Whimbey, A. E. *Development of Problem Solving Skills for Vocational and Educational Achievement.* Washington State Superintendent of Public Instruction. Reprinted by the Center for Undergraduate Education, Bowling Green State University, 1976a.

Whimbey, A. E. "You Can Learn to Raise Your I.Q. Score." *Psychology Today,* January 1976b, pp. 27–29; 85–89.

Whimbey, A. E. "Teaching Sequential Thought: The Cognitive Skills Approach." *Phi Delta Kappan,* 1977, *59,* 256–259.

Whimbey, A. E., and Barberena, C. J. *A Cognitive-Skills Approach to the Disciplines.* Bowling Green, Ohio: Competency-Based Undergraduate Education Project, Bowling Green State University, 1977.

Whimbey, A. E., and Whimbey, L. S. *Intelligence Can Be Taught.* New York: Dutton, 1975.

Whipple, G. M. *How to Study Effectively.* Illinois: Public School Publishing Co., 1916.

Whyte, C. B. "Effective Counseling Methods for High-Risk Freshmen." *Measurement and Evaluation in Guidance,* 1978, 10, 198–200.

Widick, C. "The Perry Scheme: A Foundation for Developmental Practice." *Counseling Psychologist,* 1977, *6,* 35–38.

Wilburn, A. Y. "Current Status of Ethnic/Racial Minorities in Science and Engineering Professions." *Journal of the Society of Ethnic and Special Studies,* 1977, *1,* 31–35.

Willcox, A. B. "Mathematics: To Know Is Not to Teach." *Change Report on Teaching #3,* January 1977, pp. 26–27.

Williams, B. "Readability Interference in Reading Mathematics Texts." In B. S. Schulwitz (Ed.), *Teachers, Tangibles, Techniques: Comprehension of Content in Reading.* Newark, Del.: International Reading Association, 1975.

Willie, C. V. "Perspectives of Black Education and the Education of Blacks." In L. C. Solomon and P. J. Taubman (Eds.), *Does College Matter? Some Evidence of the Impacts of Higher Education.* New York: Academic Press, 1973.

Wilson, B. J., and Schmits, D. W. "What's New in Ability Grouping?" *Phi Delta Kappan,* 1978, *59,* 535–536.

Wilson, J. T., and Koran, J. J. "Review of Research on Mathemagenic Behavior: Implications for Teaching and Learning Science." *Science Education,* 1976, *60,* 391–400.

Wilson, R. C., and others. *College Professors and Their Impact on Stu-*

dents. New York: Wiley, 1975.

Wine, J. "Test Anxiety and Direction of Attention." *Psychological Bulletin,* 1971, *76,* 92–104.

Wirtz, W., and others. *On Further Examination.* Report of the Advisory Panel on the Scholastic Aptitude Score Decline. Princeton, N.J.: College Entrance Examination Board, 1977.

Witkin, H. A., and others. "Role of the Field-Dependent and Field-Independent Cognitive Styles in Academic Evolution: A Longitudinal Study." *Journal of Educational Psychology,* 1977, *69,* 197–211.

Wolpe, J. *Psychotherapy by Reciprocal Inhibition.* Stanford, Calif.: Stanford University Press, 1958.

Wolpe, J. *The Practice of Behavioral Therapy.* New York: Pergamon Press, 1969.

Wolpe, J., and Lazarus, A. *Behavior Therapy Techniques.* New York: Pergamon Press, 1966.

Wood, E. N. "A Breakthrough in Reading." *Reading Teacher,* 1960, *14,* 115–117.

Wood, N. V. *College Reading and Study Skills.* New York: Holt, Rinehart and Winston, 1977.

Wood, P. A. "Judging the Value of a Reading Program." *Journal of Reading,* 1976, *19,* 618–620.

Wood, R. L. "Attrition as a Criterion for Evaluating Non-credit College Reading Programs." *Journal of Developmental Reading,* 1961, *5,* 27–35.

Woolley, J. "A Summary of Tutorial Services Offered by California Community Colleges." *About Tutoring,* October 1976, pp. 1–7.

Woolf, M. D., and Woolf, J. A. *Remedial Reading: Teaching and Treatment.* New York: McGraw-Hill, 1957.

Wright, R. M. "The Effects of Organized Tutoring and Advising by Upperclassmen with 'Predicted Unsuccessful' Freshmen." n.d. (ERIC Document Reproduction Service No. ED 059 696) HE 002866.

Young, S. M. "Teaching the Underprepared College Chemistry Student." *Abstracts of the 161st American Chemical Society National Meeting, Chemical Education Division,* Washington, D.C.: American Chemical Society, 1971.

Yuthas, L. "Student Tutors in a College Remedial Program." *Journal of Reading,* 1971, *24,* 231–271.

Index